Light and Life Publishing Company
4818 Park Glen Road
Minneapolis, Minnesota 55416

Second Edition
Library of Congress Card Number: 91-60187
ISBN 0-937032-81-6

All those desiring to correspond with the author may contact him at: 2136 Sheffield Drive, Fort Collins, CO 80526. 970 221-4847

ACKNOWLEDGMENTS

My thanks to the late Rev. John Meyendorff, former dean and professor of Church History and Patristics at St. Vladimir's Orthodox Theological Seminary, Crestwood, New York. This book extensively cites his works because both his understandings of Early Christianity, and his sensitivity to the questions often asked by the American culture regarding Eastern Christianity are incisive. My special thanks to him also for his personal interest in this work, and his personal encouragement.

There are others too I must acknowledge: the members of Holy Trinity Orthodox Church for their patience and understanding while their pastor squirreled himself away to complete this book, Rev. Randall Evans, Mrs. Anne Winkelmeyer, and Mr. Adrian Valentino for their proofreading, and editing labors, and for all those who have prayed and financially supported this work for the past three years. In this my last respect, my thanks to Mr. and Mrs. Kenneth and Mary Ellen Khouri, Mr. and Mrs. Charles and Julie Dalgarno, Mrs. Kathryn Spero, and Mr. and Mrs. John and Theresa Stavros.

Lastly, and most importantly, I would like to thank Geralyn, my wife. She has been a great help in assisting me on the details of this book (through research, proofreading, editing, etc.), and a great *personal* support to me. I will never forget her love throughout these past years. If it were not for her, this book would have taken two to three times longer to finish (If I would have been able to finish at all!). My thanks to her, and to the Lord Who made her a priceless crown upon my head (Proverbs 12:4).

TABLE OF CONTENTS

SACRAMENTS AND SALVATION

A VERY IMPORTANT PREFACE

HOW TO BEST UNDERSTAND THIS BOOK

This is a book about understanding our common Christian heritage — the Bible, the history of the Church and, most importantly, the truth of the Gospel. I make no attempt to persuade the reader that a proper understanding of these things is essential. I assume you already believe this. (If you did not believe this, I don't think you would have bought the book.) But before many can penetrate to the core of the Christian Faith, they will have to hurdle the tall, and wide obstacle that presses in on them at every step: the biases of their own culture.

THE DANGERS OF CULTURAL BLINDNESS

Have you ever embarrassed someone from a different country because of your lack of sensitivity to their culture? I must admit that I've done this many times. On one memorable occasion, while traveling on a train in London, I asked a fellow passenger what he did for a living.

> With a sigh of disgust, he asked me, "Are you an American?"
>
> I said, "Why yes I am. How did you know?"
>
> "Because that is what Americans always ask," he said irritably.
>
> "Is that an improper question?"
>
> "Well," he said, "it is about as proper as asking someone how much he paid for his house."
>
> I stopped my line of questioning, and apologized. I thought it best not to ask my next question ("Where do you live?").

My English traveling companion found my question offensive because he saw it as an invasion of privacy. In England, one's class standing is a sensitive issue. Unlike this country, one's status in England depends not on the money he or she makes, but the degree of prestige the job carries. While intending to initiate a friendly gesture, I made a rude, intrusive remark.

Of course, misunderstandings do not occur only when one is trying to speak with someone from a different culture. Miscommunication can happen even within the most intimate of families. One cannot understand one's own brother or sister, if he does not first seek to understand the other's frame of reference, experience, feelings and beliefs. Just think how much more difficult it would be to understand *another culture* if one did not first take the time to figure out its beliefs and practices.

This is the challenge the Western Christian must accept if he is to fully embrace the Christian message, to give himself to the task of understanding a culture different from his own. He must recognize that the original Christian sociological context is different from his own. He must admit that the native languages of the Scriptures are different from his own. He must accept that the philosophies prevalent in Biblical times are different from his own. He must acknowledge that Christianity began in a place thousands of miles from his own birthplace. And on top of all this, he must realize that Christianity began some nineteen hundred years ago.

I want to encourage you to resist doing what I did with my British acquaintance (and, perhaps, what he did with me). He was British, I an American. To understand each other, we needed to be sensitive to the fact that our cultural backgrounds were different. If I interpreted his answers from an American context, I would see him as an arrogant snob. If he were to evaluate me by a British standard, I would be an intrusive busybody. Both interpretations are wrong. The key that would make it clear that each other's viewpoint was wrong lay in understanding the other's reference point. It is the same in one's approach to Biblical Faith. If one tries to understand the teaching of the Scripture outside it's cultural context, he will be left with wrong interpretations.

If you grew up, as I did, in the Western hemisphere, particularly in America, you may find it nearly impossible to resist the temptation to interpret Eastern Christianity from a "Western" slant. As I will discuss later, Eastern Christianity is the Christianity of the early Church. This is not the way one understands it today, however. An American looks at the Eastern Church today (whether Eastern Orthodox, Armenian, or Coptic) and sees either a "Pope-less" Roman Catholicism, or a "High Church" Protestantism. Eastern Christianity is different from either.

Misunderstandings of the cultural context of the Early (Eastern) Church appears in how people interpret terms like "Eucharist," "tradition," and "sacrament." These and other such theological words do not mean entirely the same thing to an Eastern Christian as they do to most Protestant or Catholic Christians.[1] When persons from Roman Catholic or Reformed traditions use these terms, they find it easier to understand one another. A shared philosophical and historical background gives them a sense about what the other probably means. For reasons I will discuss later, Eastern Christianity did not share in this context.[2] It would, therefore, lead to a wrong interpretation to see the Eastern Church through a Western context.

Practically speaking, American Evangelicals will misunderstand Eastern Christians if they hear them say the word "Eucharist" and associate their beliefs with the Roman Catholic Church because it *sounds* Roman Catholic to their ears. Roman Catholics likewise, will commit a similar error by labeling Eastern Christians "Protestants" because they do not accept the office of the Pope.

Most American readers will find information in these pages they have never read elsewhere. To grasp the message of this book, the Protestant and Catholic reader will have who to put aside preconceived evaluations. To put it bluntly, those who have a tendency to instinctively arm themselves with ammunition from a stockpile of anti-Catholic or anti-Protestant arguments to protect their own biases, must pause, put down their weapons for a moment, and be willing to listen. Hopefully, such attentiveness will cause each party to draw closer to one another in their common pursuit of Christ. At the very least, such caution will prevent needless confusion and help insure a deeper breadth of Christian understanding.

BOTH REASONABLE, AND BEYOND REASON

Throughout this book, I've tried to share the Eastern Christian perspective in a somewhat systematic manner. **BUT BEWARE:** One cannot freeze Middle Eastern ways of thinking into systematic, ordered molds (Anyone who has ever visited that culture, even today, will certainly confirm this!) The Eastern mind is comfortable in expressing itself in parables, pictures, and stories. The Western mind, conversely, generally prefers to express itself through formulas and "hard" logic.

Here then is my problem: How does one communicate the intuitive perspective of the East in a way that the rational mind of the Westerner can grasp? How do I convert a picture into a thousand words? The answer is, I cannot! At least not with total faithfulness. A book can never summarize a painting. One does not understand a painter's creation through an understanding of the physical properties that distinguish one color from another. One perceives the message of a painting by the sight one receives through a heart shaped by life experiences.

Another way of putting it is that it is impossible to *capture* the Eastern Christian view by intellect alone. Anyone who studies Eastern Christianity as if it were but a system of ideas will always misunderstand it. One understands Christianity as he trusts Christ with his entire life, not just his head. So, from the start let it be known: this book will require you to be both intellectually *and intuitively* open to God's Spirit. Such a person doesn't merely ask, "Does this make sense?", but also, "Is the Eastern view of the Christian life consistent *with my experience of Christ?*"

THERE IS MUCH OF THE EAST WITHIN THE WESTERN CHURCHES

Though I draw contrasts between the Christian denominations of the West and earlier Eastern Christianity throughout the book, in no way do I intend to condemn Evangelical-Fundamentalism, Roman Catholicism, or any other Christian configuration. Without a doubt, there is a solid core within Western Christianity that is valuable, bears witness to the

Spirit, and still testifies to its early Eastern roots. The Church that existed in both the East and the West certainly shared a common frame of reference at one time. It is only as they grew apart that this outlook gradually dissolved. [3]

I do not write this book to advance any particular denominational position, as if one denominational perspective were superior to another. Christian Truth by its very nature is above denominational loyalties. No "denomination" can possess it.

This book presents an ancient view of Christianity that is both familiar and yet unfamiliar. It is familiar because each Christian finds his birth from within its womb. It is unfamiliar because this culture has not had the ancient perspective presented to it.

Eastern Christianity is not an alien philosophy seeking to take us by force. It is the *natural* birthright of *every* believer. It is not East *verses* West, but Christianity within the West rediscovering her own Eastern heritage. It is each Christian's task and duty (no matter where he lives) to lay claim to that heritage. May this book be a help in that task.

THE AUTHOR'S FRAME OF REFERENCE: MEANING OF TERMS, WHAT THE BOOK IS AND ISN'T

Fundamentalism, Evangelicalism, and Roman Catholicism: what do these terms mean? Authors have committed *entire* books to discussing their exact meanings. This book is not going to add a great deal to that debate. My main purpose is to outline the thinking of Eastern Christianity, not to detail every stream that has flowed out from it. Since I do use the above terms frequently throughout the book, however, it would be good for the reader to be aware of my *working* definitions.

FUNDAMENTALISM: When I speak of Fundamentalism, I am referring to the conservative theological movement that began in the 1920's. Fundamentalism's initial concern was to protect the authority of the Bible, and a specific literalistic interpretation of its texts. The Fundamentalist sees the Bible as having sole authority on all matters, not just areas of faith and ethics. On all points the Bible is to accurately represent the truth, no matter what contemporary scientific, historical, or geographical research may seem to say. To the Fundamentalist, the Bible is inerrant, authoritative and all-sufficient.[4]

EVANGELICAL-FUNDAMENTALIST: The Evangelical-Fundamentalist is generally more conciliatory toward other Protestant groups than is the Fundamentalist. Evangelical-Fundamentalism is more open to entertain the discoveries of modern Biblical scholarship, whether the source be secular or religious. In general, I see Evangelical-Fundamentalism holding common ground with straight line Fundamentalism in many areas: an "authoritative" view of the Scripture (though understandings of Biblical inerrancy can differ), a belief in the Bible's sufficiency, and in its own theological and sociological beginnings.[5]

EVANGELICAL: I use the term evangelical (lowercase "e") in its most basic, Christian sense. To be evangelical is to be a believer in the "good news," one who is "born anew" through faith in Christ. An evangelical believes in the traditional teachings of the Faith (as symbolized in the ancient Nicene and Apostolic Creeds), and earnestly desires to see both his neighbors and those around the globe embrace the One Who embodies these teachings. Lastly, an evangelical is one who seeks the will of God, and is firmly committed to pattern his or her life in conformity to God's will. In this sense, every genuine Christian is an evangelical.

ROMAN CATHOLICISM: The Roman Catholicism I speak of within this book is not necessarily the Roman Catholicism of today. It is the Roman Catholicism that characterized the Council of Trent (1545-63) and the First Vatican Council (1870). I choose this approach for two reasons: (1) as the Roman Church of today is in great flux, it is extremely difficult for me to say authoritatively what it does or does not believe, and (2) despite recent changes, numerous people both in and out of the Roman Catholic Church relate to its teachings through Medieval lenses. In most cases, Roman Catholic and Evangelical debates concern themselves with these earlier perspectives.

I would also like to explain another writing convention I have used in this book. Throughout these pages the reader will find the personal pronoun "he" and words such as "man" or "mankind" used extensively. These terms intend to convey their original *generic* meanings (i.e., "he", "his", "mankind," etc., refer to humanity, not to the male sex.).

SOME LIMITATIONS. . .

Lastly, the reader should be aware that this book has many limitations. First, this book is not a thorough exposition on Eastern Christianity but only a sketch of its vision.[6] Second, I purposely do not outline every Evangelical and Catholic position. Again, my main purpose is to describe the Eastern vision of Christianity, not offer a comparative review of it against every stream of the faith. And third, although the perspectives represented in this book are sympathetic to those of the Eastern Orthodox Churches, I confine my comments to that denomination's theology, not to its present government or practices (many of which ignore its own teachings).[7]

NOTES TO PREFACE

1 Alexander Schmemann, an Orthodox theologian who was heavily involved in inter-church dialogues, often commented on this dilemma whenever Orthodox were invited to discuss their viewpoints with Protestant/Catholic bodies:

> "For us Orthodox one of the most agonizing aspects of the ecumenical encounter lies very often precisely in this inability of the 'West' to grasp anything 'Orthodox' unless it is reduced to Western categories, expressed in Western terms and more often than not, altered in its true meaning. ...we were caught in the essentially Western dichotomies—Catholic versus Protestant, horizontal versus vertical, authority versus freedom, hierarchical versus congregational—and were made into representatives and bearers of attitudes and positions which we hardly recognized as ours and which were deeply alien to our tradition."

Alexander Schmemann, *Church, World, Mission* , "Freedom in the Church," (Crestwood, New York, St. Vladimir's Press, 1979) pp. 25, 200

2 Though there exist many disparities, and even contradictions, between Roman Catholicism and Protestantism, they both share a common Western outlook which makes them more similar to each other than dissimilar. Because the Eastern Christian perspective stands outside this context, it is often difficult for it "to get a hearing" in contemporary Christian dialogues. When it is heard, it is often misunderstood.

> ...the Roman Catholic and Protestant 'lived situations' are much more comparable and compatible with each other than either is with the Orthodox. This may not seem so on the surface of things because of the external similarities between Roman Catholics and Orthodox, ... But the theological struggles between Catholics and Protestants, with their common Western European and American histories, their common ways of approaching theological and sacramental issues, their common manner of treating the bible and their common definitions, categories and general ways of thinking—even with all of the disagreements *within* these ways— does make for greater understanding and agreement between them, even when their understanding is that there is a real disagreement. This does not exist between members of these churches and the Orthodox.

Thomas Hopko, ed., "Women and the Priesthood: Reflections on the Debate," Thomas Hopko, *Women and the Priesthood,* (Crestwood, N.Y., St. Vladimir's Seminary Press, 1983) p. 172

3 Eastern Orthodox theologian Georges Florovsky has noted as much:

> The "permanent separation between East and West was preceded by the decay of the common mind and of the sense of mutual responsibility within the one Body. When unity was finally broken [in the schism of East and West], this was not so much because agreement could not be reached on certain doctrinal issues, as because the universe of discourse had already been disrupted ...In all ecumenical conversations today, the greatest difficulty of all is the recovery of common universe of discourse."

Christianity and Culture (Belmont, MA., Nordland Publishing Company, 1974) pp. 161, 162

4 Although all will not agree with his understanding, in the main, I have adopted the definition of Fundamentalism which Louis Gasper uses in his book (*The Fundamentalist Movement: 1930-1956* [Grand Rapids, Baker Book House, 1963, p. v.]):

> Religious Fundamentalism is rooted in apostolic doctrine, Medieval-Reformation theology, and American revivalism. Since 1910 it represents an interaction against twentieth century liberalism and modernism, particularly against the teachings of science

and the higher criticism in Biblical research which tends to undermine certain fundamentalist tenets.

5 I've opted to link the terms Evangelical and Fundamentalist together for three reasons:

1) Despite the differences, the origins and perspectives of both Fundamentalism and Evangelicalism show that they've more points in common than they have in disagreement. *The Fundamentalist Phenomenon* (Ed Dobson, Ed Hindson, Jerry Falwell [Grand Rapids, MI., Baker Book House, 1986], a book advocating Fundamentalism's relationship with Evangelicalism re-enforces this impression in its quotation of James Barr:

> It is not clear that the modernized and updated Evangelicalism has yet attained to any conceptual framework intrinsically different from the Fundamentalist one, or that it has even tried." ...we too must face the fact that we [evangelicalism and fundamentalism] share a common heritage which goes back to the fundamentalist controversy of the 1920's.

The Fundamentalist Phenomenon, pp. 7, 8 citing James Barr, *Fundamentalism* [Philadelphia, The Westminster Press, 1978) p. vi, vii])

2) The second reason that I have decided upon this approach stems from the fact that Fundamentalism often embraces the broad set of Reformed positions typical of Protestant Evangelicalism. The following definition of "Evangelical" summarizes this point :

> Derived from *evangelion* (evangel, gospel, good news), the term came into use at the Reformation to identify Protestants, especially as they held to the belief in justification by grace through faith and the supreme authority of scripture... Subsequently, the meaning tended to narrow, with evangelicalism referring to those who espoused and experienced justification and scriptural authority in an intensified way: personal conversion and rigorous moral life, on the one hand, and concentrated attention on the Bible as guide to conviction and behavior on the other, with a special zeal for the dissemination of Christian faith, so conceived (evangelism). Anabaptism, Puritanism, Wesleyanism, Continental pietism, converts of the American Great Awakenings, and all their heirs represent variations on these themes. Today evangelical continues as an adjective in the name of some Protestant denominations and is also used in theology to identify Reformation doctrine (viz. Karl Barth's *Evangelical Theology*), but it is more generally associated with the aforementioned subsidiary meaning of interiorization and intensification as in "born again Christianity."

Alan Richardson, John Bowden, eds., "Evangelical, Evangelicalism", *A New Dictionary of Christian Theology* (London, S.C.M. Press Ltd., 1983)

3) The last reason why I frequently join Evangelical and Fundamentalist together is a practical one. Although there are indeed differences between these two schools of Christian thought, they often "blend" in to each other. If I became focused on the varying nuances between the Fundamentalist-Evangelical worlds, I expect that few readers would be willing to endure such subtleties. (In examining only Evangelical groups, Robert Webber, in his book *Common Roots: A Call to Evangelical Maturity* [Grand Rapids, MI., Zondervan Publishing House, 1978, pp. 30-34], identifies as many as fourteen different varieties of Evangelical alone!) Besides, a thorough analysis of the differences within and between Fundamentalism and Evangelicalism is not the point of this book, but an explanation of the Eastern Christian mind is.

6 If the reader wants to pursue a particular aspect of Orthodox Christianity at greater length, I suggest the recommended reading list at the end of the book.

7 Orthodox theologian Alexander Schmemann states the dire case well in his book *Church, World, Mission* (Crestwood, N.Y., St. Vladimir's Seminary Press, 1979) p. 130

> Whatever its 'key' or orientation, Orthodox theology seems deeply alienated from the Church, from her real life needs. Although taught in official ecclesiastical schools, its impact on students usually evaporates on the day of graduation. It is viewed as an intellectual abstraction nowhere to be really applied; as an intellectual game which the people of God—clergy and laity—simply ignore. In our

CHAPTER ONE

THE SIGNIFICANCE OF EASTERN CHRISTIANITY

This book imparts a vision of the Christian faith that is virtually unheard of in America — a perspective that can dramatically affect how each Christian can experience His walk with Christ.

The subject of this book is not a "new and improved" version of the Faith. On the contrary, over 1900 years of history, centuries of Biblical study, and ages of theological inquiry form the foundation for the approach described in these pages. Yes, Eastern Christianity offers a unique vision, but not an untested one.

Someone may ask, "How can *Eastern* Christianity offer such a contribution? Isn't there only *one type* of Christianity? The Scripture proclaims, '*One* faith, *one* Lord, *one* baptism!'" Accordingly, the suggestion that *Eastern* Christianity holds special significance troubles some people.

THE "ONE FAITH" IS EASTERN

Yes, there is only *one* Faith. But few realize that the *roots* of this one Faith lead us back to Middle Eastern and Semitic ways of thinking. The Early Church was an *Eastern* Church. By "the East" then, I'm not referring to Indonesia or China but to the East with which those in the Scriptures were familiar: Southern Italy, Yugoslavia, Bulgaria, Romania, Greece, Asia Minor, and the Middle East. It was here -- not Europe -- where Christianity began. This is obvious to anyone who takes the time to briefly trace Christianity's birth and formation:

- Jesus and His disciples were "Eastern" by birth, culture and language i.e., the Middle East.

- The Bible is an Eastern book, its entire cultural context speaks of it: its languages (Hebrew and Greek), the authors and peoples it primarily addresses, (again, Jewish and Greek), and the philosophy it is familiar with (Semitic).

- The "headquarters" of the Christian faith was in the East. The apostles founded forty-four Local Churches in the East (only two in the West). Clearly, it was from *here*, not Rome, that the apostles were *sent out* with the Gospel. The West was not the center of the early Christian movement; it was the mission field.

• For more than 1,000 years, with the exception of Rome, all the major centers of Christian belief were found in the East, in Jerusalem, Alexandria, Antioch, and Constantinople.

• All the fundamental dogmas regarding the faith were formulated and defended in the East e.g., that Christ is "of the same essence" with the Father, that He is fully God and fully man, that the Holy Spirit is a divine Person, the nature of the Trinity, etc.).[1]

• The first schools of Biblical interpretation, Antioch and Alexandria, were in the East. Their perspectives of interpretation still influence much of our understanding of the Scriptures today.

• The East was the site for all the fundamental Church Councils (that is, the first seven, from 325 - 787 AD). The overwhelming majority of the bishops represented at those councils were Eastern as well.

Denying our Eastern roots is like denying our parents. To live the Christian life in such cultural and historical ignorance is to lose a great part of our identity. The journey back to Christianity's beginnings not only leads us to a place foreign to today's American, but also to a culture and way of thinking about life very much different from ours. Most of us have forgotten the *Middle Eastern and Semitic* core of Christianity, and we are suffering the consequences. There is much at stake here.

WHAT ARE THE CONSEQUENCES OF OUR IGNORANCE?

What do we risk losing? We first lose a correct interpretation of the Scriptures. Instead of interpreting the Bible with the mind of the Early [Eastern] Church, we end up seeing it as 15th Century Europeans. A Renaissance mind set that contradicts the Early Church's understandings at several points.

To most people in America, Christianity is a Western faith. We dress it in Western clothes, make it communicate in Western ways of thinking, and evaluate it with Western rules of logic. By doing so, we impose something strange upon it. Our cultural blindness forces it to labor under chains of bias and ignorance. This error makes it difficult for us either to accurately preach the Gospel or rightly teach the Scriptures.

Let me suggest a shocking conclusion to what I am saying: If Christianity is Middle Eastern in nature, we must adopt a Middle Eastern world view to understand it. Or to put it negatively, unless we embrace the decidedly Eastern disposition of Scriptures we will never be able to fully embrace its message.

This book is to reintroduce the Christian to the Eastern Biblical thinking that characterized the Early Church. Is this difficult? Not as difficult as one might think. Christianity isn't complicated. It's our unconscious projection of Western philosophy on it that sometimes makes it hard for us to understand. Actually, many American Christians already have an intuitive familiarity with Eastern Christianity. Once presented with the earlier perspective, many Christians have said to me "I never thought of putting it like that before. That's it! That's what I believe!"

WHY LEARN ABOUT CHRISTIAN DOCTRINE?

Why does anyone need to concern themselves with Christian doctrine? Isn't doctrinal precision just another needless excuse for division? Yes, doctrine apart from one's union with Christ can easily become a barrier to God's purposes. True Christian doctrine, on the other hand, is genuinely liberating. Ignorance and false belief hold people in bondage, not knowledge and awareness (John 8:31, 32). Genuine doctrine presented and received with a right attitude is not an obstacle to fellowship with God and each other; it's an encouragement for it.

Doctrine is not an end in itself, but the means to a wonderful end: communion with God and man. When we emphasize marginal religious ideas over true doctrine, we often become sidetracked from knowing God. The Early Church only considered teaching about the Trinity as "theology." Indeed, that is what theology literally means, "the study of God."

The Early Church's perspectives are more than just a "neat" way of stating things. Their outlook opens horizons most of us never thought existed. The Eastern outlook offers fresh solutions to many doctrinal conflicts that have divided Protestant and Roman Catholic Christians for centuries. Richer understandings regarding baptism, the interpretation of Scripture, the Church, and redemption become apparent. The ancient understanding of the Church opens opportunities for a deeper relationship with God, and a deeper communion with God's people. I believe most American Christians would embrace these Eastern answers, if given the chance.

Why have a concern for the Eastern-ness of our Christianity? An Eastern perspective allows us to rediscover the faith of the Early Church, by re-acquainting us with our common origin and history. The Eastern orientation gives us another opportunity to share the faith with a generation tired of Western apologetics. The Eastern approach broadens our relationship with Christ and our Christian brethren. And lastly, our Eastern ancestry is worthy of attention because in it we find sincere Christian unity without the compromise of either theological integrity or love. All the above expresses the reasons for this book. May God grant this, and be glorified!

NOTES FOR CHAPTER ONE

1 "Much of Christian liturgy (forms of worship) and most of Christian dogma had arisen in the East... The principal symbol of the superiority of Eastern over Western theology was the preeminence of Greek as the language for expressing Christian doctrine with due precision. Various doctrinal controversies showed that 'there are not even any Latin terms to correspond to the more subtle conceptual distinctions of Greek theology." Jaroslav Pelikan, *The Christian Tradition: The Spirit of Eastern Christendom (600-1700)* (Chicago and London, The University of Chicago Press, 1974), p. 3 citing Werner Elert, *Der Ausgan der altkirchlichen Christologie: Eine Untersuchung über Theodor von Pharan und seine Zeit als Einführung in die alte Dogmengeschichte*, Edited by Wilhelm Maurere and Elisabeth Bergsträsser, Berlin, 1957, p. 186

CHAPTER TWO

AN INTRODUCTION TO THE EASTERN CHRISTIAN MIND

It is extremely important that we take time to become re-acquainted with the Christianity we profess. We need not merely to ask questions, but to ask the *right* questions. We need to ask questions about Christianity's history and the cultural womb from which it was born. Only this kind of inquiry will give us insight into the Eastern Christian mind, and the firery faith which filled their hearts.

By *Eastern* Christian mind I do not mean a breed of "Hindu Christianity." I am not asking the reader to visualize a long, grey bearded master, sitting cross-legged, and barefooted on top of a Tibetan mountain. I am referring rather to the *mind set* of the early Christian in the Middle East — the home of Jesus and His Jewish Disciples. The birth, history and doctrinal development of Christianity leads *every* Christian concerned with his birthright here. One cannot confine the Eastern Christian mind to a specific geographic area, however. For although Christianity arose in the East, the "Eastern Christian mind" transcends time and place. When I speak of "Eastern Christianity," therefore I do not refer to Christians from the Mediterranean or Middle East, but to the outlook that characterized that land during the time of Jesus.

The Eastern Christian mind is an *outlook and way of thinking which can exist among any people and within any locale*. One can be a Jewish Christian, live in Jerusalem, speak Hebrew and still hold a Western understanding of Christianity. Alternately, one can be a Christian of Swedish descent, live in Minnesota, know neither Hebrew nor Greek, and maintain an Eastern Christian perspective.

God does not call us to move to either Israel or Minneapolis. He is not asking us to take up either Jewish or American citizenship. He does call us to be "rooted" in Christ (Col. 2:7), and an aspect of being so rooted demands an understanding of His revelation — the revelation delivered *within an Eastern* context. To live in the light of this revelation, we must be willing to enter into its frame of reference.

THE EASTERN CHRISTIAN PERSPECTIVE

A very important point of difference between the Eastern and Western mind is in the way each tends to analyze a subject. The West typically studies a subject by dissecting it into smaller units and then classifying each unit by a set of definitions. The East, on the other hand, studies a matter by observing how the *entire* subject relates to each of its parts. With this latter approach, a Christian adopting an Eastern perspective would seek to understand a particular Christian teaching from *within the context of all Christian doctrine, not as an isolated unit.* Thus, one cannot study the Eucharist, for example, by itself, but only in *its relationship to* the Church, in *its relationship to* the ministry of the Holy Spirit, in *its relationship to* the two natures of Christ, in *its relationship to* the meaning of salvation, and in *its relationship to* other chief Christian doctrines.

Throughout the book, I have observed this inclusive approach to doctrine. The later chapters build upon the foundation of the beginning chapters. Each chapter clarifies and expands upon all the other chapters. So, if one looks at the table of contents, says to himself, "Hmmm, 'Baptism': that looks like an interesting subject..." and then begins to read those chapters without having read the previous ones, he will very likely misunderstand what he reads. (Therefore, one should read the book as *a unity.* No chapter — even if read in proper sequence — can be clearly understood outside the context of the others.)

There are many other perspectives where the Eastern Christian view appears distinct from the Western one. Although I will discuss these much more at length throughout the book, an outline of some of these distinctives follows:

EASTERN CHRISTIANITY IS COMMUNAL The Eastern Christian perspective sees the individual *with others*; he is never alone. This is because Eastern Christianity views the Church and the individual as a reflection of the relationships that exist among the Persons of the Trinity (John 17: 22, 23). As no Divine Person can exist outside communion with the other, so no human person can exist as an isolated individual. The bond that unites and sustains the Persons of God (Father, Son, and Holy Spirit), is to be the same bond that unites and sustains those within the Church — namely love (I John 4:7&8, and Colossians 3:14). Where there is love, there is self discovery and union. Where there is selfishness and pride, there is deceit and division.

EASTERN CHRISTIANITY IS INTUITIVE Although firmly supported by scholarship, Eastern Christianity does not trust in scholarship per se as its basis of faith. The Eastern thinking Christian would say that it is impossible to encapsulate the Christian faith into intellectual propositions.[1] Doctrines have value in that they can protect "the mystery" of Christ and redemption from heretical twistings, (1 Corinthians 2:6-8; Ephesians. 4:4-11), but they can never communicate the faith so well that one could experience God by studying them alone (Mark 12:24; 1 Corinthians. 1:22-24; 2:14). God will always transcend every one of man's finite doctrinal formulations.[2] For this reason, Eastern Christianity shies away from making "exhaustive" doctrinal confessions [3] and would never put forward any creed or "confession" as *the definition* of Christianity. [4]

Words will never be able to have a tight hold on the Faith. Reason will never be able to fully comprehend the things of the Spirit. Job recognizes one of his sins in exactly this error; being too quick to explain what he does not understand (Job 42:3). The Eastern minded Christian would not want to repeat his error; to make dogmatic statements about things left undisclosed by the Spirit.

EASTERN CHRISTIANITY IS HOLISTIC Everything stands in relationship to the other. I have already touched on this when I spoke of Eastern Christianity's refusal to separate Truths into categories and then study them as self-contained units. The Christian of New Testament sees the world as a whole; as a revelation of God in all places. He sees body, soul and spirit as distinct, yet inseparable. He sees the nature of faith, love, and service as belonging together. He sees all truths as a revelation of Him Who is Truth.

Christ came to redeem the *whole* person: body, soul, and spirit (1 Thess. 5:24), and it is this *whole* person who will One Day be seated with Christ in heaven for all eternity (1 Cor. 15; Rom. 8:11-30). Christ likewise will redeem all of creation as well, in the Last Day summing up all things in Himself (Eph. 1:9, 10). It is for this reason that the Eastern Christian does not erect an impenetrable wall between what is sacred ("spirit") and what is profane ("matter"). God has created both, sustains both, and one day will restore both. (I will speak much more about this when discussing the Eucharist and the sacraments.)

EASTERN CHRISTIANITY SEES THE CHURCH AS A LIVING ORGANISM OF WHICH CHRIST HIMSELF IS A MEMBER. The Eastern Christian recognizes that the Church's membership includes both those within a specific place and time as well as those who now exist outside time; the Church exists as a mystical and concrete reality in both places. In other words, the Eastern Christian does not see the church as existing more in one place (heaven) and less in another place (earth). The Church is *One*.

For the Eastern Christian, the Church reflects the awesome truth of the incarnation. The Church is where God dwells among men as Emmanuel — "God is with us", and where He shows Himself in intimate communion with His people.

EASTERN CHRISTIANITY SEES THE CHRISTIAN FAITH AS RELATIONAL, PERSONAL AND EXPERIENTIAL Christianity is chiefly a relationship with the Persons of God (Father, Son and Holy Spirit), with and among the people of God (brothers and sisters in Christ); together, their communion is the Church. No Creed or set of doctrines; no matter how comprehensive, can ever fully explain the life in Christ.[5] It is not the intellect that brings revelation, but union with Christ and His brethren. Doctrine can be a "symbol" that *points to Him* Who is the Way, but it is not the way. Doctrine may be a vessel, but it is never the Water the vessel contains.

To the Eastern Christian, theology is a *means* toward communion with God and others, never the end.[6] Theology is a search for words appropriate to God. It "fulfills its mission not [7] with the help of definitions, [or] 'words about words'" , but in words that lead to life and love.[8]

> Faith is not a logical certainty but a relationship. ... It is to know God not as a theory or an abstract principle, but as a person. To know a person is far more than to know facts about that person. To know a person is essentially to love him or her; there can be no true awareness of other persons without mutual love.[9]

EASTERN CHRISTIANITY SEES THE GRASP OF TRUTH AS DEPENDANT UPON ONE'S MORAL AND SPIRITUAL SENSITIVITY. The pursuit of Truth is chiefly a *spiritual* task, one more taxing to a person's depth of character than his mind (2 Peter 1:5-7). The reason for this is clear. One's life always more accurately represents Truth than one's thoughts. A person who is willing to accept correction and is open to rethink issues has access to Truth. Those who refuse to embrace change, reject Truth and its ability to see.

The first century Christian knew only those of spiritual maturity can receive the Truth. Pre-eminently, only those who are lovers of God have free access to the Truth, those who are willing to zealously labor for communion with God. Sight is only given to those who have the humility to admit the implications of the Fall within and among themselves. These people welcome change, intellectually and spiritually. These are the ones who are able to put aside the prejudiced persuasions of their particular culture. One cannot confine this person's vision. Those who remain locked to their opinions and culture, will only see through a small hole.

The Liturgy of John Chrysostom (a fourth century worship service) emphasizes the integral tie between faith and love. Before the recitation of the Nicene Creed, the worship leader exhorts the faithful, "Let us love one another, so that we may with one mind confess Father, Son and Holy Spirit, the Trinity: one in essence and undivided." Note the words "*so that* we may confess." The service rightly underscores that only those who love in the likeness of God can confess the Truth about God.

Theology does not answer an unbeliever's questions.[10] It does not mean to. The intention of theology is to lead the one with an open spirit into *a meeting with God.* The mind cannot grasp the message of doctrine, but a mind and heart in communion with God can.[11] One is changed by *Who* he knows, not what he knows.[12]

Knowledge gained through this *relationship of love* with God and the brethren is the spiritual "knowing" of which the Apostle John spoke. A knowledge gained through a relationship of love.[13] For this reason Eastern Christianity sees every true believer as a "theologian," one who knows God and is personally taught by Him. "And as for you, the anointing which you received from Him abides in you, and you have no need for anyone to teach you; but as His anointing teaches you about all things, and is true and is not a lie, and just as it has taught you, you abide in Him." (1 John 2:27).[14]

CONCLUSION

The Eastern Christian's vision of the Faith is in a number of respects different from the Western world view. I will begin to outline this Western Christian perspective and how it came into being in the next chapter. But before I do, I would like to suggest that there is something familiar in this Eastern way of looking at things — something that feels at home in every believer's heart (no matter where he or she was born). Indeed, this outlook on the Faith is not reserved for a special class, or for those dwelling only within certain parts of the world. This view of the Faith belongs to all those who can call Jesus "Lord."

NOTES FOR CHAPTER TWO

1 Unlike religious practice that has grown out of the Roman Catholic-Reformation debates, Eastern Christianity avoids reliance on academic statements to defend its theology. This is primarily true because the Semitic world view refuses to see the human mind as capable of defining God. For this reason, Eastern Christianity emphasizes a "theology of negatives" (an *apophatic theology*). God is infinite, eternal and beyond mortal comprehension. One can say *definitively* only what God is *not* , but not what He is. [For example, to say "God *is* good", does not *define* Him, for our understanding of "good" is finite and imperfect.). God can only be "known" in personal relationship.

> The whole of Eastern Christian theology has often been called 'mystical.' The term is correct, provided one remember that in Byzantium 'mystical' knowledge does not imply emotional individualism, but quite the opposite: a continuous communion with the Spirit who dwells in the whole Church. It implies as well the constant recognition of the inadequacies of the human intellect and of human language to express the fullness of truth, and the constant balancing of positive theological affirmations about God [i.e. doctrine] with the corrective of apophatic theology .

2 "Every antinomic opposition of two true propositions (e.g.,. Trinity, One and Three) gives way to a dogma, *i.e.* to a real distinction, although ineffable and unintelligible, which cannot be based on any concepts or deduced by a process of reasoning, since it is the expression of a reality of a religious order. If one is forced to establish these distinctions, it is precisely to safeguard the antinomy... The antinomy, on the contrary, raises the spirit from the realm of concepts to the concrete data of Revelation." Vladimir Lossky, *In The Image and Likeness of God* , (Crestwood, New York, St. Vladimir's Press, 1974) p. 52

John Meyendorff, *Byzantine Theology* (New York, Fordham Press, 1979) p. 14

3 "Greek Christians firmly confessed the incapacity of conceptual language to express the *whole* truth, and the incapability of the human mind to attain the essence of God...God has revealed Himself in Christ Jesus, and the knowledge of His truth is essential to salvation, but God is also above the human intellect and cannot be fully expressed in human words." John Meyendorff, *Byzantine Theology,* (New York, Fordham Press, 1979) p. 5

4 "The term 'Creed,' derived from the Latin 'credo' [belief, trust] is of Western origin. The term used by the East to designate the official or formal statement of faith is 'Symbolon' [symbol]." The reason for this distinction is that the East never believed that any "creed" could define the Christian faith, they could only grant "impressions" of it. Christianity is life with the Trinity in fellowship with other brethren. This experience cannot be given anyone unless he first repents and is born anew (Jn 3: 5), not through a mere intellectual assent to a creed or a particular set of doctrines. The fact that God can't be known by what we reason but only through an experience of faith explains the relative scarcity of Orthodox creeds and confessions as compared to the Protestant or Roman Catholic churches." Stanley Harakas, "Creed and Confession in the Orthodox Church", *The New Man: An Orthodox Reformed Dialogue* , John Meyendorff, Joseph McLelland eds., (New Jersey, Standard Press, 1973) p. 42

5 It is for this reason why the councils of the early Church did not propose any creed as a "summary" of the Faith. "The councils of the early Church never produced exhaustive 'confessions,' but rather condemned individuals or doctrines which were seen as incompatible with the Apostolic Tradition. The Apostolic Tradition was always considered to be inexhaustible in human words." John Meyendorff, "Church and Ministry," *Catholicity and the Church* , (Crestwood, New York, St. Vladimir's Seminary Press, 1983) p. 61

6 "Every truth of the faith is revealed, not as a response to mere curiosity, nor to increase some philosophical knowledge, but for the sake of an *existential communion of life and love...* It is only within this communion that the truth of faith is manifested as the truth of life. ... Thus every true theology in the Church is a reflection inspired by and springing from the theology accomplished in and by Christ. *Therefore every Christian theology must have as its point of departure and destination the divine-human communion revealed in Christ* [italics mine]." Dan-Ilie Ciobotea, "The Role of the Liturgy in Orthodox Theological

Education", *St. Vladimir's Theological Quarterly* , (Crestwood, New York, St. Vladimir's Seminary Press, 1960) Vol. 31, No. 2, p. 103

7 The "theologians" of the first centuries (the Fathers) did not attempt to define everything pertaining to the Faith in exacting detail. The Fathers theologized, as St. Gregory of Nazianzus put it, "in the manner of the Apostles, not in that of Aristotle" (Hom. 23. 12). To them Christian doctrine was not merely a catalog of "definitions" or a science of religious facts, *but a vehicle to help us better know and experience God.*

8 Alexander Schmemann, *The Eucharist* , (Crestwood, N.Y., St. Vladimir's Press, 1988), p. 149

9 Kallistos Ware, *The Orthodox Way* (Crestwood, New York, St. Vladimir's Seminary Press, 1980) p. 19, 20

10 "[Theological] formulas are fully meaningful only for those who have encountered the Living Christ, and have received and acknowledged Him as God and Saviour, and are dwelling by faith in Him, in His body, the Church. In this sense theology is never a self-explanatory discipline." Georges Florovsky, *Orthodoxy: A Faith and Order Dialogue,* (Geneva, Switzerland, WCC, 1960), Faith and Order Paper #30 p. 41

11 "This dialectic between faith and knowledge has only one purpose, to strengthen our faith in God, and, by the same token, to enrich our knowledge of God, not only from an intellectual, but also from an experiential view. The purpose of this dynamic relationship between faith and knowledge is not to reduce the one to the other, but to allow both to grow stronger and stronger. Maximos Aghiorgoussis, "Trinitarian Theology", Lecture Notes, 1978, p. 49

"'Faith needs knowledge, in a like manner that knowledge needs faith. Faith cannot be understood without knowledge, and knowledge cannot exist without faith. Faith precedes knowledge, and knowledge follows faith'." (*Stromata* 7. 10; 2.4; ct. Theodoret, *The Healing of Greek Lessons,* Sermon I) Kallistos Ware, *The Orthodox Way* (Crestwood, New York, St. Vladimir's Seminary Press, 1980) pp. 48, 49

12 "It [theological inquiry] is an existential attitude which involves the whole man: there is no theology apart from experience; it is necessary to change, to become a new man. To know God one must draw near to Him. No one who does not follow the path of union with God can be a theologian." Vladimir Lossky, *Mystical Theology in the Eastern Church,* (Crestwood, New York, St. Vladimir's Press, 1976) p. 39

13 (Jn. 3:35; 13:1ff, 5:26; 1 Jn 4:7-8; 10:14-15, 27) The biblical scholar F. F. Bruce explains:

> We are those who have come to know God, or rather to be known by God'" (Gal 4:9). And "'If one loves God, one is known by him' (1 Cor. 8:3)—and to be known by him is the antecedent to knowing him." The disclosure of the eternal mystery is no object of mere intellectual comprehension, although it calls for all the intellectual power at one's command; it requires personal acquaintance with the revealer, whose nature is perfect love.

F. F. Bruce, *The New International Commentary on the New Testament: The Epistles to the Colossians, to Philemon and to the Ephesians* (Grand Rapids, MI., Wm. B. Eerdmans Publishing Company, 1984) p. 329

14 "...*ginoskein* [to know] ... denotes personal fellowship with God or Christ. The relation between Father and Son is a knowing, and so is that between Jesus and His disciples (Jn. 10:14-15, 27). Because the Father and the Son have life, to know them is to have eternal life (5:26; 17:3). Knowing God also means being determined by love (1 Jn. 4:7-8). Love governs the relation between both the Father and Son (Jn. 3:35 etc.) and Jesus and His disciples (13:1 etc.)... Thus *ginoskein* means the recognition and

reception of love, i.e., faith. ... Knowing Christ is more than having information about his life (6:42; 7:28). It is a knowledge of his unity with the Father (10:38), of his obedience and love as the one whom God has sent (14:31 etc.)." Gerhard Kittel, Gerhard Friedrich, eds., Geoffrey W. Bromiley, trans., *Theological Dictionary of the New Testament : Abridged In One Volume* , *"ginosko"*, R. Bultmann (Grand Rapids, MI., William B. Eerdmans, 1985), p. 122

CHAPTER THREE

THE REFORMATION: RESPONSE AND REACTION

Before one can understand the frame of reference of another it is helpful to understand one's own outlook. What we have seen in the past often shapes what and how we see today. Given this, it is important for the Western Christian to look at the events and ideas that surrounded the Reformation.

Historians have referred to the Reformation as "the most profound spiritual revolution ever experienced by a people in so short a period of time."[1] Not *every* aspect of this revolution was "spiritual," however. Although clearly led of the Spirit, one can detect the fingerprints of man's imperfection on the Reformation. This should not offend any of us. *No* segment of Church history has ever been a time of complete purity. Even in the Church of the New Testament, there were evidences of "the works of the flesh": the immorality of the Corinthians, the legalism of the Galatians, the assorted failings of the churches admonished in the book of Revelation, etc. If we assume perfection in the case of the Reformation, such a prejudice will make it difficult for us to sift lessons of the Spirit from our own self projected illusions.

THE MEDIEVAL SETTING

THE CLIMATE OF THE TIMES

The Reformation was not just a forum for differing theological positions. The movement reflects the sociological, economic, political, religious, and philosophical climate of an entire era. One cannot understand the Reformation outside of this *human-historical context*. The Reformation certainly expressed a dissatisfaction with the church,[2] but other factors created a climate for the movement as well. Many were oppressed and persecuted in "the name of the Church." The people of that time experienced severe human and economic tragedies. War and famine were commonplace. Yes, religious issues were important, but they would not have seemed so significant if death, tyranny and ignorance had not given them a voice.[3]

> Throughout the Reformation Era, from the Peasant's Revolt to the Puritan Revolution, the most radical political theories did not evolve from the necessity of logic, but grew out of the demands of the dissatisfied minorities. In most cases, their religious and political views coincided. [4]

THE RELIGIOUS SENTIMENT OF THE PEOPLE

One of the most religious periods of European history occurred before and around the time of the Reformation. Historians see two major reasons for this: (1) The famine, moral devastation, and hopeless poverty result of continuous warfare and (2) the effects of the bubonic plague (which in some areas, killed as much as two thirds of the population). On numerous occasions, such tragedy led people into hysterical fanaticism.[5] Historian R. W. Southern captures the motivations of the people in the following:

> The chief sources of mass religious movements were disease and despair, and the two generally went together. ... [For] *all the religious movements of the later Middle Ages were an attempt to harness, guide, and express some elements in popular religion which drew their strength,* not from ... worship of the church, *but from pressures in ordinary life which were beyond all control.*[6]

Generally, the temperament of medieval piety was one of great superstition and simple-minded acceptance. Few could read, fewer still could afford the price of a book.[7] In the hopes of averting natural disasters, the people freely mixed Astrology and pagan customs together with Christian ceremonies. To obtain healing, peasants consumed the dust of saints' tombs and paid homage to bizarre relics.[8] People received sacraments to get "wishes granted."

These superstitions and abuses made up the "theology" of the masses. It is not unlikely that these abuses affected the Reformers thinking. How could it not have affected them? These practices were everywhere! It would certainly be difficult to distance oneself from the abuse and try to get a clear head about the true nature of sacraments. Certainly it is not unreasonable to wonder how much the Spirit shaped their views, and how much their own horror shaped them.

THE STATE OF THE CHURCH

The devout French preacher Michael Menot summarized the state of the Medieval Church by saying, "Never could less devotion be found in the Church."[9] Another contemporary echoed his sentiments, "Has not the entire state of the church become somehow brutal and monstrous?"[10] What were the reasons for these evaluations? Priests got drunk in public taverns. Clergy openly kept mistresses. Pastors abdicated their spiritual and pastoral responsibilities.[11] No wonder the humanist Desiderius Erasmus stated a man was "insulted unpardonably" if he was called a cleric.

Unfortunately, this sorry complexion typified not only the local cleric, but the entire leadership of the Church.[12] The Church's critics made the accusation that everything in the Church had a price: pardons, masses, ceremonies, parish positions, bishoprics, even the papacy itself.[13] Popes and Cardinals built their own palaces with the money. It seemed as if the major priority for the Church's hierarchy was to amass wealth, certainly, this was their greatest motivation for corruption.[14] "While the great threat to the primitive church had been persecution, the new enemy was hypocrisy and greed."[15]

During the latter fifteenth century, complacency not only typified church leadership, but the average professing Christian as well. As William A. Scott in his *Historical Protestantism* observes...

> It had become too easy to see Christianity as something into which one was born, in which one lived and died without ever having to face the necessity of making a personal commitment to being a Christian. In this world everyone was Christian and the way to live the Christian life was clearly spelled out. One said these prayers, received these sacraments, performed these works of piety...[16]

How could a dedicated Christian look at this immorality, greed and apathy and remain calm? It is one thing for the Church to be a witness *to* the world; it is quite another for the Church to be a witness *of* the world. It is understandable why many of that era would want to remove themselves from this Church. This was certainly the sentiments of the Radical Reformers, a reform movement that immediately followed the Reformation. These zealous reformers deduced that the evil within the church was a direct consequence of the church's partnership with the state.[17] How could a Christian have anything to do with religious compromise and for the sake of attaining worldly power? The only course for the true Christian, they reasoned, was to "come out" and "be separate" (2 Corinthians 6:17).

One can easily sympathize with the Radical Reformers. The Apostle Paul asks "What fellowship has light with darkness (2 Corinthians 6:14? The answer: "Nothing." But was the Medieval Church total darkness? Unquestionably, *much* of it was corrupt, but surely not *all* of it. Is it not likely that there was at least *something* about that church that could still provide *some* witness to the Early Church? Is it possible that in rejecting the Medieval Church outright, the Reformers may not only have rejected corruptions, but also rejected some good elements as well? Is it possible that some of the teachings they rejected — *if seen from another perspective* —could have borne witness to Christ in a more powerful way than the teachings that were to take its place? To say that such possibilities are impossible, would be to deify these men. I do not question the Reformers' devotion, but their sincerity does not make them less fallible.

WORKS AND INDULGENCES

A chief focus of protest by Martin Luther (1483-1546) was the Roman Church's use of the *indulgence*.[18] Originally, a person was granted an indulgence when he *repented*.[19] Later, under the influence of Thomas Aquinas (1225-1274), the doctrine allowed anyone the privilege to buy the forgiveness that the indulgence had previously symbolized.[20]

According to Aquinas, the Church was a "treasury of grace," its vaults brimming full of saints' good deeds.[21] Those who had committed serious sins could make withdrawals from these accounts, but only doing other good works or making monetary contributions to the Church could authorize such withdrawals. The logical conclusion of this thinking led many to believe one could *buy* forgiveness.[22] Although the official teaching of the Roman Church never stated grace could be purchased, this was the way many clerics advertised the indulgence.[23]

Many Evangelicals today certainly see good works as a testimony to one's salvation, but there are others who believe works have nothing to do with redemption. "How can works have anything to do with one's salvation?", they ask. "Christ's work on the cross was *all* sufficient." The current "Lordship salvation" debate among Evangelicals today is the popular variation of this theme. I cannot help think that some of the emotion around this subject today still stems around the Medieval abuse of the indulgence. If the popular piety of the Roman Church had not allowed such a practice, I wonder how differently the subject of works and faith would be discussed today.

THE INTELLECTUAL AND PHILOSOPHICAL CLIMATE

AUGUSTINIANISM

"The continent of Western Europe was withered by a blight of intellectual sterility."[24] Few priests were university trained. Few clerics knew the Bible, the Latin of the services,[25] or the meaning of the mass.[26] The meager numbers who had theological training were cast in the image of Augustine of Hippo (354-430 AD).[27] The opinions and teachings of this North African Bishop influenced Western Christian theology more than any other. "There was no important doctrinal issue in the fourteenth and fifteenth centuries that was unaffected by the study of Augustine..."[28] How the West viewed (and, still views) the Church, the sacraments, grace, original sin, the natural state of man, and salvation is traceable to him. What is wrong with this? The Church in the West has narrowed its frame of reference by relying on only one Christian teacher.

Some may counter, "I do not look to Augustine for theology, I look to the Bible." Though many may believe this, most can see the similarity between Augustine's interpretations and their own when they study him. It is more than coincidence that *both* Protestant and Roman Catholic use his thinking to support their differing stands.

SCHOLASTICISM

Scholasticism strongly shaped the way almost everyone understood theology.[29] This way of thinking was characterized by two schools, *theologism* and *nominalism.* The two scholasticisms were antagonistic to each other. Theologism maintained one could understand God's revelation through *reason.* Nominalism, on the other hand, taught that neither God nor Reality could be in any way understood, and therefore must be accepted "*by faith alone.*" The Medieval Roman Catholic, and second generation Reformed theologians employed theologism to explain the sacraments through reason.[30] The first generation Reformers borrowed from nominalism to explain salvation primarily through personal experience.

Theologism led to forced and technical theological definitions. Scholastic theologians were not beyond debating anything from the number of angels who could dance on the head of a pin, to the degree of consecratory power remaining in a crumb of Eucharist eaten by a mouse.[31] In the end, theology becomes an absurd religious "science."

At first glance, nominalism seems the better choice between the scholasticisms, but its subjective and relativistic philosophy is not Biblical. According to nominalism, all that is necessary for something to be "real" (true) is for someone *believe* it. In other words, there is no reality outside of one's faith. What one believes *makes* something real. Nominalism goes even further when it demands that one cannot exercise such "belief" unless he is willing to abandon reason all together.[32]

Thomas Aquinas pressed for a compromise between nominalism and theologism. Aquinas advocated a marriage for both a reason *and* faith oriented scholasticism. He maintained that reason had the ability to understand all objects of *science* (nature), whereas, all matters regarding *revelation* (doctrine) could be known only "by faith."[33] Through his influence, Christian dogma was to be explained through both reason (theologism) and subjective experience (nominalism).[34]

Although some interpret Aquinas' ideas as an attempt to balance nominalism and theologism, in reality, he fused both schools. Aquinas still saw "faith" in a nominalistic light. His attempts to define, and systematize Revelation was still wet with theologism.

Many became fed up with the scholastic theologies of theologism and Aquinas. Those who looked elsewhere, looked to scholastic nominalism. By 1500, nominalism and humanism become the dominant teaching in the universities of Germany and France. Together, these philosophies would help ignite the fires of the Reformation. Nominalism's influence was evident in Luther,[35] and its teachings deeply touched the other Reformers as well. It was this philosophy, for example, which led many within the Reform movements to interpret Biblical faith in nominalistic ways. Its appeal lay in its simplicity, and in its promise to answer the average Christian's hunger for "straight practical Christian life, and nothing else."[36]

Although the average American Christian would not ascribe to traditional nominalism, it seems that its philosophy still heavily biases many. How many Christians would not say, "Christian doctrine does not matter. All that matters is that one *believes* in Jesus (One rarely discusses *how* they see Jesus)." How many others would affirm, "God does not care about the specifics of your belief, *as much as* He cares that what you believe is *sincere.*" Where *believing* and the *intensity* of belief is more important than *what* one believes, there is nominalism. And to the degree one is a nominalist, to that degree Reality will be hidden from him.

HUMANISM

Renaissance humanism was a very powerful force behind Reformation thinking—perhaps, it was the most powerful force.[37] Calling people to rediscover the thought and method of Aristotle, humanism redefined man's place in the world.[38] Where mankind had at once seen God as the center of the world, man now begins to see himself as the center of all things. The philosophy was clearly individualistic: it insisted that each individual determine one's own destiny, that each should decide upon the nature of truth for himself, and that the individual has the power to judge the ethics of religion against his own convictions.[39]

The Reformers did not agree with every point of Renaissance humanism,[40] but they found a lot they liked about it. They respected it for the value it placed on studying ancient texts in their original languages (i.e., the Greek of the Bible). They also favored it in its contempt for external forms of religion, and religious traditions. The Radical Reformers would affirm humanism's stress on piety over doctrinal definition; [41] seeing "good deeds," not intellectual speculation, as "the test of creedal truth."[42] The affection of the Reformers for humanism should not surprise us. As stated, humanistic schools were responsible for the education of the majority of the Reformers.[43]

What is "humanistic" about Evangelical-Fundamental Christianity today? I would say its major affinity with humanism lay in its cultural self centeredness. Many Christians relate to God as if *their* time, place and customs were the center of all things. Instead of the seeing the Church as a manifestation of God's kingdom in and throughout time, many imprison their Christian experience to personal boundaries. As a consequence, few recognize the relevance or the importance of what God has spoken to His Church throughout its existence.

PROTESTANTISM'S TIE TO ROMAN CATHOLICISM

Roman Catholic thinking and Reformation thinking are not that different. Seminaries were teaching Reformation doctrine years before the Reformation. It is true that the language of the Reformed theologian broke with traditional terminology, but when he did use a "new" language, he merely "uttered old ideas in new words."[44] The Reformers simply opposed "Roman Catholic" Augustinianism with a "Reformed" brand of Augustinianism.[45] "In the sixteenth century both Roman and Reformed were content to argue about the same problems ... Both shared the assumptions of Western theology, Latin theology."[46] In many cases, the Reformers merely painted over Roman theology with a different color; one need only to scratch the surface to get to the old paint again.[47]

One can neither condemn the Reformers nor the Roman Church for how they dealt with the moral and theological crisis each faced. The perspectives of their culture limited their options. What else could they do? They had been raised on Augustinianism. Many had been trained in humanism. Each was confined to choose between a multiple choice of scholastic alternatives.

EASTERN EMPATHY AND ESTEEM FOR THE REFORMATION

The Reformation was a movement of the Holy Spirit. The Reformers were men moved by a desire to give God glory, and to set men free in Christ. There is no question about this. The Reformation successfully protested the popular doctrine of indulgences. The movement countered distorted teachings and traditions unique to the papacy. In these respects the Eastern Orthodox Christians see the Reformation as "...a great movement of liberation from false categories imprisoning the Christian gospel."[48]

From an Eastern point of view, the *theological* consequences of the Reformation are the inevitable result of the separation of the Christian East and West. Instead of Rome limiting itself to one historic tradition, she could have had the historic consensus and continuity to speak from other views as well. For example, the Medieval Church could have had a living reference to many early fathers who wrote in Greek. Unfortunately, Rome's detachment from the East led it to center its vision solely on Augustine. This vantage point alone could have suggested correctives that may have changed the whole course of the reform movement.

Had the Church of the West been in conversation with the East, perhaps the it could have pursued another other than schism. But such communication would have been nearly impossible. Eastern Orthodox nations were virtually cut off from the Western world. The Moslem conquest of the Middle East, and Constantinople (the center of Eastern Orthodox Christianity) preoccupied the attention of Eastern Christians. The pillaging that occurred against Orthodox Christians during the Crusades made them distrustful of the West. Russia, a huge nation consisting of vast numbers of Orthodox, technologically and culturally isolated itself from the West. All this did not allow for theological dialogue. For all practical purposes, the West did not even know that the Eastern Church existed, much less have opportunity to think about her perspectives.

LESSONS FROM THE REFORMATION PERIOD

THE REFORMATION: RESPONSE *AND* REACTION

The Reformation was not only a *response* of the Spirit, but a human *reaction* against evil. The medieval Roman Church was in desperate need of reform. The superstitious piety of her people, the immorality of her clergy, the authoritarianism of her popes, and her doctrinal deviations, all demanded a response. In this environment, it was quite natural to emphasize doctrines that seemed to be the opposite of Roman abuses: Scripture/not tradition, faith/not sacraments, Christ/not the Church, priesthood of all believers/not a clerical elite. Certainly, many of these doctrines carried more of an anti-Roman flavor than they would have had they been forged in another setting.

I think we must admit that there may be some validity to the criticism that Protestant doctrine has a tendency to *protest* more than *profess*. Unquestionably, in certain Evangelical-Fundamentalist circles, one's *opposition* to Roman doctrine is more of a proof of his orthodoxy than what he *proposes* in its place. Agreed, the Reformation was a revolution. But a revolt *against* something does not automatically make a clear statement as to what one is *for*.[49]

As for the Christians of the East, the Roman Catholic-Protestant (Reformation-Counter Reformation) debates had virtually no influence.[50] From the Medieval period on, Eastern Christians had little or no communication with their brethren in the West. Certainly, today, they recognize the intensity and seriousness of these historical controversies, but their *different ideological, philosophical, historical and cultural context* finds them emotionally removed from them. Even prior to the Medieval period, the East was isolated from the West due to differences in language (Greek vs. Latin), culture (Semitic vs. Roman), Church administration (collegial vs. Papal) and a political rivalry (Constantinople ["New Rome"] vs. Rome).[51] Thus, while Protestantism and Roman Catholicism were profoundly influenced by a combination Scholastic theology, the Renaissance, and Papal abuses, the East remained relatively unaffected by these Western trends.

THE EAST AND WEST BELONG TOGETHER

We might have avoided the bizarre breed of multi-denominated Christianity that exists today if the East and West had stayed in fellowship. Today, there clearly exists a difference in how the East and West think. These opposing viewpoints, however, do not need to exist. In spite of all their peculiarities, East and West organically belong together.[52] They share a *common* ground in a *common history*. Though the Reformers were generally ignorant of the East, some pointed to the Eastern Church as an example of an ancient Church other than Rome.[53]

The Reformation stands for the love of truth and a willingness to change in light of it. This is the major lesson that this generation must relearn. The Reformation is to be *ongoing*. It teaches each person the need to be constantly open to the leading and illuminating ministry of the Spirit.[54] When we think that we need learn nothing more, we have lost touch with the Spirit Who inspired the Reformation ... and we have lost touch with the Spirit of the Church.

"Breakdowns in human relationships, heresy, and schism do not really spring from different beliefs and opinions ... [but] from pride, arrogance, or other sins; from our failure to accept, from our distrust, intolerance, and self-righteousness."[55] We need to rediscover and integrate the Christian perspectives of the East into our way of thinking. This will not happen if we give our loyalty to a tradition, or a particular denomination, before we give our loyalty to Christ.[56] Let us put aside the past prejudices that have blinded us; and with open mind and open heart let us "pursue the things that make for peace and the building up of one another" (Rom. 14:19). Then let the Spirit of the Reformation continue.

NOTES FOR CHAPTER THREE

1 At least this is the opinion of Leopold von Ranke, the founder of modern critical history, an assessment which Lewis W. Spitz in his *The Renaissance and Reformation Movements* agrees. (Chicago, IL., Rand McNally and Company, 1971, p. 306)

2 Joseph Lortz, "Why Did the Reformation Happen?",*The Reformation: Material or Spiritual?* , Lewis W. Spitz, ed. (Lexington, MA., 1962) p. 59

3 It is clear that the development of Christian doctrine, by its very nature as thought, "is bound simultaneously to each of the particular cultural situations within which men have reflected on the Christian message and to the successions within these men have stood." Jarosalv Pelikan, *Development of Christian Doctrine,* (New Haven and London, Yale University Press, 1979) p. 46

4 Harold J. Grimm, *The Reformation Era 1500-1650* (New York, The Macmillian Company, 1965) p. 570

5 An illustration of their frenzy is well depicted during the Great Plague of Normandy (1348-1349). During this time, masses of people would parade through the streets whipping themselves. These people, referring themselves as the "Red Knights of Christ", believed that this blood letting granted them salvation as it somehow mystically united them to Christ's blood.

6 R. W. Southern, *Western Society and the Church in the Middle Ages* (Hammondsworth, Middlesex, England/New York, 1970), pp. 304-305, italics are mine.

7 Books were hard to come by for two reasons: 1) Books were scarce. The printing press was was not invented until the eve of the Reformation so every book had to be reproduced by hand. 2) The cost of books was so high, only the very wealthy could afford them. In the Tenth Century a countess of Anjou is said to have given 200 sheep, three barrels of grain and some marten furs for a single book of sermons, and at the end of the 14th century a prayer book in two volumes was bought by the Duke of Orleans for 200 gold francs. See Svend Dahl, *History of the Book* , (N.Y., The Sacrecrow Press Inc., 1958) pp. 66-67

8 It is no wonder that Protestantism reacted to the idea of relics when one sees what was being presented as sacred remnants. Here is a partial list of some of these incredible artifacts:

- A vial which contained a portion of the bread that the Lord chewed with his very own teeth
- The baby teeth of Christ
- The foreskin of Christ after His circumcision
- The collection of Frederick the Wise in Saxony [which included five thousand relics] boasted the straw from the manger in Bethlehem, wood from the true cross, and the thumb of St. Anne
- The swaddling clothes in which Christ had been wrapped and two pieces from His manger
- A piece of Aarron's rod and a shoulder blade from one of the holy innocents
- The "holy house at Loreto", which was believed to be the Lord's home miraculously transported by angels from Nazareth
- Of the Virgin Mary there were pieces of her veil, the very nightdress she was wearing the night she gave birth to Jesus, and even drops of her milk (these were found in many places).

9 Heiko Augustinus Oberman, *The Harvest of Medieval Theology* (Cambridge, MA, Harvard University Press, 1963) p. 325. Oberman sees this as indicative of the Donatistic wave that began to move in certain areas towards the end of the late Middle Ages.

10 Jaroslav Pelikan *The Christian Tradition: Reformation of Church and Dogma (1300-1700)* (Chicago and London, The University of Chicago Press, 1983) p. 86 citing Jean de Gerson's *Sermons*, Palémon Jean Glorieux, ed. Jean Gerson. *Oeuvres compleétes.* 10 volumes. Paris, 1960-73, vol. 5, p. 74

11 A well-known churchman remarked, "Which shepherd today would give his life for his sheep? In fact, which shepherd has not been transformed into a wolf that devours their souls?'" Pelikan, *Reformation of Church and Dogma,* p. 86 citing Alvaro Pelayo's *Epistles,* 13. 31 in Vittorino Meneghin, ed. *Scrittti inediti di Fra Alvaro Pais.* Libson, 1969, p. 129

12 Even the Dutch Pope Adrian VI, moments after the initial outbreak of the Reformation, confessed that the Church's failings in leadership were primarily responsible for the outbreak of this movement. He instructed his legate to the Diet of Nuremberg in 1522 and 1523 to declare the following to all present:

> God has let this persecution of His church occur because of men and especially because of the sins of the priest and prelates. The Holy Scriptures loudly proclaim that the sins of the people have their origin in the sins of the religious leaders. We know all too well that also in the case of this Holy See for many years many reprehensible things have taken place: abuses in spiritual things, breaking of the commandments, yes, that everything has taken a turn for the very worst! We therefore have no cause to wonder that the disease has been transplanted from the head to the members, from the popes to the prelates.

Lewis W. Spitz, *The Renaissance and Reformation Movements* (Chicago,IL., Rand McNally and Company, 1971) p. 318. cited from Carl Mirbt, ed., *Quellen zur Geschichte des Papsttums und des römischen Katholizismus,* 4th edition (Tübingen, 1924) p. 261

13 Owen Chadwick, *The Reformation* (Baltimore, MD., Penguin Books, 1972) p.19 Pope Leo X (1513-1521), for example, advanced the members of his family and others by selling Church offices to them at a great price; with him the number of church offices available for sale broke records. The saying *Radix Omnium Malorum Avaritia* (the love of money is the root of all evil) became popularly abbreviated by the first letter of each word: ROMA ."

14 A third of Europe was owned by the church and it was popularly believed that two-fifths of the German income from these properties was stolen off to Rome through "ecclesiastical channels." Great creativity was exerted in developing new wells which the church could pump for revenues. Some of these were the practice of reservations [the payments for nominations to vacant benefices], the collection of annates [the first year's revenue from a benefice] and opportunities for simony [the act of buying and selling church offices or pardons]. Spitz, p. 313.

15 Jaroslav Pelikan, *The Growth of Medieval Theology (600-1300)* Vol. 3 of *The Christian Tradition: A History of the Development of Doctrine*, (University of Chicago Press, 1978) p. 301

16 William A. Scott, *Historical Protestantism: An Historical Introduction to Protestant Theology* (Englewood Cliffs, N. J., 1971) p. 13

17 I do not use the term 'radical' in a negative sense here. Radical is a derivation from the word "root" and, in this context, expresses the desire to go back to the Church's primitive roots. The Anabaptists of which I will be referring in this book are of the mainline 'evangelical' stream, i.e., those represented by such figures as Menno Simmons, Conrad Grebel, Balthasar Hubmaier, Pilgram Marpeck, Dirk Philips. Their chief distinguishing characteristic (for which baptism was the outward symbol) was a withdrawal from the world, (which they believed were inclusive of the Catholic and Reformed Churches) and their formation of closely knit brotherhoods which stressed "Biblical faith" and the regenerate life of discipleship. (See

Franklin H. Littell, *The Origins of Sectarian Protestantism* [New York,The Macmillan Company, 1964] p. xv; Austin P. Evans, *An Episode in the Struggle for Religious Freedom: the Sectaries of Nuremberg, 1524-1528* [New York: Columbia University Press, 1924) pp. 14-15], John Tonkin, *The Church and the Secular Order in Reformation Thought* [New York, Columbia University Press, 1971] p. 198; Kenneth Ronald Davis, *Anabaptism and Asceticism* [Scottsdale, Pa., Herald Press, 1974])

18 Karl H. Dannenfeldt in *The Church of the Renaissance and Reformation* (St. Louis, Concordia Publishing House, 1970) pp. 13-14 summarizes the evolution of the doctrine well:

> During the Crusades a plenarym or full indulgence was granted to those who died fighting the infidel-a good recruiting device. This was then extended to all who participated in a crusade and then to those who contributed a certain amount to send a soldier in their place. After the Crusades the use of indulgences was extended in various ways. While originally indulgences were granted for virtuous deeds, they soon were sold for money. Then agents spread the highly marketable wares throughout Europe. By drawing on the treasury of "surplus merits" accumulated by Christ and the saints, the popes could issue indulgence letters and release the purchaser from temporal punishment both on earth and in purgatory. In 1247 Sixtus IV promised the purchaser the immediate release from purgatory of someone already dead. Although this papal power was questioned by some and although canon law did not legalize such indulgences, the sale of indulgences among the simple people increased rapidly. Gone was the initial emphasis on contrition and confession; the monetary aspect of the traffic became uppermost.

19 An indulgence was " to grant remission of a part or all of the temporal punishment imposed by the church of a *confessing* sinner." Karl H. Dannenfeldt, *The Church of the Renaissance and Reformation* (St. Louis, Concordia Publishing House, 1970) p. 13. Italics mine.

20 In 1343 Pope Clement VI gave official endorsement to the principle. In the thirteenth century the belief spread that one person could obtain an indulgence for another, and that the living might even obtain indulgences for the souls in purgatory. (Kenneth Scott Latourtette, *A History of Christianity Volume I: Beginnings to 1500*, Revised Edition [New York, Harper and Row, 1975] p. 530)

21 Aquinas' theory well complimented Anselm of Canterbury's (1033-1109) teaching of salvation. For Anselm taught that the "fruit" of Christ's sacrifice was bestowed through a special grace which first justifies (legally), and then creates in us a capacity that transforms our works into ones which acquire a *meritorious* character. The merit is a product of the grace which the sacramental powers of the church dispense. Here it becomes clear how this teaching was only a half-step away from the doctrine of indulgences.

22 It is important to note, however, that the doctrine demanding faith *and* works was not universally accepted by the Roman Church. This later position was solidified in Rome's Counter Reformation Council of Trent (1545 -1563). Jaroslav Pelikan, *The Growth of Medieval Theology (600-1300),* p. 25

23 Religious professionals clearly played upon the people's ignorance and were not afraid to make great promises for those who would "donate" to the Roman Church in order to receive an indulgence. It became a proverb among the preachers of the movement to proclaim, "The moment the money tinkles in the collecting box, a soul flies out of purgatory." Even a papal official was quoted to have distorted the passage of Ezekiel which read "The Lord desireth not the death of a sinner ...but rather that he should repent and live" to read "The Lord desireth not the death of a sinner...but rather that he should *pay* and live.'" See Chadwick, *The Reformation,* p. 42; Bernard M.G. Reardon, *Religious Thought In the Reformation* (New York, Longman Inc., 1981) p. 1)

24 Jaroslav Pelikan, *The Growth of Medieval Theology,* p. 7, 8 in ftnes: Laistner (1966) p. 136, and Lot (1961) p. 371 respectively.

25 In a number of cases, "an illiterate devoid of any knowledge of the Latin tongue was ordained to the priesthood, and could be heard mumbling nonsensically through his prayers at the altar.." Owen Chadwick, *The Reformation* (Baltimore, Maryland, Penguin Books, 1972) p.14

26 Rosalind and Christopher Brooke, *Popular Religion in the Middle Ages: Western Europe 1000-1300* (London, Thames and Hudson 1984) p. 1

27 The *Sentences* (a compilation of quotations from the Fathers arranged by Peter Lombard) was the foundation from which the theological tradition of the Middle Ages largely drew. That work, inclusive of those who later added their commentaries to the text, firmly established Augustine's perspectives in the Church of that era. In Lombard's compilation "Augustine is quoted most often, in about 950 passages, or, if one includes the quotations from the writings that are certainly ascribed to him falsely, in more than a thousand passages, i.e., more than twice as often as all other Fathers combined." Jaroslav Pelikan, *The Growth of Medieval Theology (600-1300)* p. 270, ftnte: Baltzer (1902) p. 2) It is interesting to note that Augustine's thinking significantly influenced both Roman Catholic *and* Reformed theologians equally.

28 Pelikan, *Reformation of Church and Dogma (1300-1700)* p. 32

29 I will speak more specifically about his system of thought in the discussion of the sacraments.

30 The starting point of theologism is faith, but then it proceeds on to reason. It was this approach that allowed Anselm of Canterbury to offer *rational* proofs to support the truth of *revelation.* Etienne Gilson, *The Reason and Revelation in the Middle Ages*, (New York, Charles Scribner's Sons, 1938) p. 27

31 Desiderius Erasmus, a Catholic scholar and humanist who was a contemporary with Luther, satirizes scholasticism's tendency in his *The Encomium Moriae* (1509) :

> "They will explain the precise manner in which original sin is derived from our first parents; they will study you in what manner, by what degrees and in how long a time our Saviour was conceived in the Virgin's womb, and demonstrate how in the consecrated wafer the accidents [appearance of the bread] can exist without the substance [the reality of the bread]. Nay, these are accounted trivial, easy questions; they have greater difficulties behind, which, nevertheless, they solve with as much expedition as the former — namely, whether supernatural generation requires any instant of time? ... Whether it would be possible for the first Person of the Trinity to hate the second? Whether God, who took our nature upon him in the form of a man, could as well have become a woman, a devil, an ass, a gourd or a stone?

Bernard M.G. Reardon, *Religious Thought In the Reformation* (New York, Longman Inc., 1981) p. 37

32 "Had we but the reason as a guide, we should think it untrue. But in such a mystery the reason is helpless." Owen Chadwick, *The Reformation* (Baltimore, MD., Penguin Books, 1972) p. 34

33 Aquinas' defense for a rational demonstration of the mysteries of the faith was based on the familiar Augustinian distinction between God's revelation via nature and the gift of grace He gives us through the sacraments and others means in the Church. God's grace can so elevate our reason that we are enabled to contemplate things which were previously beyond our reach (such as the dogmas of the Trinity and the incarnation). Pelikan, *The Growth of Medieval Theology (600-1300)* pp. 284, 285

34 In essence, what Augustine was saying was, "What resides in the realm of nature, one can know by *reason alone*, areas in the domain of revelation, can be known and accepted *by faith alone.* The logical conclusion of this method of thinking is summarized by Gilson:

> One and the same thing cannot be at one and the same time both an object of science and an object of faith. Thus it is the essence of an article of faith to rest upon divine authority alone. When something is rationally probable, its contrary also is rationally probable. It

is but an opinion. Religious faith is not an opinion. It is the unshakeable certitude that God has spoken.

Etienne Gilson, *The Reason and Revelation in the Middle Ages*, (New York, Charles Scribner's Sons, 1938) pp. 74, 75

35 Luther complimented Occam as "the only scholastic who was any good" and had practically memorized the writings of his professor Gabriel Biel who was also a strong nominalist. Luther's esteem for Occam (he had referred to Occam as his "master") certainly indicated that "he knew Occam and probably knew him better than he did the earlier theologians." Jaroslav Pelikan, *From Luther To Kierkegaard* , (St. Louis, Missouri, Concordia Publishing House, 1950), p. 6 , Louis Bouyer, *The Spirit and Forms of Protestantism* (Westminster, Maryland, The Newman Press, 1956) p. 153

36 [Nominalism] expressed the common attitude prevalent in the early fifteenth century.. All the best historians of that movement agree at least on this, that it expressed a feeling of lassitude, after the failure of so many philosophers and theologians to achieve anything like a commonly received truth. ...Many fourteenth century Christians were simply fed up with the whole business. They had no use for speculative theology...what they wanted was straight practical Christian life, and nothing else. Gilson, p. 90

37 "There is certainly no question that without the humanistic spirit that was current in Europe their [the Reformers] ideas would not have found the acceptance that they did. It seems evident, therefore, that if Luther had appeared fifty years earlier with his demands for the reconstitution of church and world, he would probably have found few supporters since he would have lacked the preparation provided by humanism... The humanists were the first to accept Luther and to give him a lasting following. ...Without them he would have failed as did many before him who had tried to stand up against the old church. One can state pointedly: No humanism, no Reformation." Ozment, pp. 34, 36

3 8 There were many different expressions of humanism, and some of the most noted historians of the period are still unclear about how to define all of its varities; the two most common divisions of humanism, however, were Italian (literary, artistic and philosophical) and Northern/ German (religious and theological). Where skeptical and rationalistic trends did occur within humanism, Protestant reformation thinking often defended itself with nominalist/"faith alone" [*sola fide*] positions. In this sense, the Reformers were actually" hybrids of scholasticism and humanism — 'half humanist' and 'half scholastic' in outlook." Ozment, p. 138 quoting Spitz, "The Course of German Humanism.," pp. 375-76

39 In this last instance, faith can be only demonstrated personally and privately, not through any outward forms such as images, music or sacraments. Grimm, p. 87

40 They particularly disagreed with humanism's stand against original sin, and its priority of life-style over truth.

41 Ozment, *The Intellectual Origins of the Reformation*, p. 139. Petrarch's statement, "It is better to will the good than to know the truth," rightly catches the sense of the moral humanist and the place where he lays his emphasis. p.140 in Ozment, Cited by Hanna H. Gray, "Renaissance Humanism: The Pursuit of Eloquence" in *Renaissance Essays,* eds. P. O. Kristeller and P. Wiener (New York, 1968), p. 203 It should be noted however, that men like Calvin, who were very much of the humanistic school, would never compromise what they believed to be "right doctrine" for right living. Calvin fought this kind of humanism through *another* kind of humanism. Erasmus, however, would seem to identify with Petrarch in his challenge to Luther on the issue of free will when "he considered Luther's doctrine of the will's bondage to sin to be detrimental to morality *even if the doctrine were true.*" (Ozment, p. 140, cited in footnote : "Figngamus igitur in aliquo sensu verum esse, quod docuit Vuyclevus, Lutherus asseruit, quicquid fit a nobis, non libero arbitrio, sed mers necessitate fieri, quid inutilius, quam hoc paradoxon evulgari mundo?" *De libero arbitrio* I a 10 in *Erasmus von Rotterdam. Augeewählte Schriften* 4 (Darmstadt 1969) p. 18

42 Grimm, *The Reformation Era (1500-1650)* , (New York, The Macmillan Company, 1965) p. 86 Scholastics, on the contrary, insisted that true *creeds* must be the fount of good deeds." (Ozment p.141).

4 3 By 1530 the ten or twenty most important intellectual leaders of the Reformation movement could be all identified as having been trained in humanism. (Ozment, pp. 35, 36) In essence the philosophical atmosphere during the time of the Reformation could be summarized as follows:

> Calvin's identification with of faith and knowledge (Augustinian position- that faith and knowledge are not mutually exclusive, excepting that rational natural theology is avoided due to man's fallen–depraved reason)..Occamists, the other extreme, separated faith and knowledge and faith and reason..Aquinas, was in between, faith and knowledge are to be distinguished, but reason leads up to and illustrates faith....Luther's view was Occamism grown religiously vital. Faith was pitted even more violently against 'the harlot reason,' but faith was mightily sure of itself. Melancthon and Zwingli, ...still held to the essential irrationality of faith.

Ronald H. Bainton, *Studies On the Reformation*, (Boston, Beacon Press, 1963) p. 131, 132

44 Oscar Cullman, F. J Leenhardt, *Essays on the Lord's Supper* , "This Is My Body", F. J Leenhardt, (Atlanta, Georgia, Lutherworth Press, 1958), p. 26

45 "For, in an epigram that may be an exaggeration but is not a total distortion, 'the Reformation, inwardly considered, was just the ultimate triumph of Augustine's doctrine of grace over Augustine's doctrine of the church'." (Pelikan, *Reformation of Church and Dogma (1300-1700)* p. 9 citing Benjamin Breckenridge Warfield, *Calvin and Augustine* (Philadelphia, 1956) p. 322)

46 "In the development of popular piety and its theological rationale, medieval Europe displays what we may call a 'naive supernaturalism' that plagues us still with the wrong questions: how can you tell a miracle? how is Christ present in the sacraments? why does the omnipotent Lord allow evil? To answer such questions an important shift took place from the position of the Early Church. John Meyendorff, Joseph McLelland, eds., "Sailing to Byzantium", Joseph C. McLelland, *The New Man: An Orthodox and Reformed Dialogue*, (New Jersey, Standard Press, 1973) p. 14

47 The reality of the Reformation theology's Augustinian and scholastic bias is even more clearly evidenced in the later Reformers who tended to base the validity of one's Christianity almost solely upon a doctrinal confession. This religious instruction indirectly communicated what the medieval theologians had said before them: "Faith" can be taught in the method of the ancient philosophers. "The Protestant reformers were truly *new* scholastics ... Aristotelianism and the humanities were 'confessionalized,' that is, taken over and integrated into the larger task of communicating Biblical doctrine to the masses." (Ozment, p. 149)

48 John Meyendorff, *The Catholicity and the Church,* "The Significance of the Reformation in the History of Christendom" (Crestwood, New York, St. Vladimir's Seminary Press, 1983) p. 76

49 The Medieval Roman Church could be cited by some as reacting as well. Before the Reformation many segments of that Church taught a doctrine of salvation by faith, were open to a more collegial form of government, allowed for various related understandings of the Eucharist, and advanced other teachings which would later be identified with the Reformers. After the Council of Trent (1545-1563), these positions were not only dropped, but a number of them were strongly opposed. The contemporary Roman Catholic Church is much more positive and open to the lessons of the Reformation today, especially since the advent of the Second Vatican Council (1962-1965). However, there are still ultra-conservative elements within Roman Catholicism today that are reluctant to recognize the existence of the Church anywhere outside her borders.

50 Reformed historian Joseph Mc Lelland explains why this is the case:

> Eastern church history lacks the entire phenomenon of our Renaissance-Reformation. That is, it lacks both the stimulus and the response, the question and its answer. It did not experience the tension of rival authorities and theories of church government, of

conflicting theologies of grace and sacraments, and therefore it cannot truly appreciate the answer of Reformation and Counter-Reformation.

John Meyendorff, Joseph McLelland, eds., "Sailing to Byzantium", Joseph C. McLelland, *The New Man: An Orthodox and Reformed Dialogue*, (New Jersey, Standard Press, 1973) p. 14

51 Besides these factors, from the Fifteenth century onward, the Moslem Ottoman Empire reigned over the East for nearly four centuries. This political-religious domination made it virtually impossible for Eastern Christians to be in contact with Christians outside their boundaries.

52 "...East and West are not independent units, and therefore are not 'intelligible in themselves.' They are *fragments* of one world, of one Christendom, which, in God's design, ought not to have been disrupted." Georges Florovsky, *Orthodoxy: A Faith and Order Dialogue,* (Geneva, Switzerland, WCC, 1960), Faith and Order Paper #30 pp. 50, 51

53 " As is well known, the early Protestants of various parties appealed to the example of the Eastern Church as a type of Catholic Christianity that was not Roman in its obedience or doctrine. Whether the reformers always understood the Orthodox tradition is one matter. That they appealed to it, however, signifies their willingness to break the theological isolation into which the West had fallen." G. L. C. Frank," A Lutheran Turned Eastward", *St. Vladimir's Seminary Quarterly* (Crestwood, N.Y., St. Vladimir's Seminary Press,1982) Vol. 26, No. 3 , p. 171

54 "The fidelity to the reformers consists in holding that the Reformation of the Reformation must always continue." Oscar Cullman, F. J Leenhardt, *Essays on the Lord's Supper* , (Atlanta, Georgia, Lutherworth Press, 1958), p. 25

55 Demetrious J. Constantelos, eds., *Orthodox Theology and Diakonia: Trends and Prospects,* Emilianos Timiadis, "The Ecumenical Movement and Orthodoxy," (Brookline, MA., Hellenic College Press, 1981) p. 311

56 Thomas Howard in *Evangelical Is Not Enough* makes a good case for Christian's to cease fighting over the past and forgive each other by demonstarting how other nations who have warred with each other are now at peace.

> We may say all we will about the bad faith at work in secular diplomacy, but it remains true that countries which have warred with each other not only sign papers of peace, but actually enter into peace despite the immense issues that have set them at each other's throats. Does Greece still war with Persia? Does Rome still send its legions through Gaul? Does England still shell Boston's harbor? Do the American and Japanese fleets still fire on each other? Little is gained by anyone's remaining fiercely loyal to his own history to the point of wishing to keep ancient flames of animosity alive.

(New York, Thomas Nelson Publishers, 1984), p. 151

CHAPTER FOUR

THE FUNDAMENTALIST-EVANGELICAL VIEW OF THE BIBLE (PART I):

UNCOVERING ITS HISTORY AND PHILOSOPHY

The next two chapters will sketch a popular outline of the American Evangelical-Fundamentalist approach to the Bible. Chapters five and six will contrast this outlook with the Eastern Christian approach. However, I must caution the reader: I will not try to define and delineate the various schools of Biblical theology that exist within Evangelicalism or Fundamentalism, nor will I make distinctions between their differing approaches. My only purpose here is to trace *popular trends* of Evangelical-Fundamentalist thinking (views which many American Christians have about the Bible), so the reader will be better able to evaluate his present understanding alongside the Eastern Christian view.

Christian integrity requires one not only to know *what* he believes, but also *why* he believes what he does. The Scriptures tell us that the foundation of wisdom is not mere knowledge but *understanding* (Proverbs 4:7). The basic underlying question one must ask oneself to grow in understanding is, "*Why* do I believe what I believe?" From this question, the following questions arise about how one views the Bible:

> Are my views of the Scripture inherently Biblical or are they a product of something else?
>
> What influence does Western culture play in my understanding of the Scripture?
>
> How do my philosophical predispositions affect the way I view the Bible? What are they?
>
> How many of my beliefs are unconsciously determined or influenced either by my family upbringing, by an uncritical denominational loyalty, or by an emotional prejudice against other denominations?
>
> Are any of my views simply the consequence of my own unwillingness to study the issues for myself?

I encourage the reader to ask himself the above questions as he reads this chapter, and the two that follow. The analysis presented in these pages can powerful impact how one sees Scripture for the rest of his life.

THE BIBLE ALONE

The central principle animating the Evangelical-Fundamentalist view of the Bible can be summed up in three words: "The Bible alone" [*sola Scriptura*]. Fundamentalist denominations and seminaries base almost every aspect of their life, government, and theology upon this philosophy. In matching spirit, many contend that their doctrinal stand is paraphrased by the slogan, "We have no need for any creed but the Bible." This contention is supported by six commonly held perspectives (a few which contradict each other): the rationalistic view, the "common sense" vision, the private interpretative outlook, the literalistic perspective, the anti-intellectual approach, and the perfect Bible doctrine. As you read the following, it will become evident that the foundation of all these views are the various forms of scholasticism I touched on in the last chapter.

A RATIONALISTIC PERSPECTIVE OF THE SCRIPTURES

By a *rationalistic* perspective, I don't mean a denial of the supernatural in the Scriptures, but that reason alone can give a full and accurate understanding of them. *Reason* is *the authority* in determining what the Bible says. Rationalism, therefore, highly respects the method of Scripture study which puts a premium on analyzing, categorizing, and ordering Biblical facts. It generally distrusts any knowledge of the faith which relies too heavily on emotions, or experience. Thus, the task of the conservative Evangelical-Fundamentalist theologian is...

> ... to systematize the teachings of Holy Scripture the best he can. He is to aim at a final system of theology deduced from Sacred Scripture even though he knows that he could never in this life attain this final system.[1]

In such a theological system, the basic message of Christianity can be deduced by simply comparing one Scripture with another. Through this method, one would use those passages of Scripture whose meanings are "clear and obvious", to gain the meaning of those which are less certain. By such a procedure, "Scripture interprets Scripture."

This system of Biblical study found favor at Princeton Theological Seminary in the early 1800's, where A. Hodge, Charles Hodge, Archibald Alexander, and B. B. Warfield articulated a "scientific" doctrine of Biblical inspiration. Their conviction about Scripture "never wavered from the fundamental tenet that if the Bible was proven to be God's inspired word, the demonstration must be made on the basis of reason through the use of external marks of authenticity—not inner convictions."[2] Charles Hodge was able to compare his rational view of the Scriptures with the system of Newtonian physics.

Warfield went on to maintain that unaided reason put both the believer and the non-believer on equal footing in their respective abilities to interpret the Scriptures:

> Reason is as necessary to faith ... as light is to photography. It is the distinction of Christianity that it has come into the world clothed with the mission to *reason* its way to its dominion. ... And it is solely by reasoning that it will put all its enemies under its feet.[3]

Given their bias that reason is the key to Bible interpretation, the Princeton professors believed that God would never reveal His truth through a book containing errors. From this platform, they constructed what they believed was the "shock proof" doctrine of biblical authority. This theory taught "...that God had so inspired the biblical authors that their every word as recorded on the original autographs [the very parchments upon which the Biblical authors themselves wrote] was inerrant— a term more specifically rationalistic than the word infallible."[4] In essence, these men became responsible for the late stage development of what is often referred to as the Fundamentalist view of the Scriptures: the Bible is verbally inspired and inerrant in its every reference, statistic, and quotation.

THE BIBLE IS INTERPRETED BY "COMMON SENSE"

The Reformers were suspicious of the interpretations of the Roman Church and what they believed were their handed down "traditions of men." In their view, the Roman Catholic Church had manipulated the Bible to support its own political agenda. But what if the Bible was given into the hands of the common man, and what if he were given authority to interpret the Bible for himself? Certainly that would take the hierarchy down a peg. But how could such a move be philosophically justified? By appealing to the *common sense* method of Biblical interpretation.

The common sense perspective assumes that *any* person can readily understand the Scriptures. This philosophy is based in Scottish Common Sense Realism, a school of thought which taught that "any sane and unbiased person of common sense could and *must* perceive the same things ..."[5] Accordingly, when it comes to the Bible "the common sense perceptions of the common man could be relied upon."[6]

Related to this ideology is the belief that the Bible's meaning is "transparent", that none of its teaching is "hidden" to the common observer. The premise was that the Scriptures could be understood well enough without the need of a scholar to decipher its message. From this vantage point, there is neither a need for an elite teaching authority (such as a bishop or Pope), nor for the academic. The Bible is able to be readily understood by "the man on the street."

PRIVATE INTERPRETATION OF SCRIPTURE

As could be predicted, the common sense view of Scripture interpretation encourages an individual to interpret the Bible without the help of anyone.[7] Dr. William Angell, a contemporary Southern Baptist and professor of Religion, seems to agree with the essence of this perspective.

> Baptists insist not only on the primary authority of the Bible but also on the right and duty of individual interpretation. That right, Baptists have generally held, springs from the fundamental principle that every person is of infinite worth to God: and the correlate to that principle is that every person is competent and responsible to stand before God without any intermediary except Jesus Christ. This is why Baptists have always suspected and avoided required creeds, efficacious sacraments, and priestly hierarchies.[8]

Dr. Angell's position is commonly held by many Fundamentalists and Evangelicals today.

A "LITERAL" INTERPRETATION OF SCRIPTURE

A literal interpretation of Scripture becomes a strong argument in support for the common man to interpret his Bible. This view argues that the literal interpretation of a passage be preferred over an allegorical or symbolic meaning. The following definition typifies what most Evangelical-Fundamentalists mean by a "literal interpretation" of Scripture:

> *Literal Sense* of any place of Scripture is that which the words signify, or require in their natural and proper acceptation, without any trope [figure of speech], metaphor, or figure, and abstracted from mystical meaning.[9]

Dispensationalism underscores this literal emphasis. This theological system believes that God's relationship to man has differed in accordance with one of seven distinct periods of history. For example, "under the dispensation of Grace [the sixth dispensation], men are required to repent and turn in faith to Christ, while under that of Law [the fifth dispensation] they were commanded to obey the law."[10]

Biblical literalism and dispensationalism often claim to see doctrines in the Scriptures which other perspectives overlook. This is especially true in regard to teaching about Christ's return and other "End-Time" teaching. Biblical prophecies are to be understood to mean "exactly what they say" and nothing else (e g. "Israel" must mean the Jews, never the Church). Numbers used in prophecy must be interpreted as clear references to exact periods of time.[11] By using such an approach, a Fundamentalist affirms that only literal-dispensational methods of interpretation can accurately disclose the biblical references to the future. Examples of such a method of interpretation, lead one to identify the manner and historic sequence of Christ's coming and the nature and length of His reign on earth.

ANTI-INTELLECTUALISM

A further justification for the private interpretation of the Bible is given through anti-intellectualism. This anti-intellectual approach expresses itself in two primary ways: (1) a distrust of the principal assumptions and conclusions of recent science which conflict with their interpretations of the Bible and (2) an assumption that graduate theological preparation makes it difficult for one to understand the simple message of the Bible.

Bernard Ramm offers an example of this later mind-set in his book, *After Fundamentalism.* Ramm not only readjusts some of his own past Fundamentalist interpretations in the book, but he also reevaluates one of the men credited to be a pillar of the Fundamentalist school: Lewis Sperry Chafer. Chafer was the author of *Systematic Theology* (8 volumes), still the standard reference work of many Evangelical and Fundamentalist schools today.[12] Ramm points out that despite his reputation in the Evangelical community, Chafer had no formal theological education, nor linguistic training. Chafer was also decidedly unfamiliar with the teachings of the Church's early and great theologians. The significant point of all this is not Chafer's lack of preparation, but his *justification* of it. As Chafer himself states in his voluminous work, "The very fact that I did not study a prescribed course in theology made it possible for me to approach the subject with an unprejudiced mind, to be concerned only with what the Bible actually teaches."[13]

An anti-intellectual approach is the child of nominalism. It does not matter what one discovers from research or study. All that matters is that one is sincere, and that he truly believes. This is an important point, and for this reason I will return to it in a later section in this chapter.

THE PERFECTION OF SCRIPTURE

Another defense for reading the *Bible alone* (while alone) can be seen in Scripture's perfection. The perfection doctrine is not a protection of the Bible's theological accuracy, but maintains that each word of the Bible is perfect. The Bible is a *vehicle* of revelation regarding Christ but, in a sense, has become *the revelation.* The generation of theologians following the Reformers upheld a view which saw the Bible as a near extension of divinity. In this view, human contribution to the Bible is negligible, for "the Holy Spirit actually supplied, inspired and dictated the very words and each and every term individually."[14] They saw the Bible as nothing less than an "'absolute transcript" of God's mind, 'dictated inspiration' and ... 'a Book dropped from heaven'."[15] Many Fundamentalists still sympathize with this seventeenth century perspective today.

Hodge and Warfield were noted for their defense of the Bible's sole authority and inspiration. Although they may not have adopted the *dictation* view of the Scriptures, they claimed there was no difference between the Scriptures and the Word of God.[16] From this premise, there is no room for enlightenment other than what was expressly stated in the Bible.[17] As I shall show later, such an outlook would have left the Early Church defenseless against the heretics of their day.

The six approaches to the Scripture did not spontaneously explode upon the scene. Underneath each underpinning of the *Bible alone* doctrine lay the roots of scholasticism. The rationalistic, literal and perfectionist views are clearly inspired by theologism. The views which allow "the average person" to use an anti-intellectual bias to interpret the Bible "on his own" are clearly nominalist.

THE WHY AND HOW OF SOLA SCRIPTURA

The doctrinal and moral abuses within the Roman Catholic Church led the Reformers to rethink the place of the Scriptures within the Church. The Roman Church's hierarchical view of authority challenged the Reformers, "If the Roman Church has been given authority by God, who are you to protest it?" The Reformers had various answers to this question, but the most popular rejoinder would come from the Reformers of another generation.

These later Protestants found their rebuttal in a reinterpretation of the doctrine of *sola Scriptura*. The doctrine of *sola Scriptura* had previously represented the teaching of the Bible as it had rightly been taught by past teachers of the Church (East and West). The doctrine gets redefined by later reformers to mean that the Bible is *the sole* authority in the Church, in and of itself. If the Bible alone is the sole authority in the Church, the reformers could now offer a challenging question to the Roman Church of their own design, "Our authority is the Bible. What authority do *you* have?"

Before exploring the *contest of authorities* (Roman Church verses the Bible), it is important that I take a moment to outline some of the arguments behind the Roman Church's claim to authority. By doing this, it will then be apparent how the doctrine of *sola Scriptura* changed, and why this change was a reaction as well as a response to Rome's stilted view of authority.

THE MEDIEVAL ROMAN CATHOLIC VIEW OF DIVINE AUTHORITY AND *SOLA SCRIPTURA*

The Roman Catholic Church taught that *she* was the source of the Bible's authority. She contended that if it were not for *her* verification and decree, the Bible would not exist as an authoritative book.[18] In other words, since the Church *gave* the Bible authority, therefore, the Church is more authoritative than the Bible. Thomas Aquinas' teaching on *relative* and *direct knowledge* gave this view even further support.

Relative knowledge is knowledge gained through the observation of creation. Direct knowledge comes only through divine revelation, and is the *only* knowledge where one can learn about God. Direct knowledge is the knowledge of "theology." Aquinas taught that the natural, fallen mind cannot be trusted to discern the proper meaning of spiritual truth. The solution to this human fallibility was the God ordained *magisterium* [the council of cardinals headed by the Pope]. God gave the *magisterium* direct knowledge of Himself that the Roman Church could rightly interpret the Faith [i.e., the Scriptures, Fathers, and Creeds], and no one should challenge that authority. In this view, the *magisterium* becomes the singular possessor of the mind of Christ and the mind of the Spirit. The Christian who follows the *magisterium* is assured of walking in the Truth.[19]

The Roman teaching office further underscored its exclusive ability to interpret the Scriptures by stressing that the Bible could not be interpreted without "tradition." Tradition, according to the Medieval Church, was understood as the oral teachings of the apostles; teaching which the *magisterium* alone had access. The hierarchy claimed their intimacy with the apostolic "secrets" gave them a *unique* ability to interpret the Scriptures. The Reformers protested to this distorted idea of Tradition, and to the *magisterium* 's claims to spiritual power. Scripture and Magisterial tradition was countered with the cry "Scripture alone!"

Here it is important to once again mention that the Reformers' affirmation of *sola Scriptura* meant something quite different than what it means to today's Evangelical-Fundamentalist. The Reformers neither intended *sola Scriptura* to be equated with a private approach to the Scriptures, nor as a denial of any teachings which the Christian Church had gained from *legitimate* Tradition (something of which we will speak about in a later chapter). The Reformers wanted the Medieval Church to cease their creation and enforcement of arbitrary and excessively allegorical interpretations of the Bible. They asserted that the teachings of the *magisterium* had no objective bearing in the Church's history, and went counter to the teaching God had given the Church.[20]

Luther and Calvin were well aware that to know the Scriptures alone was not sufficient.[21] *Sola Scriptura* was not a call to see the Bible as the authority of the Church, but a call for the Church to once against interpret the Scriptures *in accord with the Fathers of the Church.*[22] The First Generation Reformers were not against true Tradition, they sought to recover it by uncovering the Biblical message the fathers had faithfully defended. Protestant Church historian William Scott summarizes the stand of the first Reformers when he affirms that they believed "One had also to know what the great voices in the church's history... have said is the Bible's meaning."[23]

SCRIPTURE EMERGES AS A DISTINCT AUTHORITY IN ITS OWN RIGHT

The "Orthodox" Reformers [a title ascribed to the "second-generation" theologians who attempted to systematize Luther's and Calvin's teachings] lost the sense of Tradition that the first Reformers sought to restore. As a result of their ignorance, they sought to give the Bible an authority which their forefathers never thought of giving it.

The Roman Church constantly attacked the legitimacy of a "Church" outside her boundaries. The later Reformers had no defense, unless of course the Bible itself becomes the authority and basis of their movement. The Reformers that were to succeed Luther and Calvin had to answer Rome in two areas: (1) The Roman claim that their recognition of the Bible *imputed* authority to it, and (2) their accusation that the Reformation's absence of [Roman] "Tradition" meant that all Protestant doctrine was merely the bad harvest of subjective interpretations. To leave the first contention unanswered would be an indirect admission that the Roman Church's authority was indeed superior. And if that was the case, Reformed Christianity had no right to exist. To ignore the second accusation would be tantamount to admitting that Reformation teaching was not based on absolute Truth, but relative truths which vary from individual to individual.

The men who followed the first generation of Reformers replied to these challenges by formulating a doctrine which affirmed the Scriptures to be an *external*, *independent*, *self-contained* revelation. Scripture was an *independent* authority. In respect to doctrine, this teaching would insure that the Bible would neither need confirmation nor commentary from Rome. In a manner similar to the way the Roman Church promoted itself, these Reformers now heralded the Bible as the *supreme* authority. According to this teaching, the Church's role and influence in Christian doctrine would be minimal. Who or what could compete with an infallible, independent and authoritative text?

The theological heirs of Luther and Calvin succeeded. *Sola Scripture* (revised) countered Rome's assaults by counter-attacking the Medieval Church's claim to authority. If the Bible was a *self-standing* revelation, its very existence certified its truth. This teaching challenged the Roman Church's claim that it authenticated the Bible, and her right to be its exclusive interpreters.[24]

SCRIPTURE BECOMES "SCIENTIFIC" (THE FURTHER EVOLUTION OF RATIONALISM)

Given that the Roman Church no longer had any authoritative say in the Bible's interpretation, the Protestants saw the need to answer another problem: "How can contradictory interpretations of individuals be guarded against?" Luther had never addressed the problem. He did not think he would need to. He believed that if one was sufficiently illumined by the Holy Spirit, Scripture's meaning would always be clear and beyond debate. This naive view left an aching vacuum which rationalism would attempt to fill.

Phillip Melanchthon (1497-1560), the Reformer-theologian destined to inherit responsibility for the Reformation in Germany, saw the flaws of such a subjective approach. He constantly felt the cross fire of the later anti-Lutheran reform movements that spread across his continent. He had no response to the claims of these groups. Each rival sect declared its uncompromising faithfulness to the Bible.

In an effort to resolve the conflict between opposing Biblical interpretations, Melanchthon enthroned *reason* as the guiding principle for understanding the Bible. Contrary to the teaching of either Luther or Calvin, this view makes Spirit-inspired illumination practically insignificant. It stresses a Christian's ability to logically use creedal formulas as the means to understand Scripture. One's spiritual maturity is not important. Oddly enough, Protestantism here reverted back to "old school" scholasticism of the pre-Reformation Church,[25] "...the faith can now [again] be defined, understood and be made openly intelligible solely through reason."[26]

It was later, under the same influence of rationalism that the doctrine advocating a "divinely perfect" Bible appeared. This tenet stated that *every* word and punctuation mark of the Scriptures was fully divine and perfect, i.e., without human flaw. In fact, this teaching even went so far as to deny *any* human participation in the Bible's style and message. Obviously, this doctrine bolstered the Scripture's independent authority, and thereby underscored the reasonableness of appealing to "the *Bible Alone*." It is important to note that this "absolute divinity" doctrine of the Bible was something neither the Early Church nor the first Reformers believed.[27]

THE ORIGINS OF THE "FAITH ALONE", ANTI-INTELLECTUAL AND INDIVIDUALISTIC APPROACHES TO SCRIPTURE

As mentioned earlier, just before the Reformation, the Christian in the West generally approached revelation in one of two ways: (1) with the belief that *every* part of the revelation should be understood (*theologism*) or (2) with the assumption that *no* part of revelation could be understood (nominalism).[28] The Reformers felt sympathetic to the latter nominalist perspective, asserting that revelation could be perceived by faith alone (*sola fide*).

"Christian" nominalism was taken to even greater extremes by a movement that quickly began after the Reformation, the Radical (Anabaptist) Reformation. For example, the Anabaptists typically believed Biblical scholarship should be discarded altogether as mere "human learning."[29] Therefore, they ridiculed men like Luther, Calvin, and Zwingli for depending too much on scholarship and not enough upon the Spirit.[30] In this same vein, they abstained from adopting creeds or confessions, either those of the ancient Christian Church or the newly Reformed Churches. They believed that all doctrinal formulation was a "human invention." [31]

Anabaptists were certain that all such academic notions polluted the pure faith. One needed only to be a disciple of Jesus, not a theologian. In this respect, the Anabaptists' perspectives stand as forerunners to many Fundamentalist views today. [32]

> The radicals [Anabaptists] never tired of pointing out that the men who knew Jesus were simple, unlettered, anonymous. Only those schooled in the wisdom of this world could write the commentaries ... which corrupted and rendered null and void the simple Gospel truth.[33]

The Anabaptist view was a practical application of nominalist philosophy, pure and simple.

"FAITH ALONE" AND WILLIAM OF OCCAM

William of Occam (1300-1347) was the founder of Medieval nominalism, the historic predecessor of the "by faith alone" approach. Occam claimed that one cannot know God as concrete, objective reality. He also stated that neither intuition nor reason were adequate channels for knowing God. What, then, is left for the Christian? He must be satisfied only with what "faith" *subjectively* tells him about God. One's acceptance of God's revelation "by faith"— whatever that revelation *personally* means to him — is how one knows God and reality.

By such an approach, Occam denied the possibility of *any* rational demonstration of truth. Revelation is accepted with unreasoning submission, for this is what it means to "believe." Revelation is not to be questioned or challenged; it is to be accepted "by faith" without comment or explanation. In this, Occam gave people a philosophical foundation for naive, unquestioning faith in something which may or may not exist.[34] The connection between this kind of thinking and the Radical Reformers' own attitudes is especially evident in regard to their beliefs concerning the Scriptures and salvation. [35] Philosopher-historian Etienne Gilson summarizes the nominalism of Occam:

> ... since God has spoken to us, it is no longer necessary for us to think ... now all that we need to know in order to achieve it [salvation] is there, written down in the Holy Scriptures ... since he who merely believes in the word of God knows more than the greatest philosophers ... the simplest among the Christians has a philosophy of his own, which is the only true philosophy, and whose name is: Revelation.[36]

From this foundation, the revolution progressed, spurred on by the *individualistic* philosophies of Renaissance humanism. With respect to the study of the Scriptures, these individualistic philosophies naturally exalted private interpretation over any form of external or corporate authority. Why would a Christian need to consult other "authorities" for a correct interpretation? Each person was an authority in his own right; no one needed another to tell him what was or was not true.

Renaissance thinking had a monumental effect on the way people read and understood the Bible. From an individualistic vantage point, those within the Scriptures were no longer seen as members of a community. Instead, each individual described in the Scriptures as well as each person reading the Scriptures came to be viewed as independent — as having his or her primary identity without reference to or connection with the larger community. This emerging view came to have direct ramifications on how both Church and sacrament were reinterpreted by later reformers. Even in matters of religion, the "renaissance doctrine" would affirm the individual to be "the measure of all things"

ULRICH ZWINGLI, HUMANISM AND MODERN FUNDAMENTALISM

Ulrich Zwingli (1484-1531), the leading figure behind the Reformation in Zurich, was a man deeply moved by the humanist spirit. His impact was significant in that he not only inspired the Reformed movement there, but was also the initial catalyst behind Anabaptism. All of his interpretations of Scripture were strongly fortified by an individualistic humanism.[37] Modern Fundamentalism will identify Zwingli as its "spiritual father" in this respect.[38] Zwingli, like many modern Evangelical-Fundamentalists today, was an advocate of the revised *sola Scriptura* doctrine. The following statement of Zwingli's captures his sentiments, in this regard:

> All human traditions, authority of Councils, Fathers and papacy, are as nothing before the all competent self-authenticating authority of the Scriptures. The Bible has no need to be confirmed by the authority of the Church; the Word of God speaks directly from the Scripture to the individual heart and mind.[39]

This perspective forms the bedrock of early American Fundamentalism. Liberal theologies which questioned the veracity of the Bible were allowed entrance into many of the mainline churches of the later 1800's - early 1900's. The American revivals of the late nineteenth and early twentieth century responded to this challenge by preaching a nominalist gospel outside the confines of the "institutional Church." The response of the people to the non-denominational message would be the catalyst for the later Fundamentalist movement.[40]

Individuals were called to make "decisions" for Christ apart from any denominational connection. They had no awareness of the ancient Church, her teachings, nor the Biblical injunction for every Christian to join themselves to other Christians. Salvation was preached as something personal, private, and individualistic. All a believer needed was the Bible, and the Bible ... alone. In a spirit similar to that which dominated nominalist and Renaissance philosophies, each believer saw himself as his own authority in interpreting the text.

SUMMARY AND CONCLUSION

One of the greatest "inspirations" for the evolution of the *Bible alone* doctrine lay in the Medieval Roman Church herself. Her distortions of Christian truth moved the Reformers to action. At least seven specific aspects of Rome's skewed concept of Tradition and spiritual authority demanded a response: (1) the claim that *she* had the power to invest the Bible with authority; (2) her affirmation that she had "exclusive" possession of the Spirit, and thus she alone could accurately understand and interpret Scripture; (3) her dogma that the *magisterium* was the only body with which God had entrusted authority to formulate infallible Christian doctrine; (4) her doctrine asserting the existence of a "secret" oral tradition to which only her hierarchy had access; (5) her teaching that "Tradition" was distinct and separate from the Biblical tradition; (6) the tenet which preferred her own self-created "tradition" in favor of the Scriptural exegesis of past Fathers, and; (7) the belief that *magisterial* pronouncements stood equal to the Bible's teachings.

As a defense against these doctrines, the Reformers held up the Bible and the doctrine of *sola Scriptura* as a shield. Reformers of later generations reshaped this shield into a sword against Rome by proclaiming the Bible as *the sole* authority of the Church. Each of the teachings that reinforced this refashioned view of *sola Scriptura* were drawn from the philosophies of the day: the rational-scientific approach, literalism, Scottish Common sense philosophies, and the nominalism inherent in anti-intellectualism. They all represent the Renaissance humanism and scholasticism of the day.

Before ending this section, however, it must be said that Rome's abuses were not the only factors which incited the redesign of *sola Scriptura.* Three other key elements must be noted: (1) Renaissance humanism which stressed individualism and the distrust of past authorities (here, the fathers of the Church), (2) the scholasticism of the rationalists who believed they could deduce the faith through analysis and (3) the nominalists who interpreted and accepted subjective interpretations of revelation by "faith alone."

NOTES FOR CHAPTER FOUR

1 Bernard Ramm, *Protestant Biblical Interpretation* (Grand Rapids, Michigan, Baker Book House, 1970) p. 108

2 Ernest R. Sandeen, *The Origins of Fundamentalism* (Philadelphia, Fortress Press, 1968) p. 13

3 George M. Marsden. *Fundamentalism and American Culture* (Oxford, Oxford University Press, 1980) p. 115 citing Introduction to Francis R. Beattie's *Apologetics: or the Rational Vindication of Christianity* (Richmond, Va., 1903) *Selected Shorter Writings of Benjamin B. Warfield,* vol. II, John E. Meeter, ed. (Nutley, NJ., 1973), pp. 98, 99-100 Italics his.

4 Ernest R. Sandeen, *The Origins of Fundamentalism* (Philadelphia, Fortress Press, 1968) p. 13

5 George M. Marsden. *Fundamentalism and American Culture* (Oxford, Oxford University Press, 1980) p. 111 citing Charles Hodge, "The Inspiration of Holy Scripture," *Biblical Repertory and Princeton Review* XXIX (October, 1857), p. 664, quoted in Stewart, "Princeton," VI, p. 10, Italics mine.

6 George M. Marsden. *Fundamentalism and American Culture* (Oxford, Oxford University Press, 1980) p. 111 citing Charles Hodge, "The Inspiration of Holy Scripture," *Biblical Repertory and Princeton Review* XXIX (October, 1857), p. 664, quoted in Stewart, "Princeton," VI, p. 10

7 'The Bible is a plain book,' said Charles Hodge. 'It is intelligible by the people. And they have the right and are bound to read and interpret it for themselves; so their faith may rest on the testimony of the Scriptures, and not that of the Church.' George M. Marsden. *Fundamentalism and American Culture* (Oxford, Oxford University Press, 1980) p. 111 citing Charles Hodge, "The Inspiration of Holy Scripture," *Biblical Repertory and Princeton Review* XXIX (October, 1857), p. 664, quoted in Stewart, "Princeton," VI, p. 10

8 J. Willliam Angell, "The Place of Authority Among Baptists", *The Greek Orthodox Theological Review: Greek Orthodox Southern Baptist Consultation* (Brookline, MA., Holy Cross Orthodox Press, 1977) Vol. XXI, No. 14, Winter, p. 462

9 Bernard Ramm, *Protestant Biblical Interpretation,* (Grand Rapids, Michigan, Baker Book House, 1970) p. 121 citing Horne, *An Introduction to the Critical Study and Knowledge of the Scriptures,* I, 322 "We use the word literal in its dictionary sense: '...the natural or usual construction and implication of a writing or expression; following the ordinary and apparent sense of words; not allegorical or metaphorical.' (*Webster's New International Dictionary*) " p. 119

10 Ernest R. Sandeen, *The Origins of Fundamentalism* (Philadelphia, Fortress Press, 1968) p. 4

11 George M. Marsden. *Fundamentalism and American Culture* (Oxford, Oxford University Press, 1980) p. 60

12 "It is heralded as the fullest text of systematic theology that we have now in print for evangelicals." Bernard Ramm, *After Fundamentalism* (San Francisco, Harper and Row Publishers, 1983) p. 206

13 Bernard Ramm, *After Fundamentalism , (San Francisco,* Harper and Row Publishers, 1983) p. 207 citing C. F. Lincoln, *Biographical Sketch of the Author,"* in Lewis Sperry Chafer, *Systematic Theology,* vol. 8 (Dallas: Dallas Seminary Press, 1948), pp. 5-6

14 J. K. S. Reid, *The Authority of Scripture: A Study of the Reformation and Post-Reformation Understanding of the Bible* (London, Methuen and Company, Ltd., 1957) pp. 83-87 Inspiration was even attributed to "...the Hebrew vowel points in the Old Testament, which had not been added to the consonantal text until well into the Christian era, after Hebrew had ceased being a spoken language.

Arguing that the providence of God would not have permitted 'the perfection of Scripture' to be compromised and that no language could exist without vowels, many (though by no means all) Protestant dogmaticians of the seventeenth century came out in favor of the authenticity, and thus the divine inspiration, of the Hebrew vowel points." Jaroslav Pelikan *The Christian Tradition: Reformation of Church and Dogma (1300-1700)* (Chicago and London, The University of Chicago Press, 1983) pp. 346-347

15 George M. Marsden, *Fundamentalism and American Culture* (Oxford, Oxford University Press, 1980) p. 122 citing "The Inspiration of the Bible," III, pp. 14-15 and "The Testimony of the Scriptures to Themselves," VII, pp. 42-43

16 "...the Scriptures not only contain, but ARE THE WORD OF GOD, and hence that all their elements and all their affirmations are absolutely errorless...." George M. Marsden, *Fundamentalism and American Culture* (Oxford, Oxford University Press, 1980) p. 113 citing "Inspiration," *The Presbyterian Review* II (April, 1881), pp. 237, 234, 243

17 "This view of truth as an externally stable entity placed tremendous weight on the *written* word. Religious experiences, rituals, traditions, even unrecorded words spoken by God or Jesus, as essential as all of these were, nonetheless were transitory." George M. Marsden. *Fundamentalism and American Culture* (Oxford, Oxford University Press, 1980) p. 113

18 Tradition for the Roman Catholic includes both divine truth passed down to the present *and* its guardianship by the body of bishops headed by the Pope (the *magisterium*). Consistent with this perspective, the Roman Church "determined" the canon of Scripture, can specify definable rules for its interpretation and can, as it has in the past, even determine to limit the Bible's publication as a means of "protecting " her faithful from deducing dangerous interpretations. Thus, the final authority in the Roman Church is the *magisterium;* a body which is not only responsible to define truth but even to impose it if necessary for her people. Bruce Shelly, *By What Authority?* , (Grand Rapids, MI., William B. Eerdman's Publishing Company, 1965) p. 142

19 John Meyendorff, *The Catholicity and the Church,* "The Significance of the Reformation in the History of Christendom" (Crestwood, New York, St. Vladimir's Seminary Press, 1983) p. 67

20 "The principle of the sole authority of Scripture (*sola scriptura)* was affirmed in opposition to the tendency of the medieval church to accord to Tradition...as a blanket justification of any course the church might choose to take, and thus rendering the church impervious to reform..." George S. Hendry, "The Place and Function of the Confession of faith in the Reformed Church", *The New Man: An Orthodox Reformed Dialogue* , John Meyendorff, Joseph McLelland eds., (New Jersey, Standard Press, 1973) p. 29

21 Luther "clearly saw the Bible and its understanding as set within the context of the Church...'God's Word cannot be without God's people, and conversely, God's people cannot be without God's Word.'" "It is not the individual believer who holds final responsibility for its meaning but the community to which it has been entrusted." William A. Scott, *Historical Protestantism: An Historical Introduction to Protestant Theology* (Englewood Cliffs, NJ., 1971) pp. 15, 115 "...his emphasis on the 'sola scriptura' and on the clarity of Scripture included acceptance of the creeds of the early Church and respect for traditions which were in accordance with Scripture." "Martin Luther-Witness to Jesus Christ" , Ecumenical Notes and Documentation, Joint Roman Catholic-Lutheran Commission Statement, *One In Christ*, 1983, p. 293

22 John Wycliff, John Huss, and Thomas Bradwine are just a few examples of some of the men which adopted this perspective. Heiko A. Oberman, *Harvest of Medieval Theology,* (Durham, N.C., Labyrinth Press, 1983) pp. 372-373)

23 William A. Scott, *Historical Protestantism: An Historical Introduction to Protestant Theology* (Englewood Cliffs, N.J., 1971) p. 15

24 Although there are distinctions as to what *sola scriptura* meant between the Reformers, the "Orthodox" Reformers, the Anabaptists and today's American Fundamentalists, each Protestant body shares

one principle in common: a rejection of the Roman Church's ability to either validate Scripture or to dictate its meaning.

25 "When medieval theologians spoke of 'the faith', it was the latter, objective sense of the word that predominated over the subjective sense. ... Therefore even an unbelieving priest could administer "the faith" to others, because it was an objectively given truth, whether the individual himself accepted it or not." Jaroslav Pelikan, *The Growth of Medieval Theology (600-1300),* Vol. 3 of *The Christian Tradition: A History of the Development of Doctrine*, p.4

26 J. K. S. Reid, *The Authority of Scripture: A Study of the Reformation and Post-Reformation Understanding of the Bible* (London, Methuen and Company, Ltd., 1957) pp. 80, 81

27 This "full-scale articulation of the doctrine of Scripture, of its inspiration and inerrancy, was completed ... *in the Protestant theologies that came out of the Reformation.*" Jaroslav Pelikan *The Christian Tradition: Reformation of Church and Dogma (1300-1700)* (Chicago and London, The University of Chicago Press, 1983) pp. 118-119. Italics mine.

Luther freely admits human characteristics, contradictions and even imperfections in Scripture: "He expresses doubt of the Mosaic authorship of the Pentateuch, the opinion that the works of the prophets are later collected into the form in which we know them, that the later prophets are of mixed quality, that here is failure in prediction as well as success, that the Book of Kings is more reliable than that of the Chronicles; and in the New Testament, he prefers the Fourth Gospel to the other Evangelists, holds Hebrews to be a composite production, throws doubt upon the value of the Revelation..." and refers to James as "an epistle of straw." J. K. S. Reid, *The Authority of Scripture: A Study of the Reformation and Post-Reformation Understanding of the Bible* (London, Methuen and Company., Ltd., 1957) p. 67 ftnte 1.

Neither was Calvin an advocate of inerrancy "being quite prepared to recognize error in Acts 7:16 and Matthew 27:9." And the Anabaptists, although they greatly revered the Scriptures, they never ascribed to them a literal inerrancy; they felt that to do such would be to fall into a legalism which had been typical of the Scribes and Pharisees. Ronald H. Bainton, *Studies On the Reformation* (Boston, Beacon Press, 1963) p. 133

28 Etienne Gilson, *The Reason and Revelation in the Middle Ages*, (New York, Charles Scribner's Sons, 1938) p. 69

29 Ronald H. Bainton, *Studies On the Reformation* (Boston, Beacon Press, 1963) pp. 124, 126 This was probably due to Erasmus' influence upon Anabaptism. We will discuss more about the vital role this man played in the shaping of Protestant thought in chapter sixteen, "Baptism (Part 1): The Difficulties With Age Restrictive Baptism".

30 "It must suffice to note here that doctrine and conduct [for the Anabaptists] were to be determined by Scripture alone, but not by Scripture interpreted traditionally (Roman Catholic), nor by technically qualified theologians (essentially the magisterial 'scribes [Luther, Zwingli, Calvin]), but spiritually, by the Holy Spirit in the context of the redeemed community." Kenneth R. Davis, "The Origins of Anabaptism: Ascetic and Charismatic Elements Exemplifying Continuity and Discontinuity," in *The Origins And Characteristics of Anabaptism,* ed. Marc Lienhard (The Hague, Marinus Nijhoff, 1977) p. 40

31 Kenneth Ronald Davis, *Anabaptism and Asceticism* (Scottsdale, Pa., Herald Press, 1974) p. 214 "Anabaptist confessions of faith were also rare and without binding quality. They were nothing more than the term implies, confessions of individuals or small groups of the Brethren." William R. Estep, *The Anabaptist Story* (Nashville, Tennessee, Broadman Press, 1963) p. 126

"Even those Anabaptists who had a humanist training such as Hans Grebel, Denk, and Balthazzar Hübmaier were indisposed to fine spun theological speculations... " Ronald H. Bainton, *Studies On the Reformation,* (Boston, Beacon Press, 1963) pp. 124, 126

32 It should be noted that Anabaptist exegesis significantly differs from the Fundamentalist approach to the Scriptures in at least three ways: 1) in its stress of New Testament revelation as the culmination of the Old Testament (E.g., Old Testament references to Israel is a type of the Church, not the Twentieth century nation state) 2) in its emphasis on the Spirit of the Scripture over its letter, and 3) in its demand that the Scriptures be interpreted only within the local community of those demonstrating the fruit of the Spirit, not by isolated individuals living in the "world."

33 Franklin H. Littell, *The Origins of Sectarian Protestantism* (New York, The Macmillan Company, 1964) p. 60

34 Occam stated that, " no universal is existent in any way whatsoever outside the mind of the knower. For whatever exists exists only because it is framed by the mind, words, such as dog, or rose, are only a sign to which we attach our "mental intuitions." In reality, these things don't really exist. "Thus, the knowledge gained in this kind of 'revelation' can be so irreducibly individual as to be unsusceptible of any intelligible relationship or connection with any other individual." David Knowles, *The Evolution of Medieval Thought* (New York, Vintage Books, 1962) pp. 321, 322, 327, 328

35 Oddly enough, the philosophy energizing "believing" Occamists also stimulated an "agnostic" nominalism. If reality and revelation found their grounding only in one's *personal* definitions and understandings, both the believer and unbeliever were correct. How could a true Occamist say one was "right" and the other "wrong", when both were basing themselves on subjective interpretations? The contradiction within nominalism challenged the absolute nature of truth itself and encouraged relativism.

36 Etienne Gilson, *The Reason and Revelation in the Middle Ages* (New York, Charles Scribner's Sons, 1938) pp. 6, 7, 8

37 Zwingli was a champion of *the Bible alone* and was ... impressed by the Stoicism of Seneca... [Though] Zwingli's theology is biblical in origin, the style of its presentation indicates an attitude of mind which is less scriptural than humanist. The Swiss reformer approaches the sacred book from the angle of humanism;...his treatment of the scriptures always remained humanist in spirit." Bernard M.G. Reardon, *Religious Thought In the Reformation* (New York, Longham Inc., 1981) pp. 97,98

38 Though it should be noted that, unlike the Fundamentalist school, Zwingli did not equate the Bible with the Word of God: [For Zwingli] "What precisely constitutes the Word ... is not necessarily the written word ... he is not apparently committed to the sort of literalism that became such a feature of later Protestantism." Bernard M.G. Reardon, *Religious Thought In the Reformation* (New York, Longham Inc., 1981) pp. 96-97

39 G.P. Fisher, Hubert Cunliffe-Jones, editor, Benjamin Drewery, assistant editor, *International Library Series: A History of Christian Doctrine* (Edinburgh, T. and T. Clark Ltd., 1978) p. 361 [See his *On the Clarity and Certainty of the Word of God*, 1522].

40 "There are, indeed, several streams of tradition that have gone into the making of modern fundamentalism; but the basic and dominant one is the religious experience of the Evangelical Revivals." James Barr, *Fundamentalism* (Philadelphia, The Westminster Press, 1978) p. 11. Complementary to this Mark A. Noll notes the significant role of individualism inherent within the American culture (*An American Evangelical Theology: The Painful Transition ,"Theoria* to *Praxis*"):

> Most important ... for the evangelical study of Scripture has been the historical shape of religious culture in the United States. That culture has long been characterized by strong strands of individualism and egalitarianism. It has been at once intensely ideological and determinedly anti-traditional. And it has been generally anti-theological.

CHAPTER FIVE

THE FUNDAMENTALIST-EVANGELICAL VIEW OF THE BIBLE (PART II):

THE INHERENT WEAKNESSES OF THE BIBLE ALONE

Even though the motives behind the defense of a *Bible alone* position are well meaning, both Church history and the problems which this generation has been unable to answer expose the doctrine's inadequacies. This chapter looks at some of those flaws and demonstrates how *sola Scriptura* not only fails to defend Scriptural teaching, but actually makes it more vulnerable to misinterpretation. The Bible has never been, nor can ever be, the *sole* standard of defense and definition of Christian faith and practice. Once this is realized, one will be better able to appreciate the approach of the early Church to Scriptures, an approach I will begin to discuss in the next chapter. In this chapter I will look into ten reasons why the *Bible alone* doctrine is inadequate to explain both Church doctrine and the Scriptures.

1) A "PERFECT" BIBLE DOES NOT ENSURE CORRECT INTERPRETATION

The hypothesis of a perfect original text was designed to safeguard the infallibility of what is divinely written, and to explain the known imperfections of the text.[1] Respected Evangelical scholars readily recognize that "Verbal inspiration is a theory about the origin of Holy Scripture but [that] it settles nothing in and of itself about the theory of hermeneutics [method of interpreting the Bible]."[2] A sharp and perfectly designed scalpel does not insure a successful operation.

There are those who believe in a perfect Bible but still disagree on the Lord's Supper (memorial/real presence), views on war (just war/pacifism), salvation (predestination/free-will), eternal security ("once saved always saved"/self determination), baptism's significance (nonessential/essential) and method of administration (infant/adult, immersion/sprinkling), etc. Neither the doctrine of inerrancy (i.e., everything it teaches is true) or perfection (that man wrote word-for-word what God dictated to him) makes the Bible's meaning automatic, nor does either guarantee its correct interpretation.[3]

2) CHRISTIAN DOCTRINE IS MISUNDERSTOOD AS SOMETHING SOLELY RATIONAL

An approach which summons people to understand the Bible by "interpreting Scripture by other Scriptures," or one that rests upon the use of a blueprint (whether creeds, dispensationalism, or anything else), can disfigure the Faith into a system instead of a relationship. Under the influence of Melanchthon and later Protestant scholasticism, faith became what it was in the Middle Ages: an intellectual concept. It was not something one understood by living its message, but *chiefly* understood by the *study* of its message. Scripture's *spiritual* message was compromised by its sacrifice to the god of reason. The Book became more a "Encyclopedia of Doctrine" meant for theological scientists, and less a "Book of *Faith*" intended for the *faith* -ful.

A rationalistic, self-interpreting, Bible may have seemed necessary for the later Reformers in defense of their doctrines against Rome, but it was an approach foreign both to the mind of the Early Church and to the Bible itself. In the Ancient Church neither the Bible, creeds, councils nor anything else — either separately or all together— were ever understood as *the* definitive statement of the Christian faith. They may have been used to *defend* the mystery of the Faith, but they were never used to *define* it. The mind can never fully grasp the Faith, no matter how brilliant it may be.

As Jesus said, *"the words that I have spoken to you are Spirit and are life"* (John 6:63). The Bible is a *spiritual* book. One can never receive life from the Scriptures unless he approaches it in spirit as well as mind. It is all a part of being a Christian. Giving intellectual assent to a *statement* of faith, while certainly integral to the faith, does not make one a true Christian. *Ultimately, Christianity is living in Christ; a union which transcends all limited conceptions.*

3) A VIEW OF SCRIPTURE WHICH DENIES ITS HUMAN ELEMENT IGNORES THE CHURCH'S ROLE IN COMPILING THE BOOKS OF THE BIBLE

Unlike the Koran of Islam or the Book of Mormon, the Bible does not fancifully claim to be dropped from heaven. The Scriptures were born and confirmed *within* a *believing community*, i.e., real, heart-beating, breathing, flesh-and-blood people. The Bible was not discovered by Peter and John at the tomb of Christ. The authors of the Bible had not worked together on a table of contents so that the Church would know which books should be included in the canon of Scriptures. The Church—the Body of Christ (clergy *and* laity)— was called of the Spirit to discern the true books from the false. To deny the historic Church's role in this discernment process would be to deny the Holy Spirit 's ministry among God's people.

It is also important to note that Church herself, both in writing the Scriptures and in confirming them, *belongs* to the revelation. This human contribution does not make the Bible any less spiritual. The supernatural does not obliterate the natural, it complements it.

> Human response is integrated into the mystery of the Word of God. It is not a divine monologue, it is rather a dialogue, and both are speaking, God and man ... it is a book which narrates the creation, fall and salvation of man. It is the story of salvation, and therefore man organically belongs to the story.[4]

It is impossible for the Bible to be viewed as a *stand alone* entity. It's authorship, confirmation and subject matter all bear witness to the fact that the Spirit has worked *in partnership* with man. It is the Spirit of God who inspired human beings to write the Bible, and it is the Spirit of God Who inspires human beings to understand it.

4) A 'LITERAL' INTERPRETATION OF THE BIBLE CAN REPLACE THE HOLY SPIRIT

Truly, even an atheist can do the work of an historian to uncover the *literal* sense of a Biblical passage.[5] But to *rightly* interpret the Scriptures, one must submit himself to the *guidance of the Spirit* — the Spirit of Truth (John 16:13ff).[6] The Christian of the early centuries knew it was essential for him to understand the Scripture according to the Spirit as well as the letter for...

> ... without the spirit, the full meaning could not be found. Anyone who paid attention only to the letter would understand only the natural, not the supernatural, meaning. This was the reason for the failure of Jewish exegesis to understand the Old Testament properly.[7]

Neither Luther nor Calvin ever confused the written texts of the Bible with "The Word of God." [8] The Bible contains words awaiting the illumination of the Spirit, the Word of God is the voice of the Spirit Himself. For this reason, Luther and Calvin realized that without the Holy Spirit's ministry, the Bible could only "potentially" reveal God's Word. The written words in the Scripture are God's Word to the reader *only as the Holy Spirit reveals them to be so.* Passages such as "Man shall not live by bread alone, but by every *word* that proceeds from the mouth of God" (Matt. 4:4) and "faith comes from hearing, and hearing by the *word* of Christ" (Rom. 4:17) illustrate this point. In these instances "word" is translated from the Greek term "rheema," (ῥῆμα) a term which is not confined to words addressed to our senses (the Greek word "logos" is usually used in those contexts), but to words which *the Holy Spirit reveals and discloses to our spirits.*[9] "Faith comes from hearing, and hearing by the *rheema* of Christ."

Luke 18:34 is a further example of how the presence of the Word of God within the

Bible cannot be *self*-revealing but is dependent upon the Spirit's illumination:

> And they [Christ's disciples] understood none of these things, and this saying was hidden from them, and they did not comprehend the things that were said.

The message in parables must be explained for those "who have ears to hear." Jesus did *not* say "I will not leave you as orphans, I will leave *the Bible* with you" but rather: *"the Holy Spirit* , Whom the Father will send in My name, *He* will teach you all things ...and will bear witness of Me" (John 14:26, see also John 15:26).

The Bible also makes it clear that, no matter how much we may listen to or read it, *a lack of faith can prevent us from extracting God's Word from its pages.* It was this lack of faith which led the disciples to completely misunderstand Jesus' words, "beware of the leaven of the Pharisees and the Sadducees." They thought He was referring to their inadequate provision of bread (Matt. 16: 6-12). In another instance, the Pharisees were rebuked by Jesus, not for an academic deficiency of the Scriptures, but *for their lack of an experiential understanding of the Scriptures and the power of God* (Matt. 22:29).

The fallacy of the entire perspective of *the Bible alone* philosophy lies in the fact that Scripture nowhere makes the claim to be *the total, self*-sufficient revelation of the Christian faith. To relate to the Bible in isolation, and to grant it self-interpretative authority, makes it a paper magisterium. The Holy Spirit is apparently not needed, for His ministry has been usurped by a text. At best, the Holy Spirit becomes subject to the defines and limits of a written word. At worst, He is not needed at all.

5) AN ANTI-INTELLECTUAL INTERPRETATION EQUATES NAIVETE WITH SPIRITUALITY

Luke 10:21 is often interpreted as an example of how Jesus valued mental simplicity over the "learned" In the passage, Jesus praises the Father for revealing the mysteries of the Kingdom to "babes" and for hiding them from "the wise and intelligent." Many read the verse to say, "Blessed are those who are *ignorant*", but this is not what our Lord is saying at all. The Scripture scholar Norval Geldenhuys gives a valid correction to the common misinterpretation:

> The contrast pointed by the Saviour is not that between 'educated' and 'uneducated' but between those who imagine themselves to be wise and sensible and want to test the Gospel truths by their own intellects ... Often 'unlearned' persons are in the highest degree self-opinionated as regards spiritual matters, and on the other hand some of the most learned are humble and childlike and accept the truths of the Gospel unreservedly.[10]

In no place do the Scriptures teach that ignorance grants one an inherent grace of understanding. Actually, the Scriptures warn quite to the contrary, "...the waywardness of the naive shall kill them, And the complacency of fools shall destroy them" (Proverbs 1:32). To declare, "I just believe what the Bible says" as a justification for ignoring any truth outside of the text, is neither wise nor godly.[11]

6) "PRIVATE" INTERPRETATIONS OF SCRIPTURE COMPROMISE THE BIBLE THROUGH INDIVIDUAL "TRADITIONS"

The right of "private judgment" — wedded together with the Bible as "ultimate and absolute authority" — results in the Scripture *losing* authority. The individual's right to defend his or her interpretation over a legion of other understandings is of greatest importance. The contradictory opinions which result from such a premise are each given the right to be called "Scriptural." The consequence: The Bible's message is weakened by a democracy of conflicting ideas.

Oddly enough, such a plurality gives permission to the religious tyrant. Now, in the name of fidelity to "the Word", he is able to impose his inaccurate interpretations and be respected as "a Bible teacher." In many cases, this means that the one who speaks the strongest, loudest and with the most influence, can get a "Christian" following — that is, as long as his ideas are footnoted with Biblical references. Mark A. Knolls, in *Evangelicalism and Modern America,* explains the problem of private interpretation in this respect:

> The naive ... American intellectual heritage leads not to depth but to superficiality. Ironically, it leads also to a perverse kind of authoritarianism, in which a leader claiming to have no guide but the Bible rigidly imposes his form of Scriptural interpretation on followers who likewise profess to be heeding no guide but the Bible.[12]

A philosophy which advocates the Bible's "independent authority" ironically ends up giving ultimate authority to "the independent." For instance, when someone says, "I believe *ONLY* in what the Bible says", isn't he really saying, "I only believe in the way *I interpret* the Bible?" Isn't he in effect stating that *his understanding* of the Scriptures *is as divinely inspired as the Scriptures themselves? In the final analysis, then, it is not Scripture which possesses final authority, but private interpretations.* Though an exaggeration, there is some truth to the saying, "Before the Reformation there was only one Pope, but after the Reformation every man with Bible in hand is his own Pope."

The Jehovah's Witnesses' and Armstrongism (both which deny the Trinity, as well as other orthodox doctrines) assert the Bible to be the *sole* and *prime* authority behind their teachings. Official literature of the Way International, a sect rejecting the divinity of Christ, affirms that the "singular purpose" of their organization is "to research the Scriptures to understand their inherent and inerrant accuracy regarding Jesus Christ..." and to be a "teaching ministry endeavoring to promote how the Bible interprets itself."[13] And Mary Baker Eddy, the founder of Christian Science claimed, "As adherents of Truth, we take the inspired Word of the Bible as our sufficient guide to eternal life."[14] Each of these groups makes it clear that although one may declare his allegiance to *the Bible alone*, there is no such thing as a "tradition free" approach to the Scriptures.

Everyone brings *something* to the text, i.e., philosophies, experiences, emotions, attitudes, etc. It is physically, psychologically, and spiritually impossible to have faith in *the Bible alone.*[15] We cannot help but bring some part of ourselves to the text we study. The only way we could bring nothing to the text— and thus be "objective"— would be to cease to be human.

It is undeniable. Reformation theologians, and every Protestant denomination since, have brought their own methods ["traditions"] to the study of Scripture. The Scriptures do not automatically dictate a Fundamentalist [Bible-alone] method of interpretation.

> ... *sola Scriptura* has not meant the same to all Protestants. Historical examination of how the Reformers used tradition in their exegesis has qualified both their own statements about *sola Scriptura* as a principle and the construction put upon this principle by later interpreters.[16]

The Bible alone hermenutic [method of interpretation] has been forged by a *variety* of influences: Augustinianism, Thomism, nominalism, common sense realism, rationalism, anti-intellectualism, Baconian categorization and an individualistic Renaissance hermeneutic which denies any continuity with past authorities. *It is most significant to note that not one of these philosophies is inherently Biblical.*

To say that the Bible *alone* is sufficient as the guide of Christian doctrine is at best inadequate. For although both the heretic and the Christian can be sincere and agree on the Bible's "infallibility" and authority, these shared perspectives do not erase their differences. They must ask themselves: *How* and *why* do I interpret the Scriptures the way I do? These questions free one to trace the rationale and development of his system of Bible interpretation and to judge its value.

7) "THE BIBLE ALONE" WAS NOT SUFFICIENT TO DEFEND THE CHRISTIAN FAITH IN THE PAST

Sola Scriptura is not an effective weapon against heretics. It never was and never will be. We must not forget that heretics during the first centuries of the Church used Scripture extensively:[17]

> ... the Bible proved to be common hunting-ground ...Heretics showed that they could be as painstaking in their use of Scripture as the saints. The fact soon became obvious to any intelligent thinker that the principle of 'the bible and the bible only' provides no automatically secure basis for a religion that is to be genuinely Christian.[18]

The idea that someone could boast of himself as being "thoroughly Scriptural", and yet turn out to be a heretic should not surprise us. Did not even Satan himself, that father of lies, also try to encourage an interpretation and application of Scripture which crossed purposes with God? (Ps. 91:11,12; Matt. 4:3-10) Surely Satan's methods of trying to destroy God's children with his lies have not changed that much in 2000 years.

When the Christian Church of the Fourth Century had to battle against the Anomoian (Christ was totally dissimilar to the Father's essence) and Arian heresies (Christ was only "like" or "similar" to God as perfect man but not of the same essence as God), she could find no Scriptures that would *conclusively* demonstrate Christ's *total* divinity as well as total humanity. This was certainly a point that needed to be clarified, for the belief that Christ was only *similar* to God but not God in the flesh would mean mankind would still be in need of a Redeemer. The heretics constantly requested that *only* the Scripture be allowed in their debates and pointed to them as proof that they were the "true believers." What made matters worse, every Scripture that the Christians used in defense of orthodoxy was turned on its head by the heretics to support their error. If nothing in the Scriptures could be found to conclusively throw down the heresy, what recourse was left to the Church?

The Christians decided to fight back not with Bible verses but with a word which captured Bible Truth. As no Scripture existed that would make the orthodox position undebatable, the bishops in council opted to defend the correct Christian teaching by using a term which appeared nowhere in the Bible: "homoousios" ["the same essence-substance"]. Jesus Christ was not a mere man of elevated morality: he was "homoousios with the Father." Although they admitted that this term may not appear in the Bible, they knew it to be entirely consistent with what the Tradition of the Bible taught.[19] This word was incorporated into the Nicene Creed, making it clear to all what Christians believed concerning Jesus. Certainly, if the Christians of the time could have defended Christ's divinity by Scripture alone, the Council of Nicea (325 A.D.) and the creed which it authored would never have been needed in the first place!

There is no question that the Bible *contains* theology. But it is also equally true that it is not a *systematic theology text.* The Bible was not written for that purpose. If one relates to the Bible as if it were a topical theological encyclopedia, he will be destined to miss its message. The epistles were primarily written to address the specific needs of the particular communities they addressed. They were NEVER intended to be approached as a complete collection of treatises detailing *everything* about the Christian Faith.

Neither the Lord nor His Apostles intended to commit *all* they knew or taught to the pages of the Scriptures.[20] Even the Bible admits this! To teach that the Bible is "the complete and full revelation of God" contradicts the Scriptures themselves.

> "And there were also *many other things which Jesus did,* which if they were written in detail, I suppose that *even the world itself would not contain the books which were written.* " (John 21:25)
>
> "To these He also presented Himself alive, after His suffering, by many convincing proofs, appearing to them over a period of forty days, and *speaking of the things concerning the kingdom of God.* " (Acts 1:3)
>
> "Therefore be on the alert, remembering that night and day f*or a period of three years I did not cease to admonish each one with tears.* " (Acts 20:31)
>
> "Having many things to write to you, *I do not want to do so with paper and ink; but I hope to come to you and speak face to face,* that your joy may be made full." (2 John 12)
>
> "If anyone is hungry, let him eat at home, so that you may not come together for judgment. *And the remaining matters I shall arrange when I come.* " (1 Cor 11: 34) [21]

8) THE BIBLE ALONE APPROACH HAS FAILED TO BRING AGREEMENT IN DOCTRINE

Luther, Zwingli, Calvin, and many Anabaptists believed that if all followed the teachings of the Scriptures, it would be *natural* for everyone to be in agreement with each another. The *Bible alone* doctrine not only failed to produce this unanimity among the Reformers, but actually *encouraged* doctrinal diversity and contradiction. "What Zwingli and most of the early Reformers had thought was impossible had happened — division!"[22]

> When the Reformation had grown from one man to an entire movement, becoming more heterogeneous and more radical in the process, the futility of 'sola Scriptura' as a means of combating false doctrine was ever more obvious: 'Who is to be the judge among them? Who will ever harmonize all of this? ... 'If Sacred Scripture is the clearest possible' authority, how was it that some who accepted it were denying the real presence [of Christ in the Eucharist] while others were affirming it? [And] It was by 'drawing upon patriarchal precedent' in Scripture that some Radical [Reformers] were advocating and practicing polygamy.[23]

It is no better now than it was then. Today, with the existence of literally hundreds of

"Evangelical" denominations affirming *the Bible alone* as their chief rule of faith, unity is simply nonexistent. *Sola Scriptura* is not a doctrine which stimulates unity among all those who champion its cause; it is a constant source of further division.

9) A BIBLE ALONE PHILOSOPHY FALSELY DENIES THE LEGITIMATE PLACE OF DIVINE TRADITION

Most Fundamentalists and Conservative Evangelicals affirm that all the significant dogmas of the Christian faith are clear and undebatable from the Bible. However, most all do not realize that some elements of Tradition have been unconsciously incorporated in their reading of the Bible. I will speak more about the proper meaning and place of Tradition in the next chapter, but suffice it to say here that Tradition is the teaching which the Holy Spirit reveals to the *entire* Church (not just a few). Church historian Dr. Jaroslav Pelikan notes Tradition's place among the Reformers when he rhetorically asks, "Does the development of the doctrine of the Trinity, whose results most Protestants accept, correspond to that conception of the authority of Scripture [i.e., *sola Scriptura*] which these same Protestants maintain? "[24]

What was before unknown is now recognized. Those Reformers declaring that Christian dogma was deducible from the Bible alone, were concealing their debt to the legitimate Tradition of the pre-Reformation Church:

> The Westminster Confession of Faith, for example, states the doctrines of the Trinity (II,3) and of the person of Christ (VIII, 2) in language taken almost verbatim from the Athanasian Creed and the Chalcedonian Definition, but with no acknowledgement, leaving the uninstructed reader to suppose that the formulas were the work of the Westminster divines.[25]

The Confession states that "The whole counsel of God concerning all things necessary for his own glory, man's salvation, faith and life, is either expressly set down in scripture, or by good and necessary consequence may be deduced from scripture' (1,6) — it omits, however, to specify the criterion of 'good and necessary consequence'."[26] This guidance into what was of "good and necessary consequence" was the result of Christian Tradition, not the Scriptures alone. Church history makes it clear that many key dogmas of the faith were not the sole conclusion and summary of Bible verses alone.

10) A BIBLE ALONE PHILOSOPHY IGNORES THE HOLY SPIRIT'S MINISTRY IN THE CHURCH FOR THE PAST 1,500 YEARS

By adopting *sola Scriptura,* we indirectly deny the reality of the Holy Spirit's inspiration through other men who helped us understand essential Christian dogmas. What about the

Christian Fathers who were used of God to illumine the doctrines of the Trinity and the divinity of the Holy Spirit (St. Gregory of Nyssa [335-399], St. Gregory of Nazianzus [328-390], St. Basil [330-379])? What about those who defended the truth regarding Christ: His divinity (St. Athanasius [295-373]), His two natures (St. Cyril of Alexandria, (370-444)], and His divine and human will (St. Maximus the Confessor, [580-662]). These dogmas certainly aren't found by simply checking the references of a good concordance. Just as possession of the New Testament in no way justifies our ignorance of God's working in Old Testament Israel, neither does the New Testament give us license to discount God's workings in the ongoing life of the Church after New Testament times.

But can't one say, "If I trust the Holy Spirit *alone*, will He not give me the correct understanding of the Bible's interpretation?"[27] True, sensitive Scripture reading does demand that each person rely upon the Holy Spirit, but *this reliance on the Holy Spirit also includes a responsible identification with His ministry within the Christian Church (both past and present).* The Scriptures tell us that "the pillar and support of the truth" is "*the church* of the living God" (1 Tim. 3:15) — the *corporate body* of God's people. There is no room here for the independent and isolated interpretation of individuals who are spiritually and psychologically removed from this context.

Yes, each Christian has the Holy Spirit, but His indwelling in the individual was never meant to substitute for His presence in the Church (the people of God). Each believer needs the ministry of the Spirit through other brethren in order to get the enlightenment he seeks (I Cor. 12). Apostolic Tradition is neither received nor possessed by an individual in isolation nor by an "elite" group of bishops. It is something in which the *whole* Church must participate.[28] To embrace Tradition, then, will not merely result in a better understanding of the Bible, but grant a better understanding of the nature of the Church, and a deeper appreciation for both.

SUMMARY AND CONCLUSION

There is something that *sounds* good about saying that one's sole reference for the Faith can be found in the Scriptures alone. It makes it appear that God alone is the One responsible for what we believe ("If you have a problem with my doctrine, argue with the Bible, not me."). Such a philosophy *seems* to make our beliefs appear systematic and objective. I can understand the desire for such security. But *sola Scriptura* cannot give it. The *Bible alone* approach is an impossibility, both spiritually and by common sense.

Christianity's defense in the past would have crumbled had it rested on the Bible *alone*. The Bible is never alone. Humankind's inability to be unaffected by cultures, philosophies, and the times in which it lives leaves no doubt about this. We *always* bring something to Bible, and that something is *ourselves*. The person, not the Bible, must take responsibility for what he or she says they believe. The Bible may be a reference, but the final word about what we believe is up to the judgments *we* make. God will never be automatically revealed by an objective, scientific text. *God is known by a life lived in communion with God and the brethren.*

We can go astray when we forget that Christ, not the Scriptures, is *the* Revelation. The Portrait presented to us in the Bible can be greatly diminished when we become overly focused on *how* it is revealed instead of *Whom* it reveals. As in the case of a painting, if we stand close enough to count the lines of a painter's brush strokes, or to see only the oil globules in its pigments, we no longer see the message of the artist. We see only his "ingredients." *The* Revelation of the Scriptures is Christ among us, not its "inerrancy" in logic, science or syntax. In some respects, this is the error which Jesus confronted in certain Pharisees: You search the Scriptures, because you think that *in them* you have eternal life; ... [but in reality] it is these that bear witness of *Me* " (John 5:39).

The *Bible alone* perspective is an *un*biblical philosophy. It distorts the Bible's true message in many ways: it *encourages* a rationalistic and simplistic view of Christian doctrine; it *ignores* the past role of the Church and the legitimate place of Tradition; it *elevates* the subjective, isolated opinions of individuals; it *stimulates* divisions within the Christian Church through contrary opinions; and it *contradicts* the Bible's own teachings regarding the limits of its revelation. By declaring that Scripture can "stand on its own" "we only expose it to subjective, arbitrary interpretation, [by]... cutting it away from its sacred source [the Church]." [29] Oddly enough the very teaching intended to support the Bible actually weakens it, as Truth can no longer be heard over the shouts of her many would-be interpreters.

Whether in the Reformation period or later, the *Bible alone* and related perspectives had a *reaction* to an abuse or distortion as their "inspiration." As is often the case, this reaction led to an imbalanced, emotionally charged posture which supported certain positions *only because* they specifically countered an abuse. It is right to address abuses, but any action, philosophy, or "theology" that is created *for the sole purpose* of addressing such abuses will always be lop-sided, negative and incomplete. In other words, 180 degrees from imbalanced is still imbalanced.

NOTES FOR CHAPTER FIVE

1 J. K. S. Reid, *The Authority of Scripture: A Study of the Reformation and Post-reformation Understanding of the Bible* (London, Methuen and Company., Ltd., 1957) p. 87

Even this claim for the Text's perfection, however, is impossible to verify. We do not possess any of the originals, all we have are "the copies of copies." The earliest known fragment of any part of the New Testament is a tiny piece of one leaf of what was once a codex of the Gospel of John; it contains only a few words from John 18 and is dated about A.D. 130. F. F. Bruce, *The Gospel of John* (Grand Rapids, MI., William B. Eerdmans Publishing Company, 1983) p. 6

2 Bernard Ramm, *Protestant Biblical Interpretation*, (Grand Rapids, Michigan, Baker Book House, 1970) p. 126. The word "hermenutics" refers to the method one employs to interpret the Bible.

3 In the following observation, Evangelical history professor, Mark A. Noll, questions both the legitimacy and method of evangelicalism's pre-occupation with the Bible's authority in respect to its accurate exegesis:

> A further sign of the [evangelical] uncertainty concerning the character and meaning of Scripture is the massive and massively diverse literature of the last decade on the inspiration, inerrancy, infallibility, and authority of Scripture. For every one effort to derive a theology from Scripture for life or thought in the late twentieth century, it seems as if there are several devoted to formal questions of biblical authority. However much at least some of the books and articles in this great outpouring may be necessary to meet the critical need of our time, the suspicion lingers that the net result is an addition of heat rather than light. Only rarely do such works carefully discriminate among the historical, literary, theological, cultural, and hermeneutical dimensions of the issue of biblical authority. A few evangelicals do write on this subject with humility, perspective, creativity, and orthodoxy. Yet tendentiousness, short-sightedness, anti-intellectualism, and a propensity to play to the galleries descend upon the evangelical world in nearly limitless quantities as well. The tragic result is that on this most fundamental issue we often communicate the impression of being wise as doves and innocent as serpents.

Mark A. Noll, "An American Evangelical Theology: The Painful Transition From *Theoria* to *Praxis* ", *Evangelicalism and Modern America*, ed., George Marsden (Grand Rapids, MI., Wm. B. Eerdmans Publishing Company, 1986) pp. 115, 116

4 Georges Florovsky, *Bible, Church, Tradition: An Eastern Orthodox View* (Belmont, MA, Nordland Publishing Company, 1972) p. 21

5 The Jewish scholar Rabbi Hillel (60 B.C.-A.D. 20), for example, advocated a literalistic interpretation of the Old Testament in a way which in many respects is analogous to the Fundamentalist hermenutic popular today. John Breck, *The Power of the Word* , (Crestwood, New York, St Vladimir's Seminary Press, 1986) p. 52

6 John Breck, *The Power of the Word* , (Crestwood, New York, St Vladimir's Seminary Press, 1986) p. 110

7 Jaroslav Pelikan, *The Christian Tradition: The Spirit of Eastern Christendom (600-1700)*, (Chicago and London, The University of Chicago Press, 1974), p. 18. Georges Florvosky explains why:

> The fathers of the Church never held to Jewish limitations in understanding the Old Testament; for them the Scriptures was a revelation which now addressed the whole world, not just the Jews. Now, in Christ, "new light has been thrown on the old revelations by Him who came just to accomplish and to fulfil the Law and the Prophets. The Scriptures are not merely historical documents. They are really the Word of God, the

Divine message to all generations. And Christ Jesus is the Alpha and the Omega of the Scriptures, both the climax and the knot of the Bible. This is the standing message of the Fathers to the Church Universal about the Old Dispensation.

Aspects of Church History (Belmont, Massachusetts, Nordland Publishing Company, 1975), p. 38.

8 "Calvin made a parallel distinction between the Word of God and the Holy Spirit, and the communication of God through the Holy Spirit is held to be something separable and in fact frequently separated from His communication through Scripture...Calvin holds that the primary function of the Holy Spirit is revelation, and the Scripture transmits this revelation through the agency of the Holy Spirit. Luther, did not believe that the Bible needed to replace the authority of a discredited Church. But he, like Calvin, believed that the primary function of the Holy Spirit is revelation, and that Scripture can transmit this revelation only through the ministry of the Spirit— something which is not confined to the written words of Scripture." J. K. S. Reid, *The Authority of Scripture: A Study of the Reformation and Post-reformation Understanding of the Bible* (London, Methuen and Company., Ltd., 1957) pp. 81, 85

9 Ephesians 6:12 is another example of such a use of rheema.

10 Norval Geldenhuys, *The Gospel of Luke* (Grand Rapids, MI., William B. Eerdmans Publishing Company, 1977) p. 307

11 The Apostle Paul was an educated man, having studied at the university in Tarsus under Gamaliel, one of the greatest Rabbis of the first century. Paul's zeal and intellectual abilities led him to excel over the majority of his peers (Acts. 22:3). Undoubtedly God powerfully utilized His intellectual gifts for the purpose of the Gospel. The Evangelist Luke —the learned physician— came from a similar educational background (some speculate that Paul and Luke might have even been classmates in Tarsus). Luke's New Testament writings — which account for more than one-fourth of the entire New Testament — are noted for their historical accuracy and sophisticated use of the Greek language. The Fathers of the Christian Church who gave their minds to the leading of the Spirit and thus mightily refuted the damning heresies that threatened the Church of their time should also be noted here for the righteous use of their intellectual abilities. Certainly, an over-reliance upon one's intellectual reasoning can definitely lead to error but, when one's studies are subjected to the Spirit of God, God can be greatly glorified through the exercise of this gift.

12 Mark A. Knoll, "An American Evangelical Theology: The Painful Transition From *Theoria* to *Praxis*", *Evangelicalism and Modern America*, ed., George Marsden (Grand Rapids, MI., Wm. B. Eerdmans Publishing Company, 1986) pp. 115, 116

13 Citing "The Way International," a statement The Way sends to those inquiring about the nature of their organization (1987).

14 M. B. Eddy, Science and Health, p. 497 cited in Bruce Shelly, *By What Authority* (Grand Rapids, MI., William B. Eerdmans Publishing Company, 1965) p. 150

15 *Protestant Biblical Interpretation*, a respected Evangelical seminary text, itself warns: "It is very difficult for any person to approach the Holy Scriptures free from prejudices and assumptions which distort the text. The danger of having a set theological system is that in the interpretation of Scripture the system tends to govern the interpretation rather than the interpretation correcting the system." Bernard Ramm, *Protestant Biblical Interpretation*, (Grand Rapids, Michigan, Baker Book House, 1970) p. 115

16 Jaroslav Pelikan, *Development of Christian Doctrine,* (New Haven and London, Yale University Press, 1979) p. 20

17 "In the earlier part of the second century the Fourth Gospel was recognized and quoted by Gnostic writers at least as much as by those whose teaching came to be acknowledged as more in line with the

apostolic tradition." F. F. Bruce, *The Gospel of John* (Grand rapids, MI., William B. Eerdmans Publishing Company, 1983) p. 7

18 G. L. Prestige, *Fathers and Heretics*, (London, Society for the Promotion of Christian Knowledge, 1984) pp. 14, 15

19 It is interesting to note that throughout the whole discussion with the Arians, not once did the orthodox refer to "traditions", i.e. in the plural. "The only term of reference was always 'Tradition,'—indeed, *the* Tradition." Georges Florovsky, *Bible, Church, Tradition: An Eastern Orthodox View* (Belmont, MA., Nordland Publishing Company, 1972), p. 83

20 A Scriptural example of oral tradition exists where Paul quotes the Lord to have said "It is more blessed to give than to receive" (Acts 20:35). No written testimony of this saying of Jesus exists any place in *any* of the Gospels.

Clement (30-100) states what should be obvious to all: "'The Message was delivered orally by our Lord to the apostles and was handed on orally by them to their successors' (I Clement xlii)." Panagiotis I. Bratsiotis, "The Fundamental Principles and Main Characteristics of the Orthodox Church," in *The Orthodox Ethos,* A. J. Philippou, ed. (Oxford, England, Holywell Press, 1964) p. 25

21 See also Acts 1:8; 20:35; and I Corinthians 7:10-12

22 "Even while agreeing on the sole authority of Scripture, evangelical believers were disagreeing, openly now, about its interpretation and implementation." Kenneth Ronald Davis, *Anabaptism and Asceticism* (Scottsdale, Pa, Herald Press, 1974) p. 80

23 "Such inconsistency in the face of a radical biblicism that was threatening those elements of the dogmatic [Reformation] consensus to which they [the Anabaptists] wanted to retain their loyalty put them into the position of violating their own principle of authority. Although 'they often speak scandalously about it,' they wanted to keep the dogma of the Trinity, which was indeed a statement of biblical teaching but did not appear in the very words of any one biblical passage; the same was true of atonement as 'satisfaction'." Jaroslav Pelikan *The Christian Tradition: Reformation of Church and Dogma (1300-1700)* (Chicago and London, The University of Chicago Press, 1983) p. 265

24 Jaroslav Pelikan, *Development of Christian Doctrine,* (New Haven and London, Yale University Press, 1979) p. 52

25 George S. Hendry, "The Place and Function of the Confession of faith in the Reformed Church", *The New Man: An Orthodox Reformed Dialogue* , John Meyendorff, Joseph McLelland eds. (New Jersey, Standard Press, 1973) p. 31

26 John Meyendorff, Joseph McLelland, eds., "The Place and Function of the Confession of Faith in the Reformed Church", George S. Hendry, *The New Man: An Orthodox and Reformed Dialogue* (New Jersey, Standard Press, 1973) p. 36

27 "The conception of the Spirit, working though Scripture to elicit faith and bring about the believer's personal justification...had definite merit. On the one hand it situated the Bible..at the very center of Christian life and faith, and thereby it managed to restore to Scripture its 'canonical' (that is, normative) value for determining Church doctrine. ...From an Orthodox point of view, however, the Protestants did not go far enough... By isolating pneumatology from ecclesiology, they lost sight of the proper context in which the message of the Holy Scriptures should be interpreted and proclaimed." John Breck, *The Power of the Word* (Crestwood, New York, St Vladimir's Seminary Press, 1986) p. 32

28 William A. Jurgens, The Faith of the Early Fathers, Vol. I, St. Irenaeus Against Heresies, 3.3.1 (Minnesota,1970) p. 89

29 Florovsky, *Bible, Church, Tradition,* p. 49.

CHAPTER SIX

ANOTHER VIEW OF TRADITION

What comes to mind when you think of tradition? Arranged marriages in the style of *The Fiddler on the Roof*? An unreasoned imitation of what one's parents and past generations did ("We have always done it this way")? Or, do you envision a body of legends which the naive blindly accept without question? Given these popular notions, it is not surprising to find many people with similar views regarding tradition. Their opinions are typically expressed something like this: "Tradition in the Church is no different. It is simply a human system of passed-down beliefs having little foundation in fact, Scripture, or common sense. Tradition is just an excuse to make up doctrines." Perhaps for some it brings to mind the warning Jesus gave concerning the religious customs of men: vain, synthetic doctrines which compete with the true commandments of God.

To an Eastern-minded Christian, however, Tradition, Scripture, and spiritual authority are all interrelated subjects. He would boldly assert that one can understand the place of the Bible in the Church only if he first has a clear view of Christian Tradition. This is not because Scripture and Tradition are two separate but equal sources of spiritual authority that somehow must be synthesized. It is, in fact, because they are inseparably related, and the goal of this chapter is to demonstrate their organic and necessary relationship.

At this point, let me remind the reader that the term "tradition," as is true with many other Christian terms, holds different meanings for an Eastern Christian than it does for the average believer in the West. There is a distinctively Christian sense to Tradition far removed from any of the stereotypes mentioned above. Furthermore, ancient Eastern Christianity's understanding of Tradition is radically different from Roman Catholic, Protestant, or superstitious ideas on the subject. Therefore, before one can understand the true meaning of Tradition, he must attempt to put aside these various popular meanings and see Tradition with fresh eyes, almost as if he had never heard of the concept before.

In this chapter, I will look into this Eastern Christian view of Tradition. In the next chapter, I will complement this vision with an examination of the Bible's place in the Church of the first centuries. To begin our discussion, I must first address the most common misconceptions of Church Tradition with which many of us have grown up. Hopefully, this will succeed in "blowing away the fog" around the subject. Then, in the later half of the chapter, I will be able to more clearly explain just what the early Church's perception of Tradition was. Throughout the presentation, however, the reader must be patient; for although each section will clarify the sections that follow, each piece will not communicate the full sense of Tradition. Therefore, a quick, easy definition will not immediately appear; only at the end will all the pieces be in place.

WHAT TRADITION IS *NOT*

TRADITION IS NOT UNBIBLICAL

Colossians 2:8 states that we must be alert to "the traditions of men" making certain that they do not take us "captive through philosophy and empty deception." This passage was an apostolic admonition against the traditions of the Gnostics[1], a heretical group teaching a secret tradition which they claimed came from either the Apostles or by way of direct revelation from God Himself. Those who were "enlightened" with this teaching, typically denied Christ's Incarnation and the basic goodness of the physical world. Obviously, this admonition in no way diminishes the place of true (Apostolic) Tradition. In fact, this exhortation is itself a divinely inspired example of the tradition Paul wants his brethren to adhere to. Only a couple of verses before this, the Apostle exhorts them *to follow the tradition they received as Christians:*

> As you therefore have *received* Christ Jesus the Lord, so walk in Him. (Col. 2:6)

Here the word "received" means more than "to have accepted" or "acknowledged." It actually illustrates ***the process*** *by which they received the teaching.* As Evangelical Scripture scholar F. F. Bruce puts it, "When he [Paul] says that they have 'received' Christ Jesus as their Lord, he uses the verb which was specifically employed to denote *the receiving of something which was delivered by tradition.* "[2]

This word "receive" is used in similar ways throughout the New Testament:

> Finally then, brethren we request and exhort you in the Lord Jesus that, as you *received* from us instruction as to how you ought to walk and please God (just as you actually do walk), that you may excel still more. (1 Thess. 4:1)

> Now we command you, brethren, in the name of our Lord Jesus Christ, that you keep aloof from every brother which leads an unruly life and not according to the *tradition* which you *received* from us. (2 Thess 3:6)

> The things that you have learned and *received* and heard and seen in me, practice these things; and the God of peace shall be with you. (Phillippians 4:9)

> As we have said before, so I say again now, if any man is preaching to you a gospel contrary to that which you *received*, let him be accursed. (Galatians 1:9)

One can see the significance of tradition in the Scriptures by looking at two other verses where the word "delivered" could be translated as "traditioned." Keep this in mind as well as what we just said about the word "received":

> Now I praise you because you remember me in everything, and hold firmly to the *traditions,* just as I *delivered* [traditioned] them to you. ...For I *received* from the Lord that which I also *delivered* [traditioned] to you...(1 Corinthians 11: 2, 23)

> Now I make known to you, brethren, the gospel which I preached to you, which also you *received*, in which you also stand, ...For I *delivered* [traditioned] to you as of first importance what I also *received*, that Christ died for our sins. (1 Corinthians 15:1,3)

Besides these passages just quoted, there are still other verses which point to the existence of an unwritten tradition within the New Testament Church.

> So then, brethren, stand firm and hold to the *traditions* which you were taught, whether by word of mouth or by letter from us. (2 Thessalonians 2:15)

> And *the things which you have heard from me* in the presence of many witnesses, these entrust to faithful men, who will be able to teach others also. (2 Timothy 2:2)

> You, however, continue in the things you have learned and become convinced of, knowing *from whom* you have learned them; (2 Timothy 3:14

It is important to note that in *all* of the above passages Paul does not equate his exhortations to hold to the "traditions" as an appeal to "keep the Scriptures" (which, at that time, would have been the Old Testament). Certainly, "No one acquainted with the facts will deny that tradition [i.e., Apostolic Tradition] was chronologically prior to the New Testament Scriptures..." [3] These passages were a call to embrace "the Apostolic witness", that which the Apostles knew was in accord with the Spirit of their Master.

DIVINE TRADITION IS NOT THE SAME AS "TRADITIONS"

Apostolic Tradition (another way of referring to the Tradition of the Spirit) cannot be *equated* with "passed on customs" or "handed down teachings", though it can and does make *use* of these. Divine Tradition (Tradition with a capital "T") searches for ways to express the message of the Gospel in ways that we mortals can receive (e.g., the words of the Bible or ancient Christian creeds). But these human means of communication are not the Tradition of the Spirit, *they are merely instruments He uses to lead us to communion.* Tradition gives *birth* to (true) traditions, but they are not one and the same.

All "traditions" (those in the plural) can be the vehicle or the "clothes" that the Spirit uses to bear witness of Christ, but they are not the Tradition itself.[4] Temporal traditions can be distinguished from *the* Tradition in at least three ways: temporal traditions 1) are objectively perceived by our senses (sight, intellect, touch, etc.), 2) they are always confined to our finite world (they are created within a specific time, culture and place) and 3) though they present a "picture" of Truth, they are never the fullness or equivalent of the picture they depict. Although Tradition may inspire various traditions, Tradition is distinct from any or all of them in that it is both timeless and beyond explanation. Tradition is the move of the Spirit, traditions are the "footprints" the Spirit may leave behind.

Let me give an example which illustrates this distinction between Tradition and traditions. The New Testament, preaching, creeds, contents of ancient worship practices, proclamations of early Church councils, the teachings of dedicated Christians throughout the centuries, religious paintings, and other Christian symbols, are small "t" traditions. They are all "windows in time" through which the believer can see timeless Truth. Not one of these windows, however, reveals the *entire* Scene. They are only the means by which we can perceive Truth, they are not Truth itself. Tradition is nothing less than the Truth itself - or better stated, *the ministry of Him Who is the Truth* (John 15:26).

TRADITION IS NOT MAN-MADE

Obviously, the Tradition I speak of cannot be man-made. If it is man-made, then there is no question about it: it is not Tradition. Tradition is not at all anything invented by mortals, nor can it ever be modified by humanity. "[C]ustoms created by us [which] cling to things that time destroys: acting, clothing, dancing, eating, building, education, painting, soldiering, entertainment, politics and etiquette. Such things are all subject to change or dissolution.[5] This is not the substance of Tradition, for it does not concern itself with arbitrary customs, only that which is central and crucial to the Christian faith."[6]

Human traditions, in contrast, can distort truth (again, the Gnostic traditions Paul condemned are a case in point [Col. 2:8]). Just because a particular teaching or practice is ancient does not automatically guarantee its truth. As St. Cyprian (205-258 AD), a noteworthy bishop of the African church, once put it: "Custom without truth is the antiquity of error."[7] *Traditions must always be evaluated against the "Tradition of the Spirit" if they are to have any significance (1 John 4:1).*

TRADITION IS NOT ANOTHER BODY OF TEACHING DISTINCT FROM THE SCRIPTURES

The Christians of the first centuries never understood Divine Tradition as a separate set of teachings alongside the writings of the apostles, nor as a "secret" Apostolic teaching only known by a hierarchy.[8] Indeed, such an "exclusive" understanding of the faith would be similar to the Gnostic position which taught that only "the elect" could know the true teachings of Christianity! [9] This misunderstanding has encouraged the Roman Church to create such dogmas as the immaculate conception of the Virgin Mary in 1854 (the doctrine that Mary was born without the taint of sin), the dogma of papal infallibility in 1870 (which attributed the Pope a divine power to define doctrine without error),[10] and the dogma of the bodily assumption of the Virgin Mary in 1950 (i.e., that upon her death she ascended into heaven, body and soul).[11] Not one of these teachings has any clear foundation within the Apostolic Tradition.

Apostolic Tradition is not an array of unwritten Apostolic teachings, nor is it a constantly evolving gospel which only clerics can interpret (Gal. 1:6). *God's saving revelation has reached its ultimate fulfillment in Christ and was sealed with the death of the last Apostle. This Revelation has been completed and it cannot be "amended" (at least not until the Day of Judgment and its last fulfillment).* Yes, the Spirit of God will be faithful to bear witness to His truth and impart the needed understanding to His Church so that *this truth can be preserved,* but He will give no new saving revelations *after* Christ (Rev. 1:17; 2 Cor. 2: 6-10).

TRADITION IS NOT CONFINED TO HISTORY

If one escapes the error of thinking that Tradition is an excuse to make up doctrines as one goes along, he may still go astray by viewing it as an irrelevant and archaic artifact of Church history. "Whatever it means, whatever it represents, true or not, it is irrelevant to the contemporary Church." Tradition lives both within the past *and* present. The reason for this is that "Tradition is a *charismatic* principle, not a historical principle."[12] Genuine Tradition stands in agreement with *the Spirit's* working in the past, but just as He is not frozen to the past, neither is Divine Tradition. Tradition, in the same way as the Spirit Who speaks it, continues to explain and illustrate the truths of God to *every* generation.

> Tradition is not a principle striving to restore the past, using the past as a criterion for the present [for] the Church bears witness to the truth not by reminiscence or from the words of others, but from its own living, unceasing experience...[13]

The "'Traditionalist' is not one who lives in the past, but the one who is open and alert to the activity and voice of the Holy Spirit ...and so attempts to live faithfully in light of God's Revelation."[14] Tradition is not the compilation of dusty, religious facts from a previous millennium, but *a living experience of God's action today.* Tradition continually renews, illumines and guides us into a deeper experiential awareness of the Truth. It was this *Living* Tradition which reminded the Reformation Church of the importance of the Scriptures, that salvation is not by works, and that the Apostolic reform of the Church is an unending need.[15]

Even though the true sense of Tradition was confused by the Roman Medieval context, the Reformers and the Anabaptists had a budding sense of it. Luther and Calvin, for instance, saw genuine value in a "passed on teaching" form of tradition, i.e., through creeds and the teachings of the fathers. They and the Radical Reformers also had a more progressive vision of Tradition in their viewing the need for both the Holy Spirit's illumination in understanding the Scripture and in the necessity for His constant leadership in the Church's faith and practice. In fact, the Reformers' main premonition regarding the reform of the Western Church bears witness to the Eastern Church's perspective of a timeless Tradition:

> ...they [the Reformers] rejected not the catholic tradition of the Church, but its one–sided and corrupt form. They were undoubtedly looking for this authentic, true tradition, and in several instances, were practically on the verge of identifying it in the same terms as does the Orthodox Church ...[for example] the idea of *Ecclesia reformata et semper reformanda* [the Church always stands in need of reform] is obviously a Protestant form of understanding Tradition.[16]

TRADITION CANNOT BE LEARNED ACADEMICALLY

Although Tradition brings to light the real meaning of the Scriptures, giving us deeper insight into the truths of the Faith, it is not an *external* criteria that can be merely studied and learned. Many have followed that dangerous path, disregarding both its spiritual nature and its abiding presence amidst the assembly of believers. Tradition cannot be summarized into "seven principles," nor is there any seminary level course one can take in order to master it. (If you find one, avoid it!).

"Knowledge" gained through Tradition is not academic in nature. Tradition is not something that can be found in a book. One does not need to read Greek, go to a graduate school, or memorize all the pronouncements of the ancient councils before one can walk in the Tradition of the Church. In fact, *no amount of rational knowledge can automatically bring anyone closer to the Divine Tradition.* The ability to live in the Church's Tradition is not based on knowledge of facts, but on an experiential awareness of God, a purity of life, and an identification and union with Christians throughout time. Tradition dwells within one's communion with God and all the members of Christ's Body.

TRADITION NEITHER ADDS TO NOR CONTRADICTS THE SCRIPTURES

Both Scripture and Tradition are two expressions of the one and same Spirit of God. Revelation can not be "graded"; *this* one is not as good as *that* one. God's revelation, if it indeed is *God's*, will never be in contradiction with itself. Thus, the Bible and Tradition are in many respects *indivisible*. They are not two *independent* sources. It is an error, therefore, to pit one against the other as if they were rival contenders. Tradition and Scripture (i.e., Biblical Tradition) are simply two reflections of the same Revelation in the Church.[17] In other words, without Tradition (Revelation), there would be no Scriptures.

When the Roman Catholic Counter-Reformation affirmed the need for Scripture *and* Tradition, they implied that Scripture was incomplete without Tradition. Henceforth, "Tradition" would be understood as being an added "extra"— an indirect admission that *each,* separate from the other, was lacking and imperfect. This thinking, however, ignores that *both* Scripture and Tradition are of the Holy Spirit and thus neither one can ever be defective.[18]

Revelation 22:18 is often quoted as a warning against those who would think that Christian revelation could possibly exist outside of Scripture's pages:

> I testify to everyone who hears the words of the prophecy of this book: if anyone adds to them, God shall add to him the plagues which are written in this book.

Moses spoke of something similar when he said, "You shall not add to the word which I am commanding you, nor take away from it, that you may keep the commandments of the Lord your God which I command you" (Deuteronomy 4:2) *but then* the books of the prophets were later "added" to the Old Testament canon. Are those prophetic books to be considered an unscriptural addition? Of course not.

The same Spirit which inspired the prophets later inspired Christians to both recognize (and canonize) the genuine books of the Bible and to reject the pseudo-apostolic books which falsely sought a place in the canon. The Apostles did not preach from a Bible containing a divinely inspired table of contents that later generations could consult. There was nothing in the Bible itself which detailed which books were "right" and that books were "wrong!" The canonization of the Bible did not even occur until almost the Fifth Century (397, at the council at Carthage). The resolve of the council itself was a consequence of the Church's long, long process of testing the texts. In fact, this was the Tradition of the Spirit which protected and confirmed the Biblical tradition.

Genuine Tradition is well illustrated by an analogy from Irenaeus of Lyons (130- 202), the bishop of Gaul remembered for both his Biblicism and his refutation of the Gnostics. Irenaeus taught that the place of Tradition in interpreting Scripture was like the guiding intentions of an artist in creating a jeweled mosaic of a handsome king. In the inspiration of the artist, the gems of the portrait render a beautiful likeness of the ruler. But in the hands of the theologically twisted Gnostics and other heretics, the portrait is rearranged. The precious stones now form a picture that looks more like a dog or fox than of a king. On top of this disgrace, the heretics further declare that *their* later creation was in reality the original picture! Such is the way the heretics handle the Scriptures, Irenaeus declared.

Throughout the story, Irenaeus does not contest the fact that the *material* these pseudo-Christians used in their monstrosity was genuine, for they certainly did use the Scriptures. But he did dispute *how* they constructed it. *Their disruption of the order and rhythm of the Scriptures redefined and mutated Biblical Truth.* Only Apostolic Tradition, he maintained, could place the gems in their right context and proper relationship to each other. Only in this way could the "image of Truth" which lies within the Scriptures be restored.[19]

Although Irenaeus firmly believed that the Scriptures were the perfect and complete (written) word of God, *he understood that perfection could only be realized when the Scriptures were seen and interpreted as an organic whole within the Church.* Only *there*, within the assembly of Spirit-led believers, could they be protected and their true meaning preserved. As one Christian thinker of the past has said, "Scripture is not in the reading, it is in the *understanding*." This understanding is only within the Tradition of the Church. Irenaeus makes it clear: no matter how many passages one can quote, to understand the Bible apart from this Tradition is to misunderstand it. To put it another way, if one is outside of Tradition one is "out of context."

TRADITION: WHAT IT *IS*

Before moving to a positive definition, let's sum up what Tradition is not. It is not unbiblical, nor is it the same as traditions. The reader should understand that Tradition is not simply man-made, nor is it a body of teaching distinct from the Scriptures. I've discussed how tradition is not confined to history, nor to an academic format. Hopefully I have succeeded in clearing away the misunderstandings that surrounding this important concept. Let's now look at what Tradition is in the Eastern Christian sense of the word.

TRADITION: THE ABIDING SPIRIT IN THE CHURCH

The fundamental meaning of Tradition is revealed within the Church, for, in its essence, *Tradition is the living experience and witness of the Spirit among God's people.* Two things are necessary for Tradition to be Tradition: 1) the presence and leadership of the Holy Spirit and 2) the Body of Christ [the Church]—the "vessel" of the Spirit. *Tradition is ultimately a continuity of the abiding presence of the Holy Spirit in the Church; a Presence which gives Divine guidance and illumination.* [20]

This view demands our attentiveness to the Spirit's voice within the shared consensus of brethren who went before us. To ignore their testimony would be to ignore the ministry of the Holy Spirit in their midst. Tradition can certainly be heard by anyone in whom Christ's Spirit abides, but a person with such a sensitivity would desire to identify with the Spirit's working among others as well. The "spiritual man" is not an isolated individual, for the Body of Christ is "*not one* member *but many.*[21]" Only as we recognize that our union with Christ also means a recognition of our union with His "members" can we be complete Christians. To borrow Paul's phrase to the Corinthians on this point, we cannot say to the Spirit-led Christians of the past "I have no need of you."[22] To do so would be to forfeit much of the spiritual blessing and wisdom the Spirit would have us enjoy.

It is precisely because we are members of *Christ* that we have an opportunity to discern the ministry of the Spirit in our midst (i.e., the message of Tradition).[23] "Tradition is not just passed on from one generation to another, it is constantly re-enacted and *re-received* in the Spirit."[24] Our bond with Christ in the Spirit is the only thing which makes such a "reception" possible. For this reason we may say that a recognition of Tradition is also a recognition that Christ is in our midst.

> We may truly say that when we accept tradition we accept, through faith, our Lord, who abides in the midst of the faithful; for the Church is His Body, which cannot be separated from Him.[25]

Christian Tradition, then, is comprised of four things: *1) our reception of God's Message,* 2) *our communion with the Author of that message (the Holy Spirit) 3) our union with Christ and 4) through Him, our union with His members, the Church.*[26] *These living relationships are the only context of Tradition.*

TRADITION IS ALWAYS IN AGREEMENT WITH SCRIPTURE

Apostolic Tradition will constantly preserve, protect and illuminate the Biblical Tradition. In fact, because it recognized the absurdity of dividing God's revelation into "two parts", the Church should make no distinction between Tradition and the Biblical canon.[27] God's Word is God's Word; whether it is spoken, heard, acted upon or expressed in worship. Just as the Truth of the Holy Spirit will never contradict Himself by presenting 'other' opposing "truths", Tradition will never challenge the teaching of the Scriptures.

The Eastern minded Christian sees how the Bible in the hands of the Spirit-led Church can be a measuring rod able to gauge false traditions from True Tradition. In fact, for the sake of preserving the Tradition, this is one of the roles which the Bible *must* perform:

> To the Church, the Bible is the unique 'canon of truth' or 'rule of faith.' This means that all tradition (the unfolding of biblical revelation within the

life of the Church) must be measured against scripture and judged in terms of it.[28]

Again, Scripture is nothing more than *a written testimony to* and *a product of* Tradition.[29] The Bible as an instrument of the Spirit "harmonizes" with anything which similarly claims its birth from Tradition.[30] Like two tuning forks set to the same note, the written record of Tradition will automatically reverberate its tone with any other valid expression of Tradition, whether Creed, sermon or anything else. If something is "out of pitch" with Scripture, it is not of Tradition. For this reason, Tradition could never produce a "Book of Mormon" or any other heretical body of teaching.

Tradition is the ministry of the Holy Spirit among His people, ever endeavoring to make clear the truths which Jesus and His Apostles embodied: truths regarding such things as God's Triune existence, the Divinity of the Son and the Spirit, the two natures of Christ, and the true interpretation of the Old Testament prophecies which pointed to Jesus as the Messiah.

The seeds of all doctrine are assuredly in the Scriptures, but the people of God need the Revealing Spirit to know how to recognize what is planted there. Tradition gives such an insight. Without it, the heretics can claim that their weeds are of the Spirit, quoting from the same Bible as the Bible-alone people use. Tradition guides the Christian in knowing how to uproot these deadly errors and to sustain the Truth. Tradition, therefore, not only stands in agreement with the Scriptures, it teaches the Christian how to correctly interpret them — how to handle "accurately the word of truth" (2 Tim. 2:15b).

Tradition is merely "Scripture rightly understood."[31] Tradition reveals the true design and intended meaning of the Bible. It is not something which obscures the Scriptures with needless complications. On the contrary, *Tradition helps us to recognize the Word of God in the Bible, not just "words."* Without it, we would be like the Ethiopian eunuch who tried to understand Isaiah 53 without Phillip's interpretation.[32] Like the eunuch, our perplexity would resign us to say, "How can I understand unless someone guides me?" (Acts 8:31).

TRADITION IS REASONABLE

Although Tradition cannot be understood by scientific observation, *it will never contradict reason.* True tradition will always be attested to by legitimate, historical Christian origins. It is not something conjured up in isolation from the historic saving event of Christ. Indeed, science can be an aide in discerning between true and false traditions: "...the use of historical methods of research are essential for separating truth from legend, content from form, essentials from futilities, holy tradition from those human traditions that Jesus condemned before the Pharisees."[33] Tradition does not encourage blind faith, it challenges it.

Although the voice of Tradition is dependent upon our sensitivity to the Spirit's leading, it is "not a mechanism which will infallibly make known the Truth outside and above the consciousness of individuals, outside all deliberation and all judgement."[34] If Tradition is really Tradition, it will be confirmed through prayer, a collective Christian mind and diligent study. God is not a God of confusion (1 Cor. 14: 33), nor does His Word call us to abandon reason in our pursuit of Him (Rom. 12:1, Jam. 3:17).

TRADITION FOCUSES ON THE ORIGIN, PRESERVATION AND CLARIFICATION OF APOSTOLIC TEACHING

In the early Church a primary meaning of Tradition was the "delivery" or "deposition" of Apostolic teaching. However, as heretical groups began to claim their teachings as true expressions of the Apostolic Tradition, Tradition came to be understood not only as the content of orthodox teaching, but also as its *origin and manner of preservation.* In part, this was discerned by asking groups such questions as: "From where and whom does your teaching come — an apostle, or a church which had a relationship with an apostle?" "Are there references to the Scriptures, early creeds and worship practices which other apostolically recognized churches can confirm in your body?" "Has your teaching ever been altered?"

The Gnostics could not justify their "unique" interpretations of the Bible. Apostolic tradition revealed their explanations as bankrupt, and them as a fraud. They could make no appeal to a church founded by an apostle in their defense. They could not historically demonstrate its purity. Tradition exposed them.[35]

TRADITION CAN ONLY BE ACKNOWLEDGED BY THOSE WHO ARE WALKING IN THE SPIRIT

As the truth of the Gospel must be received, believed, and trusted before one can experientially know that truth, so it is with other things inspired by Tradition. Of course, an unbeliever's rejection of Christian teaching does not make that teaching any less true by his rejection. But it is important to understand that the non-Christian cannot *really perceive* Christian doctrines *as truth* if he does not receive them and regulate his life by them; for the "natural [unspiritual] man does not accept the things of the Spirit of God ... he cannot understand them" (1 Cor. 2:12-14).[36] Tradition is one of the things given to the Church by the Spirit. Therefore it can never be the property of the unbeliever.[37]

The ministry of Tradition is not primarily aimed at increasing our intellectual knowledge *about* God. Rather it seeks to brings us *into communion with God.* Tradition is nothing less than the progressive, revealing presence of the Spirit Who brings spiritual life, renewal and growth. It "is not a deposit of doctrine learned by heart, but a way of life, the way of holiness (Is 35: 8).[38] This is the goal of Tradition, to bring one into a personal, face to face, communion with God: "Blessed are the pure in heart, for *they* shall see God" (Matt. 5:8) The one who lives in Tradition will demonstrate purity of heart, depth of trust in God, and genuine love.

How then can one discern what is *authentic* Tradition? Clearly, one must walk in sensitivity to the Holy Spirit. If one (along with other brethren throughout time), cannot as a son of God confirm in his spirit that what presents itself as genuine Tradition is indeed of the Holy Spirit (Rom. 8:16), then it cannot be Tradition. If the teaching does not remind him of the voice of the Shepherd (John 10:5), he should reject it as a fraud. The anointing which the Spirit has given him must lead him to say, "*This* is Truth" (1 John 2:20, 21).

TRADITION IS CONTINUALLY INSPIRED BY THE SPIRIT

Simply put, "Faithfulness to Tradition is ... a *participation in Pentecost*, and Tradition represents a *fulfillment of Pentecost.*"[39] Pentecost marks the birth of the Church. On this day the Spirit first dwelled within and among the Assembly. That first Church in Jerusalem had the assurance that it would never be orphaned by the Lord. God and His word would now dwell among them in a manner that had never before been possible in the Old Dispensation. This assurance is intended for the Church of today as well.

Pentecost makes it possible for the Church of this generation to know the same promise which Jesus gave to the First Century Church, namely, that "when He, the Spirit of truth, comes, He will guide you into all the truth..." (John 16:13). This promise of Pentecost was not the exclusive right of the Early Church; it was intended for the Church of all time.[40] As the Eastern Orthodox theologian George Florovsky notes:

> The Church is not bound by 'letter.' Rather, she is constantly moved forth by the 'Spirit.' The same Spirit, the Spirit of Truth, which 'spake through the prophets,' which guided the Apostles, is still continuously guiding the Church into the fuller comprehension and understanding of the Divine Truth, from glory to glory.[41]

The early Fathers never referred to a specific body of Christian teaching (i.e., the Bible, creed, prayers, moral instruction, etc.) as Tradition. To them, Tradition was not a motionless "deposit" of teaching, but "the *actual divine revelation.*"[42] This Revelation is the fruit of the ongoing work of Pentecost *within* The Body of Believers. It is this ministry of the Spirit which allows Christ's Church to discern God's Word from among the many other "words" it may hear.

TRADITION MOTIVATES INSPIRED DOCTRINAL DEVELOPMENT

It is the presence of the Holy Spirit within the Church which allows her to formulate doctrine. By such a "doctrinal development", the Christian with an Eastern disposition would *never* propose a view of continuous revelation where Scriptural truths grow in quantity. Tradition is not a "supplement" to Revelation. Tradition cannot add to Revelation like one adds more paper to a loose-leaf binder. Tradition simply encourages a process whereby the Church, led by the Holy Spirit, can better defend and understand the basic Christian doctrines which she *already* possesses.[43] New revelations are not added. Christian doctrine is never altered. But rather, Divine Tradition is a light turned on in the room of our Christian experience.

Although the Church of New Testament times was chronologically closer to "the spring of truth," its placement in history does not mean it "*knew and understood* the mystery of the Revelation ... 'better' and 'fuller' than all subsequent ages."[44] The formulation of the dogma of the Trinity, a term unknown to St. Paul and the Primitive Church, was not the innovative creation of later Church Fathers. It was simply another attempt at explaining the mystery which the Church from Paul's time to the present now experiences. As Vladimir Lossky states in his book, *In The Image and Likeness of God ...*

> At every moment of history the Church gives to its members the faculty of knowing the Truth in a fullness that the world cannot contain. It is this mode of knowing the living Truth in the Tradition that the Church defends in its creation of new dogmatic definitions.[45]

The Christian cannot afford to be naive here. Doctrinal development is a necessity. Christianity's theological path was not set on automatic pilot from the time of the New Testament and thus incapable of getting off course.[46] Prayer and serious thought were required by the Christian Church to defend her experience before an onslaught of heretical doctrines, and it was these attacks which prompted the Spirit to speak to the Church inspiring the key creedal statements that Christianity has today. Tradition in the doctrinal development of the Church can be explained as "the history of the right choices made by human beings confronted by the prophetic word of God..."[47] God's continual leading and man's continual response to that leading is imperative if His Word is to be preserved.

Tradition gives us insight into the practical application of Christian Truth, both in the recent past and within our own time. For instance, from the time of the Reformation to the present, the Spirit has made it clear that salvation is not confined to any one particular denomination, that every Christian has a common heritage with the Christian peoples of the first 10 centuries (not only with post-Reformation believers), and that the Holy Spirit's ministry can neither be regulated by an era of history (i.e., New Testament times) nor by any specific Christian's doctrinal statement. Some may interject that all of these things were always clear in the Scripture, but this is certainly not the case. "Bible-believing" Christians have not always agreed on these insights, and even a number today still do not agree with all of these perspectives.

THE MEANINGS BEHIND DIVINE TRADITION ARE UNCHANGEABLE

Words and other symbols can change (i.e., doctrinal development), but *Divine Meanings will never change.* A good example of how Tradition can adopt differing *ways and means* to express Christian truth is well illustrated by a story I once heard from a missionary. He explained that sometimes, due to different tribes' cultural perspectives, his mission team had to substitute the original word of a Biblical text with a completely different word so the peoples addressed could better understand the underlying meaning of the passage. In the case of an African tribe who had never seen snow, he explained, they had to translate Isaiah 1:18, "Though your sins be as scarlet, They shall be as white as snow" to "Though your sins be as scarlet, They shall be white as *coconut.* " A word was changed (certainly snow is something quite different from coconut) but the *meaning* -"forgiveness" and "cleansing" - *had been preserved* by the change.

Remember the word homoousios (same nature) in the last chapter? Few Christians today would have a theological problem with using that word when explaining that Christ is homoousios both with God and humanity. However, some Christians in the Fourth Century did have trouble with it. Why? Because that very same word had been popularized just a century earlier by another heretic, Paul of Samosata (260).[48] Certain Christians did not feel comfortable using a word which had formerly been associated with a heretical doctrine in order to now defend orthodox dogma. Nevertheless, the Church decided to use the word anyway, believing that its *application and meaning in an orthodox Christian context* made its use justifiable.

A word with a tarnished history was brushed off and used by Tradition to brilliantly testify to the miracle of the Incarnation. It's adoption in a stanza of the Nicene Creed is something which every Christian today acknowledges, "I believe... in one Lord Jesus Christ... begotten not made, of the *same essence* (homoousios) with the Father..." Here is another example of how Divine Tradition does not represent words, but the meanings behind them. "This is the tradition of the Holy Spirit."

SUMMARY

Tradition is certainly not something extra to the Bible's message. On the contrary, Tradition preserves, clarifies and protects Biblical truth. To the Eastern Christian, Tradition is *reflected* in the Scriptures. In the next chapter, will speak more about this relationship of Tradition and Bible.

Each manifestation of Tradition stands as an intertwining link forged by the joint-partnerships of Spirit and Church. It was in this manner that the books of the Bible were recognized, and it is in this manner that false traditions are even now being rejected. The apostles' knew of faulty traditions which claimed faithfulness to the Tradition, and so warned the first Christians to "hold fast" to the valid traditions which they the true apostles, had left them to follow (1 Cor. 11:2; 2 Thess. 2:15).

Tradition is more than just "passed-on" teaching: it is the Spirit's operation in and among the Christian Church of the past, present and future. The Spirit is the *fountain* of Tradition; and in Tradition He is not just "teaching" but endeavors to reveal *Himself.* Tradition's concern, then, is not merely to impart religious fact but to impart the sense and experience of Faith. *Its goal is to bring one into a personal relationship with God and those likewise covenanted to Him.* The fruit of such a union will not necessarily increase one's *academic* knowledge of Christian doctrine, but this union will bring about doctrine's true purpose within the believer: a pure heart, a good conscience and a sincere faith (I Tim. 1:6).

Christian Tradition recognizes the need to trace the Holy Spirit's ministry in the past but it does not abandon Him there. The Spirit's renewing influence is continuous, a never-ceasing energy throughout the life of the Church, that both thwarts unbiblical perspectives (inclusive of "new revelations") and brings about a deeper experiential awareness of Christian truth. The footsteps He leaves behind in the process are the testimony to Tradition.

The Reformers understanding of Tradition was in great measure muddied by Roman abuses. But even given the crooked spin on Tradition, the Reformers clearly seemed to have an intuitive sense as to its meaning. In all probability, the Eastern meaning of Tradition was the one for which the Reformers were searching. It is not unlikely to assume that Tradition would have significantly influenced their thinking had they been more directly exposed to it.

The Christian of this century need not remain in ignorance as to what Tradition is, or to its place in the Faith. Today, Tradition calls many to widen a narrow post-Reformation, Western focus into one which could more readily embrace the Spirit's working among *all* Christians— of *all* times, *everywhere.* This is something which most Christians can already intuitively confirm to be of the Spirit.

The last three chapters of this book may leave the reader with many questions. Questions such as: What effect has the Reformation/post-Reformation reaction to Rome had on my present view of the Bible? What are the practical and spiritual consequences of rejecting the place of Tradition in interpreting the Scriptures? What role does Tradition have in helping one understand the Bible? What would result if one were to interpret the Bible in accordance with Tradition? If the Scriptures are not authoritative in and of themselves then, what *is* the authority in the Church? In the next two chapters I will address these questions.

NOTES FOR CHAPTER SIX

1 Those whom we call Gnostics included a variety of groups, carrying on a variety of traditions, chief of which was that Jesus did not come in the flesh. Another of their "common claims was that they had secret, esoteric connections with Jesus through the mediation of covert teaching transmitted from one person to another and reserved for an elite of spiritual leaders ('gnostics'— 'people who have knowledge')." John Meyendorff, "Does Christian Tradition Have a Future?," *St. Vladimir's Quarterly* , (Crestwood, New York, St. Vladimir's Seminary Press, 1982) Vol. 26, p. 244

2 F. F. Bruce, "The Epistle to the Colossians", *The New International Commentary on the New Testament* (Grand Rapids, MI., William B. Eerdman's Publishing Company, 1984) p. 93 Italics mine.

3 Bruce Shelley, *By What Authority?* (Grand Rapids, MI., William B Eerdman's Publishing Company, 1965) p. 143

4 Examples of lesser traditions common in the evangelical church of today are: Sunday schools, missionary societies, the use of instrumental music in worship, visitation evangelism, Wednesday night prayer meetings/services and altar calls. None of these practices are clearly dictated by the Scriptures, but are they for this reason "unscriptural?" Divine Tradition offers the discernment we need to judge the value of these traditions.

5 Lazarus Moore, *Sacred Tradition in the Orthodox Church* , (Minneapolis, Minnesota, Light and Life Publishing Company, 1984) p. 24

6 "When we say apostolic and ecclesiastical Tradition we mean only those elements which concern the faith and the salvation of mankind, and which come from the Lord and the apostles." C. Konstantidis, "The Significance of the Eastern and Western Traditions within Christendom", *Orthodoxy: A Faith and Order Dialogue* , (Geneva Switzerland, W. C. C., 1960) p. 63

7 Alexander Roberts, James Donaldson, eds., *The Ante-Nicene Fathers* , (Grand Rapids, Michigan, Wm.. B. Eerdman's Publishing Company, 1971 reprint) Volume V, "The Epistles of Cyprian", Epistle 73, ""To Pompey, Against the Epistle of Stephen About the Baptism of Heretics," p. 389

8 Actually, the Pope's interpretations of the Scriptures and the Christian faith take precedent even over the teachings of past Church Fathers, Tradition is even understood by some Roman Catholics as being exclusively located within the papal office. In this respect, Pope Pius IX felt he was justified when he said, "I am Tradition." The Pope, as the head of the council of cardinals , has the authority to formulate the Church's doctrine in a way that no one else can contest. Although there is debate in regard to its role, this understanding of the Tradition is in practice accepted among the Roman Church's hierarchy and members.

9 Certainly, if the teaching brought forward by this "Tradition" was of any significance, why would it be kept secret from *the faithful* ?

10 The *Oxford Dictionary of the Christian Church* gives a popular definition of the Roman Catholic doctrine of infallibility as follows:

> At the First Vatican Council (1870) the Roman Catholic Church declared that the Pope was infallible when he defined that a doctrine concerning faith or morals was part of the deposit of divine revelation handed down from apostolic tradition and was therefore to be believed by the whole Church. In Roman Catholic doctrine such a definition is infallible even antecedently to it acceptance by the Church. The Roman Catholic Church also teaches that the same infallibility attaches to whatever is taught as part of the deposit of revelation by the entire body of Roman Catholic bishops in union with the Pope, whether inside or outside the Ecumenical Council, was stressed at the Second Vatican Council [1962-65]."

F. L. Cross, E. A. Livingstone, eds., *The Oxford Dictionary of the Christian Church*, "Infallibility", (Oxford, Oxford University Press, 1983) p. 701

11 "Pope Pius did not attempt to prove that the doctrine of the assumption was taught as such in Scripture or confessed in the earliest documentary witnesses to the Christian and Catholic faith. Instead, he attached his promulgation of the dogma to the development of a tradition for which there is admittedly 'no authentic witness...among the Fathers of either the East or the West prior to the end of the fifth century'." Jaroslav Pelikan, *Development of Christian Doctrine,* (New Haven and London, Yale University Press, 1979)

12 Georges Florovsky, *Bible, Church, Tradition: An Eastern Orthodox View* (Belmont, MA., Nordland Publishing Company, 1972) p. 47

13 Georges Florovsky, *Bible, Church, Tradition: An Eastern Orthodox View* (Belmont, MA, Nordland Publishing Company, 1972) p. 47

14 "It is not the sum of past experience, but a living experience of God's action today. It is not a dead dependence on the past, but a living and total dependence on the Holy Spirit." Lazarus Moore, *Sacred Tradition in the Orthodox Church* , (Minneapolis, Minnesota, Light and Life Publishing Company, 1984) p. 11

15 The Reformation slogan, "the Church reformed and always must be reformed," is a valid attempt at discerning true tradition; one which Orthodox can —and should— apply to many human elements which are abundant in the historical Church. John Meyendorff, *The Catholicity and the Church,* "The Significance of the Reformation in the History of Christendom, St. Vladimir's Seminary Press, (Crestwood, New York), 1983, p. 76

16 John Meyendorff, *The Catholicity and the Church,* "The Significance of the Reformation in the History of Christendom, St. Vladimir's Seminary Press, (Crestwood, New York), 1983, p. 76

17 "When the early Fathers referred to a set body of teaching regarding the Christian faith they did not equate it with Tradition (paradosis). Although Tradition could also mean the contents of the teaching delivered, it also included its method of delivery: via teachers, the Scriptures, creeds, etc. So far were they from distinguishing Tradition from a "deposit" of teaching (including the Scriptures), that to them "it signified...*the actual divine revelation*, the substance of which was to be found set forth in Scripture..." G. L. Prestige, *Fathers and Heretics,* (London, Society for the Promotion of Christian Knowledge, 1984) p. 6 Italics mine.

18 "Tradition in Orthodox theology is not distinguished from or opposed to Scripture because, on the one hand, Scripture itself is a part of Tradition, of what we receive in the Church, and, on the other hand, the whole Tradition is nothing else but the *reading* and the *appropriation* of Scripture in the life of the Church. Tradition, thus, is neither a complement, and addition to Scripture ('the oral teaching of Christ not recorded in writing by his immediate disciples,' as it is sometimes defined), nor a simple 'systematization' of biblical 'data' and 'materials'....It is the reading of Scripture through the 'mind of Christ' and in the light of the Holy Spirit bestowed upon the Church. In this sense, the 'proof from the Bible" is not a mere quotation, a text found as justification, but the inner consistency of all truth, life and action of the Church with the scriptural revelation." Elmer O' Brian, S. J., ed., *The Convergence of Traditions* , "The Orthodox Tradition," Alexander Schmemann, (New York, Herder and Herder, 1967) pp. 18-19

19 Another one of Irenaeus' analogies of the "canon of truth" is illustrated by the *Hemerocentones* , a composite of Homeric verse re-arranged in such an arbitrary fashion that it resulted, not in *Homer* , but a story completely foreign to it.

20 "The pure notion of Tradition can then be defined by saying that it is the life of the Holy Spirit in the Church, communicating to each member of the Body of Christ the faculty of hearing, of receiving, of knowing the Truth in the Light which belongs to it..." Vladimir Lossky, *In the Image and Likeness of*

God, eds. John H. Erickson and Thomas E. Bird (Crestwood, New York. St. Vladimir's Seminary Press, 1974) p. 152

21 1 Cor. 12:14

22 1 Cor. 12: 21

23 1 Cor. 6:16-17; Eph. 4: 15,16; 5:28-32

24 John D. Zizioulas, "Apostolic Continuity and Orthodox Theology: Towards a Synthesis of Two Perspectives", *St. Vladimir's Theological Quarterly* (Crestwood, New York, New York, St. Vladimir's Seminary Press, 1975) Volume 19, No. 2, p. 108. Italics mine.

25 Georges Florovsky, *Bible, Church, Tradition: An Eastern Orthodox View* (Belmont, MA, Nordland Publishing Company, 1972) p. 47

26 It was in this spirit that Irenaeus said that true believers had "salvation written in their hearts by the Spirit, without paper and ink, and [thus] carefully preserving the ancient tradition (*Against Heresies* III, 4, 2). This Tradition of truth was received through the Holy Spirit only in the Church. "For this gift of God has been entrusted to the Church, as breath was to the first created man, for this purpose, that all the members receiving it may be vivified; and the [means of] communion with Christ has been distributed throughout it, that is, the Holy Spirit...For where the Church is, there is the Spirit of God; and where the Spirit is, there is the Church, and every kind of grace; but the Spirit is truth." Thus, according to Irenaeus, to reject the truth is to reject the Spirit and to reject the Spirit is to reject the Church. (*Against Heresies* III, 24, 1)

27 "Right down in the eighth century it was still possible for John of Damascus, the systematizer of Eastern theology, to refer to biblical revelation in general as 'the divine tradition', to claim the Bible as the sole channel of revelation, and to urge that nobody should try to inquire too curiously into matters of religion that fell outside its venerable limits (*fid. orth.* 1.1.). ...The Bible was associated, and largely identified, with the tradition as early as Clement of Alexandria, at the turn of the century. He claims the authority of scriptural texts with the new phrase 'as the Scripture traditioned'." G. L. Prestige, *Fathers and Heretics* , (London, Society for the Promotion of Christian Knowledge, 1984) p. 13 and p. 14 citing *strom.* I. 21, 142. 2; *ib.* 7. 18, 109. 2)

28 John Breck, *The Power of the Word* , (Crestwood, New York, St Vladimir's Seminary Press, 1986) p. 105

29 "Orthodox 'tradition' was either raw material that became Scripture or the explication of what was contained in Scripture." Bruce Shelley, *By What Authority?* (Grand Rapids, MI., William B Eerdman's Publishing Company, 1965) p. 145

30 In fact, precisely because the "message" of the Scriptures was already identified with the Tradition which the Church knew as her own "there appeared at first no need of a canon... This situation [however] enabled Gnostic teachers to ascribe their own doctrines to the apostles' and to present them in the form of 'gospels' and 'epistles.' Hence, the problem of criteria became crucial for the Church in the middle of the second century." The canonization of Scripture provided an authoritative witness to and norm for the preservation of this Tradition. Alexander Schemmann, *Historical Road of Eastern Orthodoxy* (St. Vladimir's Seminary Press, 1977) p. 44

31 Georges Florovsky, *Bible, Church, Tradition: An Eastern Orthodox View* (Belmont, MA., Nordland Publishing Company, 1972) p.75

32 An analogy used by Yves Congar in *The Meaning of Tradition* , (Tr. A. N. Woodrow. New York, 1964), pp. 81 f. cited by Archimandrite Chrysostomos, Hieromonk Auxentios in *Scripture and Tradition* , (Center for Traditionalist Orthodox Studies, Etna, California, 1984) p. 26

33 John Meyendorff, "Does Christian Tradition Have a Future?," *St. Vladimir's Quarterly*, (Crestwood, New York, St. Vladimir's Seminary Press, 1982) Vol. 26, pp. 143, 144

[34] Vladimir Lossky, *In The Image and Likeness of God* , (Crestwood, New York, St. Vladimir's Press, 1974) p. 155

[35] "...already in the Apostolic age itself the problem of 'interpretation' arose in all its challenging sharpness. What was the guiding hermeneutical [interpretive] principle? At this point there was no other answer than the appeal to the 'faith of the Church,' the faith and *kergyma* [preaching] of the Apostles, the Apostolic *paradosis* [tradition]. ...it was a method to discover and ascertain the faith as it had been always held, from the very beginning... " Georges Florovsky, *Bible, Church, Tradition: An Eastern Orthodox View* (Belmont, MA, Nordland Publishing Company, 1972) p. 98

[36] See also 1 Corinthians 3:1-3; Hebrews 5:12-14

[37] "Tradition is no outward testimony which can be accepted by an outsider. The Church alone is the living witness of tradition; only from inside, from within the Church, can tradition be felt and accepted as a certainty." Georges Florovsky, *Bible, Church, Tradition: An Eastern Orthodox View* (Belmont, MA., Nordland Publishing Company, 1972) p. 46

[38] Lazarus Moore, *Sacred Tradition in the Orthodox Church* , (Minneapolis, Minnesota, Light and Life Publishing Company, 1984) p. 11

[39] Georges Florovsky, *Creation and Redemption,* (Belmont, MA., Nordland Publishing Company, 1976) p. 194. Italics mine.

[40] Note Acts 2:38 in reference to the Lord's promise of the Spirit in Luke 24:49: "For the promise is for you and your children, and for all who are far off, *as many as the Lord our God shall call to Himself.*"

[41] Georges Florovsky, *Bible, Church, Tradition: An Eastern Orthodox View* (Belmont, MA., Nordland Publishing Company, 1972) p. 106

[42] G. L. Prestige, *Fathers and Heretics* , (London, Society for the Promotion of Christian Knowledge, 1984) p. 6 Italics mine.

[43] "The meaning here is not that the Spirit communicates new revelations or doctrines to the Church. The 'truth' into which the Spirit guides the faithful is the truth of Christ Himself. Revelation concerns primarily the *person* of Jesus Christ, and not doctrine as such." John Breck, *The Power of the Word* , (Crestwood, New York, St Vladimir's Seminary Press, 1986) p. 107

[44] Georges Florovsky, *Aspects of Church History* (Belmont, MA., Nordland Publishing Company, 1975) p.19

[45] Vladimir Lossky, *In The Image and Likeness of God* , (Crestwood, New York, St. Vladimir's Press, 1974) p. 161

[46] At the beginning the theology of the early Church branched and wandered like a country lane, but steadily, as the various more important declarations of faith were made, correct paths became more distinct. The sharp, awkward theological corners in which genuine Christianity could clearly navigate would now be the place where a number of top-heavy, badly loaded heresies would meet with disastrous road accidents. G. L. Prestige, *Fathers and Heretics* , (London, Society for the Promotion of Christian Knowledge, 1984) p. 5

[47] John Meyendorff, "Does Christian Tradition Have a Future?," *St. Vladimir's Quarterly,* (Crestwood, New York, St. Vladimir's Seminary Press, 1982) Vol. 26, p. 143

[48] He denied the unique personality of both the Second Person of the Trinity (the Logos) and the Holy Spirit and taught them as only "powers" of God. He could admit that Christ was homoousios with the Father, but not in the sense that Christ's divinity was His own. He manifested and cultivated the "divinity" which God "charged" Him with, a divinity which others in former times may have also be entrusted.

CHAPTER SEVEN

THE EASTERN CHRISTIAN VIEW OF THE BIBLE

If, in fact, the rationale and method of *sola Scriptura* are inadequate, what course is one left to pursue in his desire to understand the Bible? Many logical and pertinent questions remain. If the Bible cannot interpret itself, *how can* it be interpreted? What *protection* does the Christian Church have from heretics who twist the Scriptures? If the Bible is not the sole authority in the Church, what is? Also how is the Bible related to the Church? Is the Church "under" the Bible or "over" it? In the next two chapters, I will attempt to answer these questions by presenting views rarely heard in the West: the Eastern Christian view of Scripture and authority.

Before we can understand this Eastern approach, we must first answer three fundamental questions: 1) What exactly is the "Word of God"? 2) What makes the Scripture to be "Scripture?" and 3) How exactly are the Bible and the Word of God related to one another? After addressing these questions, we will discuss Eastern Christianity's view of the Scriptures, looking more specifically at the role the Holy Spirit and the Church play in this approach. We will then examine the method of interpretation which the Eastern Christian uses in understanding God's Word.

WHAT IS THE WORD OF GOD?

GOD'S WORD: BEYOND WRITTEN WORDS

Long before New Testament times, and even before the existence of the written word, the Holy Spirit was speaking to and motivating men and women of God. The word of God was entirely transmitted by oral transmission for *centuries*. Where and how did the saints of old receive and follow God's Word if they did not have the "Parchments?" God spoke to them in their assemblies.[1]

Obviously, the Word of God cannot be restricted to printed words on paper pages between two leather covers. The message was, of course, *spoken* before it was ever written. Indeed, the Church began and flourished for years before the New Testament was actually written as we know it today. As shocking as it may seem to some, the message of the Bible could have *remained* in its oral form even until the present time. Its Truths would have continued to live, and, many would still be finding Christ.

The Apostolic message was committed to writing as a means to secure and protect its Message from deviation. Obviously, the Message would still be God's Word even if it had not been written down. Those of New Testament times *lived* the New Testament Word before they read it.

Papias of Hierapolis (70 -155 AD) was a believer who had the privileged opportunity to speak with followers of Christ's very own Disciples concerning the Master's teaching. The impression he received from them confirmed his experience: God's Word is the *voice of the Spirit*, not mere "writings":

> ... when anyone came along who had been a follower of the presbyters [Apostles], I would inquire about the presbyters' discourses: what was said by Andrew or by Peter or by Phillip or by Thomas or James or by John or Matthew or any other disciples of our Lord... It did not seem to me that I could get so much profit from the contents of books as from a living and abiding voice.[2]

Neither the Apostles nor Christ conceived the Word of God as something imprisoned within a document. The New Testament itself bears witness that the Apostles preferred to quote the Greek *translation* of the Old Testament (the Septuagint) rather than the original Hebrew texts.[3] This is an example of how the Holy Spirit was not to be confined to the exact words of a specific text. In fact, Jesus Himself did something similar when He cited a paraphrased version of Isaiah 6:9 to explain the significance of the parables.[4]

Scripture gives many other examples of the Holy Spirit using sources *outside* the Bible to convey God's Word. Here are but a few: Jude 14, 15 is a citation from the apocryphal book of *Ethiopic Enoch*, [5] Acts 17:28 is taken from secular Greek poetry, [6] Titus 1:12 is from *Epimenides* (the work of a Cretan false teacher and "self-styled prophet"),[7] and in I Corinthians 2:9 Paul quotes the *Ascension of Isaiah,* a Jewish apocryphal writing.[8]

What does all this mean? I would suggest that just as the Kingdom of God cannot be observed with "visible signs" (Lk. 17: 20), neither can the Bible be identified as God's Word simply because it is old, historical and in writing. The Word of God is not the Word of God *because* it is in the Bible. The Word of God is the Word of God because *the Spirit of God has spoken it.* And His Word cannot be contained by any Book.

LIVING IN THE NEW TESTAMENT

The Eastern Christian recognizes the same canon as the Fundamentalist-Evangelical,[9] but he does not believe that Text to be *The* Authority in the Church. For centuries, the Early Eastern Church had no clearly defined canon. It was not particularly concerned that this ambiguity would destroy the Faith. This was not presumptuous of the Eastern Church. Their confidence stemmed from the fact that they knew the New Testament [New

Covenant] *as a way of life*. In other words, the New Testament was not an *a religious reference book*, it was something that they were *living*. Their Covenant was not a covenant to paper, but to a Person—Jesus Christ. Neither did the believer *need* a Script in hand to "bear witness" of Him, His presence in their midst was their greatest witness (Matt. 28: 18).

Some might object, "Can't such a 'mystical' approach open the door to heretical interpretations of the Scriptures?" Certainly an individualistic, subjective, and private interpretation of the Bible will lead to error. The Church's interpretation of the Scripture, however, was (and is) not relative to each individual's interior, "spiritual" experience. The Church's interpretation of the Scriptures echoes the experience of Gods' people *everywhere throughout all ages.*

Let me give a practical illustration of this by way of an example from St. Vincent of Lérins, a Fifth Century teacher of Christian doctrine. Vincent affirmed that the faithful must be loyal to what was consistently taught by the ancient Church: "We must hold what has been believed everywhere, always, and by all" even though he believed that the Scriptures are "for all things complete and more than sufficient." On the surface, this principle seems fine. But, how could the Scriptures be advocated as the "sufficient" canon of truth *when the Scriptures themselves were not held "everywhere", "always" and "by all"?* Moreover, what of the many early Christian communities who possessed only portions of a Gospel or an Epistle?

In actuality, St. Vincent's rule does not advance the principle of *sola Scriptura*, but rather promotes the importance of *Living* Tradition (the Tradition with a capital "T"). His major point is that all genuine Christians everywhere —even those who do not possess the Scriptures—hold to the ancient *Biblical truths*. He well understood that the Bible could only be the rule of the Faith *if those interpreting it held a mind in symphony with the Truth.* It is this attitude which characterizes the lived-out experience of the Church:

> That whether I or any one else would wish to detect the frauds and avoid the snares of heretics as they rise, and to continue sound and complete in the Catholic faith, we must, the Lord helping, fortify our own belief in two ways: first, by the authority of the Divine Law [the Scriptures], and then, by the Tradition of the Catholic Church. But here some one will ask, "Since the cannon of Scripture is complete, and sufficient of itself, what need is there to join with it the authority of the Church's interpretation?" For this reason,— because, owing to the depth of Holy Scripture, all do not accept it one and the same sense, but one understands its words in one way, another in another; so that it seems to be capable of as many interpretations as there are interpreters.[10]

To separate the Bible from the Church is to make it a "free-floating" balloon whereby an endless number of interpreters can blow it in any direction their doctrinal biases please. However, the Spirit-led Church throughout time does not leave room for such a subjective approach. She, through the co-operation of her members, is able to discern God's Word because she is *a body*, a network of relationships which transcends "private" interpretations or limited eras. This all-encompassing union is possible because of the unique spiritual bond which exists between the Body of Christ and Jesus *the* Word.

God's Word is intended for *God's* people, not for unbelievers. *The Word of God is revealed and experienced as the Word of God only when it is received by a people of faith.* How, then, does the unbeliever hear God's Word? God's Word is spoken to unbelievers *through* believers (either via their testimony in the Scriptures, or through those now living). But in either case, God's Word is not *heard as* God's Word unless the Spirit of the Word reveals it to those who listen. This is why Jerome (342-420) stated that even though the Gnostics had Biblical texts in their possession, they still did not possess the Gospel. [11] For the same reason Tertullian (155-220 AD), a teacher and leader of the African Church, never discussed the Bible with heretics. They had no right to use the Scriptures... they did not belong to them. Scriptures are the Church's possession.[12]

ANOTHER UNDERSTANDING OF THE SCRIPTURE'S SUFFICIENCY

The Bible *is* an infallible light— when it is interpreted within it's "home", the Spirit-birthed Church. But why do we need the Church and its correct interpretations? For one reason, the Church herself is *a part of God's revelation.* How can one hope to understand the Bible apart from the people it narrates?

St. Athanasius, the key figure who championed the inclusion of homoousios (of the same essence) in the Nicene Creed, stated: "'I have nothing contrived from the outside, but whatever I learned I have inscribed according to the Holy Scriptures.'"[13] However, as has already been stated, homoousios is a word which does not appear anywhere in the Scriptures. Is the use of this "unscriptural" word a contradiction to his claim of Biblical faithfulness? Did this word "add" anything to Scripture's teaching concerning Christ? On the contrary! Those who personally knew Christ as their Redeemer knew Him to be homoousios with God the Father.

The Bible without the Spirit and Christ's Body is only potentially sufficient. *It is all sufficient only when read within the fellowship of all the saints of all time.* The ministry of Spirit in the Church (Tradition), lets us see the Biblical Message clearly. *Here*, within the Community of God, one can begin to comprehend the "breadth, length, height, and depth" of God's love in Christ (Eph. 3: 17-19).[14] *Here,* the Scriptures become self-evident to the individual believer. *Here,* they can be understood for what they really are: the revelation of God among His people.[15]

THE CHURCH AS AN APOSTOLIC WITNESS TO GOD'S WORD

An example of how the Word of God is inseparably linked to the Church is found in the teaching of Irenaeus, the early Second Century bishop and apologist. As you may remember, the Gnostics of that time claimed writings and "traditions" contradictory to the Gospel Message. Although Irenaeus did not have a personal, Apostolically certified list of the Bible's contents, he nevertheless succeeded in defending the Faith against the Gnostics' assertions. How could he do this without *written* evidence? Or, how could he demonstrate that his rendering of the Bible was accurate and the Gnostic interpretation false without such proof?

Both of Irenaeus' claims for authenticity rested upon this foundation: *The common witness of Truth attested by Apostolically verified Churches.* Irenaeus did not have an Apostolically certified text, but he could point to Apostolically certified *Churches. There* — within the community of believers founded by Apostolic doctrine — one could find out what was indeed Truth. These Communities could either trace their histories back to specific Apostles, or could clearly verify that their teachings were recognized by faithful men who did directly identify with the Apostles.[16] By tracing their historic foundations (tradition), these Churches attested to the Tradition that was alive within their midst.

In effect, Irenaeus laid down a challenge that the Gnostics could not answer. "Do you want to know how I can tell that your doctrine is a lie?", he could ask. "Go to any of the Churches which had been acquainted with the Apostles. *These* can tell you what is Apostolic and what isn't."[17]

Those who interpreted the Scriptures according to their own "enlightenment" rather than in agreement with the Apostolic Spirit were individualists, and thus heretics. This was the only logical conclusion. Both their approach to Scripture and their interpretations made it unmistakable that they lay *outside* the New Covenant Community.

Only *within* the Church is Scripture truly the "Scripture" (i.e., the Word of God). Those outside the Church follow a *different* gospel. They can not discern God's Word, for once Scriptures are removed from their environment, the Church, the Scripture "changes." In the hands of heretics, the Bible grows wild and sound teaching is disfigured into something monstrous.

THE CHURCH'S INDIVISIBILITY WITH GOD'S WORD

This Biblical theology of Irenaeus teaches an important lesson: *the Word of God is not committed to a "page" but to a "people", i.e., the Church*. It is this interpretive role of the Church which preserves the Scripture as God's Revelation. The Apostles not only passed on God's Word but they also laid a foundation in the Church which would support and defend the Bible's intended meaning.[18] It was this Apostolic Tradition which gave the Church a "canon of Truth" even before a Biblical canon was recognized.

The Church and the teachings of the Scriptures are inseparable, for the Bible is a book *for, by*, and *based on* the Church.

> In the living experience of the Church, it is not the inclusion of a book in the canon that makes it 'Holy Scripture': rather it is included in the canon because the Church has heard the Word of God in it. The Church and the Scripture are not two distinct authorities confirming each other. They are one and the same source of life, knowledge and communion, the same Word of God spoken to us and making his abode in us.[19]

THE WORD OF GOD JESUS CHRIST: THE WORD MADE FLESH

Jesus Christ, because He is the Living Word of the Father, not only spoke the Word of God, *He demonstrated* the saving revelation which He spoke. Christ speaks God's Word to us in the *event* of His coming, in His *performing* of miracles, and in the *very acts* of His death, resurrection and ascension. Lastly, and very importantly, God's word becomes perceived and heard through His sending the Holy Spirit at Pentecost. These actions are not any less God's Word simply because they are not "verbal". Can there be a Gospel without any of these things? These events "reveal" the Father. They speak to us of redemption. It is not only the words from Christ's lips, but the testimony of His *life* which teaches and saves us as well.

What it comes down to is this: the Word of God is not primarily the revelation of Truth in human language, but it is God Himself.[20] *Jesus Christ alone is the Word of God in the fullest sense (John 1: 1). He is the total revelation of God and God's will to humanity.* Although the Scriptures are a truthful revelation, they are not Truth itself. Only Jesus Christ is "*the* way, *the* truth and *the* life" (John 14:6). The Scriptural revelation is a *disclosure* of His Personal Being to His people, but it is not His very being.[21] To say that the Bible is the Word of God and that all Christian revelation is limited to it alone is to confuse the Revealer with His revelation.

It is a mistake to equate the written words of the revelation (the Bible) with *The* Word of God (Jesus Christ). Such an error leads the Church to know the Word primarily as *readers*, not as actual members of the Word's Body.[22] This way of thinking can very easily replace Christ's presence among His people with a bound collection of writings. The Word then becomes something studied, memorized, classified and scientifically "obeyed", but not a Person Who can be known in faith and communion.

Christ is *still* among us (Matt. 18:20), He has *not* left us as orphans (John 14:18). He is *now* in our midst. *It is Christ's presence which gives meaning to the Scripture*; the Scriptures do not *give meaning to Him.*

> The Kingdom has already been inaugurated ... The fixed canon of Scripture symbolizes an accomplishment. The Bible is closed just because the Word of God has been incarnate. Our ultimate term of reference is now not a book, but a living person. [23]

Because we are the very members of His body (I Cor. 12), He will *always* remain with us (Matthew 28:20). The Word of God is not "paper and ink" but Jesus Christ *present* in His Church. It is He, by the Holy Spirit, Who leads *His Body* to discern His voice over "other voices."

The Holy Spirit has disclosed Christ in the Old and New Testaments. He is still at work revealing Christ within the midst of His people today.[24]

> ...for God is not simply *speaking* to the community any more, while remaining essentially external to it. He is *present* through the Spirit in the community; and the community itself is a community of 'saints,' of adopted 'sons,' of freely loving persons who have all received 'the seal of the Spirit' (Eph. 1:13) and are 'taught by the Spirit' (1 Cor. 2:13).[25]

THE SCRIPTURES: WHAT ARE THEY? WHAT IS THEIR IMPORTANCE?

A WORK OF BOTH GOD AND MAN

Nothing I have said so far is intended to discredit the Scriptures. As shall be discussed in a moment, the Eastern Christian recognizes the Bible as an historic account of divine revelation without equal. After all, *God* is it's author. But He is not the Bible's *only* author.

God elected *human beings* to be "coauthors" with Him in writing the Scriptures. The Bible's "human" personality, temperament and style are attested to on every page. Such is the way God intended it. Why was this His design? Because the revelation was meant to be understood *by the human participants of His Covenant.* The Bible is not written for God, nor to be deciphered by angels. The Bible is primarily addressed *to* the Church, *through* the Church, and thus, the Church intimately *belongs* to the revelation, and vice versa.

To say the Bible is not *solely* God's work is not to belittle the Scriptures. As stated in the last chapter, the presence of its natural (human) element doesn't "ruin" its supernatural characteristics. The Incarnation of Christ poses an excellent analogy of this divine-human partnership within the Scriptures. As Christ did not become 50% less divine when He took on our humanity, neither does the Bible become less inspired through its human participation. The Bible, as is also true of Christ, is a manifestation of both "divinity" *and* "humanity" — a coexistence without separation, division, confusion or mixture.[26] "Christ is not simply a deity disguised as a human. Neither is the Bible a set of golden tablets dropped from heaven but disguised as human writings."[27]

THE IMPORTANCE OF THE SCRIPTURES

The Eastern Church highly esteems the Bible as a unique witness to apostolic experience and practice. It is her rule of faith, her rule of truth and her rule of life. Eastern Christians, for example, had been studying the New Testament in its original language for over a thousand years before the Reformation. They have consistently valued its contents as "the first and main source of Christian faith and doctrine, the foundation of the whole of Orthodox spirituality."[28] Theologian Thomas Hopko summarizes the Eastern Orthodox reverence of the Scriptures in the following:

> Everything in the [Eastern] Church is judged by the Bible. Nothing in the Church may contradict it. Everything in the Church must be biblical; for the Church, in order to be the Church ... must be wholly faithful to and expressive of that reality to which the Bible is itself the scriptural witness.[29]

The Fathers well expressed the respect and attitude which the early Christians had toward the Scriptures:

> "We are not allowed to affirm what we please. We make Holy Scripture the rule and measure of every tenet. We approve of that alone which may be made to harmonize with the intention of those writings." (St. Gregory of Nyssa, 330-395) [30]

> "For they [the Scriptures] were spoken and written by God, through men who spoke of God." (St. Athanasius, 296-373) [31]

> "Therefore, let God-inspired Scripture decide between us: and on whichever side be found doctrines in harmony with the word of God, in favor of that side will be cast the vote of truth." (St. Basil, 330-79) [32]

> "Look carefully into the Scriptures, which are the true utterances of the Holy Spirit. Observe that nothing of an unjust or counterfeit character is written in them." (St. Clement of Rome, 96-) [33]

> "And if an admonition can do such great things, far more when the admonitions are with the Spirit. Yes, for a word in the ear, doth more than fire soften the hardened soul, and renders it fit for all good things." (St. John Chrysostom, 347-407) [34]

The Orthodox Churches have never questioned the ancient Christian teachings of the Faith such as the Virgin birth, the divinity of Christ, Christ's Resurrection, or other central doctrines taught by Scriptures. To this day there is no attempt by anyone within those Churches to re-interpret the Scriptures in order to modify or abolish those truths. The Eastern Churches of today have never conjured up doctrines extraneous to the Scriptures; they have "never proclaimed dogmas which were not direct interpretations of historical facts as related in the Bible."[35] In other words, Tradition leads the Eastern Christian to see that there is a faithful reflection of every saving dogma in the Scriptures.[36]

HOW THE EASTERN MINDED CHRISTIAN WOULD INTERPRET THE SCRIPTURES

THE ROLE OF THE CHURCH AND THE SPIRIT

The Holy Spirit cannot be limited by any technique of Bible study. No one approach exhausts God's message in the Scriptures; there is always *more* that can be discovered within the Texts. Because of these beliefs, the Eastern Christian would not confine himself to any one, single method of interpreting the Scriptures.[37] However, a two-fold premise or undercurrent does guide his study: the role of the Holy Spirit and the intimate relationship between the Church and the Scriptures. This fundamental mind set affects his interpretation of every Biblical passage. In this section, I will explain how this conviction is practically applied in his study of Scripture.

ATTENTIVENESS TO CHRISTIAN TEACHERS OF THE PAST

In order to "read the Bible in the Church", one must recognize that the Spirit of God has indeed inspired Christians in the past to unfold the Scripture's meanings. By "the past" I do not mean only those who lived in Reformation times, but those who studied the Scriptures for the previous fifteen centuries as well. These men are popularly called "Fathers." They are called Fathers because many of their interpretations have valiantly preserved and defended the message of the Scriptures, often in the face of great persecution, and for this we respect them.[38] If we want to be in touch with the Spirit's lessons to the *whole* Church, *we cannot confine ourselves to the teachers of our own time.*

Some of these Church Fathers were *immediate* disciples and successors of the Apostles. Clement (30-100), an early bishop of Rome, was an acquaintance of both Peter and Paul, and Ignatius of Antioch (30-107) and Polycarp of Smyrna (69-155) were disciples of the Apostle John. Noted Church historian Phillip Schaff recognizes these men, and others such as Papias (70-155), Barnabas (a letter of his dating 117/132), Hermas (140/155), and the unknown authors of the *Epistle to Diognetus* (150) and the *Diadache* (100 AD - 150), as "the first church teachers after the apostles, who had enjoyed in part personal [relationships]... with them..."[39] Imagine the insight these men had! They learned from those who literally heard the very words of Christ with their own ears. Try to fathom the perspective they brought to the Scriptures! Is it really possible to consider ourselves serious students of the Scriptures if we choose to ignore what those earliest believers and martyrs had to say?

And what of the other early Christian teachers who wrote extensive commentaries on the Scriptures? Origen (185-253/254) was the first to compare and critique varieties of Biblical texts in an effort to locate the best manuscripts.[40] Jerome (342-420), authored the *Vulgate*, an extensive translation of the Scriptures into Latin from the original Hebrew and Greek. And St. John Chrysostom (344-407), the Bishop of Constantinople, a popular expositor of the Scriptures at one time memorized the *entire* New Testament. Certainly we would not agree with *everything* these men have written — and neither has the Church for that matter — but surely the Spirit of God must have revealed *something* to these men about the Scriptures worthy of our attention. At the very least, the culture, time and traditions of the Scriptures were more familiar and immediate to their own experience than they are to us today.

The authority the Fathers have among Eastern Christians is not something which was bestowed upon them by an ecclesiastical court. Nor is it a moral or juridical authority externally enforced by Church officials. In essence, their influence was, and is, a charismatic attestation *by the people of God* that the Spirit had gifted them with a valid teaching ministry. Time, Christian experience, and the Scriptures themselves continually attest to the fruit of their ministries. In the world of the Eastern Church, it has always been important that the *entire* Church be involved in this discernment process. And the task is not limited to past ages. In fact, within this century there may be "Fathers" that the Church will come to recognize in future years.

As previously mentioned, the Reformers had a respect both for the Fathers' appeal to the Scriptures, and for the continuity of their teaching within the Church. But given the residue of Roman scholasticism which still accompanied their perspective, they had little understanding of Tradition's charismatic and communal aspects.[41]

Contrary to the major Reformers, the Anabaptists ignored any teaching of the Church Fathers (including the Creeds). They would rely on the what the Spirit would speak to them within their communities, they did not feel that they needed to rely on the Fathers. With the exception of their restricting the voice of the Spirit to their own time and congregations, they had a sense of Tradition that was very similar to Eastern Christianity's. Men like Pilgram Marpeck (1495-1556), for example, a leader of South German Anabaptists, advocated a view of interpretation with which many Eastern Christians could find sympathy:

> ...the bearer of the teaching office of the church is not the Spirit-instructed individual ... but rather the community... Tradition is the living voice of the voluntary community of believing brethren as that community is instructed by the Spirit through Scripture. It is not the doctors of the church nor the bishops [as Rome understood these offices], but the community as a whole

which is the bearer of the charism of truth. [42]

Again, the East's only major corrective to this view would be to say that, because the Spirit has always been present within the Church, her interpretative ability is not limited to one particular place (i.e., Europe), to one specific community (one local church isolated from others), or to one particular era (the Reformation, Post-reformation period). Although the Anabaptists believed the Spirit spoke to *them* , most rejected the possibility of there being any testimony of the Spirit in the Church's teaching from the time of the death of the last Apostle until theirs. The Christian in the Eastern Church, contrarily, recognizes that the Spirit not only communicates the message of the Scriptures to the Church today, but that He *has also* spoken to her in the past as well.

THE CHURCH RECOGNIZES THAT *ALL* MUST BE INVOLVED IN THE BIBLE'S INTERPRETATION

The Eastern Church does not make a distinction between hierarchy and "normal Church people" in their respective abilities to understand the Biblical revelation. It is not as if the *real* Church were the clergy and that they alone had the power to "decode " the Scriptures and the laymen were lesser members of the Body of Christ, and thus incapable to grasp the Bible's teachings. Both can approach the Scriptures and learn from them.

To ask that one refer to the Church to interpret the Scriptures does *not* require one to passively accept doctrines given him by a board of "religious professionals" or to abdicate his spiritual obligation to those "more learned." In fact, to do this would hamper the Church's process of discernment. Instead, look to the Church means to intelligently investigate and personally digest the teachings which the Body of Christ has learned throughout its history. Such participation demands that *each* member be active, in both the giving and receiving of Christian doctrine, and in openly embracing people whom the Spirit of God has made his brethren.

Within the Church, *all*, not just the clergy, have received of the heavenly Spirit. As Irenaeus has written, it is possible for everyone "in every Church, ... to know the truth, to contemplate the tradition of the Apostles [Truth] which has been known throughout the whole world."[43] Thus, "the entire Scriptures ... can be clearly, unambiguously understood by *all*..." [44] Irenaeus makes it clear that the same "charisma" of truth which rested upon the Apostles, also operates upon the bishops *within* their communities to preserve and unfold the saving revelation of Christ[45] (the bishop, here, being one who both *represents*, and is himself *a part of*, the community for which he speaks). [46]

THE NECESSARY ROLE OF THE HOLY SPIRIT

The key Biblical passage providing the focus for the Eastern Christian's approach to the Bible is summed up in the words of Jesus:

> I have many more things to say to you, but you cannot bear them now. *But when He, the Spirit of truth, comes, he will guide you into all the truth;* ... He will speak; and He will disclose to you what is to come. He will glorify Me; for He shall take of Mine, and will disclose it to you. (John 16:12-14)

The Holy Spirit: without His ministry, one could never perceive the Word of God to be the word *of God*. It is *His* ministry which allows the Church to receive both "written" and "spoken" words as *God's* Word. The Spirit does this by enlightening and inspiring. His inspiration is *not* confined to the human authors of Scripture. It is just as crucial to *those "receiving"* the divine message as it was to those recording it.

Evangelical Donald Bloesch presented a paper at a gathering of other like-minded Evangelicals in which he expressed his conviction regarding the *ongoing* role of the Holy Spirit in Christ's Church. He and those gathered with him believed it to be essential if one is to properly understand the Bible's teaching. The following excerpt from that paper not only presents a good summary of the Eastern Christian vision of the Holy Spirit's ministry in clarifying Scripture, but the Eastern concept of Tradition as well:

> ... we believe that the Spirit of God is at work in the church as well as in the Bible, and that the Spirit interprets to the church the intended meaning of the Scriptures. We reject the idea of new revelation, but we affirm continuing revelation in the sense of an illumination of what has already been revealed.[47]

THE SPIRIT, *THEORIA* AND THE INTERPRETATION OF SCRIPTURE

Although I stated that there is no one particular way of interpreting the Scriptures in the Eastern Church, a certain *attitude* and *perspective* is necessary to maintain while studying the Bible. It is summed up in the Eastern Christian concept of *theoria*. Although in no way discounting the value of academics, *theoria is primarily a spiritual way of perceiving the Truth.* The one who has theoria sees history and Biblical truths through the eyes of faith and spiritual experience. Without this spiritual vision, no matter how much he or she knows, he will never understand the Bible.

The East is grateful for the benefits gained through modern Biblical research, but it is not supremely focused on data. Theoria sees value research only if it can be used to 1) increase the Church's ability to better discern what God is trying to *say* to her, and 2) if it can deepen each Church member's *love for God and his brethren.* These two goals are a work of the Spirit, above all else.

Theoria sees a message for *this* time and *this* generation of believers, a word that is *heard* and *acted* on. No one who reads the Scriptures in accord with the principle of theoria can say he knows the Scriptures but does not live them. According to theoria, the one who does not live the Word, does not know the Word. *Theoria is a vision where God's Word is personal, immediate, living and applicable.* In *Byzantine Theology*, John Meyendorff outlines *theoria's* spiritual character:

> ...Byzantines [Eastern Orthodox theologians within the Roman Empire from around the fourth to the fifteenth century] presupposed a concept of Revelation which was substantially different from that held in the West. Because the concept of *theologia* in Byzantium ...was inseparable from *theoria* ('contemplation'), theology could not be—as it was in the West—a rational deduction from 'revealed' premises, i.e., from Scripture or from the statements of an ecclesiastical magisterium... Not that a rational deductive process was completely eliminated from theological thought; but it represented for the Byzantines the lowest and least reliable level of theology. The true theologian was the one who saw and experienced the content of his theology; and this experience was considered to belong not to the intellect alone ... but to the 'eyes of the Spirit,' which place the whole man—intellect, emotions, and even sense— in contact with divine existence.[48]

Theoria is a "spiritual perception of the one sent by God, ... possible only to the believer... "[49] It is an insight into God's Word that cannot be received by one who is a "fleshly" Christian, one whose diet consists only of milk, not meat (1 Cor. 3: 1-2). This one's spiritual senses will be numbed and handicapped (1 Cor. 2:14) and will never be able to have his senses fine-tuned so as to discern good and evil (Heb. 6:13,14). The one with a *theoritic* vision has a *heart* trained to see Truth, a heart transformed by the Spirit toward purity and godliness. "Blessed are the *pure in heart* for *they* shall see God" (Matt. 5:8).

Although theoria demands that Scripture's literal and historical meanings be respected, its foremost aim is to disclose the Bible's spiritual meaning.[50] For example, it would see Christ and His kingdom as the central message of both the Old and New Testaments.[51] And if Christ the Messiah is indeed that revelation promised in the Old Testament, theoria maintains that the Old Testament could only be properly interpreted by those who have *received* this revelation, i.e., the Christian Church.[52] Thus, according to the Eastern Christian, "The Old Testament no longer belonged to the Jews...[nor could anyone] any longer claim Moses and the prophets, if he was not with Jesus the Christ."[53]

The literal meaning of Scripture alone can never achieve this spiritual end. If the

Bible's meaning were limited to what the Old Testament authors understood by their writings, many today would miss the Messianic significance of the Old Testament prophecies. Jesus, however, did not come primarily to "explain" the Old Testament to us but to *fulfill* it. And His fulfillment gives us an interpretative vision of the Old Covenant, teaching us not just the Bible's "word for word" meaning, but the *true spiritual* meaning of the Word of God.

> When for instance, we, in the Church, identify the Suffering Servant (in the book of Isaiah) as Christ the crucified, we do not simply "apply" an Old Testament vision to a New Testament event: we detect the meaning of the vision itself, although this meaning surely couldn't have been clearly identified in the times preceding Christ... Only the Church could unambiguously discern in the "type" of the "suffering servant" Christ, the Redeemer of men. In the Old Testament we had a "shadow" or image now, in the New Testament, we have the very fact and fulfillment.[54]

These Old Testament *types* (the historic events, places, objects, or people which point to Christ's coming) were discerned by the Church as a "foretaste" of the New Covenant promise.[55] The Body of Christ alone can interpret these types because, *in Christ,* she alone has literally *experienced* their fulfillment. Only *those in Christ* can understand the significance of these passages. Why? Because they relate to *Christ* — and to them *as* members of His body.

Thus, it is obvious that the interpretation of the Scriptures according to theoria mandates not only a recognition of the Bible's inspiration, but that we too, as students of the Bible, be enlightened by the same Spirit. Before Pentecost, even the Disciples were often confused as to the exact meaning of many of Christ's words. Truly, how can one ever discern the spiritual meaning of the Scriptures without the Spirit's inspiration?! Today we too will become confused if we try to interpret the Scriptures in disregard of the Spirit's ministry.

SUMMARY AND CONCLUSION

God's Word is not bound by ink or held captive by bookbinding. His Word existed before the invention of books and would continue to exist even if every Bible were destroyed. God's Word is the "Living Voice" which those who have united themselves to Christ can bear witness to as being of God. Thus, God's Word is understood in *relationship*, not in reading. The early Church was in deep communion with God's Word not because they had a Bible, but *because they had a New Covenant relationship with the Living Word, Jesus Christ.*

The Truth of God's Word has been revealed not only *to* God's people but *in* God's people (1 Cor. 2:9-13). This gives the members of the Church alone the ability to understand the Scripture *as* Scripture. This divinely orchestrated marriage of Spirit and humanity makes the Bible truly sufficient in the Church. Unlike the heretics, the Church's members recognize its true message, for the "anointing of truth" which rests upon them lets them know the teaching (1 John 3:27). The Bible is *their* book and they are of of "like Spirit" with it. Their Christian life and experience, which includes the experiences of their brethren before them, attests to the Bible's true teaching.

Without question, the Scriptures are an invaluable and essential expression of Divine Tradition. But when they are set apart from the Holy Spirit's ministry in the Church, they are no longer "a sure foundation." Outside the Church, the Bible's stabilizing legs are cut off by contradictory interpretations of "individuals." Our call to understand the Scriptures in concert with the Church prevents such an abuse. But this attentiveness to the Church is not an exhortation to sleepily submit to an ecclesiastical court. It is a call to take responsibility: to evaluate the reasons behind our present beliefs instead of accepting them without question, to take the initiative to seek the mind of those who have gone before us, and to pursue personal interaction with their perspectives. Only then will we, in union with the brethren of all ages, be able to demonstrate the Biblical Truth entrusted to us.

NOTES FOR CHAPTER SEVEN

1 In their assemblies, God's Spirit most frequently spoke to His people. This Word was subsequently orally passed down to the generations through the heads of families and tribes (Deut. 32:7; Job 8:8-9; Ps. 78:3-6; Prov. 1:8).

2 William A. Jurgens, *The Faith of the Early Fathers* , (Collegeville, Minnesota, The Liturgical Press, 1970) Volume I, p. 38 citing "Fragments in Eusebius," *History of the Church,* Bk. 3, Ch. 39

3 The Septuagint was the most common translation of the time and was popular among many of the Hellenic Jews. "As a landmark in history, the LXX [Septuagint] can hardly be overestimated. It was a major element in preserving the continuity of the synagogue worship, and therefore both the coherence of the dispersed Jews, was the Bible of the Diaspora, and as such became the Bible of the Church, which was given its global form and mission by Hellenistic Jews." E. M. Blaiklock, "Septuagint",*The Zondervan Pictorial Encyclopedia of the Bible* (Grand Rapids, MI, Zondervan Publishing House, 1975) p. 347

4 Jesus quotes the Aramaic paraphrase of the Old Testament ["Targum"] passage (Isa. vi. 9 f.) in Mark 4: 12 instead of the Massoretic text's record of the passage. (See Norval Geldenhuys, *The Gospel of Luke* , [Grand Rapids, MI., Wm. B.Eerdman's Publishing Company, 1977], p. 246 citing T. W. Manson, *The Teaching of Jesus*, pp. 75 ff.) Perhaps another example of such a paraphrase appears in John 7:38 where, although Jesus states the saying is from the "Scriptures", no such citation can be found anywhere in the Biblical canon.

5 For other examples of Apocalyptic literature in Jude, see "Use of Apocryphal Books by Jude", *The Expositor's Greek Testament,* Ed. Robertson Nicole (Grand Rapids, MI, Wm. B. Eerdmans Publishing Company, 1980 [reprint]) pp. 234-237

6 The verse includes a fourth line of a quatrain attributed to Epimenides the Cretan (For in thee we live and move and have our being") and a fifth line of the *Phanianomena* of Aratus ("In every direction we all have to do with Zeus; for we are also his offspring."). F. F. Bruce, *The New International Commentary on the New Testament: The Book of the Acts* (Grand Rapids, MI., Wm. B. Eerdmans Publishing Company, 1978) pp. 259,360

7 This verse quotes Epimenides' hexameter line and Callimachus quoted the first part of it in a Hymn to Zeus. Archibald Thomas Robertson, *Word Pictures in the New Testament* (Grand Rapids, MI., 1931) p. 600

8 See Gordon D. Fee, *The New International Commentary on the New Testament: The First Epistle to the Corinthians* (Grand Rapids, MI., Wm. B. Eerdmans Publishing Company, 1978) pp.108, 109

9 The Orthodox Church, unlike the Roman Catholic Church, only recognizes 49 books as belonging to the Old Testament canon. The Eastern Church assigns a "second" place of honor after the New Testament and Old Testament cannon, to these remaining pre-New Testament books (they are referred to as deutero-canonical books). Although these books are not valued to the same extent as other books in the Biblical canon, the East admits that they do have historical and spiritual value. These books are: Esdras I, Tobit, Judith, Wisdom of Solomon, Ecclesiasticus, Baruch, Maccabees I, II, and III, and the Epistle of Jeremiah. For further discussion see John Meyendorff, *Byzantine Theology*, p. 7-11.

10 Vincent of Lérins in his *Commonitory II* , as cited in Robert Webber, *Common Roots* (Grand Rapids, MI., Zondervan Publishing House, 1978) p. 138

11 "For they have no Holy Spirit, without which the Gospel so preached becomes human ... do not think that the Gospel consists of the words of Scripture but in its meaning." Georges Florovsky, *Bible, Church, Tradition: An Eastern Orthodox View* p. 91 citing St. Jerome in his commentary on the Galatians., I, 1. II; M. L. XXVI, c. 386

12 Georges Florovsky, *Bible, Church, Tradition: An Eastern Orthodox View* (Belmont, MA., Nordland Publishing Company, 1972) p. 76

13 Metropolitan Athenagoras, "Tradition and Traditions", *St. Vladimir's Theological Quarterly* , (Crestwood, New York, St. Vladimir's Seminary Press, 1960) Vol. 7, No. 3, p. 103 citing Chapter 33, Migne, P.G., 26, col. 605

14 Francis Folkes, *The Tyndale New Testament Commentaries: The Epistle of Paul to the Ephesians*, (Grand Rapids, MI., The Tyndale Press, 1976), pp.104, 105 in commenting on Ephesians 3: 17,18:

> He [Paul] realized that 'true knowledge', the knowledge of God, 'is unattainable without love' (Scott). If there is no love, the Spirit of Christ is not present, and there can be no understanding. ....[thus] the truth is not apprehended by an individual in isolation but *with all the saints* ....It is also true that men are limited in the very understanding of the purpose of God until they see it working out, and they themselves are parts of its outworking, in the 'fellowship of the saints'...it is no mere intellectual feat, but a matter of practical experience, a living together in love...

15 "...the witness of the Scripture is ultimately 'self-evident,' but only for the 'faithful', for those who have achieved a certain 'spiritual' maturity,— and this is only possible within the Church." Georges Florovsky, *Bible, Church, Tradition: An Eastern Orthodox View* (Belmont, MA, Nordland Publishing Company, 1972) p. 92

16 In essence, Irenaeus' position was, "If controversy should arise on some serious question, recourse should be had to the oldest churches, in which the apostles moved. [Quoting Irenaeus] 'Even if the apostles had not left us the Scriptures, ought we not to follow the line of the tradition which they traditioned to the men to whom they committed the churches"?" G. L. Prestige, *Fathers and Heretics* , (London, Society for the Promotion of Christian Knowledge, 1984) p. 16

17 Irenaeus literally tells them to go to "...the most ancient Churches in which the Apostles were familiar." William A. Jurgens, *The Faith of the Early Fathers,* Vol I., "St. Irenaeus Against Heresies," 3.4.1 (Minnesota, The Liturgical Press, 1970) p. 91

18 "Indeed, Scripture itself was the major part of the Apostolic "deposite." So also was the Church. Scripture and the Church could not be separated, or opposed to each other. Scripture, that is— it's true understanding, was only in the Church, as she was guided by the Spirit." Georges Florovsky, *Bible, Church, Tradition: An Eastern Orthodox View* (Belmont, MA, Nordland Publishing Company, 1972) p. 90

19 Elmer O' Brien, S. J., ed., *The Convergence of Traditions* , "The Orthodox Tradition," Alexander Schmemann, (New York, Herder and Herder, 1967) p. 17

20 Alexander Schemmann, *Historical Road of Eastern Orthodoxy* (St. Vladimir's Seminary Press, 1977) p. 42

21 Theodore Stylianopoulos, *Bread for Life: Reading the Bible* (Brookline, MA., Department of Religious Education, 1980) pp. 12,13

22 "In both Barth and Bultman there is the common intuition that the Word of God and the word of man remain *extrinsic* to each other." This is quite "different from the notion of a *free* mutual participation of God and man *in the Church* through the Word's historic incarnation." Thus, in most cases, whether one holds to the Neo-Evangelical or Liberal (and actually even the "conservative") Protestant position toward the Scriptures, the Christian is still wrongly viewed as being "outside" of God's Word, not within it (as members of His Body). John Meyendorff, *The Catholicity and the Church,* "The Significance of the Reformation in the History of Christendom, (Crestwood, New York St. Vladimir's Seminary Press,1983)

pp. 80, 81

23 Georges Florovsky, *Bible, Church, Tradition: An Eastern Orthodox View* (Belmont, MA, Nordland Publishing Company, 1972) p. 36

24 "Just as the eternal Word manifested Himself to Israel in the form of prophetic utterance inspired by the Spirit of God, that same Word, risen and glorified, continues His revelatory activity with the Christian community through the Person of the Spirit of Truth." John Breck, *The Power of the Word* (Crestwood, New York, St Vladimir's Seminary Press, 1986) p. 43

25 John Meyendorff, "Historical Relativism and Authority in Christian Dogma," *Living Tradition* (Crestwood, New York, St. Vladimir's Seminary Press, 1978) p. 30

26 Thomas Hopko, "The Bible in the Orthodox Church," *All the Fulness of God* (Crestwood, New York, St. Vladimir's Seminary Press, 1982) p. 55. Hopko on pp. 56, 58 continues below:

> ...a word may be at the same time perfectly divine and perfectly human without having to admit that the true humanity is lost or that the divine...can have sensual and material words. ...God and man or, more accurately, the divine and the human can exist with and in the other and penetrate each other so perfectly and truly that the attributes of one can authentically be predicated of the other, even though the divine is not changed by nature into the human nor the human into the divine.

27 George Marsden, "Evangelicals, History, and Modernity ", *Evangelicalism and Modern America*, ed., George Marsden (Grand Rapids, MI., Wm. B. Eerdmans Publishing Company, 1986) p. 102

28 Gerasimos Papadopoulos, Bishop of Abydos, "The Revelatory Character of the New Testament and Holy Tradition in the Orthodox Church," in *The Orthodox Ethos,* A. J. Philippou, ed. (Oxford, England, Holywell Press, 1964) p. 109 and A Monk of the Eastern Church, *Orthodox Spirituality* (London, S.P.C.K., 1974) p. 1

29 Thomas Hopko, "The Bible in the Orthodox Church," *All the Fulness of God* (Crestwood, New York, St. Vladimir's Seminary Press, 1982) pp. 50-51

30 Gregory of Nyssa, *De anima et resurr.*, M.G. 46,49B

31 St. Athanasius, *On the Incarnation*

32 St. Basil, *Letters,* CLXXXIX *The Nicene and Post-Nicene Fathers* , Blomfield Jackson, (Grand Rapids, MI., Eerdmans Publishing Company, 1978) p. 229

33 St. Clement, *The First Epistle of Clement to the Corinthians* , XLV, *The Nicene and Post-Nicene Fathers,* Alexander Roberts, James Donaldson, editors (Grand Rapids, MI., Eerdmans Publishing Company, 1978) p. 17

34 St. John Chrysostom, *Homily in Matthew, The Nicene and Post-Nicene Fathers*, George Prevost Baronet, M.B. Riddle (Grand Rapids, MI., Eerdmans Publishing Company, 1978) p. 13

35 John Meyendorff, "The Meaning of Tradition", *Living Tradition* (Crestwood, New York, St. Vladimir's Seminary Press, 1978) p. 18

36 "All teaching of the Church is substantially contained in Holy Scripture...[and] all teachings of the Church are acceptable because they are witnessed to by Scripture." C. Androutsos, *Dogmatics of the Orthodox Church* , Athens, 1907, p. 10 as cited in Gerasimos Papadopoulos, Bishop of Abydos, *The Orthodox Ethos,* "The Revelatory Character of the New Testament and Holy Tradition in the Orthodox Church," (Oxford, England, Holywell Press, 1964) p. 110, in ftnte 26.

37 Elmer O' Brien, S. J., ed., *The Convergence of Traditions* , "The Orthodox Tradition," Alexander

Schmemann, (New York, Herder and Herder, 1967) p. 18

38 "...the main, if not also the only, manual of faith and doctrine was, in the Ancient Church, precisely the Holy Writ. And *for that reason* the renowned interpreters of Scripture were regarded as 'Fathers' in an eminent sense." Georges Florovsky, *Bible, Church, Tradition: An Eastern Orthodox View* (Belmont, MA, Nordland Publishing Company, 1972) p. 102, italics mine.

39 Phillip Schaff, *History of the Christian Church* (Grand Rapids, Michigan, Wm. B. Eerdman's Publishing Company, 1910) Volume II, p. 633

40 Origen is not considered by the Church as a Church Father because of some of his doctrinal errors and I do not intend to elevate him to this status by mentioning him in this context. My only point mentioning him here is to provide an example how the Church was able to glean insight from teachers of the past. In Origen's case, his terminology and some aspects of his thought provided a base from which the Church's teaching on the Trinity, the tripartite nature of man, creation and redemption could later be more fully and accurately developed.

41 "..the Reformation is...the consequence-and also the victim- of the great fundamental divide between the Christian East and the Christian West. The reformers sought the fulness of the Holy Spirit, but they sought it with the same mental processes as their adversaries [i.e. the Augustinian scholasticism of the Roman Church]." Constantine Patelos, *The Orthodox Church and the Churches of the Reformation: A Survey of Orthodox Protestant Dialogues*, "Some Remarks of the Dialogue Between the Orthodox Church and the Reformation Churches (Geneva 1975, Faith and Order Commission, WCC), paper number 76, p. 63

42 David C. Steinmetz, *Reformers in the Wings* (Philadelphia, Fortress Press, 1971) p. 229

43 William A. Jurgens, *The Faith of the Early Fathers* , Vol. I, St. Irenaeus Against Heresies, 3.3.1 (Minnesota,1970) p. 89

44 John Lawson, *The Biblical Theology of Saint Irenaeus* , (London, 1948) p. 101 Italics mine.

45 Irenaeus states his belief regarding the manifestation of apostolic truth in the Church in a similar way in the following:

> The true gnosis ["knowledge", this in opposition to the "gnostics" false knowledge] is the doctrine of the Apostles, and the ancient organization of the Church throughout the whole world, and the manifestation of the body of Christ according to the successions of bishops, by which succession the bishops have handed down the tradition of the Scriptures, which have come down to us by being guarded against falsification, and which are received without addition or deletion; and reading without falsification, and a legitimate and diligent exposition according to the Scriptures, without danger and without blasphemy...

William A. Jurgens, *The Faith of the Early Fathers* , Vol. I., "St. Irenaeus Against Heresies, 4. 33. 8 (Minnesota, Liturgical Press, 1970), p. 97]

46 According to the theology of the Eastern church, a bishop cannot speak authoritatively outside the context of, or in contradiction to, the orthodox community of which he himself is a member. We'll speak more about bishops and their pastoral role in the Church in a later chapter.

47 Robert Webber, Donald Bloesch, eds., Donald Bloesch, "A Call to Spirituality," *The Orthodox Evangelicals*, (Nashville/New York, Thomas Nelson Publishers, 1978) p. 158

48 John Meyendorff, *Byzantine Theology* (New York, Fordham University Press, 1979) pp. 8, 9

49 William F. Arndt, F. Wilbur Gingrich, *A Greek-English Lexicon of the New Testament and Other Early Christian Literature* , "Theorao", 1., b., (London, University of Chicago Press, 1957) p. 360

50 Theoria takes into account the spiritual and historical background of a passage. John Breck clearly summarizes the interplay between science and spirituality when interpreting the Scripture in his book, *The Power of the Word* , (Crestwood, New York, St Vladimir's Seminary Press, 1986) pp. 111, 112:

> It begins with scientific research of the passage in question, in order to understand and clarify it's literal sense: the historical situation of the author and his community; the various motives which led to composition of the text; the origin and nature of independent sources and their kergymatic [use in preaching], liturgical or catechetical use... Once he [the interpreter] has determined the literal sense of the passage (the sense of the author himself understood and intended to communicate), the exegete moves to the question of the spiritual sense which the passage reveals for the present life of the community of faith. These two stages in the work of interpretation are distinct, but they are by no means separate. They do not involve pure scientific interpretation on the one hand and pure spiritual interpretation on the other. For *both the literal and the spiritual sense derived from the divine activity within history* . Therefore both senses are discerned by the Spirit-given grace of *theoria* .

51 "He is the fulfiller of the old dispensation and by the same act that he fulfills the old...he inaugurates the new, and thereby becomes the ultimate fulfiller of both..." Georges Florovsky, *Bible, Church, Tradition: An Eastern Orthodox View* (Belmont, MA, Nordland Publishing Company, 1972) pp. 22, 23

52 The Orthodox Church's approach to the Scriptures is a "dynamic conservatism" whereby "the plain meaning of Scripture is generally accepted as authoritative but with the awareness that the individual parts must be seen in the light of the whole... [that is the] *skopos* (the central aim or overall message) of the Bible." Theodore Stylianopoulos, *Bread for Life: Reading the Bible,* (Brookline, MA., Department of Religious Education, 1980) p. 15

53 Georges Florovsky, *Bible, Church, Tradition: An Eastern Orthodox View* (Belmont, MA, Nordland Publishing Company, 1972) p. 33

54 Georges Florovsky, *Bible, Church, Tradition: An Eastern Orthodox View* (Belmont, MA, Nordland Publishing Company, 1972) pp. 31, 33

55 Examples of such "types" are the image of the "spiritual rock" from which the Israelites drank in their desert wanderings which Paul affirmed was Christ in pre-incarnate form ["the Rock was Christ"] (I Cor. 10:4 ff), the manna in the desert [a type of the paschal lamb] (John 6:38-50), the brazen serpent which Moses set up to heal those who had been smitten by "fiery serpents" [Christ's redemptive crucifixion] (Jn 3:14), Jonah's internment in the whale [speaks both of Christ's burial and resurrection] (Matt. 12:39,40) and the sacrifice of Isaac by Abraham is too seen as a type of Christ's sacrificial death (Gen. 22:1-10; Heb. 11:17-19) Jesus' own typological references to Himself as the Son of Man, Servant of God, Davidic King or Son of God and the Church's reference to Him as the Second Adam, the new Moses and as the "Suffering Servant" are all examples of Old Testament types fulfilled in Him.

CHAPTER EIGHT

THE REAL AUTHORITY IN THE CHURCH

If the Bible is not *the* Ruler of Truth in the Church, what is? What is it that *safeguards* the Church from heresy? *To whom or to what* should the Church turn to as *the* authority? Many would argue that these are important questions, claiming that such a standard could determine what was or was not true. In this chapter, I will discuss why such a rationalist approach is impossible, and will suggest the radically different view of the Early Church in its place.

THE MYTH THAT "AUTHORITIES" CAN CERTIFY TRUTH

Many Western Christians look to an external, "objective" authority to find Truth. For Roman Catholicism, the guideline of authority is the papacy/magisterium.[1] For most Protestant Evangelicals, the Scriptures alone are authoritative. However, history shows the unreliability of either approach. The moral and political transgressions of certain past pontiffs, together with the false teaching of Pope Honorius I (625-638), contradict Rome's claim to be an infallible guide to Truth.[2] In regard to the Scriptures, the New Testament was not canonized for centuries. Thus, there was no way an early Christian could have said, "I believe this teaching because it is in the Scriptures."[3] And even if that were not the case, I hope I have demonstrated in the last two chapters that it is a practical impossibility for the Bible to stand alone as an "infallible authority." The Bible does *not* "speak for itself"; fallible interpreters speak for it.

THE FLAW OF "APOSTOLIC SUCCESSION'S" AUTHORITY

Many Anglo-Catholic Christians attempt to prove the rightness of their teaching by drawing a chart demonstrating the historic succession of their priests and bishops back to specific Apostles. This view of "Apostolic Succession" teaches that those who can historically trace their ordinations back to an Apostle have "valid" sacraments, thus making their Churches "valid." However, no historic record could either prove a person's "apostolicity" or insure that the church congregation which had such an "apostolically verified" pastor still possessed Apostolic faith.[4]

Many times in the past, a person's merely trusting in a bishop's "Apostolic line" would have led him into heresy. There *always* have been bishops of "Apostolic descent" who have succumbed to heresy. Bishop Ignatius of Antioch (30-107 A.D.), for instance, was succeeded by Paul of Samosata (a man noted for denying Christ's divinity) just one hundred and fifty years after his pastorate. [5] In the middle of the Fourth Century *most* of the "Apostolic" bishops and clergy of the East held a sympathy for Arianism. The Sixth Ecumenical Council (681) posthumously excommunicated no less than five bishops of significant, historic Churches (patriarchal sees) for teaching serious error.

THE INABILITY OF CREEDS, CONFESSIONS AND "FATHERS" TO GUARANTEE TRUTH

A number of Reformed and Liturgical denominations appeal to creeds, confessions, or to "the teachings of the Fathers" as guidelines for Christian Truth. Certainly, there is value in being aware of what our brethren before us have taught. But no human being - even a Father - has ever demonstrated infallibility. Besides, even if a "Father of the Church" were to teach only truth, by what criteria do *we* determine who is a Father and who is an imposter? To the Jehovah's Witnesses, Arius was a venerable Father, and Athanasius a rank blasphemer. Similarly, *whose* creed does "logic" compel one to recognize? Ireneaus' or the Gnostic Valentinus'?

In the debates regarding Christ and the Trinity, the heretics made many appeals to "tradition". This was the pattern of the Arians, the Nestorians (those teaching that their were two *persons* in Christ), the Monophysites (those believing that Christ had *only* a divine nature), and the Iconoclasts (those who denied that Christ's humanity was co-inherent with His divinity and thus prohibited pictorial representations of Him). These, and many other examples from history, clearly demonstrate the insufficiency of "tradition" as an indisputable barometer of Truth.

THE IMPOSSIBILITY OF "CHURCH" COUNCILS TO ENDORSE THE TRUTH AT ALL TIMES

Lastly, there are Church bodies which find their reference for Truth in *Ecumenical* Councils [those representative of the whole Church]. However, what is it that makes one Church council "Ecumenical" and another fraudulent? What about the many councils throughout history which *claimed* to be "Ecumenical, but were heretical? Many such councils had all the external, juridical characteristics of a true Council— they were legitimately called, their participants came from many segments of the Church, all the bishops present were in agreement— yet they were still ultimately rejected by the Church.[6] Why? Didn't they meet the criteria of a proper Church council? According to a legal view, yes.[7] In respect to their adequately bearing witness to the Church's experience of Christ, no.

Although there is "wisdom in numbers," there can be no magic assurance that Truth will always follow majority vote. Both St. Athanasius and St. Maximus the Confessor were called by God to stand against the *majority* of "churchmen" in their day: St. Athanasius in his defense of Christ's eternally begotten divine nature, St. Maximus in his affirmation that Christ had *both* a divine *and* human will. In these cases, Truth was defended and presented by an almost singular minority, not by huge "numbers."

WHERE INFALLIBILITY LIES: THE MINISTRY OF THE HOLY SPIRIT IN THE CHURCH

Neither Pope, Church structure, the Bible alone, "Apostolic Succession", "tradition", or councils can be trusted to always testify to the Truth. This leads us again to the question which began this chapter: "What is the authority in the Church?" According to the Eastern Christian view, the answer is *the Holy Trinity — the Father Who is the Father of His People, the Son Who is the Head of the Church, and the Spirit Who's home is in the Church.*

Irenaeus stated, "For where the Church is, there is the Spirit of God; and where the Spirit of God is, there is the Church, and every kind of grace; but the Spirit is truth."[8] The Spirit of God—*as discerned by and in the Church* —is the unshakeable Foundation of Truth for God's people. Who or what could be more sure than the Living God in the midst of His own? It is for this reason that "the Eastern Church will not commit supreme authority to any document, governmental office, councils, or to the Pope, or to any agency through which doctrinal authority would become legally defined."[9] *The Holy Spirit is the ultimate criterion of truth for Christians.* [10] No extrinsic authority can take the place of Christ's reign as manifested by the Spirit in the Church.

This perspective suggests a radical alternative to the traditional Protestant—Catholic debate: "Which is of greater authority? The Church (to Rome, the magisterium)? or the Word (to the Evangelical-Fundamentalist, the Bible)?" "To one the Church is under the Word; to the other, the Word is under the Church."[11] The Eastern Christian rejoinder is starkly different from either option: *the Holy Spirit is over all.* What warrants such a deduction? Three irrefutable truths: 1) Without the Holy Spirit the Church could not be the Church (i.e., constituted as the Body of Christ)[12] 2) Without the Holy Spirit the Bible could never have been written and 3) Without the Holy Spirit the Bible would never be perceived by the people of God as God's Word.

Because Christ's Lordship is made manifest among us by the Spirit (not by authorities) [1 Cor. 12:3].[13] Within the Eastern Church there has never been ... a clearly defined, precise, and permanent criterion of Truth besides God Himself, Christ, and the Holy Spirit." [14]

> The ancient fathers of the Church agree in rejecting any external organ, authority or mediation which is set above the Church rather than in the midst of the Church. In their view the Church's infallibility cannot be that of a 'separate organ'—of a council, for example— but only the truth of the Church itself as lived by the whole body. [15]

The basis for this position is that Christ—not anything else—is the Church's Foundation (1 Cor. 3:11). And His will is known only through a *relationship* of faith, not by authorities. If indeed the Church is "rooted and grounded in Christ" (which it must be if it is the Church), then God gives the Church confidence to believe that whatever she discerns to be God's Truth is, indeed, His Truth. How can it be otherwise? *Christ Himself* is a member of His Church!

THE PERSONAL GOD: AN AUTHORITY BEYOND WORDS

Although God uses written and spoken words, people, events, objects, and symbols to communicate His Word, He cannot be *fully* apprehended by these, nor can they be reliable standards in and of themselves. No doctrine or "system of truth" was ever meant to communicate such a fullness of knowledge.[16] If such was the case, one would not need God; he would have doctrine instead. However, God is known only in *personal relationship with His people*, a direct, immediate experience. Similarly, God's authority is not to be experienced as an inanimate law — but in *relationship*. He does not give "rules," He gives Himself. A Christian's authority is not a some-*thing,* it is a *Someone.*

It is this conviction that causes Christians of the East to resist "summarizing" the Faith. The question "What are the *essentials* of your faith?" implies that the Faith can be categorized, prioritized, and defined intellectually. But no *relationship* can be so blueprinted. It is like being asked, "Define the *essence* of your wife and the 'bare minimums' you need in order to have a relationship with her." The question presupposes that a *person* can somehow be *encapsulated* by a description or that love has "minimums." Both assumptions are false.

Because of this perspective, when asked about the sources of their faith, Eastern thinking Christians will answer in *expansive* terms. They can never say too much, they will always say too little. When asked to describe the essence of their faith, they will answer something like, "The whole of Scripture, seen in the light of the Tradition of the ancient councils, the Fathers and the faith of the entire people of God, expressed particularly in the liturgy [worship]."[17] But even in this "answer," they realize they have not captured the experience of Christian communion.

HOW GOD'S AUTHORITY IS MANIFESTED IN THE CHURCH

Given that God is the Authority in the Church,[18] how are Christians practically to understand and perceive His authority? Each person experiences God's authority *as a member of His Church.* He speaks Truth *in* and *through a people united to Him and one another.* For this reason *every Church member* is actively involved in the process of discerning His voice, and *every Church member* personally experiences the fruit of His government.

God's authority is real and absolute, but *it can only be communicated and encountered personally.* It is *not* an abstract, de-personalized legal decree, something standing aloof from one's need to be personally receptive. Parents are to use their authority to love, care for and nurture their children. If the children ignore or misunderstand that authority, however, they will never *experience the good fruit of that authority.* It is an authority *in principle*, not *in application.*

In the same way, the Authority of God is borne witness to only when each of His children is in *responsive communion with Him.* Here, each Christian from a mutual love, takes a responsibility to be aware, sensitive and receptive. Apart from such an attentive love, *God's* authority will *not* be *manifest* within humanity. The Father's authority is intended only for those who desire to live as His children. *Outside of the context of this familial relationship*, God's authority is mutated. From a *personal* authority of *communion* it becomes a *legal* authority of *laws*.. Authority again becomes an "it" instead of a "who."

THE WITNESS OF THE SPIRIT AMONG ALL

Let me give a Biblical example of how the Church personally recognized God's Truth. There was a fervent debate within the first century Church about what was specifically required of Gentile converts: "Must circumcision be required or is their faith in Christ enough?" (Acts 15) Do you remember how that controversy was resolved?

> Paul found a Scripture in Matthew and said, "It says right here in the Word..." No.
>
> Peter stood up and said, "As *the* representative of Christ on earth, I declare..." No.
>
> The argument was settled when the Elder James referred to an oral saying of Jesus, "The words of our Lord, handed down to us, are very clear regarding this matter; we should..." Again, No.

No one could make any reference to the words of Jesus to settle the controversy. No specific Scripture could be cited which immediately addressed the problem.[19] No particular person was looked to as if he had been given God's authority to declare the right teaching.

How then did they come to a decision on the matter? They heard the testimony of the brethren gathered there and then looked to God's Spirit to discern that testimony. Their resolve? "For *it seemed good to the Holy Spirit and to us* to lay upon [them] no greater burden than... [they] abstain from things sacrificed to idols and from blood and from things strangled and from fornication" (Acts 15:28). The Church may not have had the written cannon or an oral tradition, but she had the Spirit Christ promised. This promise was verified in their midst. They were not left as "orphans"; the Spirit of God gave them a firm witness to the Truth (John 15:26,27).[20] As this promise proved true in that first council, so it would hold true in later centuries as well.

EACH CHRISTIAN'S RESPONSIBILITY

There is nothing unconscious or robotic about the process of discerning Truth. The *entire body of the Church* is needed to discern how and when the external criteria (the Bible, creeds, councils, etc.) can indeed be "witnesses" of the Spirit. *Each* member has both the *ability* (as a "Spirit-bearer") and the *duty* to verify Christian Truth.[21]

During the early Councils, the lay Christian people were actively *involved* and *interested* in the theological debates of their day. The Church's interest was intense because each member realized that he held a joint responsibility for what the Church taught.[22] Gregory of Nyssa, in his trip to one of the Ecumenical Councils, records that one could become easily involved in discussions about Christological controversies with the money changer, the baker, and at the baths. Virtually everyone wanted to know what was going on, and virtually everyone had an awareness of the theological questions being discussed. So great was the public interest, shorthand reporters took careful notes at the councils, and then read them aloud in public squares. Gregory's own theological addresses concerning the Arian controversy (inclusive of the finer dogmatic points) were given publicly in the capital.

It is true that doctrinal Truth was normally explained by the pastor-teachers (i.e., the bishops of congregations), but this never precluded the people's involvement. *Everyone* in the Church was involved. The whole body had not only the right, but the duty to certify the Faith.[23] Besides, the bishops' individual opinions did not hold any special authority. They, like any laymen, could represent the Faith only in so far that they spoke of the faith which they experienced *within their communities.*[24] *Each* Christian's responsibility to reflect Truth can be received only if he or she speaks from *within his own congregation.*

The bishop's theology was *his people's lived-out* theology. Theology was never a matter reserved for the "professional," nor was there ever a dichotomy between a "teaching Church" [the clergy who alone are responsible for directing the Church] [25] and an "obedient Church" [the laity who must passively obey]. There is only one Church, lay people and clergy both being *equal* members. As recorded in Acts, the Spirit's testimony is given to "the apostles, the presbyters, *and the whole Church* (Acts 15:22)." The Christians of the first centuries were aware of their responsibility; from 325 to 1054, laymen were active in either supporting or challenging the decrees of every Church council.[26]

Within the entire Spirit led Church, God's Word can infallibly be discerned, but again, this process is not automatic.[27] The Church's infallibility can only be manifest as God's people are responsive in mind, soul, and heart to the Spirit.[28] This demands that the people be informed, be given to prayer and foremost of all, that they be a people in communion with God and their brethren.

Eastern Christianity's awareness of this mutual responsibility for the Church of both "clergy *and* laity" is reflected in a response to Pope Pius IX. The pontiff's letter declared that the East stood in need of his oversight, and that without it, would fall prey to error. In 1848 the Patriarch [head bishop] of Constantinople, Anthimos VI, countered the Pope's claims by way of an encyclical letter. In the letter he affirmed that "the people itself," i.e., the *body* of the Church, "was the guardian of piety." [29] The encyclical was confirmed and signed by all the patriarchs of the East as well as twenty nine other bishops. An excerpt from it follows:

> "Infallibility has resided only in the universality of the Church united by mutual love; and the invariability of doctrine as well as purity of worship were entrusted to the keeping not of any hierarchy but to that of the whole ecclesial [church] people which is the Body of Christ. In our Church, neither patriarchs nor councils could ever introduce any novelty, because the protector of the faith among us is the very body of the Church, that is, our people themselves..." [30]

THE WITNESS OF THE SPIRIT THROUGH CHURCH COUNCILS

The entire Church's participation in hearing the voice of the Spirit can be symbolized by a true Church Council. The idea of a Church council receives Biblical testimony not only from Acts 15 (the Council of Jerusalem), but also in Acts 6:2. In this instance, "The Twelve" convoked the council which included "the multitude of the disciples." At this council the Church of Jerusalem discerned whom God was calling to be deacons within their flock. This pattern for making corporate decisions occurred within each Local Church throughout early Christianity.

The early councils held before the Constantinian era (325) were spontaneous, occasional events. They were convened only when and where they were needed to address pastoral issues of concern. The council was not used to *insure* any sense of "institutional unity" within the Church, nor was it the Church's locus of power.[31] The local Church was a Church because it embodied Apostolic Tradition, not because a Council gave it the permission to be a Church. For these reasons, the local Church never felt obliged to accept any particular decision of a Council *defacto.*

How, then, is a Council determined to be "Ecumenical" and thus applicable to the entire Church? The question itself reflects the answer. If a council reflects *the life and experience of the entire Church,* it is Ecumenical.[32] When the formulations of a Council are *received* and *confirmed by each Local Church,* then it, of course, represents the Church.[33] Without this acceptance, no Council can be considered Ecumenical. The "amen" of the People of God is always essential.[34]

Because the whole Church (of *all* times, *everywhere*) is involved in the ongoing process of protecting and certifying Christian truth, it often takes decades before the people of God can say of a particular decree, "This is of the Holy Spirit."[35] History shows that not only the First, but also the Fourth (451) and Seventh Ecumenical Councils (787) took a great number of years before they were received by all of the Church.[36] Each local Church must have the opportunity to digest and test what is being proposed to them as the voice of Tradition.[37] Truth is the property of the Church, and the Church must hear all her members (of different times and from different places) to know if indeed she "owns" what some say she owns. This process of "testing Truth" cannot be hurried.[38]

All of this does not mean that God's Truth is not Truth until it is received by the Local Churches. Truth is Truth; one's response to it does not change it one way or another. The bishops of Ecumenical Synods never assumed that they were making *new* truths. Their responsibility was to *preserve, guard and clarify* the one Faith entrusted to the Church.[39] Their call was to *discern* the Word, not *create* it. This is why in all conciliar proclamations one finds phrases appealling to continuity: "'following previous synods,' 'continuing their deliberations,' 'in conformity with them,' etc."[40]

Because of this perspective, the ancient Church never related to a Council as if it were something *over* the Church.[41] Even into the Third Century when the General Council first appeared, the local Church knew it had no power to prescribe specific models of procedure over local Churches. Similarly, the local Church never thought of "an authority of conciliarity," as if the processes within a council *guaranteed* Truth to be revealed through them.[42] On the contrary, the Church never accepted any council simply because it claimed to represent the Church. The Church accepts only *specific* councils—those which the Spirit had *already* made clear to her members were genuine reflections of Tradition.[43] A Council's decisions are recognized by the Church because *the Spirit* reveals what they have spoken to be true. No local Church is forced to agree with the decrees of a council simply because it is a gathering of bishops.[44]

No one, nor any organization, can *make someone* accept the Truth. Christians know their Father as the Father of Truth. They, by the promise given to them by Christ, can bear witness of the Truth (John 14:17, 1 John 2:8, 21). It is natural for the Christian to receive the Truth. No one needs to force feed them the Truth. Besides, Truth — by its very nature — can never be imposed. When it is forced on someone it ceases to reflect Him Who is True. I will speak more about this later.

What is little realized in this society is that Christ's promise to bear witness to the Truth was not given to the individual alone. In fact, as the next three chapters will show, it was not intended for anyone in isolation at all. It is a promise intended for the Christian community (individuals *in communion*), for a fellowship of brethren made up of those now and throughout time (Acts 2:39). The Holy Spirit has united many members into the one "many-membered" Body of Christ in order that all may *together* drink of the same Spirit (1 Cor. 12:12,13). In the drinking of this Cup, God's gifts and communion are given to strengthen the *complete* Body of Christ. The Spirit is given *to the Body* —not to lone individuals—so that the *Body* can experience and testify to the Truth (Eph. 4:4-14).

AUTHORITY AS SLAVERY

External authorities can never be *the source* of spiritual life, for they can never, in and of themselves, bring one into communion with God. If we do not obey authorities, we are penalized for our disobedience. If we obey them, our obedience still does not insure us that we will be brought closer to God. A non-Christian can be "obedient" to authorities and not have a change of heart. A Christian can obey "authority" and forfeit both freedom and intimacy with God (Gal. 3:23, 24; 4:1). Authorities can even become *substitutes* for our faith in God. Authorities are things we see, test and prove; things which fallen natures are comfortable trusting. [45] Such a view leads to the following absurdities: one does not need God, he has His Word (the Bible). One does not need to know Christ to know the Truth, he has apostolic teaching (the Creed). Communion with God is reduced to an *external* relationship of laws and principles. This is the way of the Fall.

Someone may ask, "How can good (i.e., the authorities of Scripture and the Creeds) be evil?" Paul rhetorically asked a similar question regarding the Law, "Is the Law sin?" (Rom. 7: 7) His answer: "May it never be!" No, external authorities are not evil. Yes, they can serve a crucial purpose in the Church (Rom. 3:31; 4:14). But when they are related to *as an end* instead of as a means to an end (i.e., union with Christ, Gal. 2:16, 21) they, like the Law, become as a golden calf. As Paul made it clear in Romans, even God-given testimonies can lead one into "slavery" (Rom. 7: 23-25, also Gal. 4: 8-11) .[46]

Truth can only be received *personally* from the Holy Spirit (John 16:13) as He brings us into a real, existential union with Christ — Him Who alone is the Church's only incontestable Authority (Jn 1:16; Eph. 3:3-5; Col. 2:2-3; Rom. 10:4). In this relationship, we see that there are not really sources of authority, but a spiritual experience which is our singular, authoritative guide: *life in and through Christ*. Where this is not recognized, Christianity degenerates into a system of doctrine where theological "proofs" become the primary way to know Truth. This is simply another version of Adam's sin, i.e., seeking knowledge in a way other than through communion with God (Gen. 3). This is not the way of a *Christian*, it is the way of a *rationalist*.[47]

THE SPIRITUAL IMPLICATIONS OF CHRISTIAN AUTHORITY

The Early Church was not concerned with finding a "Final Authority" to *support* its teachings. It was concerned with Truth. Truth does not *need* to be subjected to an empirical test and thus *proven* as Truth before it can be called Truth. Certainly, something can be true without an external authority verifying it. Are not love, faith, and honor *real* (true) though neither science nor logic can prove them? Actually, the same Greek word can be translated as either *real* or *true* (*aletheia* [αλήθεια]). There is a good reason for this: *what is real is true, and what is true is real.* Thus, the Christian life is *true* life, and a life lived in sin is a *false* life. Eternity will show the reality of this claim.

The experience of Christ, given by the Holy Spirit, transforms "objective" truth into *experiential* truth — a Truth which gives freedom. The jailed prisoner knows that he will not experience freedom by studying about it from within his cell. The steel gates must be opened. He must be allowed to live, work and play in freedom before he can really know what freedom is. The same is true for one who would want to know the Truth of the Gospel; he must experience Christ, (the Author of Truth) if he is to *really* know His liberating power.

FREEDOM - UNION WITH GOD

Man is *self*-ruling, a characteristic of being made in the image and likeness of God (Gen. 1:27, 28). Before the Fall, man *freely* chose to harmonize his will with the God's will. Hence, God did not need to dictate over His creation. God could work *along side of it* via His partnership with Adam (Gen. 1:26). God said to Adam, "Oversee My creation. Be fruitful and multiply." Adam was initially pleased to do the will of the Father. It was *his* will as well. *Together* Adam and God had fellowship.

Here God's great love for man is clearly demonstrated: He makes man in His image, entrusts to him authority and responsibility, and most of all, nurtures an ongoing close relationship with him. Adam's sin, however, distorts the union. Now, instead of an intimate communion of spirits, man's will becomes separate, distinct, and external from His Creator's. In place of the former union, God gives only what man can now receive: the Law. Man receives a partial revelation of God's will, but no longer a disclosure of His Person (Rom. 8:2-4,11).

The Law was given to perform two functions: 1) it would *command* obedience by designating a boundary around sin ("Thou shalt not" ... "Thou shalt") and 2) it would be "a tutor" which would point mankind to Christ—the One through Whom our union would once again be restored (Gal. 3:24). The Old Testament saints such as Moses, David, the prophets, and others would know God, but they would never know the union Adam enjoyed.[48] From that time until the time of Christ, God would reign *over* His people, not *in and along side of them* as He had with Adam.

In Jesus, man is given the opportunity to know the Lord *in a real, integral union* (2 Cor. 5:17; Rom. 6; 7:4-6; Col. 3:3). In the unification of Christ's divinity with humanity, God invites His creation back into His intimacy. Before, there were two options: "obedience" to the Law or revolt. God's love provided another choice: *union in Christ.* [49] Now those in Christ not only have their union with God restored but, unlike Adam, they become "partakers of the divine nature" and members of Christ's body (2 Peter 1:4; 1 Cor. 12).

What does all of this mean for us in regard to God's authority in the Church? God's authority is no longer *external.* He is no longer simply *speaking to* the community, He is *present within it* (2 Cor. 6:16; Eph. 2:21&22).[50] This makes it absolutely certain that the people of God—the Church—can indeed hear, know and experience God's Word of Truth *in their midst.* This is not fantasy, or the hyper-spirituality of a mystic. It is as real as the ground we walk on.

THE WAY OF LOVE

The way of love does not force anyone's obedience. Love is never *imposed* (Gal. 5:13). Once there is a command, either the recipient of the command ceases to love because he *must* obey, or the giver of the command ceases to love by taking away the person's free will to respond. But how can a command be a threat to freedom? One has the choice to obey or disobey doesn't he? Yes, but a command says, "You must do this, or else." You must obey *or* you will be punished, *or* your privileges will be taken away, *or* I will not love you anymore.

This latter obedience is the obedience of a *slave.* A slave is one who "obeys" his master *because* he does not have the freedom to do as *he* pleases. He must obey he is a captive. In Christ, the believer is no longer a slave, but a *son.* God takes no prisoners. Every one of His children has been given the gift of choice and freedom. And God's love allows us to use this freedom to *willingly* follow Him —from a heart full of love, not fear.

Christian authority is a "union of love", and love always appeals to *freedom* and *responsible participation.* The Church is an environment of love where each is called into a deeper union with God through Christ. He does not "make" anyone do or believe anything. "The role of the Church is not, therefore, to impose upon man's mind some truth which he is otherwise unable to perceive, *but to make him live and grow in the Spirit, so that he himself may see and experience the Truth.*" [51]

"Yes, but does not such freedom give one 'leeway' to disobey the Law?" Yes, but where there is no "leeway"—i.e., *freedom* — there can be no love. One cannot love unless he has been given the freedom to give him or herself freely. One cannot experience another's love against his will. God can only have communion with freedmen. And it is this freedom which gives each an opportunity to *surpass* the Law (1 Cor. 13). But this is not all. Our freedom in Christ is the fulfillment of God's purpose in us, a realization of His "image and likeness" in us. For the Father's love encourages His own not only to *avoid sin*, but to imitate Him by *initiating acts of love* (Eph. 5:1).

OBEDIENCE

Obedience to Christ demands more than outward actions of subjection to the Scriptures or to any other "authority"; it calls for *unity with Him—as a Person —in mind and heart.* [52] This union brings about a freedom unique to those in Christ: *a freedom from* the imprisoning pull of the world (lust of the flesh, envy, pride of life, etc.) and *a freedom to* choose the way of God *voluntarily.* A woman's "Biblical obedience" to her husband does not make it a Christian marriage. While respecting each person's freedom and uniqueness, both spouses must strive to be in symphony with the mind, heart, body, and soul of the other. It is this *union* which leads each partner into a deeper love with God and each other. This is the way of Christian communion—a way far superior to mere "obedience." This union is what makes a marriage uniquely Christian.

This is the way Christ relates to us as His bride, the Church (Eph. 5: 28-31). God's love for *us* is given in order to lead us into a *continual* conversion toward Him; one where our will, heart, soul, and mind work in harmony and co-operation with Him. In-Christ ("Christian"), obedience is not passive resignation. He wants to relate to His people as *people*, not as mindless robots who will turn right or left at the touch of a control.

The Christian is not called to *surrender his freedom* to an ultimate "objective" Authority. We are not to be as Israel who asked to be under the subjection of an earthly King's "authoritative" rule, in lieu of the Lord Himself (1 Sam. 8:7). The way of discipleship is not in "abandoning" our will, but in responsibly using it to love God and others.

The Lord desires that we know Him as sons and daughters, and as co-heirs with Christ (John 8:34,35; 15:15; Rom. 8:17). We are to be "obedient" to Him in a relationship of friendship; He speaks to us in the love friendship, we listen as those who consider themselves his friends. Our love leads us to take responsibility for this relationship of love; one where we actively *co-operate with* God's will, not to*capitualte to* it (Eph. 4:13,14).

Love gives us freedom to choose Him. There are no "subjects" in God's Kingdom; each will reign *with* Him (2 Tim. 2:12; Rev. 5:10; 20:6; 22:5) not *under* Him (Eph. 2:4-7; Col. 3:1,4). Christ's "decision" to be Incarnate was *not* a subordination or surrender of His will to the Father's and the Spirit. It was a *free* expression of His love toward Each Person (and to us). He did not do what He did because He was threatened if He failed to "oblige." We too are called to be one with the Trinity (and one another) by participating in that same, free, unrestrained love (Jn 17:21-23). This love leads us to *freely* "obey."[53]

> In communion there is no externally super-imposed authority. If there are orders and commandments in the life of the Spirit they are not there to be *obeyed* as if they possessed an authority themselves, but to give expression to communion, to invest love with a form...[54]

LOVE: THE SPIRIT'S PROTECTION OF THE CHURCH FROM HERESY

As it is the nature of love to "bring together" (Col. 2:14) those in love, the Spirit of God's love draws His people to unite. The result of such love continually bonds the believer into God's *commun* -ity, i.e., the Church (Eph. 1:7-10). For this reason, I have said that the Christian Community is the residence of the Spirit (and God's love) *par excellence.* And only here, in the context of loving relationships, can God's Word be rightly understood (Eph. 3:16-19).

The Church's safeguard against heresy is not an *objective* criteria, it is a spiritual one. It is this fellowship of love in Christ. When this environment of love ceases, we are in danger of twisting the Faith to our own selfish ends; the works of the flesh are unleashed ("disputes, dissensions, factions" [Gal. 5: 19]) and "disorder and every evil thing" [James 3:16]) is allowed to work.

Paul said the proof of true doctrine is the love it produces ("The goal of our instruction is love from a pure heart and a good conscience" [I Tim. 1: 5]). True doctrine does not exist within the heart of one who lives an insincere or corrupt life. To speak "correct" doctrine yet live in contradiction to it, James tells us, is to " *lie* against the truth" (James 3:14). The Truth Christ gave is only adequately witnessed in the life of one who knows the freedom of loving (Gal. 5:1, 13). Only in the context of the Church (the loved and loving people of God of all ages), can doctrine be Life and Truth. Similarly, only in this context of love can the Church be "protected" from heresy.

A contemporary Eastern Orthodox bishop has summed it up this way: "'The faith is not preserved where love has become impoverished'."[55] The flesh *cannot* advance the things of the Spirit, they are *opposed* to each other (Gal. 5: 17; Rom 8: 5, 6). This leaves us with one conclusion: there are no guarantees from doctrinal error when we do not walk in the Spirit of love. *God did not intend any insurances for a church which does not love*

Christ and one another. Indeed, a loveless but "doctrinally sound" assembly is not His Church. For where there is no love, His headship is not present (1 John 4:16).

SUMMARY AND CONCLUSION

History has consistently demonstrated that external standards are unreliable and inadequate measurements to defend and proclaim Truth; even worse, they can become *substitutes* for the only Authority in the Church: God Himself. And here we must be quick to say that even His Authority cannot be called upon as if He were a reference book, a foolproof guide where the Christian reader "looks up" Truth. Truth is more than data. Truth is a spiritual experience, an experience which gives us the insight to know how to *understand* the data. Truth is not just facts, it is *reality, and reality cannot be grasped by man's mind alone; it must also be grasped by his spirit* (1 Cor. 2:10-15).

To put it another way, Truth is Jesus Christ, and He can only be known in *relationship* (John 14:6). Christ is not "authoritative" in the Christian's life because of rational arguments "proving" His divinity. He is the guide of truth because He is the believer's Savior and Brother. Only in such a *relationship* does the Christian realize the blessing of God's authority in his life.

Christ is the Man Whom the Spirit of God has united with us in our "humanness." He is not removed and separate from us. We now have *communion* of heart, soul, and body with the Son of God. Amazing! So deep is this spiritual bond that Paul says that the Church has "become one flesh" with Christ (Eph. 5:29-31; I Cor. 12:12). Because of this relationship, both our humanity and personal freedom can be restored in His likeness. This union leads us to love, not because commandments declare we should, but because we want to love Him Who brought us into His Family.

An historically naive person might think that relying on "authorities" instead of one's relationship with God is less "risky." However, the opposite is the case. The one who believes he can know Truth through external criteria will always be the one most vulnerable to deception. For if one thinks He can know God and Truth without basing his faith *on relationships of love* (with either Christ or his brethren), he will only know God as "The Authority" not as the God of love. And not to know God as love, is not to know Him at all (I John 3:7-12).

In short, the chapter can be summarized by the following answers to two brief questions. What is the authority in the Church? God. How is His authority discerned? Within the Church.

But this answer leaves us with another question, "What *is* the Church?" That will be the subject of the next few chapters.

NOTES FOR CHAPTER EIGHT

1 Roman canonists taught that the continuity and strength of the Church could be *guaranteed* only through infallible authority. This concern was enhanced by the prevalent Augustinian concept of man as intrinsically sinful and liable to errors. John Meyendorff, "Historical Relativism and Authority in Christian Dogma", *Living Tradition,* (Crestwood, New York, St. Vladimir's Seminary Press, 1978) p. 43

2 Honorius taught that Christ had only *one* will, not two (human and divine). Pope Leo II (682-684) himself later concurred with the Church at large in condemning Honorius' teaching as heretical.

3 John Meyendorff, "Does Christian Tradition Have a Future?," *St. Vladimir's Quarterly* , (Crestwood, New York, St. Vladimir's Seminary Press, 1982) Vol. 26, p. 144

4 Although the East has respect for the historicity of the Church, it does not confine its understanding of Apostolicity to something which can be verified by historic records of ordination alone. In the Eastern view, a Church is not Apostolic because its pastor can trace his ordination back to an Apostle, but because the *entire congregation* testifies to the Apostolic *faith.* A *Church* may be within Apostolic succession (i.e., Antioch), but an individual cannot possess this character in his own right. One man's "pedigree" cannot make an entire Church "Apostolic." It is for this reason that the East never had a major concern about "who's who" lists of the ordained, but that the faith of the ordained (as one who *represented his congregation)* was truly Apostolic. Where a Church was a fruit of an Apostles ministry, well and good. But if that Church ceased to bear witness to the Faith, even though it has a "valid" Apostolic history, it is no longer Apostolic. Which Local Church is Apostolic? The Church which proclaims the faith of the Apostles, lives that faith, and can confirm that faith amidst sister congregations (past, present, future). See Ephesians 2:19-22.

5 Ironically, Ignatius was a man noted for exhorting the Second Century Church to follow the bishop without question. The exhortation, in his case, was intended to protect the faithful from the false teachings and traditions of the Gnostic heresies which were circulating at the time. A bishop in communion with other Local Churches which recognized Apostolic teaching was a good safeguard against heresy. Those today who quote Ignatius to defend the doctrine that only those who lay within the verifiable, historic, "genealogy" of the Twelve Apostles are true Bishops, quote Ignatius out of his historical-theological context. It is similarly inappropriate to cite Ignatius to prove a bishops' right to require a personal, pastoral obedience from each member of his congregation.

This is not all that only crisis of "Apostolic Succession" one finds in Antioch:

> Another century later we find three, and for a time even four, bishops opposing one another for decades in Antioch. These pronounced one another heterodox or schismatic. All claimed the Antiochian apostolic succession which would make them the legitimate successors of Ignatius. This was the time of the Meletian schism. Every Christian in Antioch who remembered Ignatius' admonition to obey the bishop could not help asking, "Which one?

Werner Elert, *Eucharist and Church Fellowship in The First Four Centuries* (St. Louis, Missouri, Concordia Publishing House, 1966) p. 50

6 Examples of just a few of these false councils are: the Jerusalem council in 335 (overturning the orthodox decrees of the Nicean council just ten years earlier), the "Robber Council" in Ephesus (449), the Iconoclastic Council of Constantinople in 754, the councils in Lyons (1274) and in Florence (1439) which called for the Eastern Orthodox Church's union with Rome.

7 Councils were always related to "legally" by the Emperors which existed at the time they were convened. The Empire thought in legal categories and saw the Councils as a means whereby the faith could be legally defined and then legally defended by force if necessary. The pre-Constantinian bishops had never seen the Church in this way before, but given the heresies and the new role of the Emperor as "the defender of the faith" (to the benefit of the Empire's political unity, I might add), the Emperors began to change the

character of the synods by "pressuring" for unanimous decisions in artificial ways. Oftentimes this kind of "unanimity " would come about by the government exiling dissenting factions before the event of a council. Such a way of conducting a council could hardly be a guarantee that its decisions would automatically be accepted as valid.

8 Alexander Roberts, James Donaldson, eds., *The Ante-Nicene Fathers*, (Grand rapids MI., Wm B. Eerdmans Publishing Company, 1973) Vol. I, *Adversus Haereses* , III, 24, p. 458

9 Gustaf Aulen, *Reformation and Catholicity* , (London, Oliver and Boyd Ltd., 1962) pp. 11,12

10 This is what Thomas Hopko, in his article "Criteria of Truth in Orthodox Theology", deduces as the unanimous position of the Orthodox Church, a position which well reflects the understanding of the early Eastern Church. Summarizing the perspectives of a great number of Orthodox theologians, professor Hopko's paper concludes the following on their understanding of authority and Tradition in the Church:

> For each of the authors directly studied on this point, and there are about twenty to whom concrete reference could be made here, the Holy Spirit alone remains the ultimate criterion of truth for Christians even though other eternal institutions in the Church, such as [the Tradition of the Church, including the Holy Scriptures]; the Councils; and the Church itself are named as the 'highest' and the "supreme" authorities providing formal authorities in the Church and the Church itself taken as a whole cannot and must not remain "external" to the believer, and indeed not the theologian!

Thomas Hopko, in his article "Criteria of Truth in Orthodox Theology", (Crestwood, New York, St. Vladimir's Press, 1971) Vol. 15, No. 3 p. 123

11 Bruce Shelly, *By What Authority?* , (Grand Rapids, MI., William B. Eerdman's Publishing Company, 1965) p. 142

12 "His [the Holy Spirit's] presence, as the giver of life, is not to be interpreted in terms of an immanent principle by which the Church succeeds to the authority of her Lord ... This conviction is the root of the Orthodox difference with Rome over the question of authority in the Church and the nature of primacy." Angelos J. Philippou, "The Mystery of Pentecost," *The Orthodox Ethos,* (Oxford, England, Holywell Press, 1964) p. 91

13 "Neither individuals, nor a multitude of individuals within the Church preserve tradition or write the Scriptures, but the Spirit of God which lives in the whole body of the Church." Georges Florovsky, *Bible, Church, Tradition: An Eastern Orthodox View* (Belmont, MA, Nordland Publishing Company, 1972) p. 46 citing Khomiakov's *Russian and the English Church* p. 198

14 John Meyendorff, "The Meaning of Tradition", *Living Tradition* , (Crestwood, New York, St. Vladimir's Seminary Press, 1978) p. 20

15 Emilianos Timiadis, "'Consensus in the Formulation of Doctrine," *The Greek Orthodox Theological Review* (Brookline, MA., Holy Cross Orthodox Press, 1980) Spring, Vol. XXV, No. 1, p. 29

16 "Not Scripture, not conciliar definitions, not theology can express Him fully; each can only point to some aspects of His existence, or exclude wrong interpretations of His being or acts. No human language, however, is *fully* adequate to Truth itself, nor can it exhaust it." John Meyendorff, *Byzantine Theology* (New York, Fordham University Press, 1979) p. 11

17 John Meyendorff, "Does Christian Tradition Have a Future?," *St. Vladimir's Quarterly* , (Crestwood, New York, St. Vladimir's Seminary Press, 1982) Vol. 26, p. 152 "This appears to outsiders as nebulous, perhaps romantic or mystical, and in any case inefficient and unrealistic. The Orthodox themselves defend their position as sacramental and eschatological. But are the other, supposedly clearly defined criteria more realistic and less mystical?" *ibid.,* p. 153

18 It is not just the Holy Spirit's ministry, but the Trinity in His entirety. Each Person of the Godhead ministers in complement, not one of Their ministries are completely separate and isolated from the Other Persons'.

19 James refers to the Old Testament in Acts 15:16-18 in affirming that the Gentiles have a place in the Christian fellowship. But these passages do not specifically address *how* the Gentiles will be allowed to enter (circumcision?, which, if any laws should they follow?), and this was the *key* question under discussion at the council.

20 See Veselin Kesich, "Criticism, the Gospel and the Church," *St. Vladimir's Seminary Quarterly* , vol. 10:3 (1966), pp. 144-145

21 "For by one Spirit we were all baptized into one body, whether Jews or Greeks, whether slaves or free, and we were all made to drink of one Spirit." (1 Cor. 12:13)

"But you have an anointing from the Holy One, and you all know. And as for you, the anointing which you received from Him abides in you, and you have no need for anyone to teach you; but as His anointing teaches you about all things, and is true and is not a lie, and just as it has taught you, you abide in Him." (1 John 2:20, 27)

22 "Theology first became a secret science when it became scholastic and a craft of interest only to the guild. This was far from the case at the time of the great doctrinal controversies..." Werner Elert, *Eucharist and Church Fellowship in The First Four Centuries* (St. Louis, Missouri, Concordia Publishing House, 1966) pp. 144-145

23 Georges Florovsky, *Bible, Church, Tradition: An Eastern Orthodox View,* (Belmont, MA., Nordland Publishing, 1972) pp. 52-53

24 "The conviction of the Orthodox Church that the "guardian" of tradition and piety is *the whole people, i.e.* the Body of Christ, in no wise lessens or limits the power of teaching given to the hierarchy, It only means that the power of teaching given to the hierarchy is one of the functions of the catholic completeness of the Church; it is the power of testifying, of expressing and speaking the faith and the experience of the Church, which have been preserved in the whole body. The teaching of the hierarchy is, as it were, the mouthpiece of the Church ... But [for this to be the case] the bishop must embrace his Church within himself; he must make manifest its experience and its faith. [It was for this reason that the Early Church never knew of a bishop to exist as an *individual* privilege, there was no such thing as a bishop "at large."] He must speak not from himself, but in the name of the church, *ex consensus ecclesiae.* This is just the contrary of the Vatican formula: *ex sese, non autem ex consensu ecclesiae.* [From himself, but not from the consensus of the Church]. ...He [the bishop] is limited by this experience, and therefore in questions of faith the people must judge concerning his teaching. The duty of obedience ceases when the bishop deviates from the catholic norm, and the people have the right to accuse and even to depose him." Georges Florovsky, *Bible, Church, Tradition: An Eastern Orthodox View,* (Belmont, MA., Nordland Publishing, 1972) p. 53, 54

25 "The result of this distinction is often its presentation as an opposition between a more privileged directing Church and a directed and 'obedient' Church, or again, between an 'active' and a 'passive' Church." Emilianos Timiadis, "'Consensus in the Formulation of Doctrine," *The Greek Orthodox Theological Review* (Brookline, MA., Holy Cross Orthodox Press, 1980) Spring, Vol. XXV, No. 1, p. 32

26 "During the entire Byzantine period (325-1054), no church council went unchallenged, and attempts by several emperors to regulate their subjects' consciences by decree were checked not so much by a consistently independent hierarchy as by the tacit opposition of the entire body of the Church." John Meyendorff, *Byzantine Theology,* (New York, Fordham Press, 1979) p. 5

27 "Only within the Church, within the continuous life of the Body, does the final discrimination between true and false take place. It is not the synods which do this, or any other official authority." Emilianos Timiadis, "'Consensus in the Formulation of Doctrine," *The Greek Orthodox Theological Review* (Brookline, MA., Holy Cross Orthodox Press, 1980) Spring, Vol. XXV, No. 1, p. 29

28 As Edward J. Kilmartin, a Roman Catholic, rightly notes this distinctive of Orthodoxy from the Roman Church's teaching in this respect: "The teaching expressed by the episcopacy within a general council of the Church or outside a council needs confirmation by the whole Church before it is recognized as an object of assent of saving faith. This position is opposed to the official position of the Roman Catholic Church, which holds that the teaching office of the Church, in the person of the bishop of Rome as head of the episcopal college or in the form of a general council with the bishop of Rome as head, can make dogmatic statements which are, from the moment of their solemn pronouncement, to be considered as infallible statements of saving faith." Edward J. Kilmartin, "Orthodox - Roman Catholic Dialogue on the Eucharist', *Journal of Ecumenical Studies,* Vol. 13, (Spring, 1976) p. 345

29 Georges Florovsky, *Bible, Church, Tradition: An Eastern Orthodox View,* (Belmont, MA., Nordland Publishing, 1972) pp. 52-53

30 Serge Verhovskoy, *The Light of the World,* (Crestwood, New York, St. Vladimir's Seminary Press, 1982) p. 9 Similarly, when someone asked the Russian Orthodox bishop, the Metropolitan Philaret, "Does a true treasury of sacred tradition exist?" he answered, "All the faithful, united through the sacred tradition of faith, all together and all successively, are built up by God into one Church which is the true treasury of sacred tradition..." Georges Florovsky, *Bible, Church, Tradition: An Eastern Orthodox View* (Belmont, MA., Nordland Publishing Company, 1972) p. 53

31 The situation changed with the conversion of the Empire when the Church was seen as co-extensive with the Commonwealth....The General Councils as was inaugurated at Nicea within this setting may be described as "Imperial Councils,"...and this was probably the first and original meaning of the term "Ecumenical" as applied to the Councils....Georges Florovsky, *Bible, Church, Tradition: An Eastern Orthodox View,* (Belmont, MA., Nordland Publishing, 1972) pp. 95

32 The Eastern Orthodox Church presently recognizes seven councils as "Ecumenical", these are: 1) Nicea (325) which condemned Arianism in its proclamation of Christ as "homoousios" with the Father, 2) Constantinople (381) which expanded and adapted the Nicene Creed in its affirmation of the Holy Spirit's divinity, 3) Ephesus (431) affirming One Person in Christ (the real union of God in Man in Christ), 4) Chalcedon (451) which affirmed Christ's two natures (human and divine) in union "without confusion, unchangeably, indivisibly, inseparably," 5) Constantinople (553) condemning Origenism, and a formulation defending how the two natures of Christ unite to form a single Person 6) Constantinople (681) where Monothelitism (that Christ had only one will) was condemned and Christ's two wills (where each acts in accord with the two natures) is affirmed and 7) Nicea (787) the condemnation of iconoclasm through the formulation which declared that Christ's divinity co-inhered His humanity and could thus be pictorially represented. The Coptic (Egyptian) and the Armenian Orthodox Churches stand also in principle agreement with these doctrinal formulations.

33 "This original function of the councils is obviously different from the conceptions of Western 'conciliarist' of the fifteenth century, who conceived the council as a ruling committee supplanting and replacing the Pope. The original council, however, fell essentially in the biblical category of 'witness.' Agreement on a given issue was considered to be a *sign* of the will of God, to be received by the Church with discernment and to be tested against other 'signs': Scripture, Tradition, other councils." John Meyendorff, "What is an Ecumenical Council?," *Living Tradition,* (Crestwood, New York, St. Vladimir's Seminary Press, 1978) p. 36

34 "So high an estimation of the people's endorsement of a synod is easily explained when we consider that the definitions and formulas of the holy synods are taken in accord with the written and unwritten apostolic Tradition....[as] attested and shaped by the practical faith of all its active members. The treasure of faith....is meant to be the possession of every Christian and to be lived in the life of each one of us." Emilianos Timiadis, "'Consensus in the Formulation of Doctrine," *The Greek Orthodox Theological Review* (Brookline, MA., Holy Cross Orthodox Press, 1980) Spring, Vol. XXV, No. 1, p. 28

35 "The only thing approaching a 'magisterium' in the Orthodox Church... is the universal agreement of all of her members, which is normally arrived at only after decades, if not centuries, of controversy—and,

at least in the past, seldom without dissension, division, persecution and even blood." Thomas Hopko, *Women and the Priesthood* (Crestwood, New York, St. Vladimir's Seminary Press, 1983) p. 178

36 It should be noted here that the confirmation of these Councils was not a democratic process —something dependant upon a general balloting of the entire Church— but it was a confirmation of the Spirit given in the context of Communities. In *relationship* , both on the Local and the universal level, the people of God *together* were engaged in "listening" to the voice of the Spirit. While in this process, they were able to eventually testify to what they saw the Spirit was saying to them through one another. "This assent of the whole Christian people is an assent which, as a rule, is not expressed formally and explicitly, but *lived.*" Timothy Ware, *The Orthodox Church* (Harmondsworth, Middlesex, England, Penguin Books, 1981) p. 257

37 Church history shows that a Council cannot be admitted as Ecumenical unless it penetrates the consciousness of the people, who recognize it and assimilate its resolutions. The supreme organ of infallibility is therefore the entire body of Christ. Emilianos Timiadis, "'Tu Es Petrus': An Orthodox Approach," *Patristic and Byzantine Review* (Kingston New York, American Institute for Patristic Studies, 1983) Vol. II, No. 1, p. 20

38 "Orthodox ecclesiology..can never admit of the action of the Holy Spirit being concentrated, or exclusively present, in one single aspect of the Church." Archimandrite Chrysostomos, Hieromonk Auxentios in *Scripture and Tradition* , (Center for Traditionalist Orthodox Studies, Etna, California, 1984) p. 42

39 There was never any suggestion that truth was the result of the partial or complete consensus achieved among the delegates themselves. The ruling concern was to reach agreement with the Truth transmitted through the centuries from the very beginning. From this not the least departure was permissible." Emilianos Timiadis, "'Consensus in the Formulation of Doctrine," *The Greek Orthodox Theological Review* (Brookline, MA., Holy Cross Orthodox Press, 1980) Spring, Vol. XXV, No. 1, p. 21

40 Emilianos Timiadis, "'Consensus in the Formulation of Doctrine," *The Greek Orthodox Theological Review* (Brookline, MA., Holy Cross Orthodox Press, 1980) Spring, Vol. XXV, No. 1, p. 21

41 "The universal episcopate never expressed itself in the form of a General Assembly of all the bishops of the Christian world, which would rule the whole Church as its highest authority. The canons explicitly recognize the episcopates of individual Local Churches only." Alexander A. Bogolepov, "Which Councils Are recognized As Ecumenical?" *St. Vladimir's Quarterly* , (Crestwood, New York, St. Vladimir's Seminary Press, 1963) Vol. 7, No. 2 p. 59

42 "The right understanding of religious truth is given only to those who live a holy life. This understanding does not belong to an office, as is taught in the Roman Church, nor to correct scholarship, as is often implied in Protestantism." Carnegie Samuel Calian, *Icon and Pulpit* (Philadelphia, PA., The Westminster Press, 1968) p. 62 citing Serge Bolshakoff, *Eastern Churches Quarterly,* Vol 10, (1953-54) p. 233

43 It is for this reason Orthodoxy appeals to conciliar debate or consensus in order to discern the Tradition, for the Holy Spirit works within the entire Church. Any reference to a tradition which claims to be apostolic yet advocates a "teaching elite" fails to recognize this indwelling and ministry of the Spirit within the Body of Christ, it isn't Divine Tradition.

44 Alexander Schmemann, "The Idea of Primacy in Orthodox Ecclesiology," *The Primacy of Peter* (Bedfordshire, England, Faith Press) p. 45

45 John Zizioulas, "Appendix—The Authority of the Bible," *The Ecumenical Review* , Vol. XXI, No. 2, April, 1969 pp. 161, 162

46 "Man by seeking security enslaves himself to objective "authorities and, when one in a desire to bring about reform appeals to another authority [i.e. Scripture over the *magisterium*] a change of objective

authorities becomes only a change of masters." John Zizioulas, "Appendix—The Authority of the Bible," *The Ecumenical Review* , Vol. XXI, No. 2, April, 1969 pp. 161, 162

47 Alexander Schmemann, *Church, World, Mission* , "Freedom in the Church," (Crestwood, New York, St. Vladimir's Press, 1979) p. 188

48 Although such men of God as Abraham, Noah, Enoch, etc. lived before the Law, neither would they know God *in* communion as did Adam. Only the Second Adam, Jesus, could bring mankind back into union with His Father. For although they "gained approval through their faith, they did not receive what was promised" (Heb. 11:40). See also 2 Cor. 3:7-14

49 But it is the very "function" of the Holy Spirit to abolish authority, or rather to transcend it, and He does this by abolishing the *externality* which is the essence of authority and the essence of "this word" as the fallen world." Alexander Schmemann, *Church, World, Mission* (Crestwood, New York, St. Vladimir's Press, 1979) pp. 186, 187

50 John Meyendorff, "Historical Relativism and Authority in Christian Dogma", *Living Tradition* , (Crestwood, New York, St. Vladimir's Seminary Press, 1978) p. 30

51 John Meyendorff, "Historical Relativism and Authority in Christian Dogma", *Living Tradition* , (Crestwood, New York, St. Vladimir's Seminary Press, 1978) p. 38, 41

52 "Once authority has become an external power, once knowledge or religious truth has become independent of the religious life, once man is no longer linked to man except by bonds of common submission instead of by a common soul ... Unity now is nothing more than an appeal to the 'external' reason, to an 'external' authority, to an 'external' institution." Emilianos Timiadis, "'Consensus in the Formulation of Doctrine," *The Greek Orthodox Theological Review* (Brookline, MA., Holy Cross Orthodox Press, 1980) Spring, Vol. XXV, No. 1, p. 30

53 Jesus' agony in the Garden of Gethsemane ("My Father, if it is possible, let this cup pass from Me; yet not as I will, but as Thou wilt" (Matt. 26:39) was an expression of horror of Christ's human will in the light of the knowledge that He would have to be cursed for our salvation (Gal.3:13), it was not a "giving up" of His will to the Father. Christ's human will always followed (freely and without hesitation) His divine will. If His human will had "hesitated" to follow the divine will than Christ would of had to sin (given that He would have entertained the thought of *not* going to the Cross in order to save His "own skin"). On the other hand, if this passage expresses Christ's divine will than one must conclude that there was not one shared will in the Godhead (as is the case) but *three* separate wills, thus the unity of the Trinity would be violated and there would not be three Persons but *three Gods* ["will" following"nature"].

54 John Zizioulas, "Appendix—The Authority of the Bible," *The Ecumenical Review* , Vol. XXI, No. 2, April, 1969 p. 163

55 Emilianos Timiadis, "'Consensus in the Formulation of Doctrine," *The Greek Orthodox Theological Review* (Brookline, MA., Holy Cross Orthodox Press, 1980) Spring, Vol. XXV, No. 1, p. 31

CHAPTER NINE

WHAT IS THE CHURCH?

The Church. Which one is the right one? Where is it? Is it invisible, or visible? Just what exactly, is the church, and what is it not? Can one be a member of the Church and not be a believer? Christians have fervently fought over these questions for centuries. And, unfortunately, these skirmishes rarely benefit either party. Most of the time, all parties leave such discussions more angry and divided in heart than when they first began. Much of this conflict is based on a murky understanding of the Church.

Unquestionably, the meaning of the Church is often blurred and confused in our culture. We are asked, "What Church do you go to?" and this question really means, "What *denomination* are you affiliated with?" The words "Church" and "denomination" are used inter-changeably, as if they both meant the same thing. They don't. As the next few chapters will show, the Church is the *united, indivisible Body* of Christ. A denomination is an administrative fragment which contradicts that Biblical truth. There may be many different "denominations", but the Bible makes it plain that there is only *one Church.*

What is the exact definition of the Church? The East offers none.[1] This should not be surprising. The Christian people formulated no rational definition of the Church, *for the first fifteen hundred years of its existence.* [2] The New Testament calls the Church a divine "mystery" (Eph. 5:32). It does so for good reason: the Church is the miracle of *Christ in us* and *us in Christ.* This mystery will always be beyond explanations.

In keeping with the Hebraic thought and culture of the times, the New Testament writers depicted the Church in "spiritual images", not rationalistic formulas. The Church is: *the Bride of Christ* (Eph. 5:23; Rev. 22:17), *the True Vine with its branches* (John 15: 1-7), *the Body of Christ* (Eph. 1:22), *the Temple of the Holy Spirit* (1 Cor. 3:6), *the Household of God* (Gal. 6:10) and *Living Stones* (1 Pet. 2:5). These and other New Testament figures speak not only to reason, but to our hearts, spirits, and human life experience. Each vision gives us a deeper insight into the truth that the Christian has been made a member of a divine-human community. Yet not one of these images (by itself or all together) can ever succeed in communicating the full reality of that union.

In the next three chapters I will discuss some of these images of the Church. But I would ask that you please keep the above point in mind: the Church is a spiritual entity. Therefore a spiritual sensitivity is necessary to see the pictures the Spirit paints for us to ponder. The mind alone will never be able to fully grasp any one of these illustrations.

HOW THE CHURCH BOTH IS AND IS NOT AN INSTITUTION

The Church is a human institution in that it exists within this world, has order, history, and is made up of people. The Church is a divine institution in the sense that her government is Divine, she exists eternally, and God dwells within her.

The Church is not an institution as the word is popularly understood to mean, i.e., a bureaucracy concerned with getting a job done. When the Church is thus spoken of by what it *does* rather than by what it *is*, it is reduced to a mere factory or academy.[3] Some aspects of the Church's *mission* may call it to serve as a "teaching forum," a "soul-winning center," or as a counseling clinic, *but* these things do not constitute the nature of the Church.[4] Her *being* is not defined by activities, but by *communion* with Christ and the brethren.

The love of God is the "heart-beat" of the Church, it is her very life. This divine power transforms the church as institution into the Church as a divine living organism, the Life of God. How is this so? By the fact that "*God so loved the world* that He gave His only begotten Son." Christ has come not only to provide us forgiveness, but fullness of joy through *life in, with, and through Him.* [5] Christ, "the firstborn" of the Church (Rom. 8:29; Col. 1:15, 18; Rev. 1:5), is the one Who shares membership with us in the Church. It is He who unites us in love to Himself and to the brethren. He is the Vine, we are the branches (John 15:5).

The Church is more than an association of believers, [6] and more than a collection of religious individuals working together. [7] The Church is the community of *Christ Himself.* [8] It is *Christ* who gives the Church her existence. The Church's nature and essence are totally dependent upon His nature and essence. For this reason, one's perception of the Church must rest squarely on who Christ is. "The nature of the Church is the nature of Christ because it is His body."[9] A faulty view of Him will, therefore, yield an equally defective view of the Church.

One of the most significant Church councils pertaining to the doctrine of Christ was the Council of Chalcedon (451 A.D.). In its profession, we gain not only a great insight into the nature of Christ, but also a perception of the Church as well.[10] The following is an excerpt from one of its declarations:

> [Christ is] to be acknowledged in two natures [divine and human], without confusion, without change, without division, without separation; the distinction of natures being in no way abolished because of the union, but rather the characteristic property of each nature being preserved, and concurring into one Person and one subsistence, not as if Christ were parted or divided into two persons, but one and the same Son and only-begotten God, Word, Lord, Jesus Christ; even as the Prophets from the beginning spoke concerning Him ...[11]

Just as Christ, the God-Man, has both a divine and a human nature, so the Church likewise manifests divinity and humanity. Of course, Christ's humanity differs from the humanity constituting the Church in that her members are not yet complete and perfect. This, however, in no way detracts from the fact that the mystery of Christ's presence fills the Church. As it is within the Person of Christ, the Church's human will lives and acts in cooperation with the divine. Such a cooperation results in the Christian becoming more and more like Him Who is the Church's Head.

One's affiliation with the Church's outward expressions (in clergy, membership, government, doctrine, etc.) does not automatically provide one with an assurance that he has a reserved seat at the heavenly banquet. The Church is a *Community of the Spirit*; her essence transcends denominational boundaries and earthly authority. To be a member of a "religious" body is not always the same thing as being a member of the Church. Such a religious group grants membership when one conforms to its rules (e.g., no dancing, smoking, drinking), obligations (tithing), and doctrines (subscription to a "statement of faith," professing Christ as Lord).

However, to be a member of the Church is not so simplistic. Membership in the Church requires a life of love lived with God and the brethren. *This communal life in the Spirit is the Church (1 Cor. 12:12,13).* [12] The Eastern Church is "aware of being clearly differentiated from the more or less institutional conception of the church which characterized the development of the medieval Roman church."[13] Christ came not to found a "Standing Executive Committee" or a "Divine Religious Jurisdiction." He came to bring man into communion with God and others.

In other words, Church membership is not given to those who trust in "churchly" forms, but to those who live in communion with the Spirit Who fills some of those forms.[14] When these forms become ends in themselves, the danger of religious institutionalism appears.[15] This occurs when people relate to the observable structures as if they guaranteed God's indwelling (e.g., "God must be with us, our bishop is within the historic line of the Apostles.").[16] However, no outward structure—no matter how ancient or modern—can command the presence of the Holy Spirit. The Spirit may use structures, but He can never be manipulated by them. We must not confuse one for the other.

God's Church is where truth and love are; His Church is not where structures are revered no matter how beautiful,"religious" or "effective" they may be. In fact, even if the "organization and discipline of the earthly church ... be perfect, ... if its life and activity are not inspired by the Spirit of God, they are not even Christian."[17] As Orthodox theologian Serge Verhovsky notes:

...what we call the life of the Church is very often the life of our sinful human society having but the appearance of Christianity...there is no Church where the will of God is not done. The presence of grace and of true Christian faith and love are the best criteria of the reality of the Church. "Where there is the Holy Spirit, there is the Church," says St. Irenaeus of Lyon and, 'Where there is the Church, there is the Holy Spirit! And He is Truth'."[18]

The Church does not exist to perpetuate its own institutional structures. She *uses* them to administer, to secure, and to promote the *koinonia* [communion] of man with God and with his fellow man. When they are not used to this end, they become obstacles to union. Such a misuse is no less than "blasphemous."[19]

VISIBLE OR INVISIBLE?

Discussing the institutional element of the Church naturally brings up another question: "Is the true Church visible or invisible?" In general, the Reformation tradition promoted the doctrine that the true Church was the invisible Church.[20] According to this teaching, God was the only One Who could identify the real Christian from the false; no religious structure could be trusted to make the recognition.[21] The emphasis for this view of the Church was a direct reaction to the Roman Catholic teaching on the Church. Rome's hierarchy claimed to be *the* representatives of the Christ's Church. If you wanted a chance at being a member of the Church in heaven someday (the invisible church), you had to be a member of the Church on earth (the visible Church).[22] This visible Church, Rome taught, was none other than the Roman Catholic Church.

How did the concept of visible and invisible Church first develop? Ironically, the foundation for the doctrine of the invisible Church evolved from within the Roman Church, or at least as it was expressed through Augustine of Hippo. In this famous bishop's writings titled *City of God,* a basis was built for a conception of the Church as a spiritual-material *dualism.* This perspective viewed the invisible things of the Spirit as distinct, separate and unrelated to the material things of creation.[23] Luther, echoing Augustine's dualism some thousand years later, not only asserted that the true Church was the invisible one, but that the visible and the invisible Church may be held in outright opposition to each other.[24] Ulrich Zwingli, a key figure of both the Reformed and Anabaptist traditions, affirmed that because only God knew whom He had elected to salvation, the true Church's membership would of necessity be invisible. The logical implication of this reasoning was that unity, holiness, catholicity, and apostolicity applied only to this specified "mystical" body.[25]

Generally speaking, contemporary Evangelicalism and Fundamentalism are very much in sympathy with the Reformed and Zwinglian perspective. The true Church is something mystical, spiritual, unknowable, and "heavenly", whereas the "earthly" church, whose membership is composed of both Christians and non-Christians, is but a passing, fallen institution. Certainly those who are members of "physical" churches can receive encouragement, teaching, and moral discipline through them, but only one's membership in the heaven-based Church has any eternal significance.

THE EASTERN APPROACH: VISIBLE, INVISIBLE, AND *INDIVISIBLE*

The Eastern minded Christian takes a different approach to the matter. He finds no Biblical reason either to *divide* the Church into two "parts" as the Catholics do (visible/invisible), or to believe it exists only in heaven (the invisible "mystical" body of Christ) as many Evangelical-Fundamentalists do.[26] Eastern Christians believe that dividing the Church into visible and invisible parcels actually contradicts the very nature of the Church. The Church is *one, whole* organism. *The visible is inseparably linked to and a part of the invisible, and vice versa.* If the Church is indeed *the* Body of Christ (not two different bodies, one in heaven and one on earth), then her nature must be an *undivided whole.* In short, Eastern Christianity holds to a visible yet mystical body of Christ.

It is impossible to view the Church as only invisible. Although the Church exists outside of time and space, its historic origin at Pentecost was clearly a divine *and* human event, i.e., the Church was born *in time* at a specific place, Jerusalem.

Even Christ's membership in the Church makes the claim of the invisible Church impossible. He did not poof into an invisible, divinized mist after His ascension. Christ's humanity was not erased after His resurrection (just as ours will not be in our glorification on the Last Day [I Cor. 15:20ff]). At the right hand of God Christ can still be seen in His glorified humanity (flesh, bones, teeth, etc.).

Christ's Covenant makes one a member of the Church, and that Covenant applies to the earthly saint as much as it does to the heavenly believer. The two realms of the Church are *indivisible* for Christ is the common foundation for both heaven and earth. Clearly, the Bible makes it plain that the Church is *of* heaven and *of* earth.

But you have come to Mount Zion and to the city of the living God, the heavenly Jerusalem, and to myriads of angels, to the general assembly and church of the first-born who are enrolled in heaven and to God the Judge of all, and to the spirts of righteous men made perfect, and to Jesus the mediator of a new covenant .... (Heb. 12:22-24).

WHY THE CHURCH CANNOT BE A DENOMINATION

The Church is *one* organism within the *one* Christ: "There is *one* Body, *one* Spirit, *one* Lord, *one* faith, *one* baptism, *one* God and Father of all who is over all and through all and in all" (Eph. 4: 5, 6). This intrinsic *wholeness* of the Church leads Eastern Christians to refuse to see Christianity as a *collective* of denominations.

The Lord is the shepherd of "one flock" (John 10: 16). Dissensions and factions are a work of the flesh (Gal. 5: 19, 20f), not an administrative division of the Church. The Church's internal *being* can neither be reduced nor altered. The divisions between East and West, the Reformation, the Radical Reformation, or other such reform movements, have neither decreased nor increased the number of "pieces" making up the Church. *Christianity is not the sum total of all denominations.*[27] *The Church is one* and Christ cannot be divided (1 Cor. 1:13).

In essence, the Church cannot be in dissension with itself. The Church embodies the Truth, and the Truth can never oppose itself with "many" truths for there is only *one* Truth. Since the Truth is whole, the Church can not be sliced and diced into competing denominations. A differing doctrinal confession does not create *another* "Church," it creates another *denomination.*

As the Church cannot be *administratively divided*, neither can it be *administratively reunited.* One does not "bring the Church together." The Church is *already* together. One cannot divide God and His Truth, and then through later efforts restore them to unity. Those who read John 17 ("that they may all be one") as a mandate to "put the Church together" ignore the unity and union which is *already an inherent characteristic of the Church*.[28]

One does not work for "Church unity" by trying to assemble all denominations under one administrative roof; each group is not a "state" within the Church Kingdom that can be united in a kind of federation. The Body of Christ exists concretely on the earth, but we do not *organize* the Church. With Christ, we *compose* the Church!

The earthly administration of denominations is not the same thing as the earthly administration of the Church. For the most part, the purpose of a denomination's government is to perpetuate its distinctives and defend its exclusive loyalties. On the other hand, the purpose of the Church's administration is to bring humankind into union with God. One seeks to distinguish and separate, the other to bring Divine-human harmony and communion.

THE CONFESSIONAL "CHURCH" VERSES THE CHURCH

THE ORIGIN OF "THE CONFESSIONAL" CHURCH

Both during and after the Reformation, Protestants formulated many of their doctrines *in protest* to what Catholics believed, and later Catholics developed much of their teaching *in opposition* to Protestants positions. Aspects of both theologies were being defined in *contradiction* to the other, each body trying to affirm only *its* doctrines as representative of the true Church. The result of such a battle was that true Christianity came to be equated with a particular breed of doctrine. To the Roman Catholics, one could not espouse Protestant doctrines and be a true Christian; and to the Protestants, Roman Catholic thinking prohibited one from entering into the Kingdom.

Thus began the "confessional" view of both Church and doctrine. Where the Early Church maintained that it was impossible to objectively define the mystery of this union in Christ, the confessional groups now believed that the Church could be sufficiently explained through encyclicals and "statements of faith." Hence, doctrine became something one can define, defend, and propagate through propositional logic. Whereas the early Church used doctrines only as a means of *defending* the faith, the confessional groups now used doctrines as a way to exhaustively *delineate* the Faith.[29] Instead of doctrines being a means to deepen one's experience of God, each doctrine became merely another "theological brick" cemented in the confessional barrier. Christians now had a "theological" reason for their fleshly divisiveness.

THE FALLACY OF THE NON-CONFESSIONAL CHURCH

The Reformation period's stress upon doctrine *as a means of defining the Church* is rejected by many ecumenically minded Christians today. To these Christians, ones doctrine is not as important as Christian "unity." Where for one person, confessionalism is a sign of orthodoxy; for another, a lack of theological awareness is an expression of "love."[30] Those who have a concern for doctrinal clarity and precision are judged as cold, prejudiced, individuals on the hunt for a reason to exclude others.

Such thinking replaces confessionalism with *doctrinal minimalism.* The argument becomes: "If division was mothered by exacting confessionalism, why not create a confession of 'bare essentials' in which all Christians could agree and be unified?"[31] The "*confessional* church" one belongs to is unimportant. Now the only thing that matters is that one "believes in Jesus."

The nature of the Church of God, however, can never be minimalistic. It must always be *maximalistic.* Why? The Church cannot *prioritize* Truth, because *Truth cannot be abbreviated.* To confine Truth to its "Top Ten" propositions implies that the other eleven to infinity are not *really* important. Thus, according to this reasoning, there is such a thing as *irrelevant* Truth. All Truth, however, is relevant, for where there is Truth, there is a revelation of Him Who is the Truth. Actually, to say that Truth has a minimal expression is a contradiction. Truth, to be Truth, hides nothing; only in ignorance is falsehood permitted to reign. Where there is Truth there is Light, and darkness, by necessity, must be dispelled.

The call of the Church is to manifest the Truth in its *fullest, not its least, expression.* Truth is the very foundation and nature of the Church, *its Head being Truth Himself* (John 14: 6). It is not our option to give Truth a "crew cut" simply to encourage a "practical," confessional unity. It is a fallacy to assume that a common confession will guarantee *real* unity. Despite the doctrinal agreement each confessional group maintains among its membership, the multitude of divisions existing *within* both "non-denominational" and "Brand Name" denominations sufficiently proves this point.

An agreement based on "minimums" is either a commitment to bridle one's pursuit of Truth, or an admittance that a fuller measure of truth is insignificant (at least in respect to the promotion of unity). In this latter case, Truth and the disclosure of God is not the goal of doctrine, but a superficial, administrative unity. Such a compromise is contrary to the purpose and character of Christ and His Church. *We are not to find our unity by limiting ourselves in the fear that our "unity" will be "ruined" through greater insight into the things of God . We "are to grow up in all aspects into Him"* (Eph. 4:15).

The spiritual reality of the Church is *never realized confessionally* — by either definitions *or* through minimizing Truth. The Church is actualized only in *communion with God and the brethren* (Eph. 3: 18, 19; 4:13-16). This neither denigrates or exalts the place of doctrine. It puts it in its proper perspective: *within the context of love.* This *relational* (as opposed to confessional) environment will always lead us to live more compatibly with God, i.e., to live in *Truth* .[32] Only in this setting of communion and love will we rightly understand the purpose and end of doctrine: to emulate God's love (I Tim. 1:5; Eph. 5:1, 2).

Because confessionalism distorts the vision of the Church as a divine-human *community,* its major premise is unbiblical. Christianity cannot be shrunk down to a few fundamentals. The Church is life in God, a supernatural and human society which seeks to embrace all of creation in the redemption given to her by her Head.[33] Confessionalism, on the other hand, depicts the Church as an institution of confessing individuals. The *church of confessionalism* inevitably ends up competing with the *Church of communion.*

THE CHURCH AS THE BODY OF CHRIST

CHRIST'S INSEPARABLE UNION WITH THE CHURCH

Because the Church is the *body* of Christ, it is an *organism.* It is a *living* entity. In 1 Corinthians 12: 12 Paul says,

"For just as the [human] body is one and has many members, and all the members of the body, though many, are one body, *so it is with Christ.*"

What can we conclude from this passage? *Christ and the Church (His body) are intimately united to each other.* How deep is this union? *His union with us is as intimate as the relationship we have with our own physical members... actually, even deeper.* This is a profound mystery! Christ's closeness to us is such that Paul can speak of our relationship with Him as *union* (Rom. 6:5). We are joined *into* Christ (Rom. 6:3. We are member of the very Body of Christ (1 Cor. 12:12). [34]

The body of Christ is the realization of Christ's promise to be with us even unto the end of the ages (Matthew 28: 20). When Christ ascended into heaven, he did not *leave* the Church. He kept His promise to remain with us at Pentecost in the pouring out of the Spirit. On that day, Christ made His people His body, an "incarnation" of His very being. [35] This is the "intimate union which constitutes the mystery of the Church."[36] The Spirit has made the Church and Christ *inseparable*, a genuine union emphasized time and again in Scriptures:

"He that is joined unto the Lord is one spirit with the Lord." (1 Cor. 6:17).

Our bodies are "members of Christ" (1 Cor. 6:15).

"For by one Spirit were we all baptized into one body ... and we were all made to drink of one Spirit" (1 Cor. 12:13).

We are all one body, in the one Christ (1 Cor. 12:20-27).

"...we, who are many, are one body in Christ, and individually members one of another." (Rom. 12:4, 5).

The mystery of our union with the Lord in the Church is as intimate as the one a believing husband and wife are to share (Eph. 5:29-32)— in some respects it is even richer. In this union Christ can honestly say to us, "He who receives you receives Me, and he who receives Me, receives Him who sent Me." (Matt. 10:40, Matt. 25:40). It is an identity so strong that Jesus can say that He experiences what even the least of His brethren experience at the hands of others (Matt. 25:40). It is this bond which made Paul's persecution of the Church a persecution of *Christ Himself* ("And he said, 'Who art Thou, Lord?" And He said, 'I am Jesus *whom you are persecuting*' [Acts 9:5]).

The Church can never be separated from Christ, for "She cannot exist without Him from whom she received all fullness."[37] The book of Ephesians says this very thing when it refers to the Church as "His body, the fullness of Him who fills all in all" (Eph. 1:23). The Word "fullness" here is the Greek word *pleroma* (πλήρομα), which means "that which makes something full or complete."[38] In this light, the Ephesians passage reveals an amazing and incomprehensible mystery: we, *as* the Church, somehow actually supplement, and complement Christ Himself! How can this be? In Christ, the Church stands as a *new* humanity (1 Cor. 15:20-23), redeemed and reborn through her Head.[39] The depth and intensity of our intimacy with Christ unfolds the mystery of His existence within the Church. In this context,

... the Church is Christ Himself, in His all-embracing plenitude (cf. 1 Cor. 12:12). ... For if He is the Head, we are the members; the whole man is He *and* we... 'For Christ is not simply in the head and not in the body, but Christ is *entire* in the head *and* body'.[40]

In some wonder of God, we —the Church— will complete His work of redemption on that Last Day when He restores all creation in Himself.[41] How? We do not know exactly, but we do know that the answer lies somewhere in our genuine union with Him. As our union in His Body restores us, [42] so His union within us will be used to restore creation itself. [43] In this awesome wonder to be unveiled on the Last Day, the truth is again clear: "Christ is never alone. The Redeemer and the redeemed ...[are] together inseparably."[44]

THE SPIRITUAL RAMIFICATIONS OF BEING THE BODY OF CHRIST

The Church's being the body of Christ strongly emphasizes that the Church is Community. In every place but one where the phrase "the body of Christ" is found in Scripture, it is used in direct connection with the Eucharistic gathering, [45] the gathering where "the many become one" in the communion of Christ.[46] Paul's reference to the Church as the body of Christ was not just a metaphor. It was based on the spiritual-historical reality that Christ became a Man and now shares our humanity.[47] The purpose of the Incarnation was not just to make it possible for Christ to take on our sin on the Cross, but to unite *our humanity* with His, and through Himself, to bring us *into a healing bond with one another* (1 Cor. 12:13).

The body represents the whole self, including will and heart, soul and mind, as well as the physical parts. For this reason, *membership* in the body is not a casual joining of a group of people, but an incorporation into the body of Christ, the visible body of people here on earth who belong to Him. ...there is such a solidaric relationship between these members, such an interdependence, that 'if one suffers, all suffer together; if one member is honored, all rejoice together' (I Cor. 12:26).[48]

The individual Christian is a member of a body of believers, and therefore he truly *needs* his brethren. If a glowing hot coal is taken from the fire it soon becomes cold and useless. Likewise, the Christian needs the fellowship of Christ's body to maintain the spiritual vitality that is supposed to characterize the Christian life.[49] Our union with each other in the Body is not just so we can have a more intimate relationship with *one another,* but so that we can have a more intimate relationship with *Christ*, the Head.

The truth is that our genuine communion with other Christians is actually the chief way that the Lord strengthens us, reveals Himself to us, and transforms us into His likeness. We receive the nourishment supplied by the Head through each joint (member) of the body.

"from Whom [Christ] the whole body, being fitted and held together by that which every joint supplies, according to the proper working of each individual part, causes the growth of the body for the building up of itself in love." (Eph. 4:16)

"...holding fast to the head [Christ], whom the entire body, being supplied and held together by the joints and ligaments, grows with a growth which is from God." (Col. 2:19)

We are called to actually live in such a way that this reality of our shared bond in Christ is *manifested.* When it is, we will be *living* witnesses to the truth that God is indeed among us. "The ultimate desire in the heart of God in visiting a people is not just to bless them as individuals; but His constant yearning is that they be knitted together as a functioning body through which He can express Himself to the world." [50] May the world which stands in such great need, receive this living witness soon.

NOTES FOR CHAPTER NINE

1 "No definition has been given by the Ecumenical Councils. In the doctrinal summaries drafted on various occasions in the Orthodox Church in the seventeenth century...again no definition of the Church was given ... This lack of formal definition does not mean, however, a confusion of idea or any obscurity of view." Alexander Schmemann, "The Eucharist and the Doctrine of the Church," *St. Vladimir's Quarterly* (1954) vol. 2, No. 2, p. 10

2 Alexander Schmemann, "The Eucharist and the Doctrine of the Church," *St. Vladimir's Quarterly* (1954) vol. 2, No. 2, p. 10 citing G. Florovsky, *The Church: Her Nature and Task* , in"*The Universal Church in God's Design*" The first systematic treatise on the Church was composed by Cardinal Turrecremata in the late Fifteenth Century.

3 "For the Church is an *institution,* but she is also a *mystery* , and it is mystery that gives meaning and life to institution and is therefore the object of ecclesiology." Alexander Schmemann, "Ecclesiological Notes," *St. Vladimir's Seminary Quarterly* 11 (1967) p. 35

"In the West, the Church developed as a powerful institution; in the East, it was seen primarily as a sacramental (or 'mystical') organism, in charge of 'divine things' and endowed with only limited institutional structures. The structures (patriarchates, metropolitinates, and other officialdom) themselves were shaped by the empire (except for the fundamental tripartite hierarchy—bishop, priest [presbyter], deacon—in each local church) and were not considered to be of divine origin." John Meyendorff, *Byzantine Theology,* (New York, Fordham Press, 1979) p. 215

4 This typical depiction of the Evangelical Church as existing almost for the sole sake of evangelism is more an American phenomenon than something inherent in its Reformed-Anabaptist origins.

> The main *theological* continuation of the evangelical impulse in the church during the eighteenth and nineteenth centuries is contained with the streams involved in the First and Second Awakenings. In the course of the nineteenth century, however, the American evangelical stream began to suffer constriction and reduction. This did not occur without further development and some positive gains: Charles Finney and D. L. Moody, whose native intuitions were never disturbed by seminary education, popularized the gospel in a way that brought the laity into the process of witness as never before. But there were losses in this process also . The frontline work of evangelical renewal was no longer led by men with the intellectual and theological stature of [Jonathan] Edwards and [John] Wesley, ...Revival became revivalism; what had been a comprehensive program of church renewal, evangelism and social and cultural reform, became increasingly limited to one expression of mission: mass evangelism and personal outreach through the local church.

Robert Webber, Donald Bloesch, eds., *The Orthodox Evangelicals* , "A Call to Historic Roots and Continuity," Richard Lovelace, (New York, Thomas Nelson, 1977) p. 59

5 "...seeing the Church as the locus where participation in Christ's life becomes a reality, and not so much as a human institution, where the Word is only 'heard' and where 'obedience' is required, but, in fact, never fully realized in the Body of Christ. The relations between God and man cease to be extrinsic; they are a living communion." John Meyendorff, Joseph McLelland, eds., "Conclusion", John Meyendorff,, *The New Man: An Orthodox and Reformed Dialogue,* (New Jersey, Standard Press, 1973) p. 164

6 "As the fullness of divine life communicated to men, the Church can never be totally identified with its earthly members and institutions. The Church of God is not coextensive with it's creaturely members nor is it exhausted in its being and membership by them. ...the body includes in its membership Christ Himself as its Head, and the Holy Spirit as its vivifying, sanctifying and deifying power. " Thomas Hopko, "Catholicity and Ecumenism," *St. Vladimir's Theological Quarterly* (Crestwood, N.Y., St. Vladimir's Seminary Press, 1973) vol. 17, No. 1-2, p. 64

7 "In order to understand the New Testament teaching concerning the church, we must see it as an endeavor to express a reality that transcends any concept of human community or organization." Veselin Kesich, "Unity and Diversity In New Testament Ecclesiology," *St. Vladimir's Theological Quarterly* (Crestwood, New York, New York, St. Vladimir's Seminary Press, 1975) Volume 19, No. 2, p. 109

8 "Orthodox tradition is unanimous in its affirmation of the *Church* as an organic unity. This organism is the Body of Christ and the definition is not merely symbolical but expresses the very nature of the Church." John Meyendorff et. al., "The Idea of Primacy in Orthodox Ecclesiology," Alexander Schmemann,*The Primacy of Peter*, (Bedfordshire, England, The Faith Press, 1963) p. 34

9 Serge Verhovskoy, "The Highest Authority in the Church," *St. Vladimir's Theological Quarterly* (Crestwood, New York, 1960) vol. 4, No. 2-3, p. 81

10 "The doctrine of the Church is not an 'appendix' to Christology, and not just an extrapolation of the 'Christological principle,' as it has been often assumed. There is much more than an 'analogy.' Ecclesiology, in the Orthodox view is an integral part of Christology. One can evolve the whole body of Orthodox Dogma out of the Dogma of Chalcedon." George Florovsky, "The Ethos of the Orthodox Church," *Ecumenical Review* , XII, 2, 1960, p. 197

11 J. Stevenson, *Creeds, Councils and Controversies* (London, S.P.C.K., 1966) p. 337

12 "In contrast to other Christian traditions, ours permits a diversity of life and thought, for it has never been greatly concerned to formulate dogmas concerning the nature of the Church, or to change the charismatic fellowship created at Pentecost into an institution to canalize God's grace." A. J. Philippou, ed.,*The Orthodox Ethos,* "The Mystery of Pentecost," Angelos J. Philippou, (Oxford, England, Holywell Press, 1964) p. 70

13 Gustaf Aulen, *Reformation and Catholicity* (London, Oliver and Boyd Ltd., 1962) p. 12

14 "Because it is charismatic, the institution ... is not meant to create an objectified security; it constantly depends on the Spirit ... Thus although it relies on a given form, the institution is never this form itself.; it cannot be isolated from the charismatic event of communication, it cannot exist outside the community....It is a liberation from selfhood and individualism that the Spirit grants to us in the Church, and this makes him once more simultaneously the Spirit of freedom and the creator of the community. The freedom of the Spirit means that the structure of the Church is not an objectified superimposed thing, but the fulfillment of each one's personhood." J. D. Zizioulas, "The Pneumatological Dimension of the Church," (*International Catholic Review*, Vol. II, No. 2, 1973)

15 "The problem is not so much that the church is inevitably an historical institution but that *because* it is also an institution it may lose sight of its new life in Christ at various levels with the result that its institutional aspects gain the prominence. Then the Church risks being only an institution with primary reference to itself, that is, its offices, rules, traditions, and teachings, rather than to God. ...the central problem is not structural or administrative but spiritual "Theodore G. Stylianopoulos, "Aspects of the Life of the Church," (Brookline, MA., Holy Cross Press, 1977) Vol. XXII, No. 2 pp. 203, 204

16 "The Spirit bestows upon the bishops a 'certain charisma of truth' (*charisma veritatis certum*), but He never becomes prisoner of an institution, or the personal monopoly of any human being. 'Where the Church is,' writes St. Irenaeus again, 'there is the Spirit of God; and where the Spirit of God is, there is the Church, and every kind of grace; but the Spirit is Truth.' It is not the Church which, through the medium of its institutions, bestows the Spirit, but it is the Spirit which validates every aspect of Church life, including the institutions." John Meyendorff, *The Catholicity and the Church,* "The Significance of the Reformation in the History of Christendom" (Crestwood, New York, St. Vladimir's Seminary Press, 1983) p. 28

17 Serge Verhovskoy, "The Highest Authority in the Church," *St. Vladimir's Theological Quarterly* (Crestwood, New York, 1960) vol. 4, No. 2-3, p. 78

18 Serge Verhovskoy, "The Highest Authority in the Church," *St. Vladimir's Theological Quarterly* (Crestwood, New York, 1960) vol. 4, No. 2-3, p. 78

19 John Meyendorff, *Living Tradition,* (Crestwood, New York, St. Vladimir's Seminary Press, 1978) p. 137

20 They, following Augustine, differentiated between a visible and invisible Church, "...asserting the true church to be invisible." In essence the Reformers affirmed that the nature of the Church is dominated by two fundamental convictions: 1) a necessary individual response to the Spirit's invitation and 2) because of the fall, whatever institutional forms a church will take will bear the marks of the sinfulness of their creators. William

A. Scott, *Historical Protestantism: An Historical Introduction to Protestant Theology* (Englewood Cliffs, N.J., 1971) p. 17

21 "The idea of the invisible church is found in Augustine, *City of God* ; Wycliffe, *De ecclesia* ; Luther, *Preface to Revelation* ; Calvin, *Institutes* IV 1 7....The thought that is uppermost is not to minimize the importance of church membership, but to recognize the possibility of hypocrisy and deceit. In the last analysis, those who belong to God are visible to God alone. Membership of the true church is a fact which is not visible to man. The idea recalls the statement of 2 Tim. 2:19: "'The Lord knows who are his'." Colin Brown, ed., Dictionary of New Testament Theology Vol. 1, "Church," L. Coenen (Grand Rapids, MI., Zondervan Publishing House, 1975) p. 299

22 "The essential characteristic of the Western ecclesiology is that it was built up almost exclusively in terms of *legal authority* , of 'power.' .. in other terms—a 'hierachology.' On the other hand, the Protestants in their struggle against the Roman distortions also accepted the same 'legal categories.' But, in opposition to Roman clericalism, to that reduction of the whole Church to the principle of a 'sacred power,' they reduced this organizational, 'legal' aspect of the church to a minimum..." Alexander Schmemann, "The Eucharist and the Doctrine of the Church," *St. Vladimir's Quarterly* ((1954) vol. 2, No. 2, p. 10

23 "In the West....that dualism was actively brought back in a powerful theoretical form, in St Augustine's far-reaching distinction between the *mundus intelligibilis* and the *mundus sensibilis* , reinforced by a somewhat Neo-platonic and Ptolemaic outlook upon the universe, which came to be built into the whole fabric of Western thought. ...it also had the effect of bifurcating [dividing into two parts] the religious wholeness of the Judaeo-Christian tradition into a dualism of visible and invisible, outward and inward spheres of experience, which then needed to be coordinated through a system of sacramental causal connections. ...the religious consciousness fostered by the monastic orders (especially Augustinian and Franciscan), had the effect of widening the dualism within the Roman Catholic Church as community of believers and the Church as identified with the ecclesiastical ruling class." T. F. Torrance, *Theology in Reconciliation: Essays Toward Evangelical and Catholic Unity In East and West*, (Grand Rapids, MI., William B. Eerdmans Publishing Company, 1975) pp. 31, 37, 38

24 "As Luther puts it, the Creed says 'I believe in one Holy Church', not 'I see one Holy Church'. But this distinction cannot be maintained. For although Fathers such as Origen, Jerome, and Augustine, agreed that the Church contains both false and true members, and that the latter constitute the *corpus Christi verum* , they still see the Church as a visible community with external marks which distinguish it from heretical and schismatic bodies." Methodios Fouyas, *Orthodoxy, Roman Catholicism and Anglicanism* (Oxford University Press, 1972) p. 116. See also Hans J. Hillerbrand, *Men and Ideas In The Sixteenth Century* (Chicago, Rand McNally, College Publishing Company, 1969) p.76

25 Bernard M.G. Reardon, *Religious Thought In the Reformation* (New York, Longham Inc., 1981) p. 103

26 The Eastern Church has a different view from both the Protestant and the Catholic vision of the Church. Unlike the Reformers, the East did not have to do battle against Roman claims nor was it greatly effected by Augustine's dualistic teachings. These factors allowed the Eastern Church to escape many of the philosophical and theological dilemmas within which the Reformers were born.

27 "Orthodoxy would insist on the fact that unity belongs to the one church, which essentially cannot be divided by human controversies. ...Orthodoxy prefers to allow the Holy Spirit, the inspirer of the church and the indwelling Spirit of Christ, to judge the external as well as internal visibility of the *ecclesia militans* on earth. Having said this, Eastern Orthodoxy does go on to assert that the true and actual visibility of the church within human perception is seen in the Eucharistic worship, set aside and blessed not by human hands but through the mystical act of the Holy Spirit. ...the apophatic nature of its theology in general, points toward an ecclesiology that is basically mystical, shrouded in wonder and mystery. In short, Eastern Orthodoxy holds to the visible but *mystical* body of Christ." Carnegie Samuel Calian, *Icon and Pulpit* (Philadelphia, PA., The Westminster Press, 1968) p. 75

28 This passage does not call for an administrative unity; certainly there were no "denominational" breeches at the time which would have led Jesus to ascribe this interpretation to His prayer. That the Church is called to mirror the moral and spiritual oneness which exists in God, however, is beyond question. Only in this testimony, can the world look at the Church and know that God has indeed sent His Son (John 17:21).

29 "..doctrinal definition is viewed only as an extraordinary and extreme measure, an anti-dote to heresy, and not as an end in itself. It is therefore distinct from truth, which is 'apostolic,' i.e. present explicitly or implicitly

in the consciousness of the Church from apostolic times and based upon apostolic witness." John Meyendorff, *Living Tradition,* (Crestwood, New York, St. Vladimir's Seminary Press, 1978) p. 38

30 When Dwight L. Moody (1837-99), one of the most popular and successful mass crusade evangelists in American history, was confronted by a woman who said she did not agree with his theology. Moody responded, "'My theology! I didn't know I had any.' He insisted that that instead of troubling his hearers with the disconcerting intricacies of theology, he simply stuck to the 'three R's' of the gospel: 'Ruin by sin, Redemption by Christ, and Regeneration by the Holy Ghost.'" Winthrop S. Hudson, *Religion in America,* (New York, New York, Charles Scribner's Sons, 1981) pp. 234, 235

31 Such a philosophy advocating a "pragmatic" Christian unity was underscored in the revivals which swept America's Great Awakenings:

> "In America, for the first two centuries Protestantism dominated overwhelmingly, and the Bible had played a role in shaping the culture for which there was no European parallel. Lacking a strong institutional church and denying the relevance of much of Christian tradition, American Protestants were united behind the principle of *Scriptura sola* . .. In the wake of Revolution, Americans saw themselves as inaugurators of a new order for the ages. The new order was conceived as a return to a pristine human condition. For Protestants this ideal was readily translated into Biblical primitivism. The true church should set aside all intervening tradition, and return to the purity of New Testament practice. The Bible alone should be one's guide. Biblicism was closely related to religious individualism, also encouraged by revivalism. The individual stood alone before God; his choices were decisive. The church, while important as a supportive community, was made up of free individuals."

George M. Marsden. *Fundamentalism and American Culture* (Oxford, Oxford University Press, 1980) p. 224

32 "The catholicity in minimalism, which is very popular in the ecumenical movement, contradicts the very nature of Christianity ... Jesus Christ calls us to the perfection of the heavenly Father and for the transfiguration of the whole universe in God." Serge S. Verhovskoy, "Catholicity and the Structures of the Church," *St. Vladimir's Theological Quarterly* (Crestwood, N.Y., St. Vladimir's Seminary Press, 1973) vol. 17, No. 1-2, p. 40

33 "The role of the Church is not, therefore, to impose upon man's mind some truth which otherwise he is unable to perceive, *but to make him live and grow in the Spirit, so that he himself may see and experience the Truth* ." John Meyendorff, *Living Tradition,* (Crestwood, New York, St. Vladimir's Seminary Press, 1978) p. 41

34 "As the title "son of man" is probably the most important and most comprehensive for understanding Jesus, so the image of the body of Christ is for the church. It is recognized that this image is "the most inclusive and impressive, is the most emphatic expression of the basic vision' or "the most mature result of the New Testament thinking about the Church." Veselin Kesich, "Unity and Diversity In New Testament Ecclesiology," *St. Vladimir's Theological Quarterly* (Crestwood, New York, New York, St. Vladimir's Seminary Press, 1975) Volume 19, No. 2, p. 117 citing Georges Florovsky, "The Church: Her Nature and Task," in *The Universal Church in God's Design* (Amsterdam ; London, 1948) p. 53

35 The Church is not "literally" another Incarnation of Christ as if there were now *two bodies of Christ* (One the Son of God took from Mary and the other made up of the Redeemed). Neither do we mean by Christ's union with the Church in one body that He is the head and we are the remainder of His parts (neck, arms, chest, legs, etc.). These conclusions stem from the error of trying to understand a divine mystery in rational terms (an approach which will always lead us to wrong conclusions.). Unquestionably, Christ's Body at the right hand of God is the glorified body He ascended in from this world.

Nevertheless, an actual union in the Spirit has made us members of His body. He literally dwells among and within us in a way no less intimate than the union of Christ's humanity and divinity. The only difference between our union with God and His is: 1) His union is based upon His own God-nature, ours is given to us as a gift in our union with Christ; 2) Our union with Him does not make us God (we do not lose our specific identity as persons), we can become *like* Him (1 John 3:2) not Him, and; 3), We must appropriate divine life through Him in the Spirit, we do not have any divine life to "contribute" to Him. His source of divine life is in Himself as He shares it with the other Persons of the Trinity.

36 "Christians are incorporated into Christ and Christ abides in them—this intimate union constitutes the mystery of the Church." Georges Florovsky, *Bible, Church, Tradition: An Eastern Orthodox View* (Belmont, MA., Nordland Publishing Company, 1972) p. 65

37 Veselin Kesich, "Unity and Diversity In New Testament Ecclesiology," *St. Vladimir's Theological Quarterly* (Crestwood, New York, New York, St. Vladimir's Seminary Press, 1975) Volume 19, No. 2, p. 117

38 William F. Arndt, F. Wilbur Gingrich, "πλήρομα", *A Greek-English Lexicon of the New Testament and Other Early Christian Literature* , (Chicago, Il., The University of Chicago Press, 1957) p. 678

39 George Florovsky, "The Ethos of the Orthodox Church," A Faith and Order Dialogue (Geneva, WCC, 1960) Faith and Order paper #30, pp. 47-48

40 Georges Florovsky, *Bible, Church, Tradition: An Eastern Orthodox View* (Belmont, MA., Nordland Publishing Company, 1972) p. 64, 65 citing St Augustine in *Evangelium Jannis* , tract XXI, 8 (ML., XXXV, 1568), *Ps. CXXVII* , 3 (ML., XXXVII, 1679), and *Ps. XC enarr. I,* 9 (ML, XXXCII, 1157) respectively. Italics mine.

41 Eph. 1:9, 10, Rom. 8:20-23; 1 Cor. 15:20-28, 35-58

42 "In Paul the 'body of Christ' is understood in antithesis to the 'body of death.' This contrast is expressed in Romans 5:12-21. [those not in Christ abide in the Body of death as opposed to the body of Life] ..In Christ's body the believer has 'died to sin' (6:2); been baptized 'into his death' (5:3); 'buried with him in death' (6:4). Now that the believer participates in his body (7:4) the believer is to die to the body of death and live the new life. The believer is no longer a slave to sin (6:20-23) because there has been a deliverance from 'the body of death (7:24), a freedom 'from the law of sin and death' (8:2)." Robert Webber, *Common Roots: A Call To Evangelical Maturity* (Grand Rapids, MI., Zondervan Publishing House, 1978) p. 50

43 See 1 Cor. 15:20-53; Eph. 1:7-12; Rom. 8:16-23; Philp. 3:21.

44 George Florovsky, "The Ethos of the Orthodox Church," A Faith and Order Dialogue (Geneva, WCC, 1960) Faith and Order paper #30, pp. 47-48

45 "The phrase σῶμα Χριστοῦ [the body of Christ], writes A. E. Rawlinson, 'was in the mind of St. Paul a corollary of what to him was involved in the eucharist.' In the view of H. Conselmann, St. Paul used the expression 'once outside the eucharistic tradition: 1 Cor. 12:27.' But even here the apostle 'surely cannot have helped thinking of the liturgical formula 'this is my body,' which he quotes in the same epistle.'" Veselin Kesich, "Unity and Diversity In New Testament Ecclesiology," *St. Vladimir's Theological Quarterly* (Crestwood, New York, New York, St. Vladimir's Seminary Press, 1975) Volume 19, No. 2, pp. 119, 120 citing (respectively) A. E. J. Rawlinson, "Corpus Christi," in *Mysterium Christi,* G. K. A. Bell and A. Deissmann eds., pp. 226, 230 and Hans Conzelmann, *An Outline of the Theology of the New Testament* (New York: Harper and Row, 1969) p. 262

46 "The idea of the common sharing of the Lord's supper establishes the principle of the essential oneness of the members of the community" (1 Cor. 10:17). Donald Guthrie, *New Testament Theology,* (Downers Grove, IL., Inter-Varsity Press, 1981) pp. 745,746

47 "In early Christian times the Church was not viewed as a disciplined and hierarchically ordered society, lacking in mystical and invisible characteristics; It was seen as two-fold—human and divine at the same time—and complete. It corresponded to the hypostatic union of the two natures in Christ." Metropolitan Emilianos Timiadis, "The Eucharist: The Basis of All Sacraments and Union With God," *The Patristic and Byzantine Review* (Kingston, N.Y., American Institute for Patristic Studies, 1984) Vol. 3, No. 3, p. 185, 186

48 Robert Webber, *Common Roots: A Call To Evangelical Maturity* (Grand Rapids, MI., Zondervan Publishing House, 1978) p. 50

49 William R. Davies, *Gathered Into One* (New York, Morehouse -Barlow Co., 1975) p. 23

50 Carlton Kenney, *The Church Which is His Body* (Waco, TX.) p. 4

CHAPTER TEN

THE MEANING AND IMPORTANCE OF CATHOLICITY AND THE LOCAL CHURCH

In this chapter we will press for a clearer image of the Church by examining the Local Church. In order to grasp the early Christian meaning of the Local Church, however, we must first understand another commonly misunderstood term: *catholicity*. The concept of catholicity holds a great deal of importance for the Church today because a proper understanding of catholicity can erase many popular misconceptions regarding the Church's nature.

CATHOLICITY

BEYOND 'UNIVERSAL'

To many Fundamentalists-Evangelicals, the word *catholic* is simply an abbreviation for *Roman* Catholic. The term catholic, however, can never be the property of a denomination. In fact, as I shall show in a moment, those who use it to segregate Christians from each other are actually contradicting its very meaning! The ancient Church understood catholicity to mean *wholeness*, *fullness*, *integrity*, and "totality." This is the *primary* meaning of the Greek word *katholou* (καθόλου), catholic.[1]

Another popular misunderstanding of the word catholic is "universal," as in, the church which exists throughout the world. This was not at all the early Christian understanding. The Church of the first centuries used the term as a synonym for the fullness of Truth, not as a geographical description. For example, Ignatius of Antioch (the first Christian father to use the word to explain the Church) states that the Church is *catholic* because in her assembly, the faithful welcome the presence of Christ in *all His Truth*. The idea of a universal Church understood as being constituted by all "churches" throughout the world, never occurred to Ignatius.[2]

Actually, it was not until the Fifth Century — and then only in the West— that catholicity began to take on a *geographic* emphasis.[3] For centuries, "catholicity" never implied the sum total of all individual local churches, but rather was a reference to the Church's *inner being*.[4] Catholicity is a matter of the Church's inward unity in *wholeness*, not her outward administrative structure throughout the world. Indeed, if "catholic" meant universal, even the first Church in the Upper Room could not be considered catholic.[5]

CATHOLICITY MEANS IDENTICAL FAITH, NOT IDENTICAL FORM

If the Church is catholic in its very *being*, and not because of its existence as a world-wide structure,[6] then it follows that the unity of the Church is realized through a shared

Faith, and a shared life, not just a shared administration.[7] The early Church did not believe that its doctrine was catholic because it existed everywhere, but because the very nature of Truth is catholic.[8] Its unity was based on Truth, not on form or politics. The Church was one by virtue of its possessing *the one, identical, and whole Faith of the Church, not because each Local Church submitted to a central bureaucratic structure*.

Oftentimes many modern day Christians tend to think that doctrine is divisive, unnecessary, or even an obstacle to true Christian unity. But a *catholic* understanding of doctrine leads us to the exact *opposite* conclusion. Ignorance of the Truth and false beliefs are the hindrances to unity, not encouragements to it. Catholic Truth is whole and entire, and the unity of the church must reflect this reality. "Fundamentally ... there can never be any unity without truth or any truth without unity."[9] As the presence of Christ in the Church is indivisible, so the Truth which He embodies within her is likewise indivisible. *The Church is catholic precisely because it embodies all Truth and stands "opposed to all forms of particularism and sectarian separatism or heresy which would compromise the Truth."* [10] "Unity is realized through *participation* in the one truth... *in Christ.*"[11]

CATHOLIC TRUTH VS. DENOMINATIONALISM

Catholicity cannot be squeezed into a denominational mold. The Church (not one particular denomination) sees and attests to what is of God, and bears witness to the Truth wherever it may be. The Spirit blows where He wills and He blows wherever a true witness of God's life is evident (1 Cor. 12: 3; 1 John 4: 2-6). Thus, a religious body that refuses to recognize the Spirit outside of its administrative borders is not a catholic expression of the Church: it is a denomination. Or even worse: it is a sect.[12]

This compels us to again recognize the fundamental truth that the Church is not many, but One. There are no *flavors* of Christianity. No different *shades* of truth can co-exist in the Church. Denominations do not represent a "cereal assortment pack" of the Church, each one emphasizing its own special truth (e.g., the Baptists represent "Missionary Christianity," the Pentecostals the "Christianity of Spiritual Gifts," the "sacramental" Churches offer "Liturgical Christianity," etc.). Christianity is Christianity. Truth is Truth. And the Church is *the* (one) Church. [13]

It is a contradiction to God's presence and love within the Church to say Christianity can be cut up or *denominated* according to particular tastes or functions. *We* may see the Church as divided, but *our* perception does not always accurately reflect the true nature of the Church. Certainly Christ does not see His Body this way! He has *one* Body, *not many*.

All this is not to say that Truth cannot be expressed in a diversity of cultures, styles of worship, or even theological systems, for it certainly can be, and in fact is. But this does not mean that Truth is relative to culture or anything else, only that various cultures can be used of God to speak the one same Truth to a variety of peoples. The catholicity of the Church encourages *both* the unity of faith, and at the same time, Spirit-inspired diversity. Catholic diversity, however, neither contradicts the one Truth nor divides the one Church. *Denominationalism, on the other hand, gives the impression that the Church could be divided and that contradictory doctrines are acceptable in the Church, thus denominationalism encourages neither unity nor diversity* ! [14]

Catholicity refuses to restrict the life of the Church to any one time or place in history (i.e. New Testament times, the Middle Ages, Reformation Europe, the Counter-reformation, etc.). Catholicity implies a unity with the past (in the Faith of the Apostles) and a unity with the future (the Second Coming).[15] To fragment the Church's life and experience as if the *real* Church were only in the past (30 - 100 A.D.), in heaven, or found on the Last Day, is to deny the Church's *intrinsic* catholicity (wholeness).[16] As Christ is both within and beyond time, so is His Church. "The catholic nature of the Church is seen most vividly in the fact that the experience of the Church belongs to *all times* ."[17]

CHRIST'S CATHOLICITY AND OUR TASK

Plainly stated, *the Church is catholic because Christ is catholic* . "The Church is catholic, because it is the one Body of Christ; it is union in Christ, oneness in the Holy Ghost—and this unity is the highest wholeness and fulness."[18] St. Ignatius wrote "Wherever Christ is, *there* is the catholic Church" [19] because *Christ's presence* within His Body will— and does now — unite us and all creation into wholeness and totality (Eph. 1:9, 10). By His uniting everything and all peoples in His Church, the fragmenting power of sin, satan, and the Fall are overcome in Christ's catholic nature. In Jesus Christ, all will be re-united and healed. When Jesus gathered and united a people from the diversity of humanity and culture, He performed a truly "catholic act." No longer is there any "distinction between Greek and Jew, circumcised and uncircumcised, barbarian, Scythian, slave and freeman." Now, in the Church's catholicism, "Christ is all, and in all" (Col. 3:11).[20]

Christ's presence in the Church, however, does not automatically manifest the Church's catholic nature among us. "Catholicity has been *given* to the Church; [but] its *achievement* is the Church's task."[21] We have a necessary part to play. Although the Church's inherent catholicity is founded in Christ and is not dependent upon our behavior, our *experience and participation* in His catholicity does demand our active co-operation. What does this mean?

Each is called to reveal Christ's wholeness, love, and redemption within the Church, and then to bring that catholicity into the world by loving as Christ loves. This inner "catholic consciousness" of the Church will only be *revealed* when her members take steps of faith, and when they open their lives to one another in heart and mind. Such an active Catholic Community will have no "barriers," whether they be national, regional, racial, sexual, economic, cultural, or social. All these divisions will be overcome by God's love.

There is another aspect of living a catholic life, and that is committing oneself to follow the Truth wherever it might lead. Within the catholic Church, in fellowship with one's brethren, each must take the responsibility to experience Truth in spirit, mind, and action. It is not possible for "someone else" to know the Truth *for us* (i.e. a Sunday School teacher, our pastor, a professional theologian). *Each* must make the Truth *his own* to be consciously catholic. *Each* must study, *each* must pursue Truth, *each* must give his heart in Christian discipleship.

It is the same with the responsibility to love. Catholic unity will be demonstrated only when *each* person works both to give and to receive love. This personal, responsible love manifests the Church's catholicity as nothing else can. *In this love, Truth will be perceived, shared and lived in a catholic manner* (Eph. 3: 17-20). [22] This again reiterates the truth that love and doctrine are inseparable, for one's *experience* of God's Truth *directly corresponds* to his ability to give and receive love in catholic communion. [23] Christ does not disclose Himself in one's self-imposed isolation, but in an environment of giving, sharing, receiving, and communion. In this context alone is the character of God revealed.[24]

THE CHURCH IN THE ASSEMBLY (EKKLESIA) AND COVENANT

To more fully understand what we mean by the *Catholic* Church, let us now define exactly what we mean by the term "Church." The word originates from the Greek word *ekklesia* (εκκλησία), those who have been "called out" from among others to form a union. The word is also often used synonymously for our English word *gathering*. In ancient Greece, the *ekklesia* was descriptive of the political assembly where all full citizens were *called out* to decide upon fundamental political and juridical issues.[25] In the Septuagint (the Greek translation of the Old Testament), the word was used as a rendering of the Hebrew word *Qahal* (Judges 20:2; Deut 18:16; Num. 1:16). The Qahal was the gathering which represented the *whole* nation of Israel (Deut 9:10; Ex. 19:20; Acts 7:38), placing "a special emphasis on the ultimate unity of the Chosen People, conceived as a sacred whole...".[26]

The authors of the New Testament adopted aspects of each of these meanings, but it was primarily the Old Testamental understanding of Qahal that they favored in their depiction of the Christian Church. It was this emphasis which led the first Christians to see the Church as "first of all the organic continuity of the two Covenants."[27] The Qahal, as a *community of people united to God and one another* in the Old Testament, was understood as a type for the *ekklesia* in the New (1 Pet. 2:9).[28] It was this covenanted community of God's people that the Lord Himself had in mind when He spoke of the Ekklesia - the Church.[29]

THE EKKLESIA AS A GATHERING IN "THE NAME"

The revelation of God's Name in the Old Testament as YHWH revealed something distinctly "personal" about the character of God. Chiefly it disclosed the Lord's intimate identification with Israel *as a people ... as Qahal* . God's relationship with Israel was unique; only Israel personally knew the Lord as YHWH; His Name was the special property of God's covenant people, for God bound Himself to Israel in a way which no other nation knew.

The covenantal significance of His name has not passed away with time. The Name of YHWH - the name which reveals that God gives Himself to a people - *still* holds a great deal of importance for the New Covenant Christian. Each believer's identification with *Jesus* (Aramaic for "YHWH is salvation") designates him or her as a member of *God's people* , those who personally know God *in covenant* . Like his or her counterpart in the

Old Testament, a Christian knows God within *a covenanted people* (Eph. 2:12, 13), just as the individual Jew was known in Israel. The New Testament Christian is now part of *"a chosen race, a royal priesthood, a holy nation, a people for God's own possession "* (1 Peter 2:9).

It would have been a contradiction for an Old Testament believer to say he had committed his life to YHWH but was aloof from Israel (The Qahal). Likewise it would have been inconsistent for a Christian in New Testament times to affirm his commitment to Christ yet refuse membership within the Church (ekklesia) of his town. A person did not "come to Christ" (know the Name of Jesus), by merely making a *private* decision. The nature of covenant was constant in both Old and New Testaments in this respect: *it was never something which existed solely between God and the individual believer.* If one was covenanted to God in the Name (YHWH/Jesus), he was also covenanted to his fellow *covenantors* - and joined himself *to a covenant people.*

This leads us to a stunning conclusion. If one wants to be a Christian and yet does not want to be a part of an *ekklesia —a people, i.e. the Church —* he cannot be one. Christianity is, *in its very nature, covenantal and communal.* [30] Christ established the Church in the covenant of His blood and we accept what He offered in His covenant (Heb. 12:24). To ignore the ramifications of Christ's covenant is to build on a different foundation than Christ (1 Cor. 3:11).

What is most significant for a right understanding of Jesus' view of the church is that God dealt with *a community* rather than with isolated individuals.[31] We can neither separate ourselves from others, nor casually gather together as an uncommitted body of individuals, and still say that we are living New Covenant Christianity. To gather "in the Name" necessitates that we gather as a covenanted people.

THE EKKLESIA AND THE SIGNIFICANCE OF COVENANT

We can better understand the impossibility of "Christian individualism" by taking a closer look at the meaning of *covenant* . Both Old and New Testament senses of the word communicate the idea of "binding together." The word for covenant in the Hebrew, *beriut* means "to fetter." The Greek New Testament equivalent is *diatheeke* (διαθήκη), the word is often translated *testament* . Diatheeke connotes the idea of a "contract" or "a pledge to another upon one's death." This latter conception is perhaps the best of all translations of the word.

In the Old Testament we see a foreshadowing of what Christ has done for us through covenant. A covenant was the vehicle used to established "family-like" relationships between agreeing parties.[32] Similarly, in the covenant given to us by Christ, we have been made a family. We have become brothers with Christ *and* one another, joint members of "God's household."[33] In the early years of the Church it was this brotherhood which was most observable in the Local Church, and it attracted many to Christ's love and peace. The unbeliever saw that it was in covenant brotherhood that the peace of God's family could be known.[34]

Ignatius rightly discerned each Christian gathering (the Local Church) as a focus of covenant solidarity. He expressed this most powerfully in his seeing the Eucharist as the central feature of each local church. In his letters, Ignatius uses the Greek phrase *epi tō afto* (ἐπὶ το αὐτό) as an equivalent for "assembly" , or "unite" (as "to *unite* in prayer").[35] In each usage he refers to the Eucharistic assembly. From this we can surmise that his usage of the phrase, and the meaning it held for him—the Eucharistic-covanental gathering of the Church—was that of the Christians in the New Testament period (After all, their era was *his* era [30-107 AD].). With this background, it becomes all the more clear that when the New Testament uses the Greek phrase *epi to afto* (which literally translates to come together "on the same place"), it also bears *Eucharistic* significance.[36] The implications of this will be more fully discussed in the chapter on the Eucharist, but our major point here is that the Eucharist was *the* expression of Christ's covenant and as such was the "gathering in the Name."

This insight gives us a clearer understanding of the nature of the Church. The issue is *not just coming together,*[37] but "when you come together *as a church* " (1 Cor. 11: 18). As Israel was God's people because Yahweh was present among them in the covenanted Qahal, so now *Christ's covenant makes Him present in a unique manner within the ekklesia, the gathered people of God* .[38] In this respect, each Local Church reflects the *whole (Catholic)* Church.

THE MEANING OF THE LOCAL CHURCH

Given this background of catholicity, let us now look into the last statement more fully: the *whole* Church resides within *one* specific Local body. Many are puzzled by such a statement because they see the Church as a composite, administrative string of "churches," not as the united spiritual organism she actually is. The Eastern minded Christian maintains that "the Church in its fullest manifestation is not found in some distant and exalted state of existence, but rather in the Local Church."[39] The Scriptures make it plain that the Local and the 'universal' Church *represent the same spiritual reality* (Phil. 3:6; 1 Cor. 10:32; Eph. 5:23, 27, 29). How can this be? Just as an individual person is not "a slice" of humanity but a full expression of it, so also the Local Church is not a slice of the Church, but her *fullness*. Let me illustrate this by focusing in on six ways the Local Church demonstrates to us what it means to be the Church.

(1) THE NATURE OF THE CHURCH'S CATHOLICITY

The Local Church is a true representation and manifestation of the *one* Church which exists in *many* places because each Local Church is catholic in its full expression of the Faith, teaching, life, and communion. In fact, the phrase "catholic Church" was applied almost exclusively to the Local Church within the first three centuries.[40] The notion of a *mystical* (i.e. invisible) Body of Christ as the Church was far from the New Testament writers' minds. Their usage of the term "Church" was primarily a reference to a specific, local, concrete, and visible assembly.[41]

The synagogue of New Testament times even mirrored this aspect of the Church's catholicity. Each one looked upon itself as a miniature of Judaism as a whole.[42] Paul perceived the synagogue residing within each city as the local manifestation of the whole congregation of Israel. The Apostle, seeing each Christian Assembly as a microcosm of the whole ekklesia,[43] naturally transferred this perspective to the Local Church.[44] He did not get drawn into a frame of reference which falsely divided the Church into Local and Universal.[45] Paul saw each Local Church like a full circle within a circle, every community being a concrete, specific expression of the *whole* Church. His salutations stand as revealing commentaries to this: 'the *church of God* which is at *Corinth* ,' 'to *the church* of the Thessalonians'; '*the church* in your house'..."[46]

(2) THE CHURCH AS THE BODY OF CHRIST

To ascribe anything less than wholeness to the Local Church would be to deny that the Body of Christ is present in each assembly. The Local Church is "catholic" by virtue of each Local Community being Christ's Body *existentially*. *EACH* assembly shares in *HIS* unity. *EACH* assembly shares in *HIS* catholicity. As we stated before, when St. Ignatius wrote in 100 A.D. to the Church of Smyrna that "Wherever Christ Jesus is, there is the catholic Church", he was making a reference to the fullness of Christ's indivisible Body as it existed within each Local Church.[47] The Body of Christ is *in*, *with*, and *among each* assembly.[48] This truth creates no tension between local and universal in the Church's catholicity.

(3) THE EUCHARIST MAKES THE LOCAL CHURCH *TRULY* CHURCH

Although I will take up the subject more extensively in later chapters, the meaning and significance of the Eucharist is so central an understanding of the Church that I must briefly mention some things about it now. The third reason each local community is the whole (catholic) Body of Christ, is that *each* community celebrates the Eucharist. In this celebration, the Body of Christ is revealed, not just by "symbols" of Bread and Wine, but, *by that people of God*, that particular *gathering*. Wherever the Eucharist is, there is the "whole" (catholic) Christ with the "whole" (catholic) Church. For this reason - that Christ is present within the specified assembly - all theology about the Church in the East is rooted *in the Local Church* .

The Church exists universally *only because it exists Locally* . The "universal" Church can only be manifest in the *Local* Church,[49] because the Eucharist can only be celebrated *Locally* . And it is the Eucharistic assembly, as the Body of Christ, which makes the Local Church transcend its geographical limitations. The foundation for this is seen in Paul's very description of the Church as "*the* body of Christ" (1 Cor. 12:27).[50] In fact, it is reasonable to assume that the very phrase "body of Christ" had its origin in the Eucharistic assembly: "In the eucharist the body of Christians (το σῶμα τῶν Κριστιανῶν) becomes the body of Christ (τὸ σῶμα τοῦ Κριστοῦ)."[51]

The Local Assembly cannot be only a "part" of the Body of Christ. The Eastern Orthodox Churches of today emphasize this truth in a pattern of worship they still maintain. No more than one Eucharist can be celebrated in the same parish each day, and no minister can celebrate more than once each day. The purpose of this practice is to make it clear that the *entire* body of the Local Church (not just a segment of it) must be present in the gathering. A fragment of the body cannot manifest the reality of the one, whole Church gathered in the Eucharist. If this were the case, Christ would not be *fully* present within each celebration of the Eucharist—only *parts* of Him would be. And how can you have just a *part* of Christ's presence? We, as the Church, are the members of His *Body* , not members of His *parts!* Each Assembly manifests the *whole* Christ because each is *united* to the *whole* Christ. Paul did not greet "a *part* of the Church" that met in Aquila and Priscila's home, but "*the* Church" gathered there (Rom. 16:5). That local Body was just as much the Church as The Gathering of the Christians in Rome, or Thessalonika, [52] or any other city where believers were assembled.

(4) THE LOCAL CHURCH'S EQUALITY WITH EVERY OTHER LOCAL CHURCH

As can be concluded from the above, no Local Church or group of Local Churches could legitimately claim any right of rulership over other Local Churches. Just as no one Local Church can have *more* of the Eucharist, *more* of Christ, *more* of the covenant, or be *more* catholic than any other, so no one Local Church can be *more* Church than the others.[53] Since Christ is equally present within *each* assembly, each sister Church equals all the others. The Eucharist shows each Local Church to be the *embodiment of the all-encompassing Christ,* [54] and, therefore, it is impossible for any Local Church to be "governed" by anything, or anyone else but Christ.[55] Because *Christ* is within *each* Church, the primacy of the Church must be located within each Local Church. [56]

The Church councils in early Church history are powerful illustrations of the equality and unity which each Local Church shared. In these councils, the heads of each Christian community (as representatives of their respective assemblies), protected their Catholicity by making sure that they stood in harmony with the other Local Churches. Nothing could be concluded in a council without the unanimous consent of each overseer. Each bishop was understood to be each other bishop's peer.[57] These councils were a demonstration of *each* Community's catholic expression of the Faith.

These Church councils were not standing bureaucratic structures of power, nor a religious board of directors. They were *spontaneous* events convened only *when the Local Churches sensed a crucial need for them* . Here, in the Church council, was the practical out-working of the Church which sees its existence both in the Local context *and* beyond. In essence, the council represented "the most official negation of the division between Local and universal...".[58]

(5) THE LOCAL CHURCH'S COMMUNION WITH THE CHURCH ELSEWHERE

The Local Church is not fully dependent upon another Local Church for its identity; however, neither can it ever be completely independent of it, for although the Local Church is the complete Church, it is only this *because it is mutually joined and inseparable from the Church as it exists elsewhere in the world* .[59] No truly catholic Local Church can rightly see itself as "independent" from the others. Among them stands a relationship of *inter* - dependence. Alexander Schmemann, a professor of Eastern Orthodox theology, sums up the catholicity and inter-communion of the Church, and their manifestation among the Local Churches in this way:

> ...the Church manifests itself as a plurality of churches, each one of which is a *part* and a *whole* . It is because only in unity with all churches and in obedience to the universal Truth can it be the Church; yet it is also a whole because in each church by virtue of her unity with the One, Holy, Catholic, and Apostolic Church [i.e. catholicity], the whole Christ is present...[60]

This vision of the Local Churches being "part" yet "whole" - "many" but "one" — is reflected well in the life of the Trinity:

> ..we can thus say that, as the Divine Persons, Father , Son and Holy Spirit, are not parts or portions of the Holy Trinity, as in each of them the entire Godhead is fully manifested, as each of them is true God and as neither Person *is* the Holy Trinity or *identical* with it, so in some similar way the fullness of the Catholic Church is manifested in all Local Churches which can be neither understood as 'portion' of the Universal nor simply identified with it.[61]

No One Person of the Trinity exists without the others. Similarly, the Local Church, like any Person of the Trinity, cannot exist unless it exists *in relationship* with the other Local Churches throughout the world. The Father is Father *because* of His *relationship* with the Son, and the Spirit; the Son is the Son *because* of His *relationship* with the Father and the Spirit; and the Spirit is the Spirit only *because* of His *relationship* with the Father and the Son. The Local Church exists as Church only because of its communal relationship with every other genuine Local Assembly which manifests Christ. As Each Divine Person's *very being* is *communal* so the Church is called to be a people of communion. [62]

Although the the same intensity of communion cannot be realized by us, the Local Church is nevertheless called to somehow reflect the union of the Trinity with all other truly Catholic Churches (John 17:20-23). The Trinity, though Three Persons, is Unity because of their love for each other, in the same way each Local Church, though found in many different locations, is called to express its inherent "indivisibility" by love, interdependence, and selflessness.

Each Local Church is Church because each shares a unity in the one Christ and in the life of each other's local Community. If a Local Church begins to see herself exclusively and cuts herself off from the rest, she ceases to be the Church, and to break off her *relationship* with the complete body of Christ is to become mutated, to become only a "piece" of Christ, i.e. to become something which does not exist!

(6) THE LOCAL CHURCH AS THE CHURCH IN IDENTITY OF FAITH

Finally, the Local Church is one and the same with every other local Body because of the common relationship each shares in Christ's Body. The Local Church as the Church means each "can and ... must recognize in each other the *same* faith, the *same* fullness, and the *same* divine life."[63] This identity is observable in the identical Faith which all genuine Churches demonstrate in life and in their communion in the Truth. It was for this reason Bishop Cyprian of Carthage (220-258 A.D) taught that each Local Church was *identical* with the other Local Churches, each local bishop being able to make Peter's confession of faith (Matt. 16:16).[64]

In the early centuries, the faith of one Local Church was identical with all the others, and only in this oneness of faith — not through some over-arching structure — was each united. A further illustration of "the identical faith" manifesting "the identical Church" was seen in the practice of each Local Church's refusal to consecrate any candidate for bishop unless other bishops from nearby local Communities also approved of his candidacy. This exercise is not to be misunderstood as saying that these ordaining bishops had power over the newly ordained, but merely that their testimony (again, as representatives of their respective Communities) witnessed to the fact that the faith of both the new overseer and the Community was identical with theirs, *like* testifying to *like*. If the Community's leadership, life, and witness were not in conformity with Apostolic practice, the Local Churches on its borders would not recognize it as one of theirs.

SUMMARY

The Church is whole; it defies "denominating" and cannot be delineated in purely administrative terms. Christ's presence within the Local Assembly underscores the Church's innate wholeness. The Church is whole because Christ is whole. Its call to be catholic leads the Church both to embrace all Truth and to refuse all falsehood. The Church is fullness in Life, Love, and Communion, and is open to all who would be whole. It can not accommodate those who live in isolation and prejudice. In conclusion, every Christian has a mandate to *discover* and *embrace* the Church's oneness *in her fulness and completeness*. Only in this soil can the true unity of the Church be displayed.

The experience of Church takes place not at an evangelistic crusade or in a Bible study group (as good as these may be), but when Christians come together as an *assembled people*. The Church is communion with God and one's brethren, a reality which is to be realized and experienced in the Local Church. Here, in the the Covenant Assembly, believers are gathered in Jesus' Name and manifest their union with Christ and each other as His body. Here — in a specific place at a specific time with specific people — God's love is demonstrated in a way that is impossible universally or invisibly. When this vision of the Local Church is regained, the Church will once more be "the light of the world, a city set on a hill that cannot be hidden" (Matt. 5:14).

NOTES FOR CHAPTER TEN

1 "In the West, it [the word 'catholic'] was generally understood as 'universal.' However, if this was the meaning of the word, it is not quite clear..why the early Latin translators of the creeds [like the Nicean where it reads "one, holy, catholic, and apostolic Church"] kept in the text the Greek form *catholica ecclesia* instead of using *universalis* . ....The reason for this phenomenon is that the various translators were aware of the difficulty of translating *katholike* by a single word in any language. If *katholikos* is ever to be translated by 'universal' it still does not have a geographical, but a philosophical, connotation [where it would mean "all-inclusive"]. As applied to the Church, 'catholic' first of all implies the idea of *fullness* : etymologically, it derives from the adverb *katholon* , "on the whole," opposed to *kata meros* , 'partially'." John Meyendorff, "The Orthodox Concept of the Church," *St. Vladimir's Quarterly* (Crestwood, New York, St. Vladimir's Press, 1962) Vol. 6, No. 2, p. 61

2 " On the contrary, an identification of the *whole Christ* and the *whole Church* with the *Local* episcopal community constitutes a key idea in his thought." John Meyendorff, Joseph McLelland, eds., "The Eucharistic Community and the Catholicity of the Church, John D. Zizioulas, *The New Man: An Orthodox and Reformed Dialogue,* (New Jersey, Standard Press, 1973) p. 108 italics mine.

3 "Only ... during the struggle against the Donatists was the word 'catholica' used in the sense of 'universality' in opposition to the geographical provincialism of the Donatists." Georges Florovsky, *Bible, Church, Tradition: An Eastern Orthodox View* (Belmont, MA., Nordland Publishing Company, 1972) p. 41

4 "The term derived from the Greek κάθ ὂλου = καθολικός meaning primarily wholeness, fullness, integrity not on the empirical but on the ontological plane." David Neiman and Margret Schatkin, eds., "Some Aspects of the Ecclesiology of Father Georges Vasilievich Florovsky," Peter A. Chamberas, *The Heritage of the Early Church* (Roma, Pont. Institutum Studiorum Orientalium) p. 423 ftnte 6

5 "Ecumenical" is perhaps the closest concept to a universalistic understanding of catholicity, though it is still very distinct in that it is not referring to the "jurisdictional" or "administrative" manifestation of the Church. The word comes from the Greek *oikoumene* and means 'the inhabited earth' or 'the world community'. The *oikoumene* will one day realize the Kingdom of God in her being through Christ's redemptive power. He through whom God made all worlds will gather all things to Himself in His Body and offer it back to the Father so God may be all in all (1 Cor. 15:25-28; Rom. 8: 19-23; Eph. 1:9,10, 22, 23).

6 "When... the emphasis is placed on unity [and]... based upon the dogma of the Body of Christ, the result is Christocentrism in ecclesiology. The catholicity of the Church becomes a function of her unity, becomes a universal doctrine that absorbs in imposing itself, instead of being a tradition evident to everyone, affirmed by all, at all times and in all places, in an infinite richness of living witness. On the other hand, when the emphasis is placed on diversity at the expense of unity, there is a tendency to base catholicity exclusively on Pentecost, forgetting that the Holy Spirit was communicated in unity of the Body of Christ. The result is the disaggregation of the Church: the truth that is attributed to individual inspirations becomes multiple and therefore relative..." Vladimir Lossky, *In The Image and Likeness of God* , (Crestwood, New York, St. Vladimir's Press, 1974) p. 179

7 "The idea of the visible Church and its unity has been prominent in the East since the time of Victor of Rome (A. D. 190) when, having attempted to excommunicate the Churches of Asia for keeping Easter after their own reckoning, he was reproved by Irenaeus for introducing into the Church the idea that a rigid uniformity, rather than a common faith, was the bond of union. In the West, however, Cyprian's conception of the Church was dominant. Although he regarded the church as a spiritual entity, he approached it with a practical and legalistic attitude, 'owing much to analogies borrowed from Roman Law and conditioned by the problems created by the Novatianist schism'." Methodios Fouyas, *Orthodoxy, Roman Catholicism and Anglicanism* (Oxford University Press, 1972) p. 117 citing J.N.D. Kelly, *Early Christian Doctrines* , p. 294

8 Vladimir Lossky, *In The Image and Likeness of God* , (Crestwood, New York, St. Vladimir's Press, 1974) p. 172

9 Reinhard Slenczka, "Unity in the Truth or Truth in Unity?: The Significance and Purpose of Theological Discussion with the Eastern Church," WCC paper, 1975, p. 71

10 David Neiman and Margret Schatkin, eds., "Some Aspects of the Ecclesiology of Father Georges Vasilievich Florovsky," Peter A. Chamberas, *The Heritage of the Early Church* (Roma, Pont. Institutum Studiorum Orientalium) p. 424 citing G. Florovsky, "Sobornost: the Catholicity of the Church," p. 53, italics mine.

11 Georges Florovsky, *Creation and Redemption,* (Belmont, MA., Nordland Publishing Company, 1976) p. 39. Italics mine.

12 "When it faces the present, the Church ... has two very concrete dangers to avoid. (1) It must not consider itself a 'denomination,' and (2) it must not consider itself a sect. ...Now a denomination and a sect have this in common, that both are exclusive : the first because it is relativistic by definition, since it considers itself as one of the possible forms of Christianity, and the second because it finds pleasure—a demonic pleasure indeed—in isolation, in separation, in distinctiveness and in feelings of superiority." John Meyendorff, *Living Tradition,* (Crestwood, New York, St. Vladimir's Seminary Press, 1978) p. 185, 186

13 Professor T. F. Torrence in his excellent book, *Theology in Reconciliation* , gives a good summary of catholicity in the following:

> ...the term, catholic; developed through reference both to the fulness of the Gospel in contrast to what is partial and divisive and to the integral content of the truth found in the whole historical Church in contrast to what is defective and heretical. The Catholic Church is the Church which retains in every time and place throughout the world a wholeness of life, worship and doctrine grounded in the original datum of divine revelation and embodying the permanent substance of the faith once and for all delivered to the Apostles. It is the Church which everywhere remains entire through an intrinsic relation in the Holy Spirit to its divine origin, which everywhere remains one and the same through continuous fidelity to the apostolic foundation of the Church in Jesus Christ, and is therefore the Church which everywhere remains 'orthodox', that is, 'rightly related' to the truth of the one God, Father, Son, and Holy Spirit, common to the universal Church.

T. F. Torrance, *Theology in Reconciliation: Essays Toward Evangelical and Catholic Unity In East and West,* (Grand Rapids, MI., William B. Eerdmans Publishing Company, 1975) p. 17

14 Pretending as if denominations did not exist, yet at the same time subscribing to a confessional view of the Church (whether it be adherence to only a "few" or "many" doctrines), is certainly no different— i.e. a "non-denominational" Church is merely another name for a body which denominates itself on the basis of "confession" —(even if it be the lack of one).

15 John Meyendorff, *The Catholicity and the Church,* "The Significance of the Reformation in the History of Christendom" (Crestwood, New York, St. Vladimir's Seminary Press, 1983) p. 56

16 A "universal" definition of catholicity would surely not be an adequate depiction of the Church, as the Church can never be limited only to the earth. The Church is eternal, and any understanding of the Church must include *all* believers of *all* time.

17 Georges Florovsky, *Bible, Church, Tradition: An Eastern Orthodox View* (Belmont, MA., Nordland Publishing Company, 1972) p. 45, italics mine.

18 Georges Florovsky, *Bible, Church, Tradition: An Eastern Orthodox View* (Belmont, MA., Nordland Publishing Company, 1972) p. 41

19 Ignatius, *Smyrnaens, The Nicene and Post-Nicene Fathers*, (Wm. Eerdmans Publishing Company, 1973) VIII, p. 90. Italics mine.

20 It is for this reason that "a eucharist which discriminates between races, sexes, ages, professions, social classes, etc. violates not certain ethical principles but its eschatological nature. For that reason such a eucharist is not a 'bad' —i.e. morally deficient —eucharist but no eucharist at all. It cannot be said to be the body of the One who sums up all into Himself." John D. Zizioulas, *Being As Communion* (Crestwood, N.Y., St. Vladimir's Seminary Press, 1985) ftnte. 11, p. 255

21 Georges Florovsky, *Bible, Church, Tradition: An Eastern Orthodox View* (Belmont, MA., Nordland Publishing Company, 1972) p. 55, italics mine.

22 The external witness of catholicity is always illustrated in "a call for expression and practice rather than a quality to be claimed as a possession" — and every effort to express the meaning of catholicity must be read as a reference to "wholeness in Christ," i.e. relationships of love with Him and the brethren.Carnegie Samuel Calian, *Icon and Pulpit* (Philadelphia, PA., The Westminster Press, 1968) p. 61 citing C. Welch, "Catholicity", Ecumenical Review, Vol. XVI, No. I. (October, 1963), p. 38

23 "If this opening of consciousness on the interior evidence of Truth is brought about by the Holy Spirit in each Christian person, it is nevertheless not uniform, for there is no measure common to all where persons are concerned. ...that does not mean that there is one single consciousness of the Church, which is imposed uniformly on all, as a 'supra-consciousness' belonging to a 'collective person.' If one must recognize in ecclesial reality not only unity of nature [the Church consisting of "human beings"] but also multiplicity of hypostases [i.e. personal identities, persons, "egos"] , there necessarily will be a multiplicity of consciousnesses, with different degrees of actualization in different persons..." Vladimir Lossky, *In The Image and Likeness of God* , (Crestwood, New York, St. Vladimir's Press, 1974) p. 192

24 "Christ reveals Himself to us not in our isolation, but in our mutual catholicity, in our union." Georges Florovsky, *Bible, Church, Tradition: An Eastern Orthodox View* (Belmont, MA., Nordland Publishing Company, 1972) p.55

25 Colin Brown, ed., Dictionary of New Testament Theology Vol. 1, "Church," L. Coenen (Grand Rapids, MI., Zondervan Publishing House, 1975) p. 291 A New Testament example where this secular use of ekklesia appears is Acts 19:38,39.

26 Georges Florovsky, *Bible, Church, Tradition: An Eastern Orthodox View* (Belmont, MA., Nordland Publishing Company, 1972) p. 59

27 *ibid.*, p. 58

It is important to note that the English word "assembly" which appears in our translations for the New Testament is actually the translation of *three* Greek words, only one of which is properly the Church, "ekklesia:" (1) *paneegeris* (πανήγυρις) which denotes a gathering of any or all kinds; inclusive of parades, processions or any crowd where a large number of people for any purpose are all gathered together (e.g. "*...myriads* of angels, to *the general assembly* and the Church of the first-born" Heb. 12:22,23), (2) *pleethos* (πληθός), which means a multitude, the whole number, overabundance, excess, too full, mass crowding beyond capacity, large number, throng, host, we get the English word 'plethora' from this, (e.g. "... a great *multitude* from Galilee followed..." Mark 3:7, "*... the whole body of them* arose and brought Him before Pilate" Luke 23:1; "And as He said this, there arose a dissension between the Pharisees and Sadducees; and the *assembly* was divided" Acts 23:7) and (3) the word we are here discussing *ekklesia* (ἐκκλησία: εκ - "out of", κλῆσις - "a calling, summoning") e.g."...when you *come together* as an *assembly* [Church] ..." 1 Cor. 11:18).

28 The only difference between the two is that the members of the New Testament Church can, in Christ, know a more intimate communion with God and one.s fellow believers than was ever possible before His advent.

29 "*What did Jesus mean by ekklesia?* In view of the widespread use of the word in the LXX for the congregation of Israel, it should be noted that *ekklesia* represents a Hebrew word, *qahal* , but never *'edâ* . Both of these are used of the community of God's people. If the word used by Jesus is used in the LXX sense of *qahal* , *ekklesia* refers to God's people conceived as a new community especially related to the Messiah (hence the expression 'my church' used by Jesus)." Donald Guthrie, *New Testament Theology,* (Downers Grove, IL., Inter-Varsity Press, 1981) p. 711

30 The Scriptures make it clear that the idea of salvation is indivisible from one's membership in the Local Church; fellowship with God *and* with one another are always understood by the New Testament Christian as things that go "hand in hand" with each other.

> "what we have seen and heard we proclaim to you also, that you also may have fellowship *with us;* and indeed our fellowship *is with the Father, and with His Son Jesus Christ.* " (1 John 1:3,4)
>
> "For He has delivered us from the domain of darkness, and transferred us to *the kingdom* of His beloved Son, in whom we have redemption, the forgiveness of sins. (Col. 1:12) [A kingdom which is to be experienced on earth as well as in heaven (Matt. 6:10)]
>
> "I [Jesus] do not ask in behalf of these alone [the Disciples], but for those also who believe in Me through their word [Christians of all generations]; that *they may all be one* ; even as Thou, Father, art in Me, and I in Thee, that they also may be in Us..." (John 17:21)
>
> "...the Lord Jesus Christ, who gave Himself for our sins, that He might deliver us out of the *present* evil age, according to the will of our God and Father." (Gal. 1:4)

The only way to escape that "present evil age," was to enter into another Kingdom. The Church is the environment of this deliverance..

> "And with many other words he [Peter] solemnly testified and kept on exhorting them, saying, 'Be saved from *this* perverse generation!" (Acts 2:40)

And then those who responded to Peter's invitation were baptized, "added" to their assembly, and devoted themselves to the fellowship (Acts 2:41, 42).

31 Donald Guthrie, *New Testament Theology,* (Downers Grove, IL., Inter-Varsity Press, 1981) p. 707, italics mine.

32 Such as Abraham and his descendants with God (Gen 15:18) between Laban's family and Jacob's (31: 43-54), David and Jonathan (1 Sam. 20:8), man and wife (Mal. 2:14).

33 Indeed, our Christian faith and sense of brotherhood is so intertwined that one who does not love his brother cannot possibly love his brother's Lord (1 John 4: 20). See also Matt. 28: 10; Rom. 8:16, 17; Eph. 2:19.

34 *Shalom*, the Hebrew word for peace, especially communicates how God's peace is inseparable from its covenantal realization in community. "Shalom is a broad concept, essential to the Hebrew understanding of relationship between people and God. It covers human welfare, health, and well-being in both spiritual and material aspects. [Shalom was not] mere tranquility of spirit or serenity of mind, peace had to do with harmonious relationships between God and His people. ... Unfortunately, this communal social dimension for the gospel of peace continues to evade many Christians who conceive of peace with God in individual and inward terms." John Driver, *Community and Commitment*, (Scottdale, PA., 1976) pp. 70, 74

35 This is found in his letters to the Churches of Ephesus and Magnesia (*Ephesians* 5:3; *Magnesians* 7:1)

36 Lk. 17:35; Acts 1: 15; Acts 2:1, 44; 1 Cor. 11:20; 14: 23.

37 Bible studies, "fellowship" nights, prayer meetings, etc. may be *expressions* of the Church, but they are not the Church. The word *ekklesia* is used only twice in the gospels (Matt 16:16-19; 18:17); in the first instance ("upon this rock I will build my church") it is a reference to the "faith" upon which the Church is built, in the second (" and if he refuses to listen to them, tell it to the church") it is in the context of a court similar to the Jewish synagogue which had the authority to decide and settle disputes and exercise discipline. It is this second quotation which makes it very clear that the Church is not just an occasional gathering of a few random Christians in their living room.

Certainly, a "reflection" of the Church is seen in Matt. 18: 20 where Christ states that in the gathering of two or three in His name, there He is in the midst, but the idea that this is the same thing as the Church (*ekklesia*) is countered in the statement that if a brother is not sufficiently corrected by "two or three witnesses" (Matt. 18: 16) " tell it to *the church* . " If the Church were merely the grouping of two or three brothers, why would there be need to report it "to the Church?" To borrow from Paul's description, the Church *as the Body of Christ* is not merely two or three members but the entire body *assembled* . It is the whole Body of Christ which *makes* the Church (again the significance of the Eucharistic celebration can again be seen here).

Going back to the image of the Qahal, a couple of Jews together celebrating the Sabbath did not constitute the nation of Israel (i.e. the Qahal). They *expressed* Israel, they *belonged* to Israel but *those few gathered* were not Israel. It is the same with the membership within the *ekklesia* . Two or three Christians in prayer may *testify and demonstrate* their membership in the Church, but *these few gathered* are not the Church. Besides, as we have explained, to merely gather with Christians is different than to gather *in* Jesus' name, for *to gather in Christ's name is to signify the covenantal and organic understanding of God's bond with His people ; —this is the Church* .

38 In this covenant relationship constituting His body, the significance of the Eucharistic celebration is seen once again; the covenant being represented and actualized visibly in the Eucharist — "the Covenant meal" *par excellence* . "A careful study of I Cor. 11 reveals that the term ἐκκλησία is used in a dynamic sense: 'when you come together into, i.e. when *you become* , ἐκκλησία ,' v 9, 18). This implies clearly what in the following verses becomes explicit, namely that the eucharistic terms 'coming together,' ἐπὶ τὸ αὐτό ["on this place," Acts 2: 44], "Lord's Supper,' etc., are identified with the ecclesiological terms 'ἐκκλησία or ἐκκλησία of God.' ...this local community is called *the whole Church...* (Rom. 16:23)." John D. Zizioulas, *Being As Communion* (Crestwood, N.Y., St. Vladimir's Seminary Press, 1985) p. 148

39 Stanley Harakas, "The Local Church-An Eastern Orthodox Perspective," *The Ecumenical Review* (April, 1977) p. 141

40 "It is clear from Ignatian ecclesiology as a whole that not only does a 'universal Church' not exist in Ignatius' mind but, on the contrary, an identification of the whole Christ and the whole Church with the local episcopal community constitutes a key idea in his thought..." John D. Zizioulas, *Being As Communion* (Crestwood, N.Y., St. Vladimir's Seminary Press, 1985) ftnte 3, pp. 143, 144

41 And in those places where it is a designation of the Church "at large" (i.e. in Ephesians) whatever is said is also applicable to the local gathering. As Paul uses the term in the generally accepted epistles, *ekklesia* appears fifty times. In twenty instances the term is in the plural. In the thirty occurrences of the singular it is generally evident that the term refers to a particular meeting or gathering of a small number of believers in a given locale. In only five instances (1 Cor. 15:9; Gal. 1:13; Phil. 3:6; and 1 Cor. 10:32 and 12:28) is it apparent that the primary referent *may be* the entire aggregate of believers in the whole world. The first three of these five instances all have to do with Paul as a persecutor of the gathering; 1 Cor 10:32 speaks of 'Jews or Greeks, or God's gathering'; Ephesians 4 says that God has appointed in the Gathering apostles, prophets, teachers, et al. It is evident that Paul finds it easy and congenial to use the plural and that it is the exception rather than the rule for him to speak of the *ekklesia* as the totality of believers."

John Meyendorff, Joseph McLelland, eds., "The Christian Community in the Second Century", Stuart D. Currie, *The New Man: An Orthodox and Reformed Dialogue*, (New Jersey, Standard Press, 1973) p. 94

42 Donald Guthrie, *New Testament Theology,* (Downers Grove, IL., Inter-Varsity Press, 1981) p.

43 "...not that all churches together constitute one vast, unique organism, but that each Church—in the identity of order, faith and the gifts of the Holy Spirit— is the *same* Church, the same body of Christ, indivisibly present wherever is the 'ecclesia.' It is thus the same organic unity of the church herself, the 'Churches' being not complementary to each other, as parts or members, but each one and all of them together being nothing else but the One, Holy, catholic and Apostolic Church. It is this ontological [real and actual] identity of all Churches with the Church of God that establish the connecting link between Churches, making them the Church universal." John Meyendorff et. al., "The Idea of Primacy in Orthodox Ecclesiology," Alexander Schmemann,*The Primacy of Peter*, (Bedfordshire, England, The Faith Press, 1963) p. 40

44 "It was natural that Paul should think in the same way of the new community [i.e. the Church]..." F. F. Bruce, *The New International Commentary on the New Testament: The Epistles to the Colossians, to Philemon and to the Ephesians* (Grand rapids, MI., Wm. B. Eerdmans Publishing Company, 1984) pp. 237, 238

45 For example, Paul felt no contradiction in praising Gaius for being a host to him "and to the *whole* church" (Rom. 16:23). Here he gives a direct ascription of "wholeness" (catholicity) to the *local* Church which gathered there.

46 Robert Webber, Donald Bloesch, eds., *The Orthodox Evangelicals* , "A Call to Church Unity" F. Burton Nelson, (New York, Thomas Nelson, 1977) p. 195 Rom. 1:7, I Cor. 1:2; Eph. 1:1; Philp. 1:1; Col 1:2; I Thess. 1:1; II Thess 1:1, etc.

47 John Meyendorff, "The Orthodox Concept of the Church," *St. Vladimir's Quarterly* (Crestwood, New York, St. Vladimir's Press, 1962) Vol. 6, No. 2, pp. 60, 61

48 "The Church is not simply inspired or animated or led by the Spirit; she is constituted by him *as* the body of Christ. ...this constitutive function of the Spirit transcends fully the dilemma between locality and catholicity: the two exist in each other in the very roots of the Church's existence. This is what allowed the early Church ever since the time of Paul to use the word *ekklesia* for both the totality of the Church and the local Church without any difficulty." J. D. Zizioulas, "The Pneumatological Dimension of the Church," *International Catholic Review*, Vol. II, No. 2, 1973, italics mine.

49 One cannot celebrate the eucharist "universally," at least not until Christ comes back and His Kingdom is *fully* actualized on the earth.

50 Jerome J. Holtzman, "Eucharistic Ecclesiology of the Orthodox Theologians," *Diakonia* (1973) Vol. 8, p. *10*

51 Veselin Kesich, "Unity and Diversity In New Testament Ecclesiology," *St. Vladimir's Theological Quarterly* (Crestwood, New York, New York, St. Vladimir's Seminary Press, 1975) Volume 19, No. 2, pp. 119,120 citing (respectively) A. E. J. Rawlinson, "Corpus Christi," in *Mysterium Christi,* G.K. A. Bell and A. Deissmann eds., pp. 226,230 an Hans Conzelmann, *An Outline of the Theology of the New Testament* (New York: Harper and Row, 1969) p. 262

52 Hal Miller, *Christian Community: Biblical or Optional* , (Ann Arbor, MI., Servant Books, 1979) p. 68

"The word ekklesia is predominantly used for a local church in the New Testament. However, in the letters of Paul to the Ephesians and Colossians and in some other New Testament documents, the term expresses not a local but the universal catholic church (Matt. 16:18, Acts 20:28). The same term is used for both. The local church as the eucharistic community manifests the fulness of Christ. Each of them are related to each other, and their distinctive characteristics can be seen in terms of the eucharist. The local church as the eucharistic commute manifests the fulness of Christ. Each of them represents the whole Christ, and hence incarnates the catholic church." Veselin Kesich, "Unity and Diversity In New Testament

Ecclesiology," *St. Vladimir's Theological Quarterly* (Crestwood, New York, New York, St. Vladimir's Seminary Press, 1975) Volume 19, No. 2, p. 111

53 This image of the Church is referred to as "eucharistic ecclesiology", and by its nature excludes any Local Church from exercising control *over* another Local Church. See Jerome J. Holtzman, "Eucharistic Ecclesiology of the Orthodox Theologians," *Diakonia* (1973) Vol. 8, p. 11 citing "Das Hirtenamt der Kirche: in der Liebe der Germeinde vorstehen," N. Affanassief, *Der Primat des Petrus in der orthodoxen Kirche* (Zurich: EVZ Verlag, 1961) p. 34

54 Such a eucharistic insight into the nature of the Church justifies asking the question, "Is a universal structure of the Church really necessary, although it is obviously not determined directly by the Eucharist...?" John Meyendorff, *Living Tradition*, (Crestwood, New York, St. Vladimir's Seminary Press, 1978) p. 146

55 "Power over a Local church would mean power over a eucharistic assembly, or in other words, over Christ himself." Emilianos Timiadis, "'Consensus in the Formulation of Doctrine," *The Greek Orthodox Theological Review* (Brookline, MA., Holy Cross Orthodox Press, 1980) Spring, Vol. XXV, No. 1, p. 31

56 "The moment they [the Local Churches] would admit a supra-local structure over the local eucharistic community, be it a synod or another office, the eucharistic community would cease to be in itself and *by virtue of its eucharistic nature* a 'catholic Church." John D. Zizioulas, *Being As Communion* (Crestwood, N.Y., St. Vladimir's Seminary Press, 1985) pp. 156, 157

57 "Orthodox ecclesiology does not know any divinely appointed, institutional power of one local church *over* the other local churches and their bishops. It recognizes the existence of local primacies, and it always accepted the idea that one Church, that of Jerusalem, that of Rome, later that of Constantinople, may play the role of a universal arbiter, may enjoy the right to receive appeals, a right established and regulated by the Councils, and in fact may preside over the universal episcopate. But this 'primacy' does not confer on the bishop of Rome or of Constantinople either infallibility or universal jurisdiction, but as kind of 'priority' in settling controversial matters for the common good." Such is a position to be gained by respect, it is not an "assigned" office, nor are the judgements rendered by those in this position either guaranteed as infallible or demand obedience in the juridical sense. John Meyendorff, "The Orthodox Concept of the Church," *St. Vladimir's Quarterly* (Crestwood, New York, St. Vladimir's Press, 1962) Vol. 6, No. 2, p. 70

58 John D. Zizioulas, *Being As Communion* (Crestwood, N.y., St. Vladimir's Seminary Press, 1985) pp. 156, 157

59 This perspective, of course, is much more similar to the Reformed view of the Church than it is to the Roman Catholic view: "...Orthodox and Reformed should find a basis for encounter and perhaps even for solid agreement if for no other reason than the fact that both traditions have an ecclesiology governed by the conviction that while a local church may not be the whole church, it is wholly Church." Joseph C. McLelland, "The Orthodox Church and the Churches of the Reformation: A Survey of Orthodox - Protestant Dialogues," (Geneva, WCC Faith and Order Commission, 1975) Faith and Order Paper No. 76, p. 92

60 Elmer O' Brien, S. J., ed., *The Convergence of Traditions* , "The Orthodox Tradition," Alexander Schmemann, (New York, Herder and Herder, 1967) pp. 14, 15

61 Archbishop Basil of Brussels, "Catholicity and the Structures of the Church," *St. Vladimir's Theological Quarterly* (Crestwood, N.Y., St. Vladimir's Seminary Press, 1973) vol. 17, No. 1-2, p. 46

"'As in God each one of the Three Persons, Father, Son and Holy Spirit, is not a part of the Trinity, but fully God in virtue of His ineffable identity with the One [Divine] Nature, so the Church is not a federation of her parts: she is catholic in each of her parts, since each part in her is identified with the whole, expresses the whole, has the value which the whole has, does not exist outside the whole.'" Dumitru Staniloae, *Theology and the Church* (Crestwood, N.Y., St. Vladimir's Seminary Press, 1980) p.

65 citing V. Lossky, "Concerning the Third Mark of the Church: Catholicity," *One Church* 19 (1965) p. 181-187

62 Each Person inter-dwells *within* the Other without commingling, coalescing or ceasing to be distinct. Despite its divine characteristics, the Church's human limitation prevent it from ever attaining the perfection of union existing in the Godhead.

63 John Meyendorff, "The Orthodox Concept of the Church," *St. Vladimir's Quarterly* (Crestwood, New York, St. Vladimir's Press, 1962) Vol. 6, No. 2, p. 61

64 See Cyprian's *The Unity of the Catholic Church*

CHAPTER ELEVEN

THE IMPOSSIBLITY OF "INDIVIDUALISM" - THE CHURCH AS COMMUNITY

Koinonia (κοινωνία) is the Greek word translated by our English New Testaments as *communion*, *association*, *fellowship*, *sharing*, *common*, *contribution*, and *partnership.* Not one of these words, however, adequately captures what the early Christians meant when they spoke of the koinonia they had with one another and Christ. Koinonia expressed a relationship of great intimacy and depth, one so rich in fact that it even became the "favorite expression for the marital relationship ... the most intimate between human beings."[1] The implications of this word when used to express the nature of our bond with Christ and the brethren are especially profound.

> ...κοινωνία implies a closeness of union approaching identity. Hence the significance of its use to express the believer's union with the 'Son of God, Jesus Christ our Lord' (1 Cor. 1:9), and with the Holy Ghost (2 Cor. 13:14 and Phil. 2:1)...With St. John indeed it is the predominant and determining note of Christianity. For the Fellowship as defined by him is only another word for that brotherhood or brotherly love (φιλαδελφια) which makes the difference between darkness and light (I John 2:9f), and is therefore the essential characteristic of one who calls himself a Christian..."[2]

For one to have fellowship with another Christian in the early Church meant much more to him than what it means today to many contemporary Christians. (i.e., Christians having donuts and coffee together in the "fellowship" [social] hall after the Sunday service). Genuine fellowship demonstrates "that bond which binds Christians to each other, to Christ and to God."[3] Fellowship is all inclusive, deep, personal and intimate. The "meaning of 'fellowship' or 'communion' in the New Testament relates to sharing one common life within the body of Christ at all levels of existence and experience — spiritual, social, intellectual, economic. No area of life can be excluded."[4]

The Church is not simply a society; it is fellowship *in* God and *with* God. Every description of the Church is simply another way of expressing the depth of this fellowship: the Body of Christ, Ekklesia, Temple of the Spirit, covenant, Eucharist, catholicity, brotherhood, the life of God, etc. [5] This is why one can say salvation is of the Church.

> Christianity from the very beginning existed as a corporate reality, as a community. To be Christian meant just to belong to the community. Nobody could be Christian by himself, as an isolated individual, but only together with 'the brethren,' in a 'togetherness' with them ... Christianity means a 'common life,' a life in common.[6]

INDIVIDUALISM: THE ADVERSARY OF THE CHURCH

The dictionary defines individualism as, "the leading of one's life in one's own way without regard for others."[7] The above description of the Church clearly leaves no room for this attitude. The Church—as community—will always be opposed to individualism. The nature of the Church is *love,* and where there is love there is union, fellowship, interdependence - not self-imposed isolation and indifference to others.

The individualistic attitudes of today have deformed our thinking about the Church, and directly oppose the Lord's greatest commandment to "love one another as oneself" (Mark 12:23). Many Christians demonstrate individualism in their Christianity, thinking it is a sign of discipleship, when in actuality it weakens them and the bond of genuine fellowship within the Church. Such a one is the independent, "spiritual" person who typically stresses private devotions, theological knowledge, or "ministries" *over* relationships of love, sharing, and interpersonal commitment. Unconsciously he has given in to a destroying individualistic spirit, one which will injure his communion with God and the saints by drawing him away from the center of life.

THE ORIGINS OF INDIVIDUALISTIC "SPIRITUALITY"

Individualistic piety had its beginnings before the Reformation, but it has been especially encouraged within Reformation philosophies, American revivalism and Dispensationalism. Let's take a brief look at each of these outlooks now, and see how they have affected today's Christian thinking. In order to fight against Rome's institutional conception of the Church (i.e., If you are not a part of the structure headed by Christ's proxy, the Pope, you are not a Christian), many in the Fifteenth Century gravitated toward nominalistic thought. The subjective individualism of nominalism advocated an "individualizing" view of the Church which not only challenged Rome's false institutionalism, but also countered the Church's true communal nature. The result of this view led the Reformers and those following them to dismiss the *inherent inter-relatedness of each member* within the Church, and to replace it with a vision which saw the Church as "only the sum of *individual* believers."[8] Both Luther and Calvin elaborated their doctrines of salvation from this individualistic premise.

Instead of seeing one's union with Christ as *inseparable* from the Church (the divine-human community where He dwells in covenant with His people), the Reformers began to imply that one's membership in Christ and one's membership to the institutional Church could be separated.[9] The "visible" Church became the Church *only* in an institutional sense. As we have already discussed, one could be a member of it on earth, for example, yet not be a member of the Church in heaven. It is this dichotomistic and individualistic emphasis which still leads many Protestants today to ignore the *inherent* communal nature of both the Church and of salvation. Salvation is communal because salvation is union with Christ (Rom. 6: 1-5), and He dwells within *His Body*, the Church.

In America, this individualization of Christianity accelerated further when *sola Scriptura* was employed to justify the legitimacy of an even more individualistic spirituality. Dr. George Marsden in his book *Fundamentalism and American Culture*, notes that the American individualistic understanding of the Church can be directly traced back to the Fundamentalist's approach to the Scriptures.

> The Bible alone should be one's guide. Biblicism was closely related to religious individualism ... The individual stood alone before God; his choices were decisive. The church, while important as a supportive community, was made up of free individuals.[10]

In this view, the Bible evolved into "the earthly essence of the church..."[11] and the argument became, "Who needs others for guidance or instruction when one has the Bible to guide and teach?" Who needs people, when one has a concordance? Thus, "each individual becomes his own church; [and] his own sanctification is the only holiness the church can know."[12]

Individualism was particularly emphasized in American revivalism, especially as it was typified by Dwight L. Moody (1837-99). This renowned preacher continually underscored "religious" individualism in his mass evangelistic crusades. Moody, having inherited only an institutional understanding of the Church, saw salvation solely as an "individual" matter. Of course, it is clear that a human organization can not save. Unfortunately, neither having witnessed nor understood the Church as a divine-human Community, Moody could not see how someone was redeemed *in* the Body of Christ. To him salvation was purely a "personal" matter. Logically, he did not call the new disciple to see his commitment to Christ as an equal commitment to his brethren in the *ekklesia.* The new convert was only taught that his primary concern was to "win the lost" and maintain his own private holiness.[13]

The Dispensational view of the Bible took religious individualism even further still. By contrasting the New Testament period with the era of the Old Testament, Dispensationalism taught that whereas the Lord had previously led *a people through the Law*, now He leads *individuals* through the *personal* indwelling of the Spirit. Where Old Testament Israel was a *united people*, the Holy Spirit of the New Covenant works with unrelated, believing "individuals." The Church as a "holy *people,*" and as "a holy *nation* " (I Peter 2:9) is ignored in favor of the autonomous "Spirit-led" individuals.[14] Thus, the Dispensationalist doctrine allowed many Fundamentalists to stand removed from the mainline religious bodies of which they once were a part, in order to claim themselves a "faithful remnant,"[15] those who separated themselves from the fallen multitudes ("church"). The consequence was that the core of the New Testament Christian experience was distorted; Christianity became a thing focused on the individual instead of a communal entity.

All the above views which undergirded religious individualism were based on the Augustinian dualism we discussed in the last chapter. Each view saw *two* churches: one visible and earthly, the other spiritual and heavenly. The "church" here (on the earth) came to be seen as a beachhead from which people could be evangelized into the "heavenly church," and as a classroom where "personal" holiness could be taught; only secondarily was it an environment of relationships. Fellowship with Christians was "nice," but it certainly wasn't *necessary* for godliness or instruction in the Christian life, nor was it a requirement for Christian service. By such a focus, the Church's call to model the communal love of the Trinity is repudiated by the greatest of contradictions: *self -focused* spirituality.

COMMUNITY: LOVE COMBATING INDIVIDUALISM

Unfortunately, most Christians see the Church only as a place where they can get their private spiritual needs met. The Church, however, is foremost to be an environment of love where brethren care about each other. It is a family in communion, not a forum. Individualism and self centered independence are not characteristics of God's Church, they are characteristics of the world outside of Christ.[16] It is *love*, for God and the people of God, which makes the Church community.[17]

Unity within God's family is not achieved by getting one member to submit to another member of a "higher spiritual rank", or by persuading numbers of people to conform to a set of laws intended to order them into oneness. The military may do this, but the Church leads us another way: the way of love— *here* is "the *perfect* bond of unity" (Col. 3:14).[18] A "unity" attained through laws, common teaching, intimidation, or anything else but participation in God's love and life is counterfeit.[19]

This brings us face to face with the reality that the Church is specifically *relationships of love*. As is true with all relationships, one can truly know the other only by the experience of relating to each other, not by academic study. It is this interaction - this communion - which makes us into the image of Christ. When one enters the Church, a spiritual encounter of knowing takes place, and in this encounter one is transformed by the love of God and His people.[20] In order to have real communion within the Church, each person must be open, trusting, and willing to be actively involved in "giving—receiving" relationships of love. Love and the voluntary, selfless sharing of our lives are the only philosophy of life appropriate in the body of Christ.

In short, "There can be no Church apart from love." [21] Paul said that we are called to be "imitators of God" in loving one another (Eph. 5:1, 2), and John tells us that love is the only way that we "behold God" in our midst:

> "Beloved, if God so loved us, we also ought to love one another. No one has beheld God at any time; if we love one another, God abides in us, and His love is perfected in us." (1 John 4:11, 12)

Without question, to love is "the *greatest* commandment" (Matt. 22: 36-40) and the intent of the entire Scriptures is fulfilled in this: "'You shall love your neighbor as yourself'" (Gal. 5:14). To be in the Church is to identify with Christ, and He made it clear that those who so identify with Him must love with divine love:

> "'A new commandment I give to you, that you love one another, even as I have loved you, that you also love one another. By this all men will know that you are My disciples, if you have love for one another.'" (John 13: 34, 35)

At the Church in Jerusalem, "all those who had believed were together and had all things in common" (Acts 2:44). Why? Because someone ordered them to give? Because they would feel guilty if they did not give? No. These Christians gave generously to their needy brethren *out of compassion.* They understood they were members of the same family.[22] This is the way of love. This is the way of the Church. This is the way of koinonia — "the spirit of generous sharing as contrasted with the spirit of selfish getting."[23]

Love is the only commandment in the Church necessary to manifest our unity (and union) in Christ. Let us *accept one another just as Christ has accepted us* (Rom. 15:7); let each member *care* for the other (1 Cor. 12:25); let us *love* one another just *as He has loved us* (John 15:10, 12). If we love in this way, we cannot help but be drawn into oneness. Love — which is vulnerable, open and accepting of all— leads each into genuine Christian unity.

> In love we are merged into one. 'The quality of love is such that the loving and the beloved are no more two but one man.' Even more: true Christian love sees in everyone of our brethren 'Christ Himself.' Such love demands self-surrender, self-mastery. Such love is possible only in a catholic expansion and transfiguration of the soul. [24]

Truly, the closer we come to Christ in love, the closer we will come to those who have similarly given themselves to Him in the open embrace of catholicity. Catholic union was manifested in that very first Church: "the multitude of them that believed were of one heart and of one soul" (Acts 2:44). Are we living catholic lives? Our love should show it. The Church never limits or restricts love, and her members must actively shun exclusivity or possessiveness. In the love of koinonia, "The cold separation into 'mine' and 'thine' disappears."[25] Each member does not forfeit the responsibility for his own spiritual growth in this communion. The striving for "perfection" in Christ is still up to each unique person but, we are not perfected as loners, we are "perfected in *unity* " (John 17: 23). [26] This holiness occurs only when each chooses to love his brethren.

In the early second century, a document known as The Shepherd of Hermas included a popular vision of the Church that underscored this aspect of union and love. In this vision, the Church was seen as a tower of stones. It was not just any ordinary tower, however. The tower was composed of rocks that were so closely fit together so that the edge of each individual stone disappeared into the borders of the others. When one looked at the tower, he got the impression that it was constructed of only one large stone instead of the thousands that actually constituted it. Naturally this caused the observer to wonder just how such a structure could be built. The answer was the point of the vision: only with stones that had both sharp edges and smooth surfaces. The builder of this unique tower had flatly rejected all round stones. What does this rejection signify?

In that time and culture, roundness was a symbol signifying isolation, self-sufficiency, and self-satisfaction. The early Christians, seeing that such round stones were unfit for the tower representing the Church, realized by analogy that people of "rounded-character" would likewise be unfit in the fabric of the Church. A "rounded disposition" made a stone unwilling to come into communion with what already comprised the structure. [27] The point in those earliest centuries was clear: there is no place in a kingdom of sharing and fellowship for the individualist. Only those "living stones" that choose to fit in with all the other stones will be built by Christ into His Body, the Church.

COMMUNITY — LOVING SPECIFIC PEOPLE ONE KNOWS

Loving one another in Community (Church) truly happens when we start to love people *whom we know personally.* It is much easier to love one's brethren in China than to love those with whom one must constantly rub elbows. Christians within the first Communities were not strangers who met only at weekly church services. They had *ongoing, significant, relationships* with people with whom they spoke, worked, lived, ate, laughed and cried. To live out such an ideal may be difficult today, but the nature of the Church makes it clear that some kind of *relational environment* should be the common Christian experience.

If it is difficult for us to live as Church, we must work at making it easier. We must accept sacrifices of time, money or convenience if we are to live as Christians embracing the mandate of the Scriptures. The pull of this present age against any kind of long term relationships makes it all the more clear that we can never be whole without a determination to pursue true fellowship and communion. Our society may have made the realization of these truths more complex, but the meaning and need of communion has not changed!

It is true that each Christian is a member of the one Church no matter how far he or she may be geographically removed from other Christians. However, one cannot *experience* the Community of Christ - the love of the brethren - "long distance." Agreed, in the End Time when Christ establishes His Kingdom in its fullness, all will have such a communion with each other. But for now, *on this side* of eternity, one can only taste this communion *within the Local Church with local people.* Only in *this* context can one experience meaningful *fellowship* with Christ and one another. Howard Snyder, in his insightful book, *The Problem of Wine Skins*, makes this point well:

> The New Testament idea of *koinonia* is not fully understood until we grasp the significance of the horizontal and vertical dimensions *together.* Typical church 'fellowship' seldom reaches the level of *koinonia* because *koinonia* is neither understood, expected nor sought. ... koinonia *is not simply some mystical communion that exists without reference to the structure of the church..* We may talk in abstract terms about 'the fellowship of the church,' as though it were something that automatically, and almost by definition, binds together. But the abstract concept is hollow apart from the actual gathering together of believers at a particular point in time and space. We cannot escape this *...one cannot have fellowship with another believer who is not present*, despite our mystical language.[28]

THE TRINITY AS THE CHURCH'S MODEL OF COMMUNITY

The perfect fellowship that the Holy Trinity experiences as Father, Son, and Spirit is ultimately represented by the same spiritual reality among the members of the Church. The same love that makes God One is the love that makes the Church One.[29] As each member of the Godhead willingly submits to the Others out of love, without yielding His unique identity, so it is to be with each member of the Church with his fellow members.[30] In many other similar respects, the Church as Community reflects the fellowship of the Trinity...[31]

> Not only do Christians 'praise the Father' and 'form the body of Christ' and 'live in the Spirit,' but in addition the Christian life is to be found in the mutuality of their shared life in God ... Just as the Trinity is a community of persons united in one essence, so too, is the Local parish ... a community of persons which finds its common life in the persons of that same divine essence by participation. [32]

The God of the Christians is *different* from the God of the Moslem or Jew who denies the New Testament revelation. The dogma of the Trinity is not an empty intellectual exercise created by early theologians with nothing better to do. The Trinity is a revelation of the very character of God inherent to the message of the Gospel, because it reveals the truth that the "Christian God is not just a unit but a *union,* not just unity but *community.* ...He is Tri-unity; three equal persons, each one dwelling in the other two by virtue of an unceasing movement of mutual love." [33] Here is the lesson for the Church. As a "one Personed" God is a contradiction to both God's love and divinity,[34] so is "Christian individualism" a contradiction to all that it means to be "in Christ." One person can not have communion alone, he must share his life with others to experience it.

The love between the Persons of the Trinity teaches us something else about our relationships in the Church. Just as each Person in the Godhead never loses His identity as their love is shared with one another, so is this truth to be fundamental for life and relationships within the Church. The personal dimension of the Christian life is never to be sacrificed at the expense of the corporate "good." What is not good for the person is not good for the Body. Conversely, what is good for the Body will always be what is good for the individual Christian. Whether the focus is on the one, the few, or the many, genuine love gives, frees, and strengthens *all those involved.*

The members of the Church are not merely indistinguishable cells within the Body, they are *complete, unique, human personalities.* Each person's uniqueness must be respected and revered as a gift of God, not obliterated in the cause of uniformity. In actuality, The Trinity, as the Church's model, shows us that there can be "no unity without diversity of persons, and no person fully realized outside natural unity. Catholicity consists in the perfect harmony of these two terms: unity and diversity...".[35] The Church may be One, but it is not one member. Each member has a place, and each person's distinctiveness is to be harmonized with the distinctive personalities and gifts of the other.

> Christian 'togetherness' must not degenerate into impersonalism. The idea of the organism must be supplemented by the idea of a symphony of personalities, in which the mystery of the Holy Trinity is reflected...[36]

The Holy Spirit did not fall upon *isolated* individuals, but upon the (gathered) Church at Pentecost. This truth, however, does not negate the fact that He did fill *each* individual person.[37] In this miracle, the Holy Spirit made it clear that the specific identity of each person *is* important, and that the Church needs *each* member. He has neither given all His gifts to one, nor has He given the same one gift to each; He has given a *variety* of gifts to *many.* This teaches us that every member of the Body is not only *different* from other members, but that each *needs* the other's uniqueness in order to be complete.[38]

The Holy Spirit did not come to bring unity by squeezing our distinctiveness into a blurred, non-personal glob. He respects our individual identities and encourages a diversity led from a love for the common good (1 Cor. 12:7). Each of us is different not only in the gifts God has given us, but in our personalities, experiences, and characters as well. This wonderful diversity is truly a gift of God to the Church. Uniformity is not at all the same as unity. In fact, it is an obstacle to it. If the entire Body were but one *uniform* member — if all were a hand for instance— how could each member be "connected" to the other? This sameness would actually *prevent* the unity of the Body, not encourage it. [39]

Even in God's creation of man and woman, this dual principle of distinctiveness and unity speaks to us. A man does not love a woman because she is identical with him; her distinct "femininity" draws him close. And it is this distinctiveness which can fill his loneliness and make him "whole" (Gen. 2:18) in a way that no one of his own sex could. The same is true for a woman in her love for a man. Lastly, only their union in diversity makes them "one flesh." This degree of union is something not possible for two of the same sex. Here yet is even a deeper significance: *only they together, united in diversity and love, mirror the image of God's love in creation* (for *both, together*, revealed His image and likeness). [40]

THE COMMUNITY AS THE TEMPLE OF THE HOLY SPIRIT

THE HOLY SPIRIT'S DWELLING WITHIN A PEOPLE

It is unquestioned that the Holy Spirit resides within each believer, and that each person is a temple of the Holy Spirit (2 Cor. 6:16). Yet, the ministry of the Spirit is not to make Spirit-filled individuals alone, but primarily to create a dwelling for Himself *within and among a people* .[41] In fact, this *corporate, communal* dimension is spoken of more frequently in the Scriptures than the personal and individual one.

This understanding of the Church *as a people* can sometimes be more apparent in the Greek text of the New Testament than it is in our English versions. The pronoun "you" in 1 Cor. 3:16, for example, is not in the singular but in the plural. Thus, although many tend to read the passage "you [as an individual] are a temple of God," it would be more accurate to read it as "*you -all [together]* are a temple of God." Let us keep this reading in mind as we look further at this and a few other similar passages.

> For we are God's fellow-workers; you [all] are God's field, God's building. ... Do you not know that you [all] are a temple of God, and that the Spirit of God dwells in you [all]?...the temple of God is holy, and that is what you [all] are. (1 Cor. 3:10, 16, 17)

> For by one Spirit we were *all* baptized *into one body* ..and we were *all* made *to drink of one Spirit.* (1 Cor. 12:13)

> And coming to Him as to a living stone, rejected by men, but choice and precious in the sight of God, you [all] also, *as living stones, are being built up as a spiritual house* for a holy priesthood, to offer up spiritual sacrifices acceptable to God through Jesus Christ. (1 Peter 2: 4, 5)

> So then you [all] are no longer strangers and aliens, but you [all] are fellow-citizens with the saints, and *are of God's household,* having built upon the

> foundation of the apostles and prophets, Christ Jesus Himself being the cornerstone, *in whom the whole building, being fitted together* is growing into a holy temple in the Lord; in whom you [all-together] also are *being built together* into a dwelling of God in the Spirit. (Eph. 2:19-22)

This inter-connectedness is further illustrated in the Old Testament where the Septuagint uses the word koinonia as a synonym for "*put together,*" "*coupled* " or "*joined.*" [42] The word was used to describe how the Temple was to be *joined* together in its construction. This usage now applies to the Temple of God of the New Covenant (Eph. 2:21). The Church of God is built in the koinonia of the Spirit, one member being "built together" with another in accord with the design of Christ, the chief Cornerstone.

"The church provides the context for spiritual growth by sharing *together* a fellowship which is at once the *gift* of the Spirit and the *environment* in which he may operate."[43] The Spirit's home ("dwelling place") is the Church. Here He works miracles, heals, speaks prophetically, delivers from evil, imparts knowledge, anoints its members to pray. And all of this is done, not for the individual (though he benefits), but that each may be edified (literally "built" together) as the body of Christ - as the People of God - as the Church. For this reason, we can say that the manifestation of the Spirit is *FULLY* expressed only in the Church. Orthodox theologian and historian John Zizioulas summarizes why this is the case:

> . . . the Holy Spirit is the bond of love and wherever he "blows" he does not create good individual Christians but *persons in communion* with God and with one another, i.e., he creates a *community.* It is in this sense that it remains a fundamental and irrefutable truth that the Spirit exists only in the Church, the community *par excellence*, the Body of Christ, and that all spiritual gifts, such as inspiration, *charisma*, ministry, etc. cannot be conceived as possessions of individuals, but can exist only in *persons in communion*, i.e., in the context of the ecclesial [Church] community. [44]

CONCLUSION

The call of the Church is to continually *realize* what it is: *the Body of Christ.* We need to agree with God's perspective concerning what He has done with humankind through Christ, and then rediscover what it means to be *a people who live in the communion of His love.* The Church is a family, an organism, a community, and unless the world is able to *see* this reality by the way we love one another, our own message of Life will mock us. Although the individualist may be popular in our culture, he is incompatible with Christ's view of the Church, and it is not our job to make him comfortable. The Church is first and last a manifestation of God's love. If we are to manifest this Church, we must love in divine measure (John 13:35).

The first step in meeting this challenge to love demands that we come against our own apathy. In our society, we have redefined "love" to mean "warmly tolerate." As long as someone does not ask *too* much of us in our relationships, and as long as the exit from intimacy remains accessible, we can be "loving." In other words, as long as we do not "hate" our brethren, we "love" them. This is not the love of communion. Christian love is not indifferent. It commits itself to others tangibly, practically, and daily. It requires interpersonal risk, it takes the initiative to heal, and it desires to meet the genuine needs of others. If we long to love with this kind of integrity and sincerity, we will love the way God does: in Community and communion.

NOTES FOR CHAPTER ELEVEN

1 William F. Arndt, F. Wilbur Gingrich, "κοινωνία," *A Greek-English Lexicon of the New Testament and Other Early Christian Literature* , (Chicago, Il., The University of Chicago Press, 1957) p. 439

2 Arthur Carr, "The 'Fellowship' of Acts 2:42 and Cognate Words," *Expositor* p. 462

3 William Barclay, "The Christian Fellowship," *New Testament Words,* pp. 173, 174

4 John Driver, *Community and Commitment,* (Scottdale, PA., 1976) p. 28

5 "While the Church cannot be fully defined, she may be described as a community of human persons in communion with the three divine persons. The Church is an expression of both horizontal and vertical relationships of love which are not bound by space and time. ....In our own day, the tendency to reduce the reality of the Church to a society of human persons gathered about a doctrine, a ritual or an ethical code is especially dangerous. In such a sociological view of the Church, she becomes simply a fraternal, political or ethnic association which is void of the transcendent reality. Viewed from this perspective, the Church is certainly not an object of faith." Thomas FitzGerald, "The Holy Eucharist as Theophany," *Greek Orthodox Theological Review* (Brookline, MA., Hellenic Cross Press, 1983) Vol. 28, p. 31

6 Georges Florovsky, *Bible, Church, Tradition: An Eastern Orthodox View* p. 59

7 *Webster's New World Dictionary* (Cleveland and New York, The World Publishing Company, 1959) p. 743

8 Joseph Lortz, "Why Did the Reformation Happen?", *The Reformation: Material or Spiritual?* , Lewis W. Spitz, ed., (Lexington, MA., 1962) p. 61, italics mine.

9 Gustaf Aulen, *Reformation and Catholicity* (London, Oliver and Boyd Ltd., 1962) p. 48 It should be noted that although Calvin had this perspective, he still stressed a covenantal view of the Church. Luther, however, did not even stress this aspect of the Church in favor of a more "spiritual" view: " The fundamental aspect of his [Luther's] view of the church is the antithesis between the external and the internal; the distinction between that which is external, bodily, and visible, and that which is Christian and spiritual. ...The church thus becomes merely something 'inward,' the spiritual fellowship constituted by the faith given by the Holy Spirit. Thus the idea of the church as precisely that body which in itself includes and fosters this fellowship is rejected." *ibid,.* p. 29

10 George M. Marsden, *Fundamentalism and American Culture* (Oxford, Oxford University Press, 1980) p. 224

11 "The Bible is ... the supreme tangible sacred reality. If you possess a Bible, you have the earthly essence of the church ... The Bible in fundamentalism is comparable to the virgin Mary in Roman Catholicism: it is the human visible symbol involved in salvation ..." James Barr, *Fundamentalism* (Philadelphia, The Westminster Press, 1978) p. 36

12 Ernest R. Sandeen, *The Origins of Fundamentalism* (Philadelphia, Fortress Press, 1968) ftne. 13, p. 6

13 "Moody rose to fame in the heyday of American individualism and his thought is pervaded by its assumptions. The sins he stressed were personal sins, not involving victims besides oneself and members of one's family. The sinner stood alone before God." George M. Marsden. *Fundamentalism and American Culture* (Oxford, Oxford University Press, 1980) p. 37

14 "The important spiritual unit was the individual. The church existed as a body of sanctified individuals united by commitment to Christ and secondarily as a network of *ad hoc* spiritual

organizations." George M. Marsden. *Fundamentalism and American Culture* (Oxford, Oxford University Press, 1980) p. 71

15 "The Church was made up of God's elect who were always only a handful and seldom if ever the possessors of power. The true church could not possibly be identified with any of the large denominations... but could only be formed by individual Christians who could expect to be saved from the impending destruction." Ernest R. Sandeen, *The Origins of Fundamentalism* (Philadelphia, Fortress Press, 1968) pp. 5, 6

16 "The individuality of the members is only a secondary characteristic of the one body ... We shall never understand Paul's concept of the church if we begin our theological thinking with the individual Christian and consider the church as something like a social gathering or an association of individuals sharing some common interests." Robert Webber, Donald Bloesch, eds., *The Orthodox Evangelicals* , "A Call to Church Unity" F. Burton Nelson, (New York, Thomas Nelson, 1977) p. 194 citing Eduard Schweizer, *The Church as the Body of Christ* (Richmond: John Knox Press, 1964) p. 63

17 To their credit Anabaptist groups have had a consistently strong emphasis on this: "' ... whoever eats and drinks alone, the same has fellowship with Judas, who [it is true] ate and drank with the other disciples from the bread and drink of the Lord. But he would not have community in the common brotherly love ... '" Franklin H. Littell, *The Origins of Sectarian Protestantism* (New York,The Macmillan Company, 1964) p. 97 citing Lydia Müler, ed., *Glaubenszeugnise oberdeutchdher Taufgesinnter* , 1938, p. 109

18 Certainly as love cannot be "commanded," neither can communion come about through laws; "... freedom and distinctiveness *define* the ontological fact of communion; there is no communion unless participation in it is free and distinctive." Christos Yannaras, *The Freedom of Morality*, (Crestwood, N.Y., St. Vladimir's Seminary Press, 1984) p. 212

19 "And unity cannot survive without charity. If anyone speaks of unity and lacks charity, he speaks in vain. Unity achieved at the expense of charity, or maintained at the expense of charity, will not survive for long and is never authentic. The most essential of all virtues then is unity—inner brotherhood and love." Metropolitan Emilianos Timiadis, "The Eucharist: The Basis of All Sacraments and Union With God," *The Patristic and Byzantine Review* (Kingston, N.Y.., American Institute for Patristic Studies, 1984) Vol. 3, No. 3, p. 186

20 Col. 3:9, 10,14; Gal. 5: 22, 23

21 Kallistos Ware, *The Orthodox Way* (Crestwood, New York, St. Vladimir's Seminary Press, 1980) citing John of Kronstadt, p. 51

22 "*Fellowship* in the New Testament describes a certain quality of richness of life, and was manifested in the experiment of holding all things in common. What is significant here is not the particular form of the experiment but the underlying concern and commitment for one another's well-being—and the dimension of solidarity that sought, by means of the bond of love, to remove all barriers of separation and hostility. ...This Fellowship binds together all Christians, not only for their own solidarity, but also for solidarity with all those for whose salvation Christ came." Metropolitan Emilianos Timiadis, "The Eucharist: The Basis of All Sacraments and Union With God," *The Patristic and Byzantine Review* (Kingston, N.Y.., American Institute for Patristic Studies, 1984) Vol. 3, No. 3, p. 179

23 William Barclay, "The Christian Fellowship," *New Testament Words,* pp. 173, 174

24 Georges Florovsky, *Bible, Church, Tradition: An Eastern Orthodox View* (Belmont, MA., Nordland Publishing Company, 1972) p. 42

25 Georges Florovsky, *Bible, Church, Tradition: An Eastern Orthodox View* (Belmont, MA., Nordland Publishing Company, 1972) pp. 41, 42

26 "Spirituality does not mean the accumulation of the experiences of a refined spirit, an undisturbed enjoyment of certain insights which can be cherished without reference to the community. True spirituality grows with the experience of the communion of many persons, with the understanding of the many

complex situations born in the life of communion." Dumitru Staniloae, *Theology and the Church,* (Crestwood, N.Y.. St. Vladimir's Seminary Press, 1980) p. 218

27 Georges Florovsky, *Bible, Church, Tradition: An Eastern Orthodox View* (Belmont, MA., Nordland Publishing Company, 1972) p. 43

28 Howard A. Snyder, *The Problem of Wine Skins*, (Downers Grove, IL., Inter-Varsity Press, 1975) pp. 91, 92 Italics his.

29 "The expression 'God is love' (I John 4:16) signifies that God 'subsists' as Trinity, that is, as person and not as substance. Love is not an emanation or 'property'...but is *constitutive* of His substance, i.e. it is that which makes God what He is, the one God. ...Love as God's mode of existence 'hypostasizes" God, *constitutes* His being." John D. Zizioulas, *Being As Communion* (Crestwood, N.Y.., St. Vladimir's Seminary Press, 1985) p. 46

30 "The Trinity is the culmination of the humility and sacrifice of love. It represents the continual mortification of each 'I', for it is the self-assertion of these 'I's' that would make the absolute unity of love impossible, and thus give birth to individualism. And it is the sins of individualism that hinders us from understanding fully that the Holy Trinity is a complete identification of 'I's" without their disappearance or destruction." Dumitru Staniloae, *Theology and the Church* (Crestwood, N.Y.., St. Vladimir's Seminary Press, 1980) p. 89

31 There is, however, a distinction to be made between the community and oneness we experience as human persons in the Church and the union and communion of the Divine Persons in the Trinity. This stems from the difference of natures. The common nature we share as human beings is distinct from the divine nature which each Member of the Trinity has in common:

> ... although Father, Son and Spirit are one single God, yet each of them is from all eternity a person, a distinct centre of conscious selfhood.. God the Trinity is thus to be described as 'three persons in one essence'. There is eternally in God ... personal differentiation ... Father, Son and Spirit are one in essence, not merely in the sense that all three are example of the same group or general class, but in the sense that they form a single, unique, specific reality. There is in this respect an important difference between the sense in which the three divine persons are one, and the sense in which three human persons may be termed one. Three human persons, Peter, James and John, belong to the same general class 'man.' Yet, however closely they co-operate together, each retains his own will and his own energy, acting by virtue of his own separate power of initiative. In short, they are three men and not one man. But in the case of the three persons of the Trinity, this is not the case. There is distinction, but never separation ... [they] have only one will and not three, only one energy, and not three. None of the three ever acts separately, apart from the other two. They are not three Gods, but one God. ..[The distinction is real but it] is beyond words and understanding. [For Each] of the Three is fully and completely God. None is more or less God than the others. Each possess, not one third of the Godhead, but the entire Godhead in its totality; yet each lives and is this one Godhead in his own distinctive and personal way. [According to Gregory of Nyssa] 'Using riddles, as it were, we envisage a strange and paradoxical diversity-in-unity and unity-in-diversity'.

Kallistos Ware, *The Orthodox Way* (Crestwood, New York, St. Vladimir's Seminary Press, 1980) p. 37, 38, 39

32 Stanley Harakas, "The Local Church-An Eastern Orthodox Perspective," *The Ecumenical Review* (April, 1977) pp. 16, 17

33 Kallistos Ware, *The Orthodox Way* (Crestwood, New York, St. Vladimir's Seminary Press, 1980) p. 33, Italics mine.

34 "The one, true and living God is not, and according to Orthodox theology cannot be, 'alone' in his divinity. If he were 'alone' he would not be God, for his very divine perfection is such that he has with himself—eternally and essentially, by nature and not by decision, by his being and not by deliberative

choice—his only-begotten Son, also called his personal Logos and Image, and his Holy Spirit, who is the hypostatic personification of his divine activity and life." Thomas Hopko, ed., "Man, Woman and the Priesthood of Christ," Bishop Kallistos Ware,*Women and the Priesthood,* (Crestwood, N.Y.., St. Vladimir's Seminary Press, 1983) p. 99, 100

35 "The relation of the work of Christ to that of the Holy Spirit in the Church would appear to have the character of an antimony: the Holy Spirit diversifies what Christ unifies. Nevertheless a perfect concord is supreme in diversity ... Without this personal diversity, the natural unity could not be realized and would be replaced by external unity, abstract, administrative, blindly submitted to by the members of a collective body." Vladimir Lossky, *In The Image and Likeness of God* (Crestwood, New York, St. Vladimir's Press, 1974) p. 178

36 Georges Florovsky, *Bible, Church, Tradition: An Eastern Orthodox View* (Belmont, MA., Nordland Publishing Company, 1972) p. 67

37 "While Christ unites us, the Holy Spirit ensures our infinite diversity in the Church: at Pentecost the tongues of fire were ... divided, descending *separately* upon each one of those present. The Gift of the Spirit is a gift to the Church, but it is at the same time a personal gift, appropriated by each in his own way. 'there are diversities of gifts, but the same Spirit' (I Cor. 12:4)." Timothy Ware, *The Orthodox Church* (Harmondsworth, Middlesex, England, Penguin Books, 1981) p. 247

38 "To desire to base ecclesiology solely on the Incarnation ... is to forget Pentecost and to reduce the work of the Holy Spirit to a subordinate role, that of an emissary of Christ, a liaison between the Head and the members of the Body. But the work of the Holy Spirit, although inseparable from the work of Christ, is distinct from it. ... As surely as she is the new unity of human nature purified by Christ, the unique Body of Christ, so she is also the multiplicity of persons, each one of whom receives the gift of the Holy Spirit. The work of the Son has for its object the common nature: this is what is redeemed, purified, and recapitulated by Christ. The work of the Holy Spirit is directed to persons, communicating the virtual fullness of grace to each human hypostasis [person] in the Church, making each member of the body of Christ a conscious collaborator (συνεργὸς) with God ... " Vladimir Lossky, *Image and Likeness of God,* (Crestwood, New York, St. Vladimir's Press, 1976) p. 177

39 "If the Body of Christ is 'unity in variety,' it cannot exist without the communion of all the members, without common love, reciprocal care, and common interdependence. " Serge S. Verhovskoy, "Catholicity and the Structures of the Church," *St. Vladimir's Theological Quarterly* (Crestwood, N.Y.., St. Vladimir's Seminary Press, 1973) vol. 17, No. 1-2, pp. 27, 28, 29

40 " ... in the image of God He created him, male and female He created *them* " [Gen. 1:27]) "If God is 'we,' then man too must exist as a multipersonal being. ... Man in isolation is both incomplete and unhappy. Only in mutual relationships do men attain the fullness of being. ...The words spoken by Adam about his wife have a much deeper meaning in the original Hebrew text than in any translation. The word 'wife' in Hebrew is *ish*ah, and husband—*ish.* The concepts of husband and wife are thus expressed by the very same word, only with the masculine and feminine word endings. This emphasizes the correspondence and unity of nature between man and woman. They are the same man, the same nature, only in two different forms—masculine and feminine, as it was said at the beginning: 'God created man in His own image, in the image of God he created him; male and female He created them'." Serge Verkhovskoy, "Creation of Man and the Establishment of the Family in the Light of the Book of Genesis", *St. Vladimir's Seminary Quarterly* (Crestwood, N.Y., St. Vladimir's Seminary Press, 1964) Vol. 8, No. 1, pp. 7, 10

41 "In the New Testament, the Holy Spirit usually was poured out upon groups of persons, be they the company of disciples or family groups. The Holy Spirit was rarely given to individuals alone, and even in these cases He was given for the edification of the body of Christ." John Driver, *Community and Commitment,* (Scottdale, PA., 1976) p. 40

42 "And thou shalt make fifty golden rings [clasps], and thou shalt *join* (or "couple") the curtains to each other with the rings, and it shall be one Tabernacle. " (Ex. 26:6). *Septuagint Version of the Old Testament* (Grand Rapids, MI., Zondervan Publishing House, 1970) p. 104. Koinonia is also used in a similar way in Ex. 26:9, 10; Gen. 14:3.

[43] Howard A. Snyder, *The Problem of Wine Skins*, (Downers Grove, IL., Inter-Varsity Press, 1975) p. 95

[44] John Zizioulas, "Appendix—The Authority of the Bible," *The Ecumenical Review* , Vol. XXI, No. 2, April, 1969 p. 163

CHAPTER TWELVE

WHAT ABOUT THE SACRAMENTS?

There are typically two main views of the sacraments held by modern Christians. One is that a sacrament is a vehicle of spiritual power that can almost magically transmit grace. The other views sacraments primarily as empty symbols (although they can be useful for strengthening or expressing one's faith). The Primitive Church, however, advocated neither of these approaches, nor a crossbreed between the two. Her understanding was a perspective not generally well known today, and reveals much about God's love in creation, His intimacy with humanity, and His nature.

What was this early sacramental perspective? Before answering this, I must address the assumptions behind the two most common approaches noted above. By doing this, I will be able to more clearly explain the Eastern view by way of contrast and comparison. In the first part of this chapter, I will analyze the philosophical foundations upon which these viewpoints rest, and then proceed to examine the assumptions of the earliest Christians. After evaluating these premises, you will be better able to understand just what the Eastern Christian view is, and how and why it differs from the modern notions.

MATTER AS "UNSPIRITUAL"

THE INFLUENCE OF AUGUSTINE

Evangelical-Fundamentalism is generally wary of *the earthly* being associated with *the spiritual*. As I have briefly mentioned, this attitude was inherited from the Reformers who, in their own way, adopted it from Rome's understanding of Augustine. [1] Let me refresh our memories. Augustine's theological system saw the world as being *divided* into two distinct parts: the world of the spirit and the world of matter. The material world was understood as something that will always be divorced, distinct, and separate from anything residing in God's realm, i.e., the invisible domain of the spirit.

In this spirit-matter division, Augustinianism has a great deal of similarity to Platonic philosophy. [2] Platonism saw the spiritual world as being the only real (or ideal) world; the material world was but an image or shadow of that reality. Augustine sympathized with this distinction. In fact, it was this division between matter and spirit that lay behind his understanding of a sacrament as "an outward and visible sign of an inward and invisible grace." To Augustine, the *reality* of a sacrament was spiritual—something which was *cloaked behind* the material and "visible sign." Not only did this formula become a popular Roman Catholic definition, but it found its way into all the major Reformation catechisms as well.[3]

What then is sacramental grace, and how is it received? The Roman Catholicism of the Middle Ages answered that question by saying that grace was the "saving power" energizing the sacraments. The Reformers held a similar view, but most of them qualified this understanding by affirming that it was one's *faith* in what the elements represented, not the elements themselves, that communicated God's grace. In both contexts, grace was not understood as "favor", its literal Biblical meaning. Grace was redefined by Augustinian-schooled scholastics as an energy able to bring the Christian *alongside* of God. The "Reformed" Augustine is little different from the "Catholic" Augustine. In both systems, grace was a *non-personal substance*, not a direct, intimate communion of God with the believer. The reason for this deduction was clear: matter is matter and God is God, and never the two shall meet. [4]

<u>THE CHASM BETWEEN MATTER AND SPIRIT: THE EVIL OF FLESH AND BLOOD</u>

In general, the various streams of Protestant Christianity have often flowed in sympathy with Augustine, Platonism, and pietistic humanism. Luther, himself a former Augustinian monk, clearly reflected an Augustinian dualism in his theological treatises and Biblical exegesis.[5] Calvin was also heavily influenced by these schools of thought, having had the opportunity to study them seriously for years.[6] The Catholic-Reformer Desiderius Erasmus (1469-1536) was another scholar who emphasized the Platonist spirit-earth dichotomy,[7] and his thinking made a significant impact on Anabaptist sacramental thinking.[8] And lastly, Zwingli, a man whose influence within Fundamentalism is still very much present, also demonstrated his allegiance to these philosophies and demonstrated it in his distrust of "outward things" in religion.[9]

As might be expected, these perspectives encouraged a very low view of *human* nature. While the *spirit* of an individual was *pure*, the tactile and sensible dimension of his personhood was ignoble and *base*. It was not just a person's "fleshliness" (i.e., carnal appetites) that was evil, but the body's very skin and bones as well! Zwingli clearly thought this way:

> The actual origin of sin Zwingli ascribes to the contrariety of soul and body, the tension between spiritual aspiration and the down-drag of carnal appetite. Thus by the 'flesh' he means the 'fleshliness' of the actual physical body, so narrowing the sense in which St. Paul uses the word. Indeed it was characteristic of Zwingli always to distinguish sharply between man's true being. That the argument is more rationalist than biblical Zwingli himself is frank enough to admit...[10]

Zwingli extended his dualistic thinking to the point of contradicting the Church's traditional teaching on the Incarnation. For example, he taught that Christ's humanity and divinity *did not* interdwell each other.[11] (Instead of understanding Christ's human nature as participating in His divine nature, he saw the two natures as merely existing "side-by-side.")

What consequence did this have on his view of the sacraments? Simply this: if divinity is distinct and does not co-inhabit the humanity given to Christ, how can any spiritual reality occupy such "lesser" material symbols such as bread, wine, or water? [12] The basic Platonist teaching is again emphasized: the material world is intrinsically incompatible with that which is Spiritual. [13]

Zwingli's aversion to the marriage of matter and Spirit was complemented and carried further by the South German Anabaptist, Menno Simons (1496-1561). Not only is this former Roman Catholic priest the "spiritual father" of most Mennonites today, but much of his thinking is still well received by many Twentieth Century Fundamentalists as well.[14] Simons was similar to Zwingli in his strong repugnance to the idea that divinity could co-reside within Christ's humanity. But unlike the Swiss Reformer, he did not divide Christ into two separate entities. Instead, he taught that Christ had only *one* nature— a *divine* one.

According to Simons, Christ's flesh was *totally* divine, not one speck of it being human.[15] This perspective seemed to address the problem left unanswered from the Augustinian interpretation of original sin he had once been taught. If, as this doctrine explained, it was impossible for man to escape from Adam's sin and guilt, how could a sinful woman (Mary) give birth to a sinless Man (Jesus)?[16] To answer this question, Simons cited John 6:63: "It is the Spirit who gives life; the flesh profits nothing...". In other words, Mary gave *nothing* of her humanity to Christ in the Incarnation; she was merely "a tube" through which Christ passed unaffected.[17]

> 'Jesus Christ is alone the Word of God, who himself became flesh through his divine power, and received nothing from the Virgin Mary; else she would not have remained a virgin. He is alone the seed of the Spirit. Even as the water in the jars at the wedding of Cana became wine through divine power, and took unto itself no wine from the jars nor from any other wine. As the Bread from heaven, he [Christ] fell from heaven and became himself a seed [corn], but received nothing from the earth.'[18]

Although Calvin clearly did not teach such an erroneous view of Christ, neither did he, in common with both Zwingli and Simons, hold a high place for the human body. He reserved honor only for "the spiritual side of man," and "considered the spirit-soul the exclusive bearer of the image of God and the essence of human personality to the disparagement of the body and its drives."[19] Once again, this entire way of thinking was "plainly a direct result of Platonism as absorbed into medieval Augustinianism."[20]

In this view, sin has defaced God's image in humanity beyond all recognition, having been passed on from one generation to another through *biological reproduction.* Therefore, man *as* a product of *human* sex, must be *depraved* (i.e., total depravity) as nothing pure could *naturally* live in his "fallen-matter" flesh. This Platonic theme was continually emphasized in Reformation theology, and, though to a much lesser degree, in Anabaptist teaching as well. [21]

This leads us back to where we began. God, as the Supreme Good, stands at an eternal arms length from anything "matter-like," either in creation or in humanity. The conclusion: anything material—in man or sacrament— has little real value.[22] Today, many Christians in the West would certainly not agree with the distorted perspectives of Christ's humanity some of the Reformers maintained, nor would they explain grace in such academic terms. But the Augustinian and Platonic prejudice against creation and the scholastic definition of grace, especially in respect to the sacraments, still has its proponents.

EVANGELICAL-FUNDAMENTALIST RESPONSES TO MEDIEVAL ROMAN CATHOLIC VIEWS

THE REACTION TO MEDIEVAL SACRAMENTALISM

The Evangelical-Fundamentalist suspicion toward anything "sacramental" is understandable. Both in Medieval times and the present day, the sacraments have been abused, and superstitious sentiments surrounding them are, unfortunately, still prevalent.[23] Without question, much within the various Reformation movements has been used by the Holy Spirit to protect the integrity of the Gospel in regard to the sacraments. The problem, however, lies in the fact that the philosophical perspectives of the Middle Ages and the Renaissance, which were not complementary to the Biblical Tradition, were the standard used by the Reformers to judge what was and was not "Biblical."

It was in this vein that Zwingli opposed any and all objectified, "mattered" expressions of Christianity as unforgivable distortions. For him, "If the sole basis for true religion is spiritual, then any attempt to embody this in concrete forms becomes idolatrous. "[24] Such a theology naturally leads one to ask, "Are the sacraments *really* necessary?" [25] To this, he affirmed that Baptism and the Eucharist were necessary because their observance is commanded by Scriptures, (not because they presented any spiritual reality). Zwingli believed that they are to be understood only as outward rites, merely "ordinances" which have no intrinsic value in and of themselves [26] But the place of faith is a different matter entirely.[27] Faith *does* have inherent value; it is the key that opens the door to God's saving grace in Christ. Therefore, Zwingli deduced, it is faith —not sacraments— that is crucial.[28]

WHAT IS A SACRAMENT?

AN EASTERN CHRISTIAN UNDERSTANDING

The Eastern perception of sacrament is different in a number of points from the common Western ones we have just outlined. To begin with, let me note that the word sacrament is found nowhere in the Scriptures. The Latin term *sacramentum*, meaning "to make holy", was a legal term belonging to the language of Roman jurisprudence. It referred to the oath taken by a Roman soldier upon his enlistment in the army, (a pledge to set himself apart for this service). Given this backdrop, Tertullian (160-225) applied the word to Baptism, asserting that each Christian's reception of the rite thus enlisted him in Christ's army. From that time on, sacramentum, or sacrament, was applied in the Church of the West to other rites believed to have been instituted by Christ.

While this use of the word sacrament came to be widely accepted in the West, Eastern Christianity was unfamiliar with both the term and Tertullian's application of it. In its place, the Eastern Christian knew the word "mystery" (*mysterion*), a Greek word holding a deeper and wider meaning than its Latin counterpart. [29] The word appears in the Scriptures, and signifies God's *entire* scheme of redemption — the new creation of all through the life, death, resurrection, and glorification of Christ. [30] From the Eastern Christian point of view, the *mysteries* of the Faith ("the sacraments") reflect the *whole Mystery* of what it means to be in Christ.

Given this broader conception, Christians of Eastern attitudes refuse to limit the mysteries to either two or seven. *Anything which reveals God's Redemptive Mystery* —words, acts, symbols, Christian relationships, etc.—*qualifies as a mystery of the Church.*[31]

> In early Christian language, 'mysterion' was applied to any sacred object, in fact to anything which as 'mirror' or 'form' of the Divine was regarded as revealing the Divine. The number of 'mysteries' is therefore potentially limitless, for everything in the cosmos in some manner mirrors or informs the Divine, and is thus a 'mysterion'.[32]

The Eastern Christian may use the word "sacrament" in conversation, but his doing so is not an admission of a Western understanding. The word is simply used because most Christians would have *no* idea of what he meant should he use the word "mystery" in instead of "sacrament."

JESUS AS SACRAMENT: MANY BUT ONE

"The Word of God Himself, the Paschal Lamb slain before the foundation of the world (Rev. 13:8), is the true and ultimate Sacrament of our salvation."[33] Everything which reveals Jesus is "sacramental." And because nothing can better reveal Christ, nor bring one into a deeper union with Him than His Body, the Church herself is considered the *chief* of sacraments.[34] This *union* of Christ with His people is *the* mystery of our redemption; as Paul states, it is a *great mystery* (Eph. 5:32).

A kind word to someone needing encouragement, a gift to a person in need, or even the warm embrace of one who feels rejected can all reveal the presence of Christ within the Church. In all of these physical expressions of the Faith, the mystery of Christ's love can be manifest. Thus, every work done in faith, love, and hope, suggested to Christians by the Spirit of God, is truly sacramental.

> Somebody coming to see you when you are sick can be a sacrament. A meal with people you love can be a sacrament. Once we recognize His Universal Presence, all our acts of love and service become sacraments. 'The whole Christian life must be seen as . . .one great sacrament, whose different aspects are expressed in a great variety of acts, some performed but once in a person's life, others perhaps daily.'[35]

Prayer, Bible reading, witnessing, "walking the aisle" to commit one's life to Christ, all have the potential of being "sacramental."[36] Prayer, Scripture reading, and witnessing, can also be truly "sacramental."[37] No act or gesture is sacramental in and of itself, however. Each must be inspired and empowered by the Holy Spirit to be a sacrament. Each must reveal Christ's presence amidst the people of God. Apart from the presence of God's Spirit, and the fellowship of Christ's Body, even the most "holy" of acts fails to reveal The Mystery of redemption.

SACRAMENTS CAN NEITHER BE SEPARATED NOR DEFINED BY "FUNCTION"

Because Jesus is *The* Sacrament which makes all sacraments possible, every sacrament finds its unity in Him. No one sacrament, therefore, can be isolated from the others, nor is each sacrament administered to perform a different "job" (i.e., baptism to erase Original Sin, confirmation to impart the Spirit, the Eucharist to communicate Christ's atonement). Each sacrament manifests Christ in His wholeness, not "pieces" of His power; each brings union in and with the one Lord.

It is for this reason that the Early Christian saw the initiatory sacraments (Baptism, Confirmation, Eucharist) as a *collective whole,* each one *standing in symphony with the others* to manifest the redemptive mystery. Thus, Baptism, Confirmation, and the Eucharist are *inseparable*, each disclosing the reality of Christ's saving union with us. Baptism reveals *God's union* with us through Christ, Confirmation (in the East, "chrismation") manifests *God's union* with us through the Spirit's indwelling within and among us, and the Eucharist actualizes the reality of *God's union* with us as the Body of Christ. What Christ is to us in Baptism, He is to us in Confirmation and the Eucharist.[38]

Each sacrament reveals the one and same mystery, "Christ in you, the hope of glory" (Col. 1:27).

From this it should become clear that all sacramental acts (if they are indeed true sacraments) are a participation *in Him* . [39] Each sacrament identifies us with Christ and realizes the truth that we, as members of the Church, actually participate in the life He shares with the other Persons of the Trinity. This Life flowing to us through the mysteries is the consequence of the Spirit— Him Who has been sent to bear witness to Christ (John 15:26).

All of this sounds so grandiose, so expansive: the sacraments as Christ, as union with God, as life in Christ. Western Christians are more accustomed to conceiving of them as spiritual entities in their own right. To do so, however, is to displace the personal presence of God with a lesser thing, a mechanical, self-contained vehicle designed only to convey a "spiritual courtesy." [40] In his book *Church, World and Mission,* Alexander Schmemann gives an excellent critique of the problem:

> Theorizing about isolated sacramental acts, we lost the sacramental sense in general. The number of these acts, their institution, the conditions of their validity and so on - we asked those questions in too narrow and concentrated a fashion, so that everything else became nonsacramental in our minds. In this situation, the idea of grace itself suffered loss. We stopped thinking of the coming of the Spirit, of the huge wind from heaven. We thought instead of something small, something attenuated and weak, something to be defined legally and measured out in small doses. God gives His grace in a great torrent, not to be measured by men; and yet, down the centuries, theology seems to have concentrated upon measuring it, and - inevitably - upon reducing it to something that men might hope to measure. What kind of grace was it? Was it preventing grace, sanctifying grace, efficacious grace? Where was it to be found in the official, numbered list? This frame of mind, this approach has had its day.[41]

Sacraments, therefore, are not empowered objects that give private blessings to solitary individuals. In no way do they fit into an individualistic frame of reference. The mysteries reveal the *bond* we share with Christ *and* the brethren (His body).

WHAT IS "THE GRACE" OF THE SACRAMENTS?

GRACE AS PERSONAL RELATIONSHIP

If one sees grace as something distinct from God Himself, or as some substance He created to save us, he is bound to misunderstand sacraments and their purpose. Grace is not a mysterious force enabling man to come to God. Grace is not something God manufactured in heaven and then sent to earth to save us. [42] Grace is *the direct and personal communion of God with His people*, and the sacraments manifest *that communion.* When someone is strengthened or saved *by grace*, he is not strengthened or saved by "a thing" but by a *Person.*

When a Christian participates in a true sacrament, *he* is changed not because of the substance of the sacrament, but because of what the sacrament makes manifest: a personal encounter with *God.* One who encounters God, encounters His *personal* love, not just "elements." Donald Baillie, in his book *The Theology of the Sacraments*, captures this personal sense of sacrament well:

> God works faith in our hearts. He bestows on us the gift of faith, by winning us, gaining our confidence, not forcing it. His graciousness overcomes our mistrust, His grace creates our faith, so that when we come to Him, it is really our faith, and we come willingly. In order to bring about this end he uses means—words, smiles, gestures, symbolic gifts, which we call sacraments. As Baron von Hugel has written: 'I kiss my child not only because I love it; I kiss it also in order to love it. ..." All such are 'means of grace', methods employed by the graciousness of God *to express and develop a gracious personal relationship between Him and us.* When we think of grace in that personal way, a flood of light falls on many questions of sacramental theology. [43]

The Eastern Christian understands grace and salvation only in terms of a *personal relationship with God.* Again, grace is neither a substitute for God, nor a conveyor of something "god-like"; *it is actual communion with God.* [44] In essence, the grace of God is nothing less than the Spirit Himself bonding us in relationship with the Father, through the Son. [45] This should only make sense to us because our natures, as human beings made in the image and likeness of God, were created to participate in this grace (God's communion). [46]

To know God intimately is not contrary to man's nature. Man is most "at home" with God His Creator. To be "God-like," [47] therefore, is for man merely to be as his true Father is. Sin, rebellion, and separation from God, on the other hand, *are* contrary to man's nature. One does not need grace to function as a bridge between his humanity and God's divinity. God has supplied the bridge *in Himself,* the divine-human Christ. In relationship with *Him* there is true grace.

THE PERSONAL AND COMMUNAL ASPECTS OF THE SACRAMENTS

If sacraments reveal and manifest the presence of God and His union with men, they *must* be communal. God Himself is Three Persons in communion, and His union with men is through Christ in the Church Community. A Christian's reception of the sacraments, then, is to manifest his participation both in God's Communal Life and in the divine-human Community (the Church). Hence, the sacraments cannot be given to the lone, "unconnected" individual; no sacrament can exist apart from Christ Who dwells *within* His body. [48]

Our participation in the life of God as manifested in the mysteries will not bring about a *total* identification with God (i.e., we will not become God). But a true union does take place, a union which allows us to grow in a deeper awareness of our relationship with Christ and those joined to Him.[49] So what "happens" to us in the sacraments? Two things: we meet God and we meet God's people.

In meeting Christians within the Local Church through the sacraments, we see the congregation not only as "fellow believers," but as who they really are to us (both now and for eternity): our brothers and sisters. In allowing us to commune with both Christ and our brethren, the sacraments give us a taste of the full and final redemption the Lord has prepared for His people.[50] When we meet Christ in the sacraments, the anointing of Jesus, "the anointed" One (1 John 2:20), is shared with the members of His Body (1 Cor. 12:13). What was hidden before the ages, the Spirit now reveals (1 Cor. 2:10). The mysteries manifest The Mystery.

Of course, the Christian's participation in the sacraments does not automatically guarantee him an increased realization of fellowship with the Trinity and his brethren. "The sacraments are not the 'machines of salvation,' or magical contacts that work automatically; they are personal encounters with Christ in faith."[51] Each believer can experience the communion of God in the mysteries, but what he does with this Presence, and how it changes him, is up to his own personal co-operation with the Spirit of God throughout his Christian life.

All of this should be obvious if we again realize that the sacraments are not something different or distinct from our relationship with Christ, and our relationships as fellow members of His body. Just as every Christian has a relationship with Christ, but it is his faith and co-operation with the Holy Spirit which determines *the extent* to which that union will be made manifest in his life and character, so it is with one's participation in the sacraments.[52] The transformation we receive in Christ is not an enchantment; it is a matter of God touching us in His love and our willingness to receive it. [53]

HOW CAN MATERIAL THINGS COMMUNICATE THE THINGS OF THE SPIRIT?

GOD ACTS WITHIN HIS CREATION

How can *material* things make us aware of the presence of *God*? This truth can only be grasped if we understand that matter is not inherently base or evil. The earth is no less good than the spiritual realm which He also created (Gen. 1:25). There is no "better-worse" distinction between the material and spiritual world; *both* were created by God, *both* co-habit the other, and *both* reveal God's presence. [54] The world is not a "failed attempt" of God. To reject creation as an inferior product is to reject the Creator Who made it. [55]

The earth has consistently been involved in the things of the Spirit. In fact, the whole scheme of salvation has been clearly "incarnated" in time and matter. [56] Creation, Redemption, the Incarnation, the Crucifixion, the Resurrection, Ascension, and Pentecost all took place within this material world. Not one of these events occurred purely in the 'spiritual' realm.

The Scriptures make plain that if the material creation and the supernatural world did not have such an integral relationship with each other, the entire creation would collapse; for "in Him all things hold together" (Col. 1:17). To pit objects we can smell, taste, and feel against those things which defy dimension, is a contest the Bible forbids us to engage in. Matter and Spirit are not enemies; they are "relatives" which have both been Fathered by the same hand.

> God created matter as well as spirit. God has created the entire world, and every ounce of matter belongs to Him. ... Therefore a certain tendency in religion which 'despises' material things, reducing religion to what is 'spiritual,' is wrong, non-Christian.[57]

As C. S. Lewis so aptly put it, "God likes matter; He invented it."

REDEMPTION: THE RESTORATION (NOT THE OBLITERATION) OF THE MATERIAL WORLD

In the Last Day, the Lord will not discard His creation; it —like all those in Christ— will be restored and redeemed to its original "newness."

> 'Behold, I make all things new' [Rev. 21:5]. These were God's last words to us, and they only say at the end, and eternally, what was in His mind at the beginning, when He looked on the sacramental world of His creation and saw that it was good. [58]

In other words, Christ may make all things new, but he will not wipe out his creation in favor of a *different* creation. After Christ's return, it will be the same world, and we will still be human beings. The difference will be that God's redemptive presence within us and the world will be more fully revealed and experienced. [59]

Nothing in creation was meant to suffer death and to be thus imprisoned by corruption.

Although the consequence of humanity's Fall has passed on to the world around us, sentencing it to the same curse (Romans 5:12), when Christ returns it will be a recipient of the same redemption we have inherited in Him (Rom. 5:17-21). [60] Until that Day, man's call is to *offer back* creation to God. Such an offering is performed through the consecration of ourselves and all of creation to God. In this consecration, all matter acquires its spiritual meaning and is blessed. [61]

The crucial truth to be understood is that created matter is not inherently corrupt, nor is spirit inherently holy. Both have been personally made by the Lord for His glory. Both can be turned away from Him and thus corrupted. The spirit world cannot be distinguished from the material world on the basis of one being more hallowed than the other.

> ...it must be remembered that corruption applies as much to the spiritual realm as to the material. The devils and damned souls in hell are, precisely, spirits in a state of corruption. Just as good food rots, and silver tarnishes, and our flesh sickens and decays, all of it because of evil, so the lordliest celestial spirits may rot and tarnish and decay into fiends in hell. It is the same process, the same fabric. [62]

THE SPIRITUALITY OF THE BODY

One's negative view of creation often leads one to discount the physical nature of man. Many within the Evangelical-Fundamentalist stream believe that the *real* person is located only within the spirit or soul. This popular teaching continues by saying that the body is merely an "earth-suit", something God gave us so we could "get along" on the earth. The philosophy is often summarized, "We *are* a spirit, we *have* a soul, and we live *in* a body." The eternal reality of the person is confined to the spirit and soul, the body will simply pass out of existence. [63]

Platonic philosophy supports such a non-matter view of man, but nowhere is this teaching supported by the Scriptures.

> The New Testament never uses 'spiritual' (pneumatikos) in antithesis to the bodily (somatikos). There is no opposition between spirit and body, for there is even such a thing as a spiritual body (soma pneumatikon) [1 Cor. 15:44].[64]

Sin was not the cause of man's material identity. God created man *both* as spirit *and* matter from the very beginning. The body is not carnal; it is just as spiritual (godly and holy) as our souls and spirits are.

Likewise, our true selves are not composed of two or three parts which can be studied in isolation. We are not parts (material + spiritual), we are *whole* beings (material interdwelling spiritual). Spirit and matter *inseparably* make up our entire identity; thus *our bodies are an inherent part of our personhood.*¨ "The spiritual man does not *have* a body, but *is* a body. Man is 'bodily' a spiritual being, and is 'spiritually' a material being."[65]

As shocking as it may seem to some of us, the truth is that our bodies (not just our souls) will be with us for eternity. And our bodies—along with the created world—will be saved...

> ...even we groan within ourselves, waiting eagerly for our adoption as sons, the redemption of our body. (Romans 8: 23).[66]

On the Last Day our bodies will not be destroyed. Far from it! They will be cast in the very likeness of Christ's resurrected body (1 John 3:2; 1 Cor. 15:42; Phil. 3:21). One day our flesh of corruption will be transformed, and it — along with all of "mattered-creation" — will experience *full* redemption (1 Cor. 15:38-45).[67] Yes, it is true that our bodies will be glorified, and yet they will still be that same "seed" of flesh we presently identify as our physical persons.

Many unintentionally deny this truth when they refer to 2 Cor. 5 where Paul groans under the burden of his "earthly tent" (here, referring his physical body). They think, "Here is proof that the body is of little value, something separate and divorced from the real person." Paul's prayer request, however, is not to be in heaven as a "disembodied spirit," but that he receive the *total* redemption of *his person* -body and all- at Christ's second coming. His prayer is not to be "unclothed, but *to be clothed,* in order that what is mortal may be *swallowed up by life*" (2 Cor. 5:4). As John Chrysostom, the Fourth Century bishop and Bible expositor explained:

> It is not flesh... that we put off from ourselves, but corruption; the body is one thing, corruption is another. ... True, the body is corrupt, but it is not corruption. The body dies but it is not death. The body is the work of God, but death and corruption entered by sin. Therefore, he says, I would put off from myself that strange thing which is not proper to me. And that strange thing is not the body, but corruption. The future life shatters and abolishes not the body, but that which clings to it, corruption and death.[68]

The word "body" in the Scriptures is most typically a designation for the *whole person,* an inclusive reference of all that makes a person to be a person (spirit, soul and body).[69] Even where the physical body was specifically emphasized, it was never separated from a person's identity. In fact, Paul warned the Corinthians not to give their *bodies* to a harlot, for to do so would have meant their becoming *one spirit with her.* (1 Cor. 6:15-20) [70] What we do with our bodies clearly has an effect on our spirits, and vice-versa.

To reject the body as a part of our identity is not to unmask our "true" selves; it is a platonic, unchristian maiming of our personhood. It is just as impossible to be a person without a body as it is to be a person without a soul or a spirit. Again, man is a *complete* being. Orthodox theologian George Florovsky stated it well: "A body without a soul is but a corpse, and a soul without a body is a ghost."[71]

Our redemption is not fully realized at the time of death (because our soul is separated from our body). Although in death our spirits can taste "home" and its joys, our person nevertheless suffers destruction. A measure of God's image has faded through our physical demise, and a dimension of our real selves is missing.[72] Only in the Second coming will *full* redemption be realized, for us and for creation. Christ came to destroy death and to undo the consequences of the Fall so that man might have communion with God *as a full man,* not as a being foreign to His original creation.[73]

Perhaps the strongest statement affirming the primary goodness of matter is Jesus Himself partaking of human flesh and blood (Heb. 2:14).[74] God in Christ has assumed material existence, and now He as God-man has knitted humanity into the Godhead.[75] In Christ, we see that Divinity does not stand aloof from His creation. It is precisely because of the union of the divine and human in the Person of Christ that the gulf created by the Fall has been closed.

WHAT IS A SYMBOL?

THE SYMBOL: DOUBLE REALITY

The people of the Scriptures saw the entire world as an integral *whole*,[76] a perspective that is being affirmed by modern physics.[77] The Biblical world view saw that the spiritual world was not distant from the material world, but was, in fact, *in union with* it. It is this integrated perspective which accounts for the Hebrew and early Christian's understanding of religious symbols. Since matter was not devoid of spiritual meaning, they had no problem seeing physical symbols as having a direct and immediate relationship to the spiritual reality they represented.[78]

In the West, a symbol is something which stands for something which does not exist, or is seen as a mere illustration of the reality (like the ball and spoke plastic model scientists use to depict a water molecule but in itself is not really a water molecule). The Biblical mind, however, saw a symbol as something which could both *manifest* and *communicate* the reality which it revealed. It is particularly interesting to note that the original meaning of the word symbol is "*to put together*" (symbolon). This is an accurate definition, for in ancient times a symbol actually stood for two different realities: the visible created reality *and* its invisible spiritual reality. Both of these realities are inseparably intertwined and together represent a double-reality.[79]

Examples abound in the Scriptures of how material symbols can make divine realities present: *a bramble bush* manifesting the presence of God to Moses (Exodus 3); *the bones of Elisha* raising a dead man to life (2 Kings 13:21); the appearance of *a star* over Bethlehem testifying to the Incarnation (Matt. 2:1-9); Christ using *clay and saliva* to give sight to a man born blind (John 9); *the fringe of Jesus' cloak* healing a hemorrhaging woman (Mark 527 ff.); *Paul's handkerchiefs* healing diseases and exorcising demons (Acts 19:12); *Peter's shadow* bringing deliverance (Acts 5:15); and God's redemptive power being manifested through *oil* (James 5:14-15). Are the uses of these symbols indicative of a superstitious attitude toward matter? Or did the early believers think that clay or cloth or oil had power in themselves? Of course not. What was clear to them was the fact that God's presence was not confined to an unseen realm but was within the very world in which they lived. Faith may be the conviction of things not seen, but through it the *material universe itself* was made (Heb. 11:1,2).

Because of this understanding, the Early Christians did not employ symbols in their worship as a mere "memory technique" to help them remember a past religious event. [80] They saw the symbol itself as making present the reality it depicted. No, not in a magical sense, for, as already stated, without the Spirit and the fellowship of the faithful, a sacrament ceases to be sacred. They did not believe that the *material* of the symbol had power, but what the *material represented* had power. As Christ Himself stated, it is not the gold part of the altar which makes an offering on the altar holy, but what the entire altar *represents* which sanctifies an offering (Matt. 23:18-20).

Christ's own baptism brilliantly illustrates this point. There, at the Jordan River, the Father, the Son and the Holy Spirit personally manifested themselves in the symbols which presented themselves; the Father, in the roar that was heard from heaven, the Son in the waters of baptism, the Spirit, in His descent as a dove. To the unbeliever, the sound, the water, the dove meant nothing. But to those who beheld these symbols in faith, the personal presence of God Himself was manifested.

THE MESSAGE OF SYMBOLS

Are symbols *necessary* to communicate spiritual realities? Does God *need* to use physical symbols to bless others or to reveal Himself? Let me answer these questions by looking at some other examples in the Scriptures.

What if one had refused to place blood on the door frame of his home on the eve of the Passover? "My faith is not in 'lamb blood', I am a believer in the God of Abraham, Isaac and Jacob. My *faith alone* will save the firstborn in this household." Would his abstinence from this rite have been an expression of this Israelite's faith in God? Or was the performance of this act to be understood precisely as an expression of faith in God alone? What would have been the result had he refused to anoint his home with the symbol of the blood of the Passover lamb? The answer is clear. The firstborn within that home would have died (Ex. 12:12,13).

Or let's take the symbol of circumcision. What if one had refused to circumcise his children? "My faith in the covenant is enough. I don't need to cut my male children's sex organ!" What would have been God's response toward that child? The Scriptures make it clear: that "person shall be cut off from his people, he has broken My covenant" (Gen. 17:14).

Other examples are plentiful. What if the lepers had refused to wash themselves as Jesus directed them to do? Why did it take the "breaking of the bread" for the disciples on the road to Emmaus to recognize Jesus? Or why use oil along with the prayer of faith for healing as it says in James?

The point in these examples is that God is not asking us to use our faith in opposition to the symbols He has given to strengthen this very same faith. We are not commanded to have faith in animal blood, surgery, or oil. We are, however, to have faith in the reality these symbols embrace: the Covenant and Christ's sacrificial death.

In this light, the water of Baptism symbolizes the cleansing of sin which only Christ can give (1 Peter 3:21). The Bread and the Cup of the Eucharist symbolize the nourishment that He alone provides (John 6: 57,58). [81] Exactly how these symbols bring us into the redemptive presence of God is a mystery that defies definition, but that is no real concern.[82] God's presence is never known by discourse; it is known only in communion.

Why then did God choose to convey spiritual benefits through these material symbols? For the same reason that the Son of God became Man: to communicate Himself in a way we matter-made mortals could best receive. This is the same reason He still chooses to use symbols (objects, actions, words and ideas) today. To say that we only need faith and not the symbol of faith, is a contradiction our brethren in the Scriptures could have never imagined. The "faith versus symbol philosophy" was forged in the fires of Medieval and Renaissance debates. It was not gleaned from the texts of the Bible. Symbols are a means of expressing our faith, not a contradiction to faith.

SACRAMENTAL SYMBOLS AND OUR UNION IN CHRIST

No sacrament can be a sacrament if it does not immediately bear witness to Christ (inclusive of His Life in the Godhead, the Kingdom and the Church). Symbols and sacraments are not something extra to our belief in Christ, but are an indivisible expression of it. No one can affirm this view of the sacraments and believe that being sacramental is a belief in salvation by works.

Our reception of Christian Baptism is not an expression of our faith in water, nor is our participation in the Lord's Supper a confession that wine and bread saves us. "The 'power of the sacrament' is derived from the 'power of the Word' [Jesus] that it enshrines and celebrates."[83] Our faith is not in an "it" but in Him. And it is *He* whom every sacrament discloses. "...Biblical Christianity proclaims, not indeed a Gospel of sacraments, but sacraments of the Gospel."[84]

THE PLACE OF FAITH

What about a person who receives the sacraments and has no faith? How does the sacrament affect him? Such questions would have made no sense to the Early Church. They knew that the sacraments were never intended for those outside of Christ. The New Testament never tried to explain what would happen if an unbeliever received the sacraments, [85] and never envisaged such a situation. Such a line of thinking is like asking, "What happens when an unbeliever 'worships' God?" Is *unbelieving* worship possible?! How does an unbeliever participate in the Mystery of salvation from which he has excluded himself!? Obviously, these questions make no sense whatsoever.

Of course faith is necessary for the proper reception of the sacraments. What is holy is intended for those who through Christ have been made *holy* (or "saints" since both words come from the same Greek word, "agios"). The sacraments are a revelation, a manifestation, and an embrace of the Kingdom of God. The unbeliever finds himself out of place here.

SUMMARY

I have sought in this chapter to disclose the early Church's view of the sacraments, a view quite different from what most understand them to be. This perspective sees sacraments not as "cuts" from a stiff cloth of grace, but as manifestations of the personal redemption of God Himself; not as empty symbols, but as the revelation of God caressing and transcending the matter He sanctified through His creation and Incarnation; and Sacraments, not as distant second-bests to God's love; they are the very communion of God with and among His people.

I have also emphasized that sacraments are communal because they actualize and disclose the love of God within the Trinity and the Church. Apart from one's communion with the brethren in the Local Church, and one's faith in Christ, sacraments make no sense. Christ is the Sacrament *par excellence*. In Him, the Christian sacramental vision becomes clear. In communion with Christ, the believer sees not merely symbols, but God's people—and all of creation—filled with the Spirit of God. To be sacramental, then, is to taste the Mystery of Christ — He who is and will be "all in all" (Ephesians 1:23).

NOTES FOR CHAPTER TWELVE

1 " ... the theologians of the Reformation sought to entrench the evangelical and doctrinal renewal of the Church and to defend it against the counter-attacks of Roman Catholic theologians deploying the legal and scholastic weapons of the mediaeval masters. This inevitably meant the taking up of the epistemological, sacramental and cosmological dualism of Augustinianism into the Reformation and the building of it into its established theological positions ... " T. F. Torrance, *Theology in Reconciliation: Essays Toward Evangelical and Catholic Unity In East and West,* (Grand Rapids, MI., William B. Eerdmans Publishing Company, 1975) p. 43

2 Many assume that Augustine's spiritually empty view of creation was a carry over from his pre-Christian involvement with the Manichaens, a Gnostic sect which saw "divinity" as "imprisoned" within but radically distinct from matter. Augustine's Platonism was compatible both with his view of God as the Supreme Good and his vision that the Good was exclusively enclosed within "the absolute and divine original being" alone. Thus, God's personal presence was normally separate and removed from His creation. In this latter sense, a residue of his Manichaenism may well have remained.

3 "A platonizing dualism in anthropology thus takes the place, for Augustine, of his original Manichean ontological dualism." John Meyendorff, *The Catholicity and the Church,* "The Significance of the Reformation in the History of Christendom", St. Vladimir's Seminary Press, (Crestwood, New York), 1983, p. 66

4 "In its criticism of scholastic theology for being too generous toward nature and reason, the theology of the sixteenth century Reformers sometimes threatened to denigrate not only reason and philosophy, but nature and creation itself, and to verge on determinism and dualism. Grace did not abolish nature, nor did it complete nature; it seemed to replace nature with a 'new creation' that was radically discontinuous with the old creation." Jaroslav Pelikan, *The Growth of Medieval Theology (600-1300),* Vol. 3 of *The Christian Tradition: A History of the Development of Doctrine*, p. 292

5 " ... Luther's experience that 'no one is sure of the integrity of his own contrition,' and that consequently there could be no assurance of forgiveness based on the quality or quantity of one's contrition, which could never be worthy or sufficient. ... was too absolute in its demands and too transcendent in its holiness to be satisfied by the works of attrition or even contrition ... To be "holy" meant to be 'separated' and set apart from everything that was profane and sinful, and the holiness of God meant that 'God alone is holy, but the whole people and whatever the people do are completely defiled." Jaroslav Pelikan *The Christian Tradition: Reformation of Church and Dogma (1300-1700)* (Chicago and London, The University of Chicago Press, 1983) pp. 131-132 citing Luther's *Lectures on Isaiah, 6:2,D. Martin Luthers Werke.,* Vol. 31-II:48

6 "'If Augustine is the theologian to whom Calvin refers most frequently, Plato is the philosopher most often cited and nearly always with favor. One can say that for Calvin Plato is, as a philosopher what Augustine is as a theologian.'" Charles Partee, *Calvin and Classical Philosophy* (The Netherlands, E. J. Brill, Leiden, 1977) p. 111 citing Jean Boisset, *Sagesse et Sainteté dans la Pensée de Jean Calvin* (Paris: Université de France, 1959) pp. 284, 221

7 Erasmus purportedly said, "'Among the philosophers I would prefer you to follow the Platonists...their opinions and in their way of speaking [in many ways] follow the gospel pattern.'" Brian A. Gerrish, ed., *Reformers in Profile* , (Philadelphia, Fortress Press, 1967) p. 77

8 "Erasmus' views on the sacraments are rather ambiguous; much is not Anabaptistic, but some vital points are. In general, his emphasis is on the internal and spiritual aspects over the external, without completely abandoning the usefulness of the latter as a starting point, and on a biblical understanding and spiritual reception of them. Therefore images, singing, and even the sacraments are not objectively conveyers of grace." Kenneth Ronald Davis, *Anabaptism and Ascetism* (Scottdale, Pa, Herald Press, 1974) p. 286

9 E. J. Furcha and H. Wayne Pipkin, *Prophet, Pastor, Protestant* (Allison Park, PA., Pickwick Publications, 1984) p. 161

10 "Death accordingly does not affect the soul except to liberate it from its physical constraints, existence in this world being captivity rather than freedom." Bernard M.G. Reardon, *Religious Thought In the Reformation* (New York, Longham Inc., 1981) p. 100

11 His "christology is in line with the distinctions he consistently draws between God and humanity, spirit and letter, substance and form." The *communicato idiomatum* (the interchange of the divine and human properties appropriate to each nature in Christ), "Zwingli explains as only a figure of speech, whereby one thing is stated but another is meant." Bernard M.G. Reardon, *Religious Thought In the Reformation* (New York, Longham Inc., 1981) footnote 38, pp. 101, 116

12 His views on the incarnation definitely influenced his views of the eucharist. Zwingli could even go as far as to use Casper Schwenckfeld's treatise on the Lord's Supper ("spiritual" Anabaptist whose teachings were clearly heretical) to deny the Lord's presence in the signs of bread and wine. The treatise affirmed this on the analogy that Christ did not have material flesh, but only a celestial flesh. Schwenckfeld taught that both Christ's humanity and divinity were of the Spirit (God the Father). "... Zwingli published it [this treatise], because it agreed with him against the Lutherans ... without knowing of the document's Christological teaching, though this was also clearly expressed in it." Alvin J. Beachy, *The Concept of Grace in the Radical Reformation* (Harrisonburg, U.S.A., 1976), footnote 81, p. 79

13 "Of all reformers (including Melancthon) Zwingli was most strongly influenced by humanism. .. The humanistic influence had grasped Zwingli while he was still attending school and the university, and as a pastor in Glarus he was already a prominent member of the Swiss circle of humanists. Erasmus, whom Zwingli met in 1515, strengthened this attitude. ... When Zwingli was asked in 1526 about works that might offer help for a preacher, he listed a great number of ancient authors with special reference to the way in which they were useful, but he included no Church Father, no theological writing. And when Zwingli depicted paradise for King Francis I of France, it contained not only Old testament heroes and New Testament apostles, but also "Hercules, Theseus, Socrates, Aristides, Antigonus, Numa, Camillus, Cato, Scipio. It is only on the basis of humanistic presuppositions that some of Zwingli's theological opinions can be explained, his view in the hotly contested dispute about the Lord's Supper, for example." Kurt Aland, *Four Reformers: Luther, Melancthon, Calvin, Zwingli* (Philadelphia, Augsburg Publishing House, 1979) pp. 90, 91

14 Simmons did not begin the Mennonite movement, however. He is its founder only in the sense that many of these later Anabaptists found in his teaching an echo of their own sentiments and thus looked to his teaching with great respect.

15 In his *The Foundation Book,* Simmons explains that "his flesh must itself be thought of as heavenly, for had he been really born of Mary 'he would have sprung from the sinful flesh of Adam' so that man's salvation would then have come through his own sin-tainted flesh, an idea totally unacceptable, Christ therefore must have been born not 'of' Mary but rather 'by' or 'through' her." Bernard M. G. Reardon, *Religious Thought In The Reformation* (New York, Longman Inc., 1981) p. 221 citing J. C. Wenger, ed., *Menno Simmons: the Complete Writings,* English trans. by L. Verduin (Scottdale, Pa., 1956) p. 797, 768

16 William R. Estep, *The Anabaptist Story* (Nashville, Tennessee, Broadman Press, 1963) p. 135

17 Alvin J. Beachy, *The Concept of Grace in the Radical Reformation* (Harrisonburg, U.S.A., 1976) p. 80

18 Alvin J. Beachy, *The Concept of Grace in the Radical Reformation* (Harrisonburg, U.S.A., 1976) p. 80

19 George Huntston Williams, *The Radical Reformation* (Philadelphia, The Westminster Press, 1975) p. 582

20 Louis Bouyer, *A History of Christian Spirituality III: Orthodox Spirituality and Protestant and*

Anglican Spirituality, (New York, Seabury Press, 1982) p. 82

21 As we shall later see in the chapters dealing with baptism and the doctrine of salvation, the Anabaptists generally had a more positive view of man than did the Reformers. Nevertheless, an Augustinian doctrine of depravity did appear in certain streams of the movement, most notably in the segments influenced by the thinking of Menno Simons. "The image of fallen man which emerges from Menno's writing is not the image of a glorious creature corrupted, but rather the image of a being who is—without qualification—"unclean slime and dust of the earth." Apart from isolated and incidental references to God's love in the creation and preservation of the world, one searches in vain in Menno's writings for any positive content to the understanding of creation. The distinction between creation and fall seems to have disappeared entirely. In creating the new Adam, Christ, by implication, does not restore and renew the first Adam, but rather destroys him." John Tonkin, *The Church and the Secular Order in Reformation Thought* (New York, Columbia University Press, 1971) p. 141

22 Bouyer summarizes why Protestantism has adopted this posture toward anything looking "sacramental": There is, firstly, the survival and the exaggeration of an Augustinian tendency, more or less Platonist, which was already pronounced all though the Middle Ages, but predominated without counterbalance in the Reformed Churches. This was the tendency to reduce the spiritual to the interior life, to look on all that as corporeal or sensible in religion as, at best, superfluous and of dubious value. The more a person discards intermediaries ... the more 'spiritual' he becomes. We have read of those ascetics who, since they could not avoid having a body, got on with it as best they could, which was rather badly at that. The Protestants generally looked askance at all asceticism, which they suspected of being an attempt on the part of man to gain salvation by his own merits. But they were instinctively in complete agreement with the ascetics, even with the strictest among them, in despising the body and viewing with suspicion any part it might play in the spiritual life. The Quakers, which have no rites at all, no external worship, are not, strictly speaking, Protestants and Protestants in general do not venture to go as far as they. But they are certainly in the instinctive line of Protestantism..." Louis Bouyer, *The Word, Church and Sacraments in Protestantism and Catholicism* (New York, Desclee Company, 1961) pp. 62-63

23 "... the suspicion of outward things needs ... to be set in the context of medieval religion, with its superstitious attachment to people, places, and things, not least to the sacraments and the financial exploitation of this by the church." E. J. Furcha and H. Wayne Pipkin, *Prophet, Pastor, Protestant* (Allison Park, PA., Pickwick Publications, 1984) p. 161

24 Robert Webber, Donald Bloesch, eds., *The Orthodox Evangelicals* , "A Call to Holistic Salvation" Lane Dennis, (New York, Thomas Nelson, 1977) pp. 110, 111, 113. Italics mine.

25 Zwingli asserted that "The Spirit breathes and works in the hearts of believers; not outward things ... " Gottfried W. Locher, *Zwingli's Thought: New Perspectives* (The Netherlands, E. J. Brill, Leiden, 1981) footnote 367, p. 226

26 "While some baptists continue to use the term sacraments (particularly in Britain). Baptists of North America generally prefer the term ordinances. To many Baptist the term sacraments communicates implications of some magical transference of power." Gerald L. Borchert, "The Nature of the Church: A Baptist Perspective", *American Baptist Quarterly* , (Dec. 1982) Vol. 1, No. 2, p. 164

27 Zwingli believed that since God is free, He will not bind His gift of faith to the outward signs of water or bread and wine. "It relates more to what the believer does and affirms than to what he is given [in the sacrament] ... they were instituted by Christ to strengthen our faith in His saving work by recalling to us the fact and meaning of His Cross. ... their value lies in their psychological and teaching power." Hubert Cunliffe-Jones, ed., *A History of Christian Doctrine* (Edinburgh, T. & T. Clark, 1978) p. 363

28 It is still debated today as to what degree Luther's view of faith was nominalistic and what portion was Biblical, but one thing does seem clear: It is not "just" Christ who redeems us, it is *our* faith *and* Christ which justifies us. "Justification taking place 'on account of Christ; but only 'through faith,' with Christ as the ground and faith as the instrument." Jaroslav Pelikan *The Christian Tradition: Reformation of Church and Dogma (1300-1700)* (Chicago and London, The University of Chicago Press, 1983) p. 150

29 "'Sacrament' too often conveys a certain accent on the external forms and the efficacy of the rite by

the pronouncement of a strict formula independent of the context of the believing community. Such an accent leads in the direction of superstition and magic." Theodore G. Stylinanopoulos,"Holy Eucharist and Priesthood in the New Testament", *Greek Orthodox Theological Review* (Brookline,MA., Holy Cross Press Summer, 1978) Vol. XXIII, No. 2, pp. 121-122

30 Mk. 4:11, Rom. 16:25; 1 Cor. 2:7; 15:51; Eph. 1: 9; 3:4-9; Eph. 5:32; 6:19; Col. 1:26-27; 2:2 ; 4:3; 1 Tim. 3:16; Rev. 10:7

31 "To place a limitation on the number of sacraments is to view them from a very narrow perspective. If a sacrament happens whenever God's grace is mediated to man through matter, then there is no limit to the number of sacraments. Indeed the whole of creation becomes a sacrament, a Theophany, through which we see God." Anthony M. Coniaris, *These Are the Sacraments* , (Minneapolis, Minnesota, Light and Life Publishing Company, 1981) p. 9

32 A. J. Philippou, ed.,*The Orthodox Ethos,* (Oxford, England, Holywell Press, 1964) p. 133

"Byzantine theology ignores the Western distinction between 'sacraments' and 'sacramentals,' and never formally committed itself to any strict limitation of the number of sacraments. In the patristic period there was no technical term to designate 'sacraments' as a specific category of church acts: the term mysterion was used primarily in the wider and general sense of 'mystery of salvation ... '" John Meyendorff, *Byzantine Theology,* (New York, Fordham Press, 1979) p. 191

33 John Breck, *The Power of the Word* , (Crestwood, New York, St Vladimir's Seminary Press, 1986) p. 21

34 "The Eastern Churches see the whole Church as a Sacrament (mystery) participating in the unique mystery of the God-Man." David J. C. Cooper, "The Eastern Churches and the Reformation in the Sixteenth and Seventeenth Centuries," *Scottish Journal of Theology,* Vol. 31, 1978, p. 432

35 Anthony M. Coniaris, *These Are the Sacraments* , (Minneapolis, Minnesota, Light and Life Publishing Company, 1981) p. 10,11

36 This is especially the case if by such a gesture one also recognizes his commitment and identification to a particular Christian people, i.e. the Local Church.

37 "Now, when the early fathers came to the new Testament, they saw that the Church was as full of sacrament as Israel. They spoke not only of Baptism and the Lord's Supper as means by which we were brought to Christ, but also the gospels, prayer, the study of doctrine, the power of a life led as a good example, as well as other visible means by which Christ was represented. ... In this view the sacrament is not a thing in itself, an end, but a means through which Christ encounters us savingly." Robert Webber, "Recovering a Sense of the Sacred", *Again* (Mt. Hermon, CA., Concilliar Press, 1985) Vol. 7, No. 4, p. 17

38 "...in the East that the three rites, Baptism, Confirmation, Eucharist, remained united in the liturgical life and that it was there, too, that no particular theology of any of these three developed, at least in the first centuries. The whole problem of the relation between Word and Sacrament as well as the particular question whether Confirmation is a sacrament at all have been unknown to the East. ...problems will arise when one attempts to isolate Baptism from the Eucharist. It is not an accident that our Lord uses the term 'Baptism' in connection with his death (Mt. 20:22; cf. Luke 12:50). The 'cup' of his death and the 'Baptism' of his death to which he refers there, can hardly be understood apart from the cup of the New Covenant of the Last Supper. And in the entire Pentecostal scene described in Acts 2 the descent of the Holy Spirit, the Baptism of the three thousand people and the participation of all in the 'breaking of the bread' form one indivisible unity. There is thus an essential unity in the origins of all three, Baptism, Confirmation and Eucharist..." John Zizoulas, "Some Reflections on Baptism, Confirmation and Eucharist", A paper prepared for the Study Commission on Worship of the Commission on Faith and Order of the World Council of Churches, pp. 644, 646. Even today the Orthodox Churches receive new Christians into the Church by administering Baptism, Confirmation, and the Eucharist within the same service, each one immediately after the other.

39 John Zizoulas, "Some Reflection on Baptism, Confirmation and Eucharist", A paper prepared for

the Study Commission on Worship of the Commission on Faith and Order of the World Council of Churches.

40 "What would really be unspiritual would be that the action of the sacraments should be conceived in a sub-personal way. When people speak of 'sacramental grace' they sometimes betray forgetfulness of the fact that grace is 'a gracious personal relationship'. That is a real danger. That would really be unspirituality." Donald M. Baillie, *The Theology of the Sacraments* (New York, Charles Scribner's Sons, 1957) p. 49

41 Alexander Schmemann, *Church, World, Mission* , "Freedom in the Church," (Crestwood, New York, St. Vladimir's Press, 1979) p. 220,221

42 "This [understanding] gave rise to all those apparently insoluble problems about the irresistibility of grace, the relation of divine grace to human freedom, the relation of grace to faith, and so forth. And though the reformers in large measure rediscovered the Pauline conception, yet they did not carry it far enough to solve those problems." Donald M. Baillie, *The Theology of the Sacraments* (New York, Charles Scribner's Sons, 1957) p. 52

43 Donald M. Baillie, *The Theology of the Sacraments* (New York, Charles Scribner's Sons, 1957) p. 54. Italics mine.

44 Grace is not a created gift given to an imperfect humanity, "It is the divine life itself given to man who has been created in order to receive it and to share in it and who, if he is deprived of grace, ceases to be consistent with his own nature." John Meyendorff, *The Catholicity and the Church,* "The Significance of the Reformation in the History of Christendom, St. Vladimir's Seminary Press, (Crestwood, New York), 1983, p.71

45 In the Old Testament the Spirit is depicted more as the Power of God rather than as a Person. The day of Pentecost, however, changes our understanding of Him just as the day of the Incarnation changed our understanding of the Son. On Pentecost, the Spirit becomes involved with us as a *Person* and, in union with Him, we become the body of Christ.

46 Man is not only "creature", but a creature made in *God's* likeness. Man's potential to commune with God (and thus His divinity) was not obliterated in Adam's rebellion. By God's grace it is still possible for all (through Christ)to become imitators and sons of God. The capacity for man to become "God-like" and "partakers of the the divine nature" (2 Peter 1:4) has not been destroyed by the fall, only the life and communion he once had in God has been corrupted. See John Meyendorff, *The Catholicity and the Church,* "The Significance of the Reformation in the History of Christendom, St. Vladimir's Seminary Press, (Crestwood, New York), 1983, p. 72

47 In the Eastern Church being conformed to Christ-likeness is commonly called "deification" or the process of "theosis" (to be divinized). These terms hold different meanings in Western vocabularies than they do in the Eastern context. Deification is not a neo-platonic pantheism nor does it claim to say that man "possesses" God, i.e., that he becomes infinite, shares in God's essence or that God's *Person* inhabits him. I will speak in more in detail about this in the salvation chapter.

48 "The Church is one in the Holy Spirit and the Spirit 'construes' it into the complete and perfect Body of Christ. The Church is predominantly one in the fellowship of the sacraments. Putting it in another way, the Church is one in Pentecost, which was the day of the mysterious foundation and consecration of the Church when all the prophecies about her were fulfilled. In that 'terrible and unknown celebration' the Spirit-Comforter descends and enters the world in which He was never present before in the same way as He now begins to dwell. Now He enters the world to abide in it and to become the all-powerful source of transfiguration ... Pentecost, therefore, is the fulness and the source of all sacraments and sacramental actions, the one and inexhaustible spring of all the mysterious and spiritual life of the Church." Georges Florovsky, *Creation and Redemption*, (Belmont, MA., Nordland Publishing Company, 1976) p. 189

49 Alexander Schmemann, *Church, World, Mission* , "Freedom in the Church," (Crestwood, New York, St. Vladimir's Press, 1979) p. 227

50 In the sacraments the Spirit discloses the *ongoing consequences* of Christ's redemptive Mystery

— consequences we *still experience today* . Christ's work of redemption may have been completed some two thousand years ago, but it's ramifications are never ending. (As George Florovsky notes, "That which took place 'in the past' was a beginning of 'the Everlasting.'") Although a symbol is not like a type in that it usually is not prefigurative, in the respect that every symbol embraces both the promise and its ultimate fulfillment in the Kingdom of God it is "typologicial." In the sacraments the Spirit allow the faithful to see redemption from *God's* point of view, from a reference both inside *and* outside of time.

51 Anthony M. Coniaris, *These Are the Sacraments* , (Minneapolis, Minnesota, Light and Life Publishing Company, 1981) p. 15

52 "The sacraments, in relation to our persons, are means, gifts which must be realized, acquired and become fully ours, in the course of constant struggles wherein our wills are conformed to the will of God in the Holy Spirit present in us. In the Church our nature receives all the objective, conditions of this union. The subjective conditions depend only upon ourselves." Vladimir Lossky, *Mystical Theology of the Eastern Church,* (Crestwood, New York, St. Vladimir's Press, 1976) p. 183

53 "The need for faith as we approach Christ in the personal encounter of the sacraments is obvious. There were many people in the crowd that day who jostled about Jesus and touched Him. Yet it was only the sick woman who managed to get close enough to touch the hem of His robe who was healed. Of all the people in that crowd she was the only one who touched Jesus with faith. The touch of Jesus in the sacraments is not magical or mechanical. It is just as personal as the touch established by that sick woman in the crowd. Thus, we must approach Jesus in the Sacraments with faith, obedience, and deep penitence for our sins. We come not just to be takers but also givers. We give ourselves to God and to our fellow humans with a deliberate act of love without which the sacraments themselves would be worthless." Anthony M. Coniaris, *These Are the Sacraments* , (Minneapolis, Minnesota, Light and Life Publishing Company, 1981) p. 16,17

54 "Man possessed the earth because God gave it to him. It was the original sacrament, for it was this means by which man encountered God, His Creator, and it would have always been so, had man used it as God intended." Bishop Dmitri, *Orthodox Christian Teaching* (Syosset, New York, Orthodox Church of America, 1983) p. 26

55 "Is God only the God of spirits or is he not also the God of all flesh? ...God-the-Trinity, living in inaccessible Light and penetration by His energies the created world—the world of pure spirits as well as that of physical beings..." Vladimir Lossky, *In the Image and Likeness of God* (Crestwood, New York, St. Vladimir's Press, 1974) p. 63

56 Robert Webber, Donald Bloesch, eds., *The Orthodox Evangelicals* , "A Call to Sacramental Integrity" Thomas Howard, (New York, Thomas Nelson, 1977) p. 123,124

57 Alexander Schmemann, *Liturgy And Life: Christian Development,* (Crestwood, N.Y., St. Vladimir's Seminary Press, 1974) p. 93, 93

58 "On the one hand, sacrament is rooted in the nature of the world as created by God: it is always a restoration of the original pattern of things. On the other hand, it is rooted in Christ personally. Only through the perfect man can the broken priesthood of humanity be restored. Alexander Schmemann, *Church, World, Mission* , "Freedom in the Church," (Crestwood, New York, St. Vladimir's Press, 1979) p. 227

59 Alexander Schmemann, *Church, World, Mission* , "Freedom in the Church," (Crestwood, New York, St. Vladimir's Press, 1979) p. 224

60 Man and creation are closely related and intertwined. Man's sin resulted in death's reign in the world ("...as through one man sin entered into the world, and death through sin..." Rom. 5:12) and man's final redemption through Christ will likewise bring immortality and life back to creation (Romans 5:17-21; Col. 1:15-20; 1 Cor. 15:53-56).

> To the universe, man is the hope of receiving grace and unity with God, and also the danger of failure and fallenness. 'Creation anxiously awaits this revelation of the sons of God,' writes St. Paul. "It is indeed to vanity that creation was made subject, not

> willingly, but because of him who subjected it; with, however, the hope that creation would also be liberated from the slavery of corruption to participate in the glorious liberty of the children of God' (Rom. 8:19-21). Subjected to disorder and death by man, creation also attends upon man, become sons of God through grace, for its liberation. The World follows man, since it is like him in nature: 'the anthroposphere,' one could say.

Vladimir Lossky, *Orthodox Theology: An Introduction*, (Crestwood, New York, St. Vladimir's Press, 1978) p. 71

61 "The 'demonic' in nature comes from the fact that creation fell out of its original meaning and direction. God had entrusted control over the world to man—His own 'image and likeness.' But man chose to *be controlled* by the world and , thereby, lost his freedom. He then became subject to cosmic determinism, to which his 'passions' attach him and in which ultimate power belongs to death. ... By sanctifying water, food, and plants, as well as the results of man's own creativity, such as works of art of technology... the Church replaces them all in their original and true relation, not only to God, but also to man, who is God's 'image.' ...Thus, sanctification of nature implies its demystification. For a Christian, the forces of nature cannot be divine; nor can they be subject to any form of natural determinism: the resurrection of Christ, by breaking the laws of nature, has liberated man from slavery to nature, and he is called to realize his destiny as lord of nature in God's name." John Meyendorff, *Byzantine Theology,* (New York, Fordham Press, 1979) pp. 135-136

62 Robert Webber, Donald Bloesch, eds., *The Orthodox Evangelicals* , "A Call to Sacramental Integrity", Thomas Howard, (New York, Thomas Nelson, 1977) p. 125

63 1 Corinthians 6: 13 is often misinterpreted because many stop at the first part of the verse where it says, "Food is for the stomach, and the stomach is for food; but God will do away with both of them" and fail to read the rest which states, "Yet the body is not for immorality, *but for the Lord; and the Lord is for the body.* " The meaning of this passage in reference to the body becomes all the more clearer in the context of the following verse, "Now God has not only raised the Lord, but will also raise us up through His power." On this passage I quote biblical commentator F. W. Grosheide: "...the word 'Lord' designates the risen and glorified Christ. In like manner it is stated that when God has raised us up, *we* are complete men. In both cases, therefore, the object of the resurrection is that which will be after the resurrection. Our resurrection is the fruit of the *power* of Christ (15:23). God raises us up through the work of Christ (Rom. 6:5; II Cor. 4:14). The dignity of the body is great. It is not destined to perish but to come to glory." F. W. Grosheide, *The New International Commentary on the New Testament : The First Epistle to the Corinthians* (Grand Rapids, Wm. B. Eerdmans, 1976) p. 148

64 Donald M. Baillie, *The Theology of the Sacraments* (New York, Charles Scribner's Sons, 1957) pp. 47-48

65 "The breath of God quickens matter and His Spirit unites them. ... God sanctifies the material nature in the human body: 'God formed man of dust from the ground'." (Genesis 2:7) A. J. Philippou, ed.,*The Orthodox Ethos,* (Oxford, England, Holywell Press, 1964) p. 51

66 "Platonism longs for the purification of the soul only. Christianity insists on the purification of the body as well. Platonism preaches the ultimate dis-incarnation. Christianity preaches the ultimate cosmic transfiguration." Georges Florovsky, *Creation and Redemption,* (Belmont, MA., Nordland Publishing Company, 1976) p. 115

67 Davids, commenting on James 1:18 ("In the exercise of His will He brought us forth by the word of truth, so that we might be, as it were , the first fruits among His creatures."), makes some salient remarks in regard to the entirety of material redemption:

> ... the author intended some reference to creation.. creation in Genesis was 'by the word' of God and κτίσμα ["creation"] does refer to the whole creation, not just humanity... Yet is it not the case that redemption in the NT is often seen as a new creation...? "We' are a "firstfruit of his creation.' Κτίσμα originally referred to the foundation of a city...but in the LXX [the Greek Septuagint translation of the Old Testament] it is frequently used of

> God's creation or creatures in it... it always has a wider scope than simply humanity...humanity can be joined in creation in redemption ... James, like Paul (Rom. 8:18-25) see Christians...as that part of creation first harvested by God as part of his new creation. They have been reborn by the word of truth, the gospel. ... But redemption does not stop here, for the full harvest will follow the firstfruits and the consummation will include the whole creation.

Peter Davids, *New International Greek Testament Commentary: Commentary on James* (Grand Rapids, MI., Wm. B. Eerdmans Publishing Company, 1982) p. 89-90

68 Georges Florovsky, *Creation and Redemption*, (Belmont, MA., Nordland Publishing Company, 1976) pp. 113, 114 citing John Chrysostom, *de resurrectione mortuorum* , 6, M.G. L, c. 427-428

69 See Romans 6:13; 12:1; 1 Cor. 6:20; Col. 3:5 for some examples of this.

> A further new factor is the modern understanding of the wholeness of man. Modern medicine unites with Bible teaching to present human nature as an integral unity, not a soul inside a body but distinct from it, nor a being with spiritual needs divorced from physical and mental needs. The modern word psychosomatic exemplifies that rediscovery. Some insights of psychology also illuminate the vital connection between what a man does and what he really is in the depths of his being. Surely this can be helpful in looking again at the whole concept of the sacramental.

Donald Bridge, David Phypers, *Communion: The Meal That Unites?* (Wheaton, IL., Harold Shaw Publishers, 1981) p. 167,168

70 "The church is the body of Christ, and so the members of the church are members of Christ (Rom. 12:5; Eph. 5:30). The coinherence is indeed most intimate, it is one life which rules both Christ and those who are His. .. If the bodies are so closely united with Christ, they are to be used in accordance with that union. It is inconsistent with the glory of a body which is linked to Christ to make it a *member of a harlot*. ... as often as a person has intercourse with a harlot, he comes one flesh with her. A union like that is not broken off, it is always existing. But there have been people, and they must have been in Corinth also, who argued that intercourse with an unchaste woman did not matter, just because she in any case lives unchastely. There is no union effected in such a case. In order to contradict that opinion Paul appeals to the Scriptures, especially to the word that God Himself instituted physical communion between men and women, where it also appears that such communion, no matter how it is realized, causes a man and a woman to be one flesh." F. W. Grosheide, *The New International Commentary on the New Testament : The First Epistle to the Corinthians* (Grand Rapids, Wm. B. Eerdmans, 1976) pp. 148-149

71 "...our last end is not only an intellectual contemplation of God but the resurrection of the total man, soul and body, the beatitude of human beings who are going to see God face to face in the fulness of their created nature." Georges Florovsky, *Creation and Redemption*, (Belmont, MA., Nordland Publishing Company, 1976) p. 222

72 "...it is not the body that dies, but the whole man. For man is organically composed of body and soul. Neither soul nor body separately represents man. ... Mysterious as the union of soul and body indeed is, the immediate consciousness of man witnesses to the organic wholeness of his psycho-physical structure. This organic wholeness of human composition was from the very beginning strongly emphasized by all Christian teachers. That is why the separation of soul and body is the death of man himself...i.e. of his existence as a man." Georges Florovsky, *Creation and Redemption*, (Belmont, MA., Nordland Publishing Company, 1976) pp. 106-108

In this light, man has been by analogy compared with the personhood of Christ, whereby He is one Person (ego) *in* (not *of*) two natures (human and divine). Applying an aspect of this christological dogma to man, one could say that although a particular man is one person, he is only "a person" as he exists in his two "natures" of spirit and matter. Neither spiritual nor material "nature" can exist separately; if separated the whole person ceases. "... in death this one human hypostasis [person] is broken up. Hence the justification for the mourning and weeping. The terror of death is only warded off by the hope of resurrection and life eternal. " *ibid.*, p.108

73 Vladimir Lossky, *In the Image and Likeness of God* , (Crestwood, New York, St. Vladimir's Press, 1974) p. 63

74 This , however, should not be interpreted in an Apollinarian sense. Jesus did not *only* take on our flesh; He identified with us completely in every aspect of our *humanity* (e.g.,. inclusive of a human intellect, rational soul).

75 "It was 'for us men and for our salvation' that the Son of God came down, and was made man ... The union, or 'communion,' with God had been re-established, and the power of becoming children of God has been granted to men, through faith. ... The Son of God, 'was made man' for ever. ... The Hypostatic Union [the union of divinity and humanity in the *Person* of Christ] is a permanent accomplishment." Georges Florovsky, *Aspects of Church History* (Belmont, Massachusetts, Nordland Publishing Company, 1975), p. 65

76 Evangelical Lane Dennis comments on this lack of perception common among evangelicals and their failure to see creation's participation in God's plan of redemption:

> For it is not just that the full meaning of salvation has somehow become reduced; rather the problem is bound up in something much more comprehensive - that the prevailing consciousness of Western culture makes it extremely difficult to affirm a holistic world-view in which the spiritual and the eternal co-inhere, such as the historic, biblical Christian understanding of reality requires. In short the modern consensus is that we live in a one-dimensional world - the reductionist reality of naturalism, positivism, and materialism. In reaction to this, we evangelicals have tried to affirm the existence of the eternal-spiritual dimension, but we have often done so without a clear understanding of the problem and have ended up fighting the battle by our opponents' ground rules. In the process we have often lost the proper understanding of the temporal-material dimension, with the result that the holistic-Christian meaning of salvation and the holistic-Christian world-view have become fragmented. The problem, I would suggest, grows out of the whole development of Western culture, especially as this can be seen in the late medieval breakdown of Western Christendom and the emergence of Reformation Protestantism.

Robert Webber, Donald Bloesch, eds., *The Orthodox Evangelicals* , "A Call to Holistic Salvation" Lane Dennis, (New York, Thomas Nelson, 1977) p. 108

77 Many physicists have determined that the particles which make up the universe are not isolated from each other, but rather are related and connected . Actually, everything in the universe is connected to everything else—past, present, future —in what is the 'the implacate order.' Particles are not really separated, but connected in a way that is invisible to ordinary concepts of reality.

Today's Einsteinian cosmology, in contrast to the Newtonian cosmology characteristic of Roman Catholic and Protestant theology, is *non-dualist* and monist in character. It challenges the view which would divide nature, a philosophy which has afflicted western science, philosophy and theology. Newtonian perspectives, contrarily, notably effect a destructive split between subject and object, form and being, structure and substance. Einsteinian cosmology, a philosophy more sympathetic with the Scriptures ...

> ... demands a thoroughly *integrative* approach in which knowledge is grounded in the *inherent relatedness that permeates the universe* , and therefore in the objective structures and transformations of the real world. A critical effect of this change in cosmological outlook is the disclosure of how deeply conditioned our traditional habits of mind have been by the paradigms of dualist structures and the pseudo-concepts they engendered, but its constructive effect is *the replacing of analytical, disjunctive modes of thought with integrative, synthetic modes of thought* correlated with the intrinsic patterns and organizations that are naturally latent in the world... "

T. F. Torrance, *Theology in Reconciliation: Essays Toward Evangelical and Catholic Unity In East and West,* (Grand Rapids, MI., William B. Eerdmans Publishing Company, 1975) p. 74, italics mine.

78 ."...the ancient meaning of the word, 'symbol' is not the modern meaning; Harnack has taught us

that the reality is present in the symbol." Yngve Brilioth, *Eucharistic Faith and Practice : Evangelical and Catholic* (London, S.P.C.K., 1953) pp. 59-60

79 Maximos Aghiorgoussis, "The Theology and Experience of Salvation", *Greek Orthodox Theological Review* , (Winter 1977) Vol XXII, No. 4, ftnte 12, p. 411

80 This is not to say that a symbol is to be confined to material things. A symbol (sacrament) can equally be expressed in actions as well. Biblical examples typifying this sense are demonstrated by the Old Testament prophets (e.g.,. I Sam. 15:27, 28; Jer. 32:6-44; Ezek. 4:4-8) as well as by Jesus Himself (multiplication of the loaves-Christ the Bread of Life [Jn 6], the healing of the man born blind-Christ the Light of the world [Jn. 9], Lazarus raised from the dead-Jesus the Resurrection and the Life [Jn. 11], Christ's washing the feet of His disciples-Christ as Servant [Jn. 13]).

81 Both baptism and the eucharist are symbolic of many other things reflective of Christ's redemptive mystery. We shall look more deeply into these in the next few chapters.

82 In a Mystery: Here is, perhaps, the key. "There are no propositions that can quite encompass the transaction that occurs in sacrament. Here we are brought up to that frontier where propositions tend to get muddled and die away. No one - no father, doctor, or council - has ever found precisely the adequate phraseology and vocabulary to define exactly what is going on in the sacraments. Any Christian knows that on every single point of the faith we come eventually to the place where we must say, 'It is a mystery. I cannot press my explanation any further than this.' Creation, Fall, Redemption - who is equal to these topics?" Robert Webber, Donald Bloesch, eds., *The Orthodox Evangelicals* , "A Call to Sacramental Integrity," Thomas Howard, (New York, Thomas Nelson, 1977) p. 122,123

83 John Breck, *The Power of the Word* (Crestwood, New York, St Vladimir's Seminary Press, 1986) p. 17

84 Donald Bridge, David Phypers, *Communion: The Meal That Unites?* (Wheaton, IL., Harold Shaw Publishers, 1981) p. 169

85 Even the instance where some of the Corinthians were receiving the Eucharist unworthily they were not rebuked for their unbelief but for their arrogance, hard-heartedness, and extreme disrespect for the less fortunate members of the Body (1 Cor. 11).

CHAPTER THIRTEEN

THE EUCHARIST (PART I):

THE EARLY CHURCH'S REPLY TO WESTERN QUESTIONS

Though unique and profound, the Early Church's perspective of the Eucharist is surprisingly simple. Unfortunately, many in the West often misinterpret her positions and this simplicity is frequently blurred. To avoid such confusion, this chapter will briefly outline the rationale behind popular Western approaches to the Eucharist, and then offer an Eastern Christian response.

THE MEDIEVAL ROMAN CATHOLIC TEACHING OF THE EUCHARIST

Though there were countering positions, the accepted view of the Eucharist within the Medieval Roman Church was that it was *literally* the body and blood of Christ, both spiritually and *historically.* The confession of Berengar of Tours (1059) sums up this teaching in a striking manner:

> ...the bread and wine... after consecration, are the real body and blood of our Lord Jesus Christ, not merely sacrament thereof; and that body is sensibly, not merely sacramentally, but in reality (*sensualiter, non solum sacramento, sed in veritalte*), handled by the priest's hands and crushed by the teeth of the faithful.[1]

As for the bread, as bread, *nothing* remained of it. After the prayers of consecration, not even a morsel of it existed.[2] It only *looked* like bread; in reality it was the *very body* of Christ which hung on Calvary. This view of Christ's presence in the Eucharist was explained as *transubstantiation.*[3] With such an emphasis, it followed that the most important aspect of the Mass were "the words of institution" ("This is My body ... this is My blood"). This phrase was believed to effect the change of the bread and wine into the body and blood of Christ.

This "Element-focus" was evidenced by the popular devotion to the Eucharist by the people. So great was their reverence, they even adored the consecrated host apart from the actual liturgy. The Eucharist was as an *object* which *individuals* received; it expressed virtually nothing about their relationship with each other. The organic connection between the Church as the Body of Christ and the Eucharist as the Body of Christ was disintegrated.

> From the 12th century the *corpus christi mysticum* (i.e., the Church) and the *corpus Christi eucharisticum* [the Eucharist] — once radically identified with one another— came to be distinguished ever more sharply. The church came to be understood above all as a divinely instituted, hierarchically ordered body politic, and the Eucharist, one of several 'means of grace' dispensed by it for the spiritual growth of individual members. [4]

Accompanying this view, the *sacrifice* of the Mass was seen as a means whereby one could receive Christ's atoning work on Calvary. Christians in this period began to view the sacrament both as *containing* grace and as the *cause* of grace. [5] This distorted understanding caused many to relate to the Eucharist as if "It" could forgive sins. Salvation, therefore, in some ways became dependent upon one's reception of the sacrament.[6] To this the Reformers protested: "Salvation is appropriated by faith, not by a rite."[7]

FOUNDATIONS OF THE EVANGELICAL-FUNDAMENTALIST PERSPECTIVE

A CHILD OF THE MEDIEVAL ROMAN CHURCH

Much of Protestant thinking on the Eucharist was a reaction to Medieval Roman Catholic ideas, and was itself born from within Roman scholasticism. Luther's arguments regarding the Eucharist were clearly scholastic.[8] Although his conclusions differed from Luther's, Zwingli's positions were likewise defended by scholastic arguments.[9] This should not surprise us. Both Luther and Zwingli were former Catholic priests, and as students, the teachings of both William of Occam and Thomas Aquinas had exerted a tremendous influence on their approaches to philosophy and theology.

Luther's view of the Eucharist was not his own invention; it was dug out of scholastic quarries. This is especially the case in his explanation of *how* Christ dwelt within the sacrament. His *consubstantial* view (where Christ is said to dwell *in and with* the bread and wine)[10] was a teaching he borrowed from the Medieval Roman Church before the transubstantiation view became its official teaching.[11] Similarly, Luther's teaching that Christ's presence in the Eucharist came in response to God's Word originated from Augustinian scholasticism. He was not the only one who quoted Augustine in this regard. Other Reformers looked to his various interpretations to support an array of opinions regarding Christ's presence in the Eucharist. Lastly, Augustine's dualistic view of the universe and nominalism was also used by Luther and the Reformers to de-emphasize the place of the sacraments within the Medieval Church. If the material universe is only a passing imitation of reality, and if faith alone makes Christ "real" to the believer, then, of course, faith alone—not the sacraments—grants salvation.[12]

Protestantism inherited the individualistic sacramental emphasis of the Medieval Roman Church and then took it a step further. From an excessive focus on the elements, many within the Reform movement called for an even greater attention on the *individual* by asking each communicant to personally reflect on his or her life's holiness. Of course there is nothing wrong with this, but to see *the Eucharist* as an exclusively *private* devotion is to once again ignore its identification with each member *within the Church.* It is to view believers as secluded individuals.[13]

Today it is still this individualistic lens which the average Evangelical-Fundamentalist adopts: "The ordinance of the Lord's Supper ... [being] a divinely appointed testimony from the believer's heart to God respecting his trust in Christ's efficacious death."[14]

LESSONS FROM ZWINGLI

Zwingli's position on the Eucharist does not parallel modern Evangelical-Fundamentalism's at every point. But because his teaching is so foundational to those views, I will take a more in-depth look at his approach here. It will not take long to discover that the energy behind his thinking was in reaction to Roman Catholicism's sacramental exaggerations, the people's hyper-pietism toward the Eucharist and claims that the sacraments could "save." His desire was to secure the primacy of faith over physical things, and he does this chiefly through his Platonic and humanistic philosophies.

ZWINGLI'S PLATONISM AND HIS REACTION TO 'GROSS MATERIALISM' IN THE EUCHARIST: CHRIST IS NOT PHYSICALLY PRESENT IN THE EUCHARIST

Zwingli reacted strongly to Rome's doctrine of transubstantiation and its related crudities ("chewing the blood and bones of Christ" in the Eucharist).[15] One of the foremost reasons for his aversion stemmed from the belief that, because Christ's body was *already* seated at the right hand of God, it was logically impossible for His body and blood to be also literally present on earth in the Eucharist as well.[16] Zwingli went so far as to say that it was even foolish to wish for such a bodily presence for "it was to the 'advantage' of his disciples and of the church in all ages that they should no longer have direct physical access to him."[17]

CHRIST'S 'SPIRITUAL' PRESENCE AT THE EUCHARIST

Despite his anti-materialist stress, Zwingli did happen to believe in the "real presence" of Christ in the Eucharist. Actually, he, the other Reformers,[18] and the Anabaptists [19] *all* believed in *some* kind of presence of Christ in the observance of the Lord's Supper.[20] But for most of them, this presence was a spiritual presence solely dependent upon one's individual faith. [21] Of course for Zwingli, a "spiritual" presence at (not in) the Eucharist was consistent with his view that Christ's "spiritual nature" can have nothing whatsoever to do with His physical nature (things fleshly). For this same reason Zwingli believed that Christ's redemption was solely a *spiritual* gift, something detached from anything physical.

THE EUCHARIST AS A MEMORIAL AND SIGN

Zwingli stressed that the Eucharist was a *memorial* of Christ's sacrifice. The sacrament was only a "public sign" of the absent Christ,[22] a token of Christ Who is present *only* by faith. [23] "He never allowed the traditional doctrine that in the Lord's Supper there is a true communication of the Lord's humanity to the faithful soul."[24]

Zwingli maintained that Christ's words in the Upper room, "This is my Body", must be understood as one of the many metaphors Jesus often used to refer to Himself (i.e., "I am the door", "I am the light of the world", etc.). In this case, he interpreted "is" (*estin*) in "This is My body" as "signifies " (*significat*).[25] This saying of Jesus, therefore, merely meant 'this is a *sign* of my Body," not "This is *actually* my body." [26] Cornelius Hoen, a Dutch humanist physician, should be credited with convincing Zwingli of this explanation. [27] When Zwingli was first exposed to this interpretation via one of Hoen's colleagues, he extolled it as "the great pearl" he had been searching for. [28] In complement to this incident, Zwingli also had a dream where he saw an unknown person point to Exodus 12:11 and say, "It is the Lord's passover." [29] This vision gave him an even greater certainty that the Eucharist was only a memorial.

SALVATION BY FAITH, NOT BY SACRAMENTS

Zwingli stood against a "fleshly" presence within the Eucharist not only because his humanism prohibited it, but because such an interpretation would encourage some to see it as a means of sacrifice for sins. If Christ's sacrificial body were *really* present, and if it were *really* offered up in the Mass, then, indeed, the forgiveness of the atonement would be available to each communicant. Zwingli could not allow for such a sensual corruption. Christ's original one-time sacrifice was valid; it did not need to be "repeated." His interpretation of Hebrews 9:24-26 made this patently clear. Zwingli firmly asserted "it is a false religion which teaches that consuming symbolic bread cancels sins. For it is only

Christ and his death that atones for sins."[30] The Eucharist, he affirmed, was only a memorial to be celebrated in response to Christ's command, thus its observance four times a year was sufficient.[31]

THE SPIRITUAL PROFITS THE BELIEVER; THE MATERIAL PROFITS NOTHING

Following Hoen's interpretations, Zwingli placed great importance on Jesus' statement recorded in John: "For it is the Spirit Who gives life; *the flesh profiteth nothing*" (John 6:63). [32] His exegesis of this verse shows us the conclusions he drew regarding the Eucharist: nothing physical could ever be a vehicle for the Holy Spirit. Zwingli concluded that whenever Jesus spoke of eating and drinking His "flesh and blood," He must have been referring to the *redemptive significance of His death,* not His *literal* body and blood. He interpreted this to mean that eating the body of Christ in the Eucharist could be of no benefit. Only "spiritual" (non-bodily) things can have an impact on the spirit of man; "flesh" cannot satisfy the soul. "For whatever is to renew and comfort and revive the spirit must be spirit..."[33]

As could be expected from this approach, Zwingli denounced transubstantiation and any claim of a change in the Eucharist. The Eucharist was spiritual, not fleshly. The flesh has *nothing* to do with the Spirit. If the Eucharist is to mean anything, therefore, it must only have a spiritual meaning. To imply that it is *both* spiritual and material is an impossibility.

> If it is the spirit that is being spoken of, then it follows, from the law of opposites, that it cannot have to do with the flesh; if it is the flesh that is spoken of, then whoever hears is sure that it does not mean the spirit. Therefore, 'to eat bodily flesh after a spiritual manner' is to maintain that flesh is spirit.[34]

Where did Zwingli get this teaching? He ends the above discourse with the answer, "I have drawn this from the [ancient Greek] philosophers' springs...."'[35]

THE FUNDAMENTALIST-CONSERVATIVE EVANGELICAL VIEW TODAY: SIMILARITIES AND DISTINCTIVES WITH ZWINGLI

Even though there are many similarities between the Evangelical-Fundamentalist perspective and that of Zwingli, there are also several significant distinctives. The Fundamentalist, for example, typically sees the Eucharist as a memorial and as a "mere symbol." [36] To him, the word symbol means something that represents an entity which *is not there*, (the dualistic-rationalistic, and non-Biblical sense). Actually, even Zwingli did not take his humanistic philosophy this far. He understood the New Testament word "remember" as signifying an actual bringing of Christ's Presence into the present time, and not just a mental contemplation of Christ's death.[37] Today's Evangelical-Fundamentalist, however, disregards any other aspect of the word's meaning but "*to recall* ."[38]

Christians of this persuasion adopt Zwingli's interpretation of the phrase "This is My body" as "This *signifies* My body." But they go further, believing that the word "signifies" does not in *any* sense communicate Christ's presence; it "removes *any* idea of identification."[39] Zwingli would have never agreed to such an understanding. This further emptying and re-interpretation of the word "remember" to mean only an individual's mental "recollection", has done much to de-emphasize the Church's communal identity, and has encouraged a pietistic individualism in its stead. [40]

In similarity with Zwingli's thought, the average Evangelical-Fundamentalist today insists that the "body and blood" of Christ in the Eucharist is "not a sharing in corporeal elements, but in an experience of Christ in terms of his sacrifice." One's reception of the elements is understood primarily as a pledge "to an identification with the mission of Christ."[41] With either vantage point, the observance of the Eucharist is not so much a statement about the Church's organic oneness with Christ and the brethren as it is a time for individual reflection.

Following this reasoning, it is obvious why many Evangelical-Fundamentalists do not think that the Lord's Supper is all that important. Most Evangelical-Fundamentalist bodies limit their observance of the rite to four times a year. Most theology texts written from this perspective pay little attention to the subject. For example, Dr. Lewis Sperry Chafer's expansive and respected eight volume set of systematic theology only dedicates a third of a page to the matter. To many, the Eucharist has no real significance how one lives the Christian life or to how the Church should see herself. It is a *personal* devotion. As we shall see, this is very different from what the Early Church believed.

THE PRESENCE OF CHRIST IN THE EUCHARIST

CHRIST'S PRESENCE IN THE EUCHARIST IS UNDEFINABLE

The Early Church believed in the actual presence within the Eucharist but not in the sense of transubstantiation. [42] How then? After all, if one believes that Christ is present in the Eucharistic elements, he should be ready to explain *exactly how* He is present. To this challenge, the early Christians would have responded, "Christ is present *in the same way* He is present in the Eucharistic gathering (i.e., the Church)." *Exactly* what manner is this? It cannot be explained, nor was it meant to be explained. [43] As is the nature of the Church, it is a mystery that defies definition.

THE SYMBOL OF THE BODY AND BLOOD IN THE EARLY CHURCH

To get an understanding of the Early Christian's sense of the literal (yet not crassly physical) sense of Christ's presence in the Eucharist, one must go back to the idea of symbolism discussed in the last chapter, i.e., symbols manifest the reality they represent. A good illustration of this symbolism is in 1 Corinthians 10, a key chapter on the Eucharist. Let us look at a few verses from this chapter and then draw out the meaning of the Eucharistic symbolism it expresses.

> For I do not want you to be unaware, brethren, that our fathers were all under the cloud, and all passed through the sea; (2) and all were baptized into Moses in the cloud and in the sea; (3) and all ate the same spiritual food; (4) and all drank the same spiritual drink, for they were drinking from a spiritual rock which followed them; and the rock was Christ.

Then, applying this symbolism in verse 16, Paul continues...

> Is not the cup of blessing which we bless a sharing in the blood of Christ? Is not the bread [loaf] which we break a sharing in the body of Christ? (17) Since there is one bread [loaf], we who are many are one body; for we all partake of the one bread [loaf]

The rock "which followed them" was not a "walking boulder"- it was Christ. Paul himself tells us this plainly. The pre-incarnate Christ was literally and actually present with the Israelites in their desert wanderings via the manna and water He miraculously provided. *He* was the "spiritual food" and the "spiritual drink" they consumed in order to live. Although the Israelites may not have been able to identify Christ's presence with them in the wilderness, Paul states that from *this side* of the New Covenant, the Church can and does identify Him. [44]

These types (rock, bread, drink) *actualized* His presence within the congregation of Israel. In the same way, the types of bread and wine in the midst of the assembly, the new Israel, actualize Christ's redemptive presence. This is why Paul later in the chapter talks about the "bread" being the body of Christ and the "cup of blessing" being a sharing in the blood of Christ.

Is not this bread *real* bread and the wine of the cup *real* wine? Of course, but they communicate Christ as well. Were the manna and the water given to the people of God in the wilderness *really* manna and *really* water? Certainly, but they were also more; they were "spiritual" food and "spiritual" drink —they *manifested* Christ in their midst. It is the same in the Lord's Supper. The elements are both signs *and* what they represent. From this vantage point, we can better understand what Jesus really meant to convey in the words of institution:

> All four accounts of the Last Supper describe how, during the meal, Jesus took bread, blessed, broke and gave it to his disciples saying, 'This is my body.' All add that later in the meal he took a cup of wine, passed it round and said, 'this is my blood of the covenant,' or, 'This is the new covenant in my blood.' Significantly, however, at the Last Supper, Jesus said neither of the phrases which developed Catholic and Protestant theology really requires him to have said. He did not say, 'This has become my body,' nor did he say, 'This represents my body.' He simply said, 'This is my body.' Indeed, if the Greek words of the New Testament are translated into Aramaic, Jesus' native language, he probably said merely, 'This my body.' So what, then, did Jesus mean? . . . Reality or figure of speech? Faced with such a question, familiar with the Passover lamb and many, many other instances in the Old Testament where a prophet took a visual aid and called it by what it signified, the disciples of Jesus would have been quite bewildered. "Both", they would have had to reply. The bread and wine are symbols, but they are also Christ's body and Christ's blood. [45]

John 6: 55 presents another Biblical example of the Eucharistic symbolism I am speaking about here:

> "For My flesh is true food, and My blood is true drink. He who eats My flesh and drinks My blood abides in Me, and I in him."

People have fought to extract either a transubstantial or a metaphorical interpretation from these words, but both understandings are more scholastic and humanistic than they are Biblical. The real-symbolic meaning is especially clear when one reads verse 35 as a part of the context. In this verse, Jesus says He is the "bread of life", while in verses 32-41, He claims to be the manna from heaven, from which all who partake will never hunger but have eternal life. Is *He* literally bread? [46] Yes, in that as a man cannot live without bread (a Biblical expression for food), neither can he live without Him who is the author of Life. Is His flesh and blood literally food? Yes, in the sense that only as we depend upon Him and the offering of His Life can our hunger for Life be satisfied. [47]

> 'Flesh and blood' in that chapter (John 6) does not mean either the material flesh and blood of Jesus, or a symbol or figure thereof; rather, the words taken together signify the wholeness of the person of Jesus; 'the living bread' is equated first with Jesus himself, then with his flesh. This is the reconciliation of the difficulty of the apparent realism of verse 53-58 ... and the apparent symbolism of verse 63 ('the flesh profiteth nothing'). Neither a purely realistic nor a *purely* symbolistic explanation [in the Western sense] does justice to the Evangelist's thought.[48]

This view of symbolism also allows us to recognize the presence of Christ in *both* the assembly and in the Eucharistic elements. Two passages in 1 Corinthians 11 make this point clearly. In verse 27, Paul states that whoever *eats the bread or drinks of the cup* unworthily shall be guilty of sinning against the body and blood of the Lord. Here is a patent reference to the profaning of Christ's body *as symbolized in the elements.* As a (physical) type the Eucharistic supper represents a spiritual reality - how one relates to that type speaks of his attitude toward the spiritual truth it embodies.[49] In verse 29 he states that this condemnation is for the one who partakes but "does not judge *the body* rightly." How is this the case? In this passage, Christ's presence in the assembly has been violated by the Corinthians' lack of brotherhood. While assembled as Church to celebrate the Eucharist, they have ignored the needs of their poor members. The symbolic connection between the Church and the elements cannot be separated.

A FULL SYMBOL, NOT AN EMPTY ONE

The Fathers of the first centuries referred to the Eucharist in ways favoring both a literal and a metaphorical interpretation,[50] and this has confused many Western Christians looking for evidence to support either of these views. In truth, the Early Church did affirm a real presence in the Eucharist, but they did not advocate the transubstantial view. They affirmed the symbolic view we have just discussed. [51] Irenaeus (120-202) summarized the Biblical physical-spiritual understanding of the Eucharist well in the following:

> But our opinion is in accordance with the Eucharist, and the Eucharist in turn establishes our opinion. For we offer to Him His own, announcing consistently the fellowship and union of the flesh and Spirit. For as the bread, which is produced from the earth, when it receives the invocation of God, is no longer common bread, but the Eucharist, consisting of two realities, earthly and heavenly; so also our bodies, when they receive the Eucharist, are no longer corruptible, having the hope of the resurrection to eternity. [52]

Irenaeus' insight into the Eucharist remains the perception of the Eastern Christian today. [53]

BREAD AND WINE DO NOT DISAPPEAR

Eastern Christianity does not define the Eucharistic elements as the body of Christ in the manner of medieval scholasticism.[54] It does not see the bread and wine as being disintegrated and then replaced with the material body and blood of Christ. Christ is not in a "house of bread." The Eastern Church, however, does see the bread and wine as symbols which speak of His presence in this matter-world in which we live. The Eucharistic elements "contain" creation, life (food), and humanity, all that this world is made up of. In these elements, the Eastern Christian believes Christ can and does manifest

Himself. John Meyendorff outlines this Eastern understanding of Christ's presence within the Eucharist by contrasting it with the classical scholastic teaching of transubstantiation:

> The Byzantines understood the Eucharistic bread to be necessarily consubstantial with humanity, while Latin medieval piety emphasized its otherworldliness. The use of ordinary bread, identical with the bread used as everyday food, was the sign of true Incarnation. The Byzantines did not see the substance of the bread somehow changed in the Eucharistic mystery into another substance - the Body of Christ- but viewed this bread as the 'type' of humanity: our humanity changed into the transfigured humanity of Christ.[55]

Christ's *incarnation* makes it clear that matter and spirit are compatible. Christ's *resurrected* body also makes it clear that Spirit can transfigure matter. Christ took on our humanity, united it to His divinity, and then raised it from the grave. In His rising, Christ's humanity was transfigured and glorified. Because of Christ's union with us, every believer's humanity is likewise promised glorification. Through our Communion with Christ and God's people, our humanity can be continually transfigured into His likeness.

"THE CHANGE"

HOW THE SPIRIT CHANGES OUR PERCEPTIONS

How do the elements change into the body of Christ? As we have previously implied, they change in the same way the congregation "changes" (manifests) the body of Christ—by the Holy Spirit. Without the Holy Spirit, neither Christ's incarnation, the birth of the Church, nor the foretaste of redemption in the Eucharistic assembly would be possible.[56]

In so many of the debates throughout the years, too much attention has been focused on the elements and not enough on the brethren gathered around them. As the Spirit reveals the elements to be the body and blood of Christ, so we too are revealed to be the body of Christ by the same Spirit.[57] In the early Church, when the presider of the worship service prayed for the Holy Spirit's presence, he did not ask Him to descend upon the bread and wine alone but upon the *people* as well. Why? So that they, like the gifts, might manifest *the real presence of **Christ***, God's dwelling in the midst of His Assembly.

WHAT "THE CHANGE" REVEALS

Am I saying by this that there is no real change, only a realization of what is? Yes and no. Yes in the sense that every time one has communion with the love of God and others, he is changed. No, in the sense that nothing becomes *essentially* different.

Many times the word "change" denotes magic *presto-changeo*— what was here is now changed into something completely different. A change *does* come about in us and in the elements, but it is *not* a physiological metamorphosis. The change occurs by way of the *communion* of creation with the Spirit. The Spirit not only "descends" upon the Church, but He also *resides within her*. The Spirit *discloses* Himself, and reveals to us the nature of His indwelling. His communion with us as Christ's Body is a never ending process of revealing, disclosing, and giving. This is never completed, let alone in an instant of change.

And here once again is the emphasis: *communion.* The Spirit comes to bring us into communion *with Himself,* and *thus effects a change.* How does He do this? By His showing us what communion is like in the Kingdom, and by allowing us to "taste" of it now. "And thus in the Eucharist it is He who seals and confirms our ascension into heaven, who transforms the Church into the body of Christ and -therefore- manifests the elements of our offering as communion in the Holy Spirit. This is the consecration."[58]

Yes, the Eastern church does believe something happens to the elements in this communion. But, as stated before, in this change the physical elements are not obliterated; they are *fulfilled.* In them we see humanity and divinity, the created and the uncreated, the now and the not yet. They speak to us of "things to come" in "the now." Just as we will be completed on the Last Day, the bread and the wine show how all creation through union with Christ will one day be restored (1 Cor. 15:22-24; Eph. 1:9,10).[59]

> The elements are thought to change into Christ's body and blood, but there is also rather more stress on what might be called the 'natural' side of it, in that all physical 'elements' are seen as parts of God's creation. The material is meant to bear the stamp of divine glory, and this fact is an additional part of the meaning of what happens in the Eucharist.[60]

Once more, back to the question: "How then do the elements change?" Frankly, Eastern Christians refuse to say exactly when and how the Eucharist is "transformed." Similarly, there exists no definition in any Eastern council, nor citation from any Eastern Father, which nails down the change to a particular moment (e.g.,. "the words of institution"). The Early Eastern Church did not rely upon any word or action as being the definitive consecrating moment. She relied upon the Holy Spirit, One Who never can be reduced to a liturgical formula.

> The real presence of Christ does not depend upon the repetition of the words of the Last Supper and of the institution of the sacrament; it is not limited to the material elements of bread and wine only. The real presence of Christ is real because in the Ecclesia [Church] He comes after Pentecost as the Father's answer to the invocation of His Name through the Holy Spirit. This presence is neither an imprisonment of Christ within our limitations nor an act of binding the Spirit, but precisely the result of His freedom as communion, based on Christ's redemption and resurrection.[61]

THE PRIESTHOOD OF CHRIST IN THE EUCHARISTIC ASSEMBLY

The manifestation of the Spirit within the Eucharistic assembly is not due to a "power" which resides within the pastor. The entire assembly's presence and prayers are needed to welcome the Spirit's activity. The clergyman has neither an ordained power "to make sacraments," nor can he perform his role as an officiating pastor-priest on "his own." Without the Assembly, his ministry does not exist. The pastor's ministry, as each member's ministry, can only manifest itself *within the context of his relationship* to the entire Church. For this reason, no individual presider-priest in the Early Church could ever have celebrated the Eucharist without the participation of his whole assembly. How could the Body of Christ be present at the altar when the Church-the body in the Assembly-was absent? [62]

Who then is responsible for the Eucharistic manifestation of the Kingdom? Jesus Christ. He is the *chief* Minister in the Church.[63] He alone is *the* Priest mediating between God and man (1 Tim. 2:5).

Christ, the High Priest, is the One Who has purchased us by His blood, the One Who has given us all we have received, and the One Who forever stands as our Intercessor. He gives us the reason to worship, the spiritual and material gifts to offer in worship, and access to the Father by which we can worship. Thus, as it appears in the Eastern liturgy of St. John Chrysostom, the Christian can attest to Christ's Priesthood and affirm, "Thou art the Offerer and the Offered, the Acceptor and the Distributed, Christ our God."

He is the Priest in the Church, and He makes His priestly ministry available to all those in the Church. As co-priests with Christ in Eucharistic worship, each Christian is able to offer himself and his service to God through the giftings of the Spirit. One of these giftings is that of pastor-presider, and it is through the one who has been given this gift that Christ's shepherding is manifest in the Eucharist. *In the context of the worshipping Assembly,* he manifests Christ's gift as Chief Shepherd, and is thus able to unite his (His) congregation in worship and dedication to God. *In this ministry of corporate worship,* every member, discloses Christ's presence through his (His) varied ministries and gifts.[64] All in all, each person's priesthood (through that one Priesthood), makes Christ's Body present.

THE EUCHARIST AS SACRIFICE AND OFFERING

Before I close this chapter, I think it is important to make a few comments concerning what the Early Church meant when it referred to the Eucharist as "sacrifice" and "offering." The Reformers rightly protested against the Eucharist as a sacrifice performed to grant forgiveness of sins for those in attendance. When many Evangelical-Fundamentalists hear the word "sacrifice" or "offering" in association with the Eucharist, their nervousness is understandable.

When the Fathers of the Early Church used these words in reference to the Eucharist, they were not referring to the "re-sacrificing" of Christ or to the rite as a means of blotting out sins. The Church of the first centuries never offered the Eucharist as a means to appease God for sin. [65] The words "sacrifice and offering" carried many meanings, none of which were juridical.[66] Of these different understandings, I would like to emphasize the one in particular: the Eucharist as a sacrifice and offering *of ourselves (in and through Christ) as members of His Body.*

In the Early Church it was understood that to be a Christian, one united himself to Christ. Christ's life was to be *our* life, and equally important, His death was to be *our* death. In the Eucharist, each Christian was identifying with Christ. His communion was to be a sacrifice of his selfish desires, pride, and willfulness, a choice to choose the way of love (Mk. 8:34-37). Similarly, when the Christian partakes of the Lord's Supper today, this must commit him to saying, "Yes, I am willing to drink the Cup that you drink. Yes, I am willing to not only live for you but to die for you" (Matt. 20:22).[67] Furthermore, to partake of the Cup means not only to live and die for Christ, but it speaks of the Christian's commitment to give his life *for his brethren* as well (John 13; 1 John 3:16). This attitude toward the Eucharist is not something "nice" to believe, without it, it is impossible to approach the Eucharist as an offering.

CONCLUSION

The true meaning and experience of the Eucharistic celebration has suffered greatly through the centuries. It has suffered through medieval superstitions and a mechanized view of grace. It has suffered through a philosophy which stressed individual blessing over communal love. And it has suffered due to scholastic and humanistic attempts to define what escapes rational definition (i.e., What changes? What remains the same? When does the change come about? What happens to the person who receives the sacraments? What kind of "grace' does he receive? Etc.). In each distortion, the Eucharistic celebration's organic bond to the Assembly (the Body of Christ) is missing. The Eucharist is misperceived as one thing, the Church as another.

The Reformers understandably reacted to a transubstantial view of the Eucharist. To adopt such a perspective would conflict with their doctrines of the Church, the priesthood of all believers, and salvation by faith. Nevertheless, the Reformers and a number of other Protestants after them believed that there was indeed something more to the Eucharist than just a memorial. The problem before them was this: How does one express a "presence" of Christ without falling back into Roman ways of thinking and therefore contradicting other Biblical teachings? Today, because of these same troubling questions, the Evangelical-Fundamentalist is still "gun-shy" about anything resembling a "real presence."

The mood behind this thinking has often led the typical Evangelical-Fundamentalist to be more concerned about what the Lord's Supper is *not* than what it is (e g., it is *not* a sacrifice, it does *not* communicate "grace," the symbols do *not* present any spiritual reality, etc.). For this reason, many see little purpose in pursuing a clearer understanding of the Eucharist. This avoidance causes many Christians to perpetuate faulty conclusions: a symbol continues to be thought of in Platonic terms instead of Biblical ones, spirit and matter remain divorced, and a holistic view of creation is persistently rejected.[68]

Since Eastern Christianity has been removed from the medieval Roman - Reformed tensions and polarities, its understandings have never been defined or refined within Reformation debates. The Eastern Christian vantage point is reminiscent of an earlier era, one much closer to the primitive Church. To them, to affirm that communion with God was a spiritual experience expressed through creation would not have struck them as a contradiction. On the contrary, to think of the redemption *as distinct* from creation would have struck them as incongruent.

The Early Church had no need for definitions, nor did they fear because their beliefs could not be contained within the sealed jars of man's logic. The presence of Christ within the Eucharistic Assembly is not a subject for debate; it is a Life to *experience, to* personally *testify* and *give thanks for.* Their communion with the Trinity and each other was real, true, and life-giving; they did not feel any lack because they did not have the "sophistication" to inquire as to *how* they could have such a communion. The Holy Spirit confirmed that they indeed did, and their lives of love demonstrated it. This was more than enough.

NOTES FOR CHAPTER THIRTEEN

1 Yngve Brilioth, *Eucharistic Faith and Practice : Evangelical and Catholic* (London, S.P.C.K., 1953) p. 86

2 "The idea of a sacramental change after consecration entered the West through the writings of Ambrose (d. 397). ...Ambrose...supplied the Latin writers of the middle ages with classical texts for the complete formulation of the doctrine of transubstantiation. Without developing a theory of Transubstantiation, Ambrose let loose ideas upon which Lanfranc and Guitmund in the eleventh century grounded their doctrine. Ambrose's teaching is ["]clearer["] than that of the Greek fathers. He describes the sacramental process or change as conversion (*conversio*) of the nature (*natura*) of the elements, a preparation (*conficere*) of the body of Christ; as a change (*mutare*) of the species of the elements; a transfiguration (*tranfigurare*) of the Sacraments into the body and blood of the Lord. In addition to the use of the terms "conficere," "commutare" in the *De Sacramentis* , which , since the recent exhaustive enquiry of Faller may be regarded as the work of Ambrose, he says that the body of Christ did not exist before consecration, but does exist afterwards. The sacramental body is identical with the body which Christ received from the Virgin." A.J. Macdonald, ed., *The Evangelical Doctrine of Holy Communion* , "Formulation of Sacramental Doctrine", A. J. Macdonald (Cambridge, W. Heffer and Sons Ltd., 1930) pp. 69, 70

3 The word was officially adopted at the Fourth Lateran Council in 1215. The scholastic formulation of this dogma of the real presence at Trent was phased in Aristotelian categories. "In an Aristotelian metaphysic, there is no super-sensory realm of metaphysical ideas as there is in Platonism. The Aristotelian philosopher worked with the two categories of *substance and* accidents . That is to say, each object consisted of two elements, a universal category that defined its identity - e.g.,. chairness, bookness, etc; and the physical components i.e., its accidents, what made it concrete. Applied to the communion, or eucharist, this implied that the metaphysical substance - i.e. breadness and wineness must have visible accident, i.e. color, weight, smell; hence, transubstantiation." Howard Ervin, "Addendum on Tradition Added for Presentation to the Pentecostal/Roman Catholic Dialogue (Venice, October 1980) as transcribed from a presentation given at the May, 1980 Charismatic Leaders Conference at Glencoe, Missouri.

4 John H. Erickson, "Eucharist and Ministry in Bilateral and Multilateral Dialogue", (Crestwood, N.Y., St. Vladimir's Seminary Press, 1984) Vol. 82, No. 4, pp. 287, 288 citing *In Quest of a Church of Christ Uniting* (Consultation on Church Union, Princeton, N.J., 1980) pp. 30ff, 19-23 respectively

5 William Barclay, *The Lord's Supper* (Philadelphia, Westminster Press, 1967) pp. 70, 71

6 "On the sacrifice of the mass the Council of Trent declared that "in eating and drinking Christ's sacrifice is renewed and commemorated sacramentally and the fruits of that sacrifice are granted to the believer'." Donald Bridge, David Phypers, *Communion: The Meal That Unites?* (Wheaton, IL., Harold Shaw Publishers, 1981) p. 118,119.

7 The reader must be reminded, however, that many of the Roman Catholic positions on the Eucharist today are much more compatible with Reformed teaching than they were during the Reformation era: "The 'Real Presence' is now rarely defined in the old terms of transubstantiation which cost so many Catholics and Protestants their lives in an earlier century [The Inquisition]. *Trans-signification* is the current expression. The really significant fact is seen as the action of the Holy Spirit in the whole eucharistic prayer rather than in the priest's words of consecration. Thus the *epiclesis*, the prayer to the Holy Spirit to "come down", has reappeared in the new prayers. Moreover, *Sacrifice* is no longer defined in terms of repetition, but in terms of *re-presentation* . The sacrifice of Christ was offered once-for-all in history on the cross ... and its re-presentation at each eucharist is seen as recalling before God and before man, his saving acts in Christ, thus making them effective again to the believing community." Donald Bridge, David Phypers, *Communion: The Meal That Unites?* (Wheaton, IL., Harold Shaw Publishers, 1981) p. 144

The weakness of transignification, however, lies in the fact that the doctrine teaches that the very "sense" of the bread and wine becomes something *essentially* different, the essence of the bread and wine becoming something else than what they inherently are, i.e. bread and wine. The physical properties of bread and wine remain but now it signifies, for *us*, something different. The flaw in this theory is that the elements are emptied of their own realism.

8 "William of Ockham was also accused of favoring the idea 'that the substance of the bread is truly annihilated in the Sacrament of the Altar.'....God's power to separate substance and accident and as a way for faith to be meritorious by believing something without the evidence of experience or reason." This perspective was passed on to Luther in his understanding of the eucharist. Jaroslav Pelikan *The Christian Tradition: Reformation of Church and Dogma (1300-1700)* (Chicago and London, The University of Chicago Press, 1983) p. 57

9 Gottfried W. Locher, *Zwingli's Thought: New Perspectives* (The Netherlands, E. J. Brill, Leiden, 1981) p. 58

10 Consubstantiation was the Medieval Roman doctrine of *impanation,* a doctrine later discarded in favor of transubstantiation.

> After Augustine's example, the distinction was made between the visible elements and the super-sensible sacramental gift, *res sacramenti;* and in the 'impanation theory' attempts were made to find a middle way between symbolism and realism: the bread is not transubstantiated, its substance remains, but the personal presence of Christ is added to it as a heavenly substance. This view was a desperate attempt, in face of great difficulties, to preserve something like a spiritual interpretation; it was to be revived by Scotus and Ockham, and passed on by them to Luther.

Yngve Brilioth, *Eucharistic Faith and Practice : Evangelical and Catholic* (London, S.P.C.K., 1953) pp. 86, 87

11 "Luther's acceptance of the real presence and rejection of transubstantiation made his position analogous to that of medieval theology before transubstantiation had become official... the Lutheran doctrine, which the Reformed came to call 'consubstantiation,' was as much a 'materialistic theology' as was the Roman Catholic doctrine of transubstantiation." Jaroslav Pelikan *The Christian Tradition: Reformation of Church and Dogma (1300-1700)* (Chicago and London, The University of Chicago Press, 1983) pp. 200, 201

12 "Perhaps the most disquieting of Augustine's statements...quoted in the *Sentences* [citations of Augustine on various subjects]complied by Peter Lombard], 'Why are you preparing your teeth and your stomach? Believe and you have already eaten.' " This could have been interpreted to either mean that it was impossible to physically ingest the consecrated elements (thus, favoring a "spiritual" eating of the sacrament) or "it could also mean that 'only he eats in reality...who believes in Christ,' thus apparently making the reality of the presence a corollary of faith." This later argument was used to justify Rome's withholding the chalice from the laity (those with faith already received the blood, they did not need to take of the Cup). Jaroslav Pelikan *The Christian Tradition: Reformation of Church and Dogma (1300-1700)* (Chicago and London, The University of Chicago Press, 1983) pp. 54-55

13 "The Reformation challenged medieval teaching on the eucharist at several specific points: the mode of Christ's presence in the eucharist was reinterpreted, the sacrificial nature of the eucharist was questioned... yet just as before, the eucharist was regarded chiefly as indicating what the church does, *not what the church is* . It was one of the church's 'corporate forms of worship', and though the church might be defined as the 'body of Christ,' this was taken as a mere metaphor, implying no necessary connection with eucharistic participation in Christ's body and blood." John H. Erickson, "Eucharist and Ministry in Bilateral and Multilateral Dialogue", (Crestwood, N.Y., St. Vladimir's Seminary Press, 1984) Vol. 82, No. 4, pp. 287, 288 citing *In Quest of a Church of Christ Uniting* (Consultation on Church Union, Princeton, N.J., 1980) pp. 30ff, 19-23 respectively, italics mine.

14 Lewis Sperry Chafer, *Systematic Theology* (Dallas, TX., Dallas Seminary Press, 1948) Vol. VII, p. 229

Mark McCully, a man standing in the Anabaptist tradition, notes that this individualism is common place in the thinking of most Baptist Americans. It is an observation which has credence not only in respect to the Baptists, however, but to many Americans of fundamentalist-evangelical sentiments.

> The American Baptists, like the earlier 'spiritualists,' did not emphasize the ordinances. Rejecting 'Reformed' notions about sacramental 'means of grace,' they often made the Lord's Supper a 'mere memorial.' The aspect of community celebration and commitment to one another in the covenant was lost. The Baptists no longer thought of themselves as a 'chosen people, a royal priesthood, a holy nation, a people belonging to God' (I Peter 2:9). Instead, they thought of themselves as *Americans* , as *individuals* , as *national citizens* , and not as a *distinct people* . Baptism and communion were 'Christian ordinances' which could be practiced at association meetings, apart from the solidarity of a local group of disciples.

Mark McCulley, *Studies in History and Ethics* ," (St. Croix Falls, WI., Searching Together, 1983) p. 19

15 "The phraseology of Berengar's confession, that 'the bread and wine are the true body and blood of our Lord Jesus Christ ... handled and broken by the hands of the priests and ground by the teeth of the faithful,' indicated to what extremes a literal doctrine of the real presence might go, and it was against such crass conceptions of eating the flesh of Christ that the word, 'The flesh is of no avail,' were directed. Calvin found the phraseology 'monstrous,' quoting it over and over again for its shock value against those who shared Luther's view of the affair." Jaroslav Pelikan *The Christian Tradition: Reformation of Church and Dogma (1300-1700)* (Chicago and London, The University of Chicago Press, 1983) p. 199

16 Instead of recognizing the ancient Christian doctrine which affirmed that Christ's two natures were inseparable, Zwingli was so intent on affirming the impossibility of Christ's physical presence on earth that he even went so far as to say that Christ's human and divine natures could be divided: in heaven He was present only in His humanity and on earth He was present only in His divinity. This is very close to the heresy of Nestorius (d. 451) who taught that there were two separate Persons in the Incarnate Christ, one Divine and the other human. This teaching is impossible for a Christian to accept, however, for if this were true it would mean that man would *still* stand in need of a saviour. It is only because Christ was one Person *in* two natures that our humanity can have communion with God's divinity. In Christ, —the One who has assumed our humanity and made it His own— we as mortals can have access to both God's healing power and His personal fellowship.

17 Jaroslav Pelikan *The Christian Tradition: Reformation of Church and Dogma (1300-1700)* (Chicago and London, The University of Chicago Press, 1983) p. 158

18 Although they disagreed on the nature of the presence, the debates between Luther, Zwingli and Calvin made their belief in "a" presence clear. "Calvin went on criticizing Zwingli and Oecolampadius for failing to emphasize that though the bread and wine in the Eucharist were 'signs,' they were 'the kind of signs with which reality' was joined.' He criticized Luther, on the other hand, for continuing to speak, despite his rejection of transubstantiation, in such a way as to give the impression that he 'intended to assert the sort of local presence that the papists dream about'." Jaroslav Pelikan *The Christian Tradition: Reformation of Church and Dogma (1300-1700)* (Chicago and London, The University of Chicago Press, 1983) p. 186 citing Calvin's *Short Treatise on the Holy Supper*, 5, from Peter Barthand Wilhelm Niesel, eds. *Johannis Calvini opera selecta.* 5 volumes (Munich, 1926-36) here volume 1, pp. 527-529

19 Conrad Grebel the chief spokesman of the early Anabaptist movement " unlike Carlstadt and much like Oecolampadius, [considered] the bread in faith the body of Christ: '.In faith, it is the body of Christ and the incorporation with Christ and the brethren. But one must eat and drink in the Spirit and love, as John shows in chapter 6....'." George Hunston Williams, *The Radical Reformation* (Philadelphia, The Westminster Press, 1975) pp. 98-99 citing George Hunston Williams, ed. "Letters to Thomas Müntzer By Conrad Grebel and Friends (Zurich, September 5, 1524)" *Spiritual and Anabaptist Writers* (Philadelphia, Westminster Press, 1957) pp. 71-85

20 "'This presence of Christ's body is of a spiritual nature'..According to Zwingli, the controversy is not about "the real presence of the body of Christ", but about the form of the presence — whether it is ' a spiritual presence of the body and blood of Christ in the souls of the faithful' or a ' corporeal presence' [ZIII 341; Z V 587, 588, Cf. Z VI, II 202; S IV 11, 32f.]." Gottfried W. Locher, *Zwingli's Thought: New Perspectives* (The Netherlands, E. J. Brill, Leiden, 1981) footnote 358, p. 224

21 "The real body of Christ is present to the eye of faith...and this means that those who thank the Lord for the benefit bestowed on us in his Son recognize that he took real flesh, in which he really suffered, and really washed away our sins by His blood, and that here the entire work of salvation which Christ accomplished is, as it were, present to the eye of faith." According to Zwingli, the controversy is not about "the real presence of the body of Christ", but about the form of the presence — whether it is ' a spiritual presence of the body and blood of Christ in the souls of the faithful' or a ' corporeal presence'." *ibid.,* footnotes 343, 358, pp. 220, 224

22 "One after another, the expositors of the Reformed view of the Lord's Supper formulated their underlying hermeneutical principles. 'Christ, who is recognized by faith alone and worshiped by faith alone,' had according to Hoen, 'withdrawn his corporeal presence from us'; hence the bread was a 'sign' of his presence." Jaroslav Pelikan *The Christian Tradition: Reformation of Church and Dogma (1300-1700)* (Chicago and London, The University of Chicago Press, 1983) p. 194 citing Cornelius Hoen's *Christian Epistle*, from *Corpus Reformatorium.* Berlin and Leipzig. (1834-) 91:516-17

23 In this sign"...we have a parable that comes very close to *Calvin* . 'If a man is about to travel to a far country, and he gives his wife his finest ring, on which his likeness is engraved, saying: 'Here you have me, your husband; hold to me even when I am absent, and rejoice in me'.....then he is giving much more than if he had merely said 'Here you have my ring'...He is really saying: 'I want you to be sure that I am wholly yours...'" Gottfried W. Locher, *Zwingli's Thought: New Perspectives* (The Netherlands, E. J. Brill, Leiden, 1981) p. 225

24 Owen Chadwick, *The Reformation* (Harmondsworth, Middlesex, England, Penguin Books Ltd., 1972) p. 79

25 "Zwingli derived his conception of the Sacrament as a memorial from Hoen in 1523 when he received a letter from him stating that the phrase, "'This is my body," was really a figure of speech, a trope, and that the word "is" must be understood to mean "signifies." "We need to differentiate," quoted Hoen, "Between the bread which is received by the mouth and Christ who is received by faith.' ... Perhaps Erasmus' most effective blow at Protestantism was ... his subtle infusion of spiritualism into Zwingli, making him susceptible to ... Hoen's highly rational solution to a mystery of faith." Lewis W. Spitz, *The Renaissance and Reformation Movements,* (Chicago, Rand McNally and Company, 1971) pp. 390, 392

26 *ibid.,* p. 392

27 An encounter with Hinne Rode and Zwingli in 1523 resulted in a major event in the development of Reformation thought on the Lord's Supper. Zwingli was introduced to the *Epistola* of Hoen through Rode and he considered it to be a revelation. The idea of taking *est* to mean *significat* then crystallized for Zwingli. George H. Williams, *The Radical Reformation* (Philadelphia, PA., The Westminster Press,1961) p. 88.

28 Actually, Johanness Oecolampadius first received the idea from Hoen, expanded upon it and then passed it on Zwingli. Basing his thinking on Christ's bodily Ascension, Oecolampadius taught that it was thus impossible to believe that it was present here on earth via the sacrament. "In sum, Christ was saying: 'When you see me ascend up to heaven, you will see clearly that you have not eaten me literally and that I cannot be eaten literally..'." Jaroslav Pelikan *The Christian Tradition: Reformation of Church and Dogma (1300-1700)* (Chicago and London, The University of Chicago Press, 1983) p. 159 citing Zwingli's *A Clear Instruction About Christ's Supper*, 2, from *Corpus Reformatorium.* Berlin and Leipzig. (1834-) 91:818:-19

29 In a dream which occurred on the night of April 12th, 1525, Zwingli was pointed by an unknown person to Exodus 12:11: 'It is the Lord's passover' (Z IV 483, in the *Subsidium*). " Locher, ftnte. 353, p. 221

30 *ibid.*, footnote 368, p. 227

31 "Indeed, Zwingli's satisfaction with a mere four celebrations each year sharpened this separation. Indeed, the eucharist virtually ceased to be a sacrament at all. It conveyed no grace, but was merely a memorial of Christ's death, celebrated in obedience to Christ's command, "Do this in remembrance of me." Later generations would make the word paramount, and many would rarely receive communion in the glad and joyful spirit of thanksgiving so apparent in the early church." Donald Bridge, David Phypers, *Communion: The Meal That Unites?* (Wheaton, IL., Harold Shaw Publishers, 1981) p. 97.

32 "....the statement in the Gospel of John concerning the Spirit [John 6:63], who alone can give life, was of cardinal importance not only for Zwingli's doctrine of the sacrament, but for the whole of his thought and action." Gottfried W. Locher, *Zwingli's Thought: New Perspectives* (The Netherlands, E. J. Brill, Leiden, 1981) pp. 228-229

33 "The Spirit breathes and works in the hearts of believers; not outward things... 'If we eat the body of Christ, then it must produce something in us. So we ask, whether the soul can be nourished with flesh? One has to answer, 'No'. For whatever is to renew and comfort and revive the spirit must be spirit, as it says in John 6:63'" (Z VI, I 476)" Gottfried W. Locher, *Zwingli's Thought: New Perspectives* (The Netherlands, E. J. Brill, Leiden, 1981) footnote 367, p. 226.

34 Gottfried W. Locher, *Zwingli's Thought: New Perspectives* (The Nether-lands, E. J. Brill, Leiden, 1981) footnote 367, p. 227

35 Gottfried W. Locher, *Zwingli's Thought: New Perspectives* (The Nether-lands, E. J. Brill, Leiden, 1981) footnote 367, p. 227

36 Hinson, Glen E., "The Theology and Experience of Worship: A Baptist View" *Greek Orthodox Theological Review,* Holy Cross Orthodox Press, Volume XXI, Winter-1977, Number 4, p. 423 This is Dr. Hinson's assessment of what he believes to be the majority Southern Baptist view on the subject.

37 "This 'remembrance' is not merely intellectual process; and it does not awaken association with the past, but rather with the present. *Memoria,* as understood by Augustine (like ἀνάμνησις in Plato) describes the soul's power of realization and of consciousness in general; it often means the same as *conscientia.* According to this tradition, remembrance does not denote our ability to set ourselves back into the immediate or the remote past, but the way in which the past is brought into our present time, becoming contemporary with us and effective in us. Zwingli thinks in the categories of this Platonist-Augustinian anthropology; though for him this power to 'render present' the death of Christ as our salvation does not lie within our soul, but in the Holy Spirit, on the basis of the eternal efficacy of the Lord's sacrifice; the organ by which it is received is faith, or rather the conscious contemplation of faith." Gottfried W. Locher, *Zwingli's Thought: New Perspectives* (The Netherlands, E. J. Brill, Leiden, 1981) pp. 222-223

38 "It was to be a strong strand of super-Zwinglian teaching throughout Baptist history. The popular Victorian preacher Dr. Alexander Maclaren of Manchester could declare in 1884, "All our theories about the meaning and value of this Communion Service must be found within the four corners of that word . . . a memorial rite, and as far as I know, nothing more whatsoever." Donald Bridge, David Phypers, *Communion: The Meal That Unites?* (Wheaton, IL., Harold Shaw Publishers, 1981) p. 116,117

39 italics mine. The full quote from Donald Guthrie, *New Testament Theology* (p. 443) appears as follows:

> The words, 'take, eat; this is my body' (Mt., Mk, Lk.), leave the precise significance unexpressed. ... We are concerned, however, to note that it is highly improbable that identification of the bread with the body is in mind. The copula (*estin*) has the force of 'signifies', which removes any idea of identification. As in the Jewish passover, which must have been in the mind of Jesus at the time, the procedure was intended to be

symbolical [here again defining the term "symbol" in the Western sense, not the ancient sense of the word] .

40 Donald Bridge and David Phypers in *Communion: The Meal That Unites?* (pp. 116-117) cite the historical evolution of this individualistic attitude within the foremost of Evangelical-Fundamentalist bodies in America, the Baptists. They especially see the roots of this perspective being reflected in *The Pilgrim's Progress* , a devotional classic still well respected in most Evangelical circles:

> The most famous of these ejected Baptists was John Bunyan, author of many books including the timeless allegory, *The Pilgrims Progress.* In this great classic there is little place for the Communion Service, and when it is mentioned (and this is the subtle development) it is recommended merely as a personal help to the believer, a means to an end. ... Elsewhere in his works, Bunyan describes baptism and the eucharist as "shadowish and figurative ordinances". By calling them "ordinances" he implies that they are not sacraments which do something, but rites to be observed as a matter of obedience because Christ commanded them...
>
> An attitude of increasing casualness towards the Lord's Table developed within many of the historic Free Churches. Bunyan's deeply personal and individualistic approach became quite common. "Communion Services" became increasingly separated from the main diet of worship; extra optional services to which those who wished remained after the normal exercises. It was an attitude which could easily develop from an exaggerated emphasis being put on personal assurance of salvation rather than on the corporate nature of the church. That exaggerated emphasis was almost bound to be seen when repeated periods of revival, renewal and evangelistic fervor overtook the churches.

41 Donald Guthrie, *New Testament Theology* (Downers Grove, Il. Inter-Varsity Press, 1981), p. 758

42 "The early Christians refused to define exactly what happened to the bread and wine. For them it was something more than a mere physical bread and wine, for Christ was actually present in a renewing and nourishing way. But it was something less than a crass physical presence like that taught later by some eleventh-century theologians who insisted that if "you bite the bread you have bitten the body of Christ.' " Robert Webber, *Common Roots: A Call To Evangelical Maturity* (Grand Rapids, MI., Zondervan Publishing House, 1978) p. 90.

43 "The Eastern Church as a whole seldom ventured beyond a positive statement of her faith in the Eucharist and did not let herself be dragged into hazardous and undesirable speculations. Whenever her theologians happened to step beyond the boundaries of the mystery, it was mostly in reaction to Western developments or on the occasion of doctrinal controversies in the wake of the Protestant Reformation." Georges A. Barrois, "Closed Communion, Open Communion, Intercommunion?", *St. Vladimir's Seminary Quarterly* (Crestwood, N.Y., St. Vladimir's Seminary Press,1968) Vol. 12, No. 3-4 , p. 145

44 "The children of Israel ate actual meat and drank actual water and yet here it is called "spiritual." What is Paul really saying? Is he telling us that the Rock which followed the Israelites was not a real rock? Did the Israelites actually see Christ? How could they drink a spiritual drink? How could they eat spiritual meat? Aren't meat and drink real, actual, tangible substances? The Rock which followed the children of Israel had spiritual merit. It symbolized Christ! This is what made it a spiritual rock! Its whole meaning was spiritual." James Lee Beall, "The Lord's Supper", (Detroit, MI., Evangel Press) p. 10.

45 Donald Bridge, David Phypers, *Communion: The Meal That Unites?* (Wheaton, IL., Harold Shaw Publishers, 1981) p. 15-17.

46 Christ, who identified Himself with the sacrifice, did not use the flesh of the lamb to signify his body, but rather chose bread. Bread was more a reference to the manner of the exodus, something which was fulfilled in Christ: "the manna from heaven" (John 6). More than this, Christ integrates the idea of the Exodus, the sacrifice, and the bread of life: "Your fathers ate the manna in the wilderness, and they died. This is the bread which comes down out of heaven, so that one may eat of it and not die. I am the living

bread that came down out of heaven; if any one eats of this bread, he shall live forever; and the bread also which I shall give for the life of the world is My flesh." (John 6:49-51).

47 "The Eucharist for them [Byzantine theologians] always remained fundamentally a mystery to be received as food and drink, and not to be 'seen' through physical eyes." John Meyendorff, *Byzantine Theology,* (New York, Fordham Press, 1979) p. 204

48 Yngve Brilioth, *Eucharistic Faith and Practice: Evangelical and Catholic* (London, S.P.C.K., 1953) pp. 57-58, italics mine.

49 Lesser examples of a bond between an image and the spiritual reality it represents might be seen in one's willful burning of the Bible or in his defiant breaking of a cross. What these images symbolize— God's Word and Christ's sacrificial death— have been profaned by the desecration of their symbols.

50 Ignatius of Antioch (30-107 A.D.) : "I have no delight in corruptible food, nor in the pleasures of this life. I desired the bread of God, the heavenly bread, the bread of life which is the Flesh of Jesus Christ, the Son of God, who became afterwards of the seed of David and Abraham, and I desire drink, namely His blood, which is incorruptible love and eternal life." *Epistle to the Romans*, VII., *The Ante-Nicene Fathers* (Grand Rapids, MI., Wm. B. Eerdmans Publishing Company, 1973) pp. 76-77

Justin Martyr (110-165) : "And this food is called among us Evxaristía [the Eucharist], of which no one is allowed to partake but the man who believes that the things which we teach are true, and who has been washed with the washing that is for the remissions of sins, and unto regeneration [baptism] , and who is so living as Christ has enjoined. For not as common bread and common drink do we receive these; but in like manner as Jesus Christ our Saviour, having been made flesh and blood for our salvation, so likewise have we been taught that the food which is blessed by the prayer of His word, and from which our blood and flesh by transmutation are nourished, is the flesh and blood of Jesus who was made flesh. For the apostles, in the memoirs composed by them, which are called Gospels, have thus delivered unto us what was enjoined upon them; that Jesus took bread, and when He had given thanks, said, 'This do ye in remembrance of Me, this is My body;' and that, after the same manner, having taken the cup and given thanks, He said, 'This is My blood;' ..." *The First Apology* , LXVI., *The Ante-Nicene Fathers* (Grand Rapids, MI., Wm. B. Eerdmans Publishing Company, 1973) p. 185

In the third and fourth centuries "there are passages in which they speak with almost literal crudeness about the bread and the wine being the body and the blood of Jesus Christ, and equally there are passages in which these same writers speak for the bread and the wine being the symbols of the body and the blood of Christ. *But it is true that within this period the symbols do tend to become more and more identified with that of which they are symbols* . [italics mine]. Hippolytos (*The Apostolic Tradition*), Eusebius of Caesarea, Cyril of Jerusalem, etc..." William Barclay, *The Lord's Supper* (Philadelphia, Westminster Press, 1967) p. 63ff

51 "At any rate in the patristic period the underlying assumption of the literature is a devotional realism which can be variously expressed. The evidence is disparate in character (exegetical allusions, homiletical explanations and liturgical material). It is of varying degrees of theological penetration. But even when it is least theologically self-conscious it would make nonsense if the real presence of Christ at the service or within the elements was not a widely accepted devotional fact." H. E. W. Turner, "The Eucharistic Presence", *Thinking About the Eucharist:: Essays by Members of the Archbishops' Commission on Christian Doctrine*, (London, SCM Press Ltd, 1972) pp. 99, 100

52 *Against Heresies*, IV. 18, 5., *The Ante-Nicene Fathers* (Grand Rapids, MI., Wm. B. Eerdmans Publishing Company, 1973) p. 486

53 "The Eucharist is neither a symbol to be 'contemplated' from outside nor an 'essence' distinct from humanity, but Jesus Himself, the risen Lord, 'made known through the breaking of bread' (Lk. 24:35); Byzantine theologians rarely speculated beyond this realistic and soteriological affirmation of the Eucharistic presence as that of the glorified humanity of Christ." John Meyendorff, *Byzantine Theology,* (New York, Fordham Press, 1979) p. 204

54 "...any physical identification of the bread and wine with the material flesh and blood of Jesus is impossible, even apart from the Jewish sentiment, which viewed the drinking of blood with abhorrence.

The words, so interpreted, would be meaningless, since at the Last Supper Jesus was sitting at the table with the disciples; and the copula—*est* , is— which has been taken in some later controversies as proof of a corporeal identify, was certainly lacking in the original Aramaic. It is the form which the words take when translated that has contributed to the localising of the presence in the elements." Yngve Brilioth, *Eucharistic Faith and Practice : Evangelical and Catholic* (London, S.P.C.K., 1953) pp. 55-56

55 John Meyendorff, *Byzantine Theology,* (New York, Fordham Press, 1979) pp. 204, 205

56 "In the celebration of the eucharist, the Church very early realized that in order for the eucharistic community to become or reveal in itself the wholeness of the Body of Christ ... the descent of the Holy Spirit upon this creation would be necessary. ...'Send down Thy Holy Spirit upon *us* and upon the *gifts* placed before thee' (Liturgy of of St. John Chrysostom, prayer of consecration). ... It is important to bear in mind that the Body of Christ, both in the Christological (incarnational) and in the ecclesiological sense, became a historical reality *through the Holy Spirit.* " John D. Zizioulas, *Being As Communion* (Crestwood, N.y., St. Vladimir's Seminary Press, 1985) p. 160

57 "The Spirit transforms the sacred gifts into the body and blood of Christ (*metabole*) in order to bring about the growth of the body, which is the Church. In this sense, the entire celebration is an *epiclesis* , which becomes more explicit at certain moments. The Church is continually in a state of *epiclesis* . ...For the *epiclesis* is not merely an invocation for the sacramental transforming of the bread and cup. It is also a prayer for the full effect of the communion of all in the mystery revealed by the Son." "The Mystery of the Church and of the Eucharist in the Light of the Mystery of the Holy Trinity", Document of the Joint International Commission for Theological Dialogue between the Roman Catholic Church and the Orthodox Church, July 6, 1982 as reported in *St. Vladimir's Seminary Theological Quarterly* , 1982, Vol. 26, No. 4 , p.

58 Alexander Schmemann, *For the Life of the World* , (New York, St. Vladimir's Seminary Press, 1973) p. 43, 44

59 "...in the Orthodox ecclesial experience and tradition a sacrament is understood primarily as a revelation of the genuine *nature* of creation, of the world, which, however, much fallen as 'this world,' will remain God's world, awaiting salvation, redemption, healing and transfiguration in a new earth and a new heaven." Alexander Schmemann, *The Eucharist* (Crestwood, N.Y., St. Vladimir's Seminary Press, 1987) p. 33

60 A. J. Philippou, ed.,*The Orthodox Ethos,* (Oxford, England, Holywell Press, 1964) p. 11

61 A. J. Philippou, ed.,*The Orthodox Ethos,* (Oxford, England, Holywell Press, 1964) p. 69.

62 Again: "The celebration of the eucharist by the primitive Church was, above all, the gathering of the people of God ... [and as such was] both the manifestation and the realization of the Church." John D. Zizioulas, *Being as Communion* (Crestwood, N.Y., St. Vladimir's Press, 1985), pp. 22, 23

63 "There is no ministry in the Church other than Christ's ministry. This assertion, which seems to go back to the New Testament Church (Heb. 3:1, Matt. 23:8, John 13:13, Heb. 5:6, 8:4, 10:21, 2:17, 1 Peter 2:25, 5:4, Heb. 13:13) is understood by the Fathers so realistically that not only the dilemma of choosing between an *opus operantis* and an *ex opere operato* is avoided but also any other question implying a *distance* between the Church's and Christ's ministry becomes irrelevant and misleading." John D. Zizioulas, *Being As Communion* (Crestwood, N.Y., St. Vladimir's Seminary Press, 1985) p. 210

64 Christ's ministry is not localized in the pastor alone, it is expressed and shared in diverse ways *throughout the entire Church's membership* .

> The text of the epiclesis, as it appears in the canon of John Chrysostom and in other Eastern liturgies, implies that the mystery is accomplished through a prayer of the entire Church ("We ask Thee. . . ") - a concept which does not necessarily exclude the idea that the bishop or priest pronouncing the words of institution acts *in persona Christi* , as Latin theology insists, but which deprives this notion of its exclusivity by interpreting the ministerial sacerdotal "power" to perform the sacraments as a function of the entire worshipping Body of the Church.

John Meyendorff, *Byzantine Theology,* (New York, Fordham Press, 1979) p. 206

65 Of course this is not to deny the way in which the eucharistic gathering symbolically allows one to enter into Christ's eternal sacrifice. But this *anamnetic ,epicletic* and *symbolic* conception is far different than the popular medieval Roman Catholic understanding of the eucharist as sacrifice.

66 "The fathers used the term in reference to various elements: (1) the offering of material gifts for use in the sacrament, for the maintenance of the ministry and for the poor; (2) the common and appointed public prayers offered by the Church; (3) the sacrifice of praise and thanksgiving, or 'Eucharist', as Chrysostom explains by saying that in the celebration, the contemplation of God's blessings, particularly his action in Jesus Christ, are placed before the Church as a challenge to thanksgiving; (4) the solemn proclamation of the passion, death, resurrection and ascension in 'unbloody sacrifice' and (5) the solemn consecration and dedication of the Church and individual believers to the Lord and to their neighbors." G.L.C. Frank, A Lutheran Turned Eastward, (St. Vladimir's Theological Quarterly, Vol.26, Number 3, 1982) p. 165, 166

67 Dom Gregory Dix summarizes Irenaeus on this point:

> Each communicant from the bishop to the newly confirmed gave *himself* under the forms of bread and wine to God, as God gives Himself to them under the same forms. In the united oblations of all her members the Body of Christ, the church, gave herself to *become* the Body of Christ, the sacrament, in order that receiving again the symbol of herself now transformed and hallowed, she might be truly that which by nature she is, the Body of Christ, and each of her members of Christ. In this self-giving the order of laity no less than that of the deacons or the high-priestly celebrant had its own indispensable function in the vital act of the Body. The layman brought the sacrifice of himself, of which he is the priest.

Dom Gregory Dix,*The Shape of the Liturgy* , (New York, The Seabury Press, 1983) p. 117

68 "Historically the Platonic affinities of the symbolic view of the communion elements were both recognized and condemned wherever in antiquity a symbolic view emerged, e.g.,. the repeated condemnation of the Messalian's - anti-sacramental monastic sect of the early centuries of Christianity." Howard Ervin, "Addendum on Tradition Added for Presentation to the Pentecostal/Roman Catholic Dialogue (Venice, October 1980) as transcribed from a presentation given at the May, 1980 Charismatic Leaders Conference at Glencoe, Missouri.

CHAPTER FOURTEEN

THE EUCHARIST (PART II):

WHAT THE EUCHARIST REVEALS

The Early Christian saw the Eucharist first and foremost as a revelation of the Kingdom of God, God's communion with His people. The entire Eucharistic celebration was seen as an unveiling of God among His people, a revelation of God's Church. How did these believers acquire such an understanding? To answer this question, I will make several observations about the background and meaning of the Eucharistic Meal. Then, in light of this context, I will illustrate the many ways the Christian Community understood the Eucharist as communion in the Kingdom.

HOW COMMUNION IS REALIZED IN A SHARED MEAL

THE THANK OFFERING

It is around the *Eucharist Meal*, that the *Eucharist of Communion* with God and the people of God is revealed. This Meal-Celebration carries with it a spiritual power and reality that few in the West realize. How can a meal be spiritual? The Eucharistic Meal is a direct parallel to the Old Testament *thank offering*, a meal of deep spiritual significance. The first Christians were clearly aware of the parallel and saw the Eucharistic Meal through this vantage point. This Old Testament sacrifice is described in Leviticus with customary attention to detail.

> If he offers it [his sacrifice] by way of thanksgiving, then along with the sacrifice of *thanksgiving* he shall offer unleavened cakes mixed with oil ... And of this he shall present one of every offering as contribution to the Lord; it shall belong to the priest who sprinkles the blood of the peace offerings. Now as for the flesh of the sacrifice of his *thanksgiving* peace offerings, it shall be eaten on the day of his offering... (Lev. 7:12-15)

This seemingly complex ordinance was worked out in an interesting way. After the priest offered the sacrifice to the Lord, he would take his portion, and he and the sacrificer would eat the thanksgiving offering in a "meal before God."

The most dramatic example of this "meal before God" occurs in Exodus 24. After receiving the covenant from the Lord, Moses and the elders of Israel were told to go up to

Mount Sinai to worship Him (Ex 24:1-2). Accordingly, they sacrificed thank offerings (v. 5), and took the prescribed offerings with them to the mountain (Ex. 24:9-11... they beheld God, and ate and drank.").[1] This is particularly significant when one realizes that the word "Eucharist" comes from the Greek word for "thankful" or "gratitude" (εὐχαριστία).[2] The Eucharistic celebration, like the thank offering, was seen by the Ancient Church as an offering of praise and thanksgiving acknowledging Christ's presence in their midst. In the meal, "they beheld God, and ate and drank" and worshipped Him.

As discussed in the last chapter, the Eucharist is sacrifice and offering. An aspect of our offering is the "sacrifice of praise" we give as we behold God in the Meal. There, while eating and communing with God and the brethren, our hearts perceive the greatness of the Incarnation. We know that Christ is *Immanuel*, because in the faces of the God people we see that "God is *with* us."[3]

THE SPIRITUAL DIMENSION OF SHARING A MEAL

In our culture, "having a bite together" symbolizes little if anything. During the time of the ancient Hebrews and early Christians, however, sharing in a meal together was an expression of each participant's fellowship with and good will toward the other.[4] Conversely, if one refused to eat with someone, or if he were excluded from another's meal, he understood this act as a personal rejection.[5] The account in I Corinthians 11 makes it clear that because this meal was an integral part of the Eucharistic service, the segregation between the poor and wealthy contradicted the meal's very meaning, and so was rightly rebuked by the Apostle. The Eucharistic Meal was the Love Feast;" a Meal celebrating the personal communion each member had with God and his brethren.

The average person in the New Testament era understood something else about a "shared meal." When partaken of in the context of religious observance, it also meant that those dining had communion with the deity in whose name the meal was eaten. Recognizing that this was commonly understood by the culture, both Paul (1 Cor. 10:19-22), and the council at Jerusalem (Acts 15:29) prohibited Christians either from sharing in the table at a pagan feast or from eating any meat which had been sacrificed to idols.[6] The message was clear: one cannot partake at a meal of sacramental quality without also having fellowship with *the person* (the demon or "being") it commemorates.

THE TABLE FELLOWSHIP: EATING A BLESSING

Let me further illustrate the symbolic significance of the Eucharistic Meal by pointing to an accepted practice familiar to the ancient Middle Easterner: the *table fellowship*. To him, the symbols communicated in a shared meal were rich, abundant, and *far* from empty. When the head of the house recited the blessing over the bread of the meal, broke it, and then handed a piece to each member, *their actual eating of the bread* was understood as making them a *recipient of the blessing.* The same was true of the "cup of blessing" (a cup of mixed wine): they believed their *drinking from it actually mediated a share in the blessing.* [7]

The significance this custom holds for the Eucharist should be quite clear. The disciples who participated in the Last Supper (a meal patterned after the Table Fellowship) fully realized that they were participating in the blessing Christ spoke over the bread and wine. This whole custom was "a familiar and self-evident idea to the disciples from their earliest childhood...."[8]

This gives us an additional insight into how the disciples understood their Master's words over the cup and the bread at the Supper. To the usual blessing over the bread and the wine Jesus "added the words which referred to the broken bread and the red wine to his atoning death for 'many'." [9] What does this mean? Jesus not only communicated a "blessing" to the disciples via the bread and the wine, but also indicated "*that by eating and drinking he gives them a share in the atoning power of his death.*" [10]

But someone may ask, "Are you saying that one cannot be saved unless he partakes of the Eucharist?" That is a strange question, one which would never have been asked had it not been for various sacramental abuses throughout history, and the concurrent non-*relational* views of salvation. Actually, if one stops to think about it, apart from the Reformation-Counter-Reformation context, the question really makes no sense.

Only when salvation is viewed as a thing, instead of as union in Christ, are such questions asked. Communion with God and each other is what salvation is all about! Therefore, to ask if one *has* to have communion with God and his brethren to be saved is bizarre. It is similar to someone asking, "Can I be married although I never intend to have intercourse with my spouse?"[11] Well, I don't know. Can you? It certainly is a peculiar way to think about marriage. One does not ask, "what is the least I need to do to be married?" Marriage is to be an opportunity for intimacy and communion without restrictions. The one who wants to know its minimums removes it from the context of communion and love.

It is the same with Eucharistic communion. One's participation in the Eucharist (which *always includes the entire gathering of the Church, not just blessed elements)* is not to "get saved," but to participate, realize, and manifest the communion Christ has made possible. This communion has no limit, and is something that will take all of eternity to fulfil.

THE PASSOVER MEAL AND WHAT IT MEANT TO "REMEMBER" IT

The most intimate link between the Eucharist and a meal is the Passover meal. [12] This is particularly evident in the way the Old Testament Jew celebrated it as a means to *remember* his deliverance from Egypt. As briefly noted in the last chapter, the word "to remember" had a distinctly different meaning to the Jew and other Eastern peoples than merely "to recount" or "to recall." This is a crucial point. When Jesus asked us to perform the Eucharistic rite in "remembrance" of Him, He obviously had the Jewish understanding of "remember" in mind.

The word "remembrance" in the Gospel accounts of the Lord's Supper is translated from the Greek word *anamnesis* (ἀνάμνησις). This word is difficult to translate into just one English word. When we use "remembrance" or "memorial" to translate it, we are often led astray from its deeper significance. These usually connote something absent—something which is *only* mentally recollected. However, they do not capture the *Biblical sense* of "remembrance" (anamnesis).

According to the Scriptures, when an event from the past is being "re-presented" before God in such a way that what is being symbolized becomes operative in the present, one "remembers" it.[13] To remember in this sense, then is to defy the historical limitations of time. When the Jews "remembered" the Passover, for instance, they *re-lived* and *re-entered* their exodus from Egypt once again. God's deliverance of them was again made real.

ANAMNESIS AND THE EUCHARIST

This background ties directly into our understanding of the Eucharist. When the Lord asked us to "do this *in remembrance*" of Him, He was asking us to remember -- "to do *anamnesis* " -- in the same sense as the Jews "remembered" their deliverance in the Passover Feast. He was not asking us merely to mentally recall His death on our behalf. In the Eucharistic celebration, we are to "remember" our salvation through Christ's offering of Himself. Through this "re-living" or "re-entering" connoted by *anamnesis*, each believer personally participates in the event of His once-for-all sacrifice.

In this Eucharistic remembrance — like the Jews in their Passover celebration— each is actively delivered afresh from slavery, sin and death. *Anamnetically,* each enters into God's salvation in the corporate celebration of the Eucharist, just as *anamnetically* each Jew entered into the experience of deliverance again and again at each Passover. And just as the Jews would not have said that the firstborn of Egypt were slain again and again because of this "remembrance" of their deliverance, so neither did the Early Church say that Christ is crucified again and again through her "remembrance" of His sacrifice.[14] The Spirit-filled celebration of the Eucharist does not re-create history. It allows the Church to experience the saving *effects* Christ accomplished in history, effects that are *now experienced* and *manifested* in the gathered Assembly's "remembrance."[15]

Anamnesis not only calls us to re-live (and thus to re-experience) what is being "remembered," it also invites us to taste the *future*. The Passover did this by foreshadowing the Eucharistic celebration not only in its rite, but also in the salvation which *was yet to come.* Passover night was the night on which the Jews had been redeemed in the past, and on which they would be redeemed in the future. "When the Jews at the first Passover 'remembered their deliverance, they also 'remembered-anticipated' their *ultimate* deliverance in the One Who was to come."[16] The Eucharist is a celebration of the Pascal mystery *now* completed in Christ.[17]

THE EUCHARIST AS THE KINGDOM OF GOD

The early Eucharistic celebration spoke of communion with God, communion with each other in Christian brotherhood, and was itself a manifestation of Christ's redemption. Given this understanding, the Eucharistic Gathering is a reflection of the Kingdom of God (Are not these chief characteristics of God's reign of love?). I will illustrate an important implication for our Christian life and experience based on this perception.

THE EUCHARIST AS A REVELATION OF THE CHURCH

How is it possible for the Eucharist to give a revelation of the Church? A partial answer to this question is found in the fact that early Christians never looked at the Eucharist as something *distinct* from the Church. Their experience of the Church was always inseparable from their experience of the Eucharistic gathering. Of course, by now this should be obvious. They are both the same, the Body of Christ—the Church—*is* the body of Christ—the Eucharist.

When an Eastern Christian receives from the Cup and the Loaf, he does not come expecting to receive "a spiritual power" different from what is already given him in his union with Christ. He sees the Eucharist as an *expression* of the Church, not "a power" of the Church. John Zizioulas, an Orthodox theologian specializing in early Christian literature, encourages us to:

> ... give up envisaging the Eucharist as one sacrament among many, as an objective act or a 'means of grace' 'used' or 'administered' by the Church. The ancient understanding of the Eucharist ... was very different. The celebration of the Eucharist by the primitive Church was, above all, the gathering of the people of God ... that is, both the manifestation and the realization of the Church.[18]

When we inquire about the meaning of the Eucharist apart from its connection to the *entire life* of the Church, its real meaning is bound to become obscured.[19] Neither the Eucharist nor any "sacrament" can be separated from the others as if they were "pieces" of sanctification. The chief Mystery is Christ in the Church. The pattern unfolded in the

Lord's Supper uniquely reveals that He holds the Church together through *communion with each believer,* and that each believer—as a *member* of His Body—stands in *relationship* to the other members of His Body. He is the Vine, we are the branches (John 15).

THE EUCHARIST CANNOT BE SEPARATED FROM THE CHURCH

It is impossible, therefore, to separate the Eucharist from the Church and relationships of Christian union. When we speak of "communion" or "Eucharist" we are not referring to the elements of the bread and wine alone, but to the *entire* Eucharistic gathering. Thus "the Eucharist ... is unthinkable without the gathering of the whole Church in one place, that is, without an event of *communion* ."[20]

In the Eucharist the Holy Spirit deepens our union and gives us the spiritual vision to recognize the union which already exists. In one of the liturgies of the Byzantine Church (St. Basil's), the presider prays for this very illumination:

> We pray Thee and call upon Thee, O Holy of Holies, that, by the favor of Thy goodness, Thy Holy Spirit may come upon us and upon the gifts now offered, to bless, to hallow, and to ... unite all of us to one another who become partakers of the one Bread and Cup in the Communion (koinonia) of the Holy Spirit. [21]

St. John of Damascus (675-745), a theologian of the Eastern Church, complemented this New Testament vision when he said, "The Eucharist is also called *Koinonia* [communion] and rightly so, for by it we have communion with Christ ---and by it we also have communion and are made one with each other, because we are part of the one body."[22]

THE EUCHARIST AS THE BODY OF CHRIST

This understanding makes it obvious that one of the key images of the Eucharist is found in *the Biblical vision of the Church as the one Body of Christ.* "The Eucharist is the Sacrament of the Church: In it the Church *realizes what she is:* the body of Christ, a new Unity of men in one divine and human life."[23]

The Church is not simply an association of believers, but a mystery of union. This perception was clear to the New Testament Church ("...we who are many are *one body.*" 1 Cor. 10:17) and was the most common understanding of the Church in both East and West until its interruption by Twelfth Century scholasticism. Again, the Eucharistic Assembly realized the truth that *they, as the people of God,* were the Body of Christ, and as such were *united with Him and one other.*

THE EUCHARIST AS RELATIONSHIP

Christ's reference to His "flesh and blood" in John 6:56, coupled with His signifying the bread of the Last Supper as His *body* (Lk. 22:19; Mt. 26:26; Mk. 14:22) did not speak only of His giving Himself up for the Church. These words also made it clear that the life of the Church would be continually dependent upon *His* life (i.e., *His* body). Hence it should not surprise us that the Church identified herself with the word "body." The word revealed something substantial about her members; each was *related* to Christ in a similar way one's members were to his own body. The Eucharist primarily tells of a *relationship* — the relationship between God and His people.

The Eucharist manifested this *organic bond* between Christ and His Body, the Church. The Early Church did not see the Eucharist as principally "holy objects", but "first of all as an assembly (*synaxis*).¨ a community, [and] a network of relations..."[24] The early Christians did not *go* to Church, they "*gathered* as Church" (cf. 1 Cor. 11:18). "They did not ' *receive* communion'; they *entered* into it, with God and with each other." [25] And in this gathering and communion, by the power of the Holy Spirit, they became what they were—one body in Christ. [26] The Eucharist boldly affirmed that each member *together,* are now bone of His bones and flesh of His flesh" (Gen. 2:23; Eph. 5:29-32).[27]

THE EUCHARISTIC GATHERING: AN EXPRESSION OF THE KINGDOM'S CATHOLICITY

As union in Christ is catholic, [28] *all Christians* who participate in the Eucharist are *to be united* (no matter what race, class, status or distinction).[29] If the Body of Christ (the Church) is one, how could any segregation, isolation, division, or alienation be allowed in the Eucharistic Assembly? [30] Each member's participation and partaking of the sacrament makes it clear that each is *joined to the other* and *thus all are equal in Christ* .[31] No member is greater or lesser than another, *each* is needed to make up the body. [32] From this perspective, the Eucharistic Gathering is an image of the Kingdom: the environment where all social and natural divisions are transcended in love. [33]

In this respect, the Eucharist testifies to both the reality of the Kingdom of God *now* and its presence *yet to come* (Mk. 1:15; Matt. 6:10). The Spirit is *engaged* to the Church, but the marriage has not been *totally* consummated (Eph. 1:7-14). Yes, we are the body of Christ, but we have not *fully realized* what we are (2 Cor. 3:18).

Marana tha, an early Christian prayer said around the Eucharistic table, aptly expresses this tension between the *now* and *not yet* of God's Kingdom in the Church. The prayer is in the Aramaic language, an expression for "Come Lord" and it expresses *both* of these thoughts simultaneously. It means both "'Come and grant us *now* Thy presence in our worship' and 'Come in power and glory [in your Kingdom]'." The "real presence" of Christ now in His Body, and the eschatological note of Christ's Second coming are blended in one.[34] Both of these manifestations are accomplished by the ministry of the Holy Spirit. [35]

THE EUCHARIST AS COVENANT

Besides a meal being able to communicate a spiritual reality, the Scriptures mention yet another meaning to eating—the covenant meal. A covenant between two parties was often sealed by their sharing in a *covenant* meal. [36] The occasion in the wilderness when the Israelites first pledged to honor and obey the Lord's covenant *was marked by a meal* in which the elders of Israel, led by Moses, saw God and ate before him.[37] The sacrifices offered by the priests for the sins of Israel were consummated *by the people actually eating portions of the sacrifice.* [38] This last example is particularly helpful in understanding the association of a covenant relationship with the experience of forgiveness in a meal. It stands as a type of the meal Christ was to have with His disciples, and from this we gain insight into how they understood their Savior when He spoke of the Cup of Covenant: "this is My blood of the covenant, which is to be shed for many for forgiveness of sins" (Matthew 26:27).

Our bond to one another in the Church is established within this divine blood Covenant.[39] When Jesus stated that his death, symbolized by the bread and the cup, would ratify the New Covenant, He was not making twelve separate covenants with each disciple. He instituted one covenant with the one Church (composed of many persons). The disciples at that covenantal meal expressed their acceptance of Christ's invitation by eating and drinking, and thus bonded themselves to each other and to Him as members of a new people for God. It is in this union, that each receives forgiveness and healing from God and one another. This is how those participating in the Eucharistic Gathering today are meant to experience this Meal.

THE EUCHARIST AS COMMUNITY AND COMMUNION

All of the above should underscore that the structure within Eucharist speaks of it (and thus the Church) as being *inherently* communal in nature. [40] The first time the word communion was explicitly used in the Church was in the context of the *community* in Jerusalem. Acts 2:43 gives us the picture of the Eucharistic Gathering:

> "And they were continually devoting themselves to the apostles' teaching and to fellowship [communion], to the breaking of bread and to prayer."

The link between the Community Gathering and "the communion" makes it clear that Eucharist is possible only in community. "There is ... no doubt at all of the fundamental importance in the early church of the idea of fellowship through communion."[41]

> The Eucharist has from the beginning been a κοινωνία, *communio*, fellowship, both between each Christian and his heavenly Lord, and of Christians with one another. In the early church these two aspects stood in no sort of opposition, nor should they today; for it is of the essence of the Eucharist, that union with the Lord and union with the brethren are inseparable from one another.[42]

As no individual alone can be the body of Christ, so no one man can have "communion" with God *as* His body. The Eucharist is not a private devotion. It is a corporate relationship, and in this relationship we learn precisely that we are not alone anymore. The body of Christ (the Church) receives the body of Christ (the Eucharist).[43]

The Eucharist illustrates two aspects of communion: communion with *God* and communion *with one another*. The Eucharist here again makes it apparent that one cannot be members of Christ' s body without being at the same time members one of another. In this union one sees the mystery of his union lifted up into the mystery of God's union.[44]

Just as, by analogy, the marriage union does not begin and end at the marriage bed, so one's fellowship does not begin and end at the table, it is only to be manifested and deepened there. To extend this analogy, a Christian who participates in Eucharistic communion (gathering, singing, praying, eating the elements, etc.) yet refuses to love or share with his brethren, is like the one who would have sex with a spouse and yet withhold love in day to day living. Both actions profane and weaken the "sacramental bond" which God's Spirit has established in the respective unions.

HOW CHRIST COMMUNICATES HIMSELF IN THE CHURCH-EUCHARIST

The understanding of the Eucharist as communion takes away the "magical" overtones sometimes associated with the sacrament. At the Supper Jesus said, "Take, eat, this is My body." He was not saying, "chew my skin." He was making a reference to His *whole person*, not to His *body parts*. The Eucharist, in this context, is symbolic of His *one united divine-human being.*

> What we rather have in the *mysterion* [mystery] of the Eucharist is the personal presence of Christ, which is real and miraculous—beyond the control or manipulation of man—but active according to the free grace of Christ in the context of faith. The Kyrios [Lord] makes Himself truly present in the Eucharist through His Body and Blood ['Body' and 'Blood" meaning here "Christ's total life."] so that He may be totally shared by the believing community.[45]

In partaking of the bread and the cup, one receives His whole reality, both the *spiritual and the physical, both the human and divine.* This must be the case for Christ is a whole Person, and a Person cannot be divided into two. Jesus' humanity and divinity are indivisible. Thus, it is impossible to relate only to the "divine Christ" and to ignore "the human Christ."

This leads us once again to punctuate that the Church's celebration of the Eucharist chiefly *realizes and deepens each member's union with Christ and one another as members of His body.* [46] Precisely because God took on our humanity, and by His Spirit brought us into communion with Him, we can share *in Him as a Person* - not just His "power" (i.e., "grace").

His Life is shared with those who have entered into communion with Him in His body. This is what the Church *thanks* God for in the Eucharistic Gathering. The Kingdom is sharing life with God and His people, this is what it will be in the Last Day. In this communion we begin to see God for Who He is, and we begin to see ourselves the way He sees us.

> "... it has not appeared as yet what we shall be, [but] we know that, when He appears, we shall be like Him, because we shall see Him just as He is." (1 John 3:2)

NOTES FOR CHAPTER FOURTEEN

1 Hal Miller, *Christian Community: Biblical or Optional?* , (Ann Arbor, MI., Servant Publications, 1979) pp. 114,115

2 "This does not happen to be represented in the New Testament in direct connection with the eucharist. But there are in the New Testament passages like 'Giving thanks (*eucharistountes*) at all times for all things in the Name of our Lord Jesus Christ to God and Father', (Eph 5:20), and 'Through Him, therefore, we present a sacrifice (*anapheromen thusian*) of praise continually to God' (Heb 13:5), which by their very language would suggest such an understanding of the eucharist." Dom Gregory Dix, *The Shape of the Liturgy* ,(New York, The Seabury Press, 1983) p. 114

3 "This equation of sacrifice with thanksgiving is the constant theme of all early writers on the eucharist. Thus Clement, bishop of Alexandria, in Egypt at the end of the second century and the beginning of the third wrote, 'rightly we do not offer God, who has need of nothing who however has given men everything, an (external) gift; on the contrary, we glorify Him who dedicated Himself to us, by dedicating ourselves to Him.' And Origen, bishop of Caesarea later in the third century said, 'we are not people with ungrateful hearts; it is true we do not sacrifice . . . to such beings who. . .are our enemies; but to God who has bestowed upon us an abundance of benefits. . . we fear being ungrateful. The sign of this gratitude towards God is the bread called Eucharist.' This early insistence on thanksgiving in the context of the eucharistic sacrifice needs to be remembered. . ." Donald Bridge, David Phypers, *Communion: The Meal That Unites?* (Wheaton, IL., Harold Shaw Publishers, 1981) p. 48,49

4 "For the oriental, every table fellowship is a guarantee of peace, of trust, of brotherhood. Table fellowship is a fellowship of life. The oriental, to whom symbolic action means more than it does to us, would immediately understand the acceptance of the outcasts into table fellowship with Jesus as an offer of salvation to guilty sinners and as the assurance of forgiveness." Joachim Jeremias, *The Eucharistic Words of Jesus* , (Philadelphia, PA., Fortress Press, 1966) p.204.

5 "Refusal to eat together severs the relationship (1 Samuel 20:34). Those who do not eat or drink together are without any obligation to one another, if not actually enemies. The worst kind of traitor is the traitor with whom one has shared food (Psalms 41:9, Obadiah 1:7, Matthew 26:21, Mark 14:17, Luke 22:21, John 13:18, 24:-27)." Gillian Feeley-Harnik, *The Lord's Table* , (Philadelphia, PA., University of Pennsylvania Press, 1981) p. 86.

6 "Pagans commonly hold that their idols are present at the sacrifices and that they enjoy the vapors which arise form the burning fat so that those who participate in the meal are actually communing with the idols (cf. 1 Cor. 10:20f)." F. W. Grosheide, *The New International Commentary on the New Testament : The First Epistle to the Corinthians* (Grand Rapids, Wm. B. Eerdmans, 1976) pp. 191, 192

7 Joachim Jeremias, *The Eucharistic Words of Jesus* , (Philadelphia, PA., Fortress Press, 1966) p. 232

8 Joachim Jeremias, *The Eucharistic Words of Jesus* , (Philadelphia, PA., Fortress Press, 1966) p. 233.

9 Joachim Jeremias, *The Eucharistic Words of Jesus* , (Philadelphia, PA., Fortress Press, 1966) p. 233.

10 We can state this all the more confidently when we remember that to orientals the idea *that divine gifts are communicated by eating and drinking* is very familiar. Joachim Jeremias, *The Eucharistic Words of Jesus* , (Philadelphia, PA., Fortress Press, 1966) p. 233.

11 1 Cor. 6:16; Eph. 5: 28-32 make it clear that the sexual union (communion) between husband and wife and the eucharistic communion among Christ and the Church is more than just an analogy: both involve our entire being and effect our identity as persons.

12 There is no need to enter here into the long and technical debate, as to whether or not the Last Supper was a Passover meal. The Passion of Jesus occurred at Passover time, thus Passover associations are inescapable. This fact is supported by the fact that the Passover theme was very apparent in the "table fellowship" of Jesus we have just explained. Joachim Jeremias, *The Eucharistic Words of Jesus* , (Philadelphia, PA., Fortress Press, 1966) p. 120

13 Dom Gregory Dix, *The Shape of the Liturgy* ,(New York, The Seabury Press, 1983) p. 161,162

14 "Protestantism, then, sets itself apart from traditional Catholicism at a moment when Catholicism has only a stammering expression of the eucharistic tradition; the Protestants maintained that the Cross was not to be begun again and that only its memorial was to be celebrated among us. This is true. But this memorial itself, in the fulness of its biblical sense, implies both a continued mysterious presence of the unique sacrifice that was offered once, and our sacramental association with it." John Breck, *The Power of the Word* , (Crestwood, New York, St Vladimir's Seminary Press, 1986) p. 467

15 "It is for this reason that Justin and Hippolytus and later writers after them speak so directly and vividly of the eucharist *in the present* bestowing on the communicants those effects of redemption - immortality, eternal life, forgiveness of sins, deliverance from the power of the devil and so on - which we usually attribute more directly to the sacrifice of Christ viewed as a single historical event *in the past* . One has only to examine their unfamiliar language closely to recognize how completely they identify the offering of the eucharist by the church with the offering of Himself by our Lord, not by way of a repetition, but as a 're-presentation' (anamnesis) of *the same* offering by the church 'which is His Body'." Dom Gregory Dix, *The Shape of the Liturgy* (New York, The Seabury Press, 1983) p. 161,162

16 John D. Zizioulas, *Being As Communion* (Crestwood, N.Y., St. Vladimir's Seminary Press, 1985) p. 254, italics mine. One of the ways this was expressed was in the Jewish expectation that the Messiah would actually come on the night of a Passover. Joachim Jeremias, *The Eucharistic Words of Jesus* , (Philadelphia, PA., Fortress Press, 1966) p. 123

17 " How is this possible? Here we touch the mystery of time and eternity, a mystery which enters into also most every theological problem. The very essence of incarnation, and indeed of all revelation, is the coming of eternity into the midst of time. God inhabits eternity, He cannot be limited by time. His existence transcends the distinction between past, present and future in an eternal present. God bore our sins incarnate in the passion and cross of Christ in one moment of history. But we cannot say that God's bearing of sin was confined to that moment. " Donald M. Baillie, *The Theology of the Sacraments* (New York, Charles Scribner's Sons, 1957) pp. 116-117

18 John D. Zizioulas, *Being As Communion* (Crestwood, N.Y., St. Vladimir's Seminary Press, 1985) pp. 20, 21

19 Alexander Schmemann rightly points out the consequences of such segregated thinking regarding the eucharist and the sacraments in general:

> It is indeed one of the main defects of sacramental theology that instead of following the order of the eucharistic journey with its progressive revelation of meaning, theologians applied to the Eucharist a set of abstract questions in order to squeeze it into their own intellectual framework. In this approach what virtually disappeared from the sphere of theological interest and investigation was liturgy itself, and what remained were isolated "moments", "formulas" and " conditions of validity." What disappeared was the Eucharist as one organic, all-embracing and all-transforming act of the whole Church, and what remained were "essential" and "nonessential" parts, "elements," "consecration," etc. Thus, for example, to explain and define the meaning of the Eucharist the way a certain theology does it, there is no need for the word "eucharist" ; it becomes irrelevant. And yet for the early Fathers it was the key word giving unity and meaning to all the "elements" of the liturgy. The Fathers called "eucharist" the bread and wine of the offering, and their offering and consecration, and finally, communion. All this was *Eucharist* and all this could be understood only within the Eucharist.

Alexander Schmemann, For the Life of the World, (New York, St. Vladimir's Seminary Press,

1973) p. 34

20 John D. Zizioulas, *Being As Communion* (Crestwood, N.Y., St. Vladimir's Seminary Press, 1985) p. 22

21 John Meyendorff, *Byzantine Theology,* (New York, Fordham Press, 1979) p. 174-5.

22 Metropolitan Methodios of Aksum, *Ekklesiastikos Pharos* (Addis Ababa, Ethiopia, 1975) Vol. LVII., I-II, p. 22 citing Book IV. 90 (Athens Ed. in Greek [1859] pp. 174-175

23 Alexander Schmemann, "The Eucharist and the Doctrine of the Church," *St. Vladimir's Quarterly* ((1954) vol. 2, No. 2, p. 12

24 John D. Zizioulas, *Being As Communion* (Crestwood, N.Y., St. Vladimir's Seminary Press, 1985) p. 60

25 John H. Erickson, "Eucharist and Ministry in Bilateral and Multilateral Dialogue", (Crestwood, N.Y., St. Vladimir's Seminary Press, 1984) Vol. 82, No. 4, p. 293, Italics mine.

26 Everything in the Early Church emphasized the integral relationship between Christ and His Church in the eucharist, especially its architecture.

> The basic model of the Christian temple in the fourth century was the basilica. This was not in origin a religious building but specifically profane, designated for large gatherings—for the court, for trade, or for politics. ....Christians deliberately rejected as prototypes both the pagan temple and the Temple of Jerusalem, described in detail in the Bible. ...the pagan temple was subordinated architecturally to its religious function as the house of a god; in its center, therefore, stood an idol or a depiction of the god. The Christian church, on the other hand, was wholly subordinate to the concept of the Christian gathering, and so was its architecture. In the center of the building stood that which transformed this gathering into a Church, uniting Christians into a living temple of the Body of Christ: the table for the celebration of the Eucharist.

Alexander Schmemann, *Historical Road of Eastern Orthodoxy* (St. Vladimir's Seminary Press, 1977) pp. 99,100

27 This profession, of course, is not a "physiological" declaration of the Church's identity with Christ, but an affirmation of the spiritual bond between Christ and His members—one no less real or organic.

28 "Already in the book of the *Didache* in the later first or early second century the idea was clearly expressed that in the celebration of the eucharist the Church experiences that which is promised for the *Parousia*, namely the eschatological unity of all in Christ: "Just as this loaf was scattered all over the mountains and having been brought together was made one, so let your Church be gathered from the ends of the earth in your Kingdom.' This conviction was not irrelevant in the application of the term 'catholic Church' to the local community. ...The eucharist understood primarily not as a *thing* and an objectified means of grace but as an *act* and a *synaxis* of the local Church, a 'catholic' act of a 'catholic' Church..." John D. Zizioulas, *Being As Communion* (Crestwood, N.y., St. Vladimir's Seminary Press, 1985) pp. 143, 145

29 "In the *Didache* , this catholicity was well expressed within the celebration of the eucharist: 'As this broken bread was scattered over the mountains, and being gathered together became one, so may thy church be gathered together from the ends of the earth into thy kingdom' (chap. 9)

30 "The primitive church was conscious of its special place, of its being the third race, different from the race of Jews and the race of Greeks. In the eucharist the church overcame any racial distinction and became the third race, which really meant a "non-racial race." ... In the eucharist the Jewish and Gentile Christians were united, When Jewish Christians hesitated to eat the meal together with their Christian brethren of gentile origin, St. Paul rebuked them as being not "straightforward about the truth of the Gospel" (Gal. 2:11ff). The unity within a local church is realized in the eucharist, as well as the unity among the local churches." Veselin Kesich, "Unity and Diversity In New Testament Ecclesiology," *St.*

Vladimir's Theological Quarterly (Crestwood, New York, New York, St. Vladimir's Seminary Press, 1975) Volume 19, No. 2, p. 113

31 "Theologically the Sacrament was always understood as binding its participants together." Werner Elert, *Eucharist and Church Fellowship in The First Four Centuries* (St. Louis, Missouri, Concordia Publishing House, 1966) p. 27

32 The entire congregation received of the eucharist, even those who for reasons of illness could not attend the gathering. We learn from Justin Martyr that the Eucharist is not only the Liturgy of the bishop, but the whole body of Christ gathered. "The service is therefore, truly a community service, corporate worship; there are no idle spectators or listeners; all are actively co-operating. This is especially shown by the fact that all receive Holy Communion and that it is brought by deacons even to the absent." J. A. Jungmann, *The Early Liturgy* (Notre Dame, IN.,University of Notre Dame Press) p. 44

33 "If the Eucharistic gathering is not such an image, it is not the eucharist in a true sense. A eucharist which discriminates between races, sexes, ages, professions, social classes etc. violates not certain ethical principles but its eschatological nature. It can not be said to be the body of the One who sums up all into Himself." John D. Zizioulas, *Being As Communion* (Crestwood, N.Y., St. Vladimir's Seminary Press, 1985) p. 254, 255

34 Donald M. Baillie, *The Theology of the Sacraments* (New York, Charles Scribner's Sons, 1957) p. 105 italics mine.

35 "...there is no Kingdom of God outside the work of the Holy Spirit, who is by definition *communion* . ...there is no Kingdom of God which is not centered on Christ surrounded by the apostles...in which the relations within the community are *definable* , and they are definable not arbitrarily but *in accordance with the eschatological nature of the community*" (Acts 2:17; 1:12-26, 2:42). John D. Zizioulas, *Being As Communion* (Crestwood, N.y., St. Vladimir's Seminary Press, 1985) p. 205

36 "It was custom to cut the animal in two or three parts ... Part of it was burnt in honour of the god and part of it was eaten at a covenantal meal." J. D. Douglas, ed., *The Illustrated Bible Dictionary (Part 1)* , (Hodder and Stoughton, Tyndale House Publishers) p. 326 (See Gen. 15; 26:30; 31:44, 54; Num. 18:17-19; Ex. 24)

37 "'Then Moses and Aaron, Nadab, and Abihu, and seventy of the elders of Israel went up, and they saw the God of Israel. . . And he did not lay his hand on the chief men of the people of Israel; they beheld God, and ate and drank'." (Exodus 24: 9-11) Gillian Feeley-Harnik, *The Lord's Table* , (Philadelphia, PA., University of Pennsylvania Press, 1981) p. 88.

38 1 Sam. 9:11-14, 25; 1 Chron. 29:21-22; 2 Chron. 7:8-10

39 "'The blood of the covenant...the most obvious source is the OT Sinai tradition, especially Ex. 24:8 'And Moses took the blood and threw it upon the people, and said, 'Behold the blood of the covenant which the Lord has made with you in accordance with all these words'. The Epistle to the Hebrews treats this Sinai covenant-making... Sinai foreshadows the 'new' covenant, mediated by Jesus and made possible by his death...making of the first covenant is seen as, so to speak, explaining why the new covenant too had to be ratified with blood, in this case the blood of Jesus; and that blood-shedding was concerned, as this one is, with purification and the forgiveness of sins. ...'This is the blood of the covenant which God commanded you'... We have, therefore, solid evidence to suggest what a phrase like 'blood covenant' could and did mean to at least one New Testament Christian [here the writer of Hebrews] when applied to the death of Jesus: a purification and expiatory sacrifice by means of which the new covenant foretold in the OT prophet was established between God and men." *Thinking About the Eucharist:: Essays by Members of the Archbishops' Commission on Christian Doctrine,* "The 'Institution' Narratives and the Christian Eucharist", John Austin Baker (London, SCM Press Ltd, 1972) p. 41

40 See Constantine N. Tsirpanlis, "The Structure of the Church in the Liturgical Tradition of the First Three Centuries", *Patristic and Byzantine Review* (Kingston, N. Y., American Institute for Patristics and Byzantine Studies, 1982) Vol I, p. 59

41 Yngve Brilioth, *Eucharistic Faith and Practice : Evangelical and Catholic* (London, S.P.C.K.,

1953) p. 29

42 Yngve Brilioth, *Eucharistic Faith and Practice : Evangelical and Catholic* (London, S.P.C.K., 1953) p. 27

43 "The Sacrament of the body and the blood is a realization of the unity of our nature both with Christ and, at the same time, with all the members of the Church. It is necessary, says St. John Chrysostom, to understand the wonder of this sacrament, 'What it is, why it was given, and what is the profit of the action. We become one body; members, as it is said, of His flesh and of His bones... this is effected by the food which He has freely given us... He has mingled His body with ours that we may be one, as body joined to head.' Or as St. John Damascene puts it: 'If union is in truth with Christ and with one another, we are assuredly voluntarily united also with all those who partake with us..' In the Eucharist especially the Church appears as a single nature and body united to Christ." Constantine N. Tsirpanlis, "The Structure of the Church in the Liturgical Tradition of the First Three Centuries", *Patristic and Byzantine Review* (Kingston, N. Y., American Institute for Patristics and Byzantine Studies, 1982) Vol I, p. 59 citing John Chrysostom's *In Ioannenm,* homil. XLVI; P.G. 59, 260 and John of Damascus' *De Fide Orthodoxa*, IV, 13; P.G. 94, 1153B respectively.

44 "...it is the special characteristic of the narratives of the institution [of the eucharist] that they set forth the Lord's presence in the midst of the gathering, and unite the social fellowship of the brethren with the Master's self-oblation." Yngve Brilioth, *Eucharistic Faith and Practice : Evangelical and Catholic* (London, S.P.C.K., 1953) p. 27

45 Theodore G. Stylinanopoulos,"Holy Eucharist and Priesthood in the New Testament", *Greek Orthodox Theological Review* (Brookline, MA., Holy Cross Press), Summer, 1978, Vol. XXIII, No. 2, pp. 121-122

46 "Common participation in the eucharistic loaf unites the many into one body (1 Cor. 10:17), the body of Christ: so with the final kingdom be the summing up of all things in Christ (Eph. 1:10), when we shall all have attained to the measure of the stature of the fullness of Christ, whose body we are" (Eph. 4:11-16). Geoffrey Wainwright, *Eucharist and Eschatology* , (London, Epworth Press, 1971) p. 148

CHAPTER FIFTEEN

SALVATION AS UNION IN CHRIST

The West often presents the doctrine of salvation as a system reflective of the logic, precision, and order of an exhaustive law text. It is clear, neat, rational, unambiguous. As you might expect, given our discussion to this point, Eastern Christianity explains salvation more in *relational* terms rather than in rational ones.[1] To the Eastern Christian, salvation is the literal reunion of man and creation in God through Christ. Salvation is the restoration of divine-human intimacy, the joy and love of interpersonal communion, and the healing of all creation. Many Christians in the West, however, frequently cast the doctrine of redemption in the legal terms of "justice", "penalty," and "commitment." As we shall see throughout this chapter, the differences between these two vantage points are not minor, and have great significance on how one expresses and experiences his Christianity.

Anselm of Canterbury (1033-1109) summarizes the popular Roman Catholic—Protestant understanding of the doctrine of redemption. Anselm learned from Augustine that man was *thoroughly* depraved, so much that not even a speck of God's image was left within him. [2] Man was unrighteous and unclean. God was righteousness, and purity. Because of this, man was an offense to God and barred from communion with Him.

This put man in a dilemma. He needed to pay his debt to God, to cancel out the penalty for his sins ("to make satisfaction"),[3] but his own spiritual contamination made it impossible for him. Anselm concluded that unless man could offer a "well pleasing sacrifice" for his offences he could never be made "right" with God, and was destined thus to receive the certain wrath and judgment of God. Anselm reasoned, however, that God Himself did provide the solution to man's problem by supplying the perfect and sufficient offering needed: the death of His Son on the cross. In this act, mirroring the sacrificial atonement rituals in the Old Testament, Christ is punished as our substitutionary sacrifice, i.e., He received the consequences of our sin in His body, and has taken the penalty and wrath of God originally intended for us.

The Eastern Christian would never deny the crucial importance of Christ's death as an offering for sins. However, he wouldn't express it in the terms of Anselm, nor would he confine God's redemptive ministry to Golgatha alone. Salvation is an indescribable mystery, one which neither angel nor man can fully comprehend (1 Peter 1:12). For this reason, the Eastern-minded believer stands aloof from any air tight definitions. God's redemptive love goes far beyond giving payment for broken *laws,* it restores *relationships;* for salvation is, foremost, communion with God and one's fellow man.[4] In this chapter, I will attempt to outline this mystery in contrast with Anselm's thesis and other popular Western interpretations.

WHAT IS SIN?

Whether in Hebrew or in Greek, sin is the failure to achieve one's goal or potential.[5] In Adam's refusal to fulfill "the image and likeness of God" within him, and in his attempt to be "god without God," the Fall stands as the portrayal of sin. Instead of agreeing with God's purpose—godliness and communion—Adam chose to be *self*-sufficient, to "go on his own," and to compete with God. In his disobedience, he said to God, "I do not *need* You. I do not *need* to be in communion with You." He who once walked with God in the Garden, now makes himself a stranger to God by his thirst for power.

CONSEQUENCE OF SIN

In the Fall, man turned his back on God's love; by doing so, every evil followed. In exchange for true life, man created an inauthentic life, only an "existence." In every respect, humanity continues to testify that the image and likeness of God within it has been distorted and muddied. Adam's selfish independence yields a rotting crop of devastation. Man's will is weakened, his reason blurred, and his moral and spiritual perceptions dimmed. His inability to live in harmony with others is clear evidence that he has been taken over by his own self-destructive desires. Man loves only himself, and seeks to order all things around himself.[6] He becomes like a river ceasing to flow outside itself; stagnation and death are the consequence. Man becomes both the author and the inheritor of death. He tastes death on every plane: physically, relationally, spiritually and eternally.

Today, the sickness of the Fall is the same disease that works destruction wherever sin is present. It is this malady, with all of its accompanying manifestations, from which Christ came to save humankind.

THE ANCIENT VIEW OF ORIGINAL SIN

Many Christians with a Western perspective agree with Anselm and Augustine. They believe that the Fall occasioned man's *total depravity,* they see it as the moment when man became entirely devoid of God's image. The Genesis account, however, does not state this, nor does the book of Romans that summarizes the event. Augustine based his interpretation of the Fall on a faulty Latin translation of Romans 5:12. It was from this text that he, and many others following him, *read an erroneous interpretation of Original Sin into* the Genesis account. *His* version of the passage reads as follows:

> "Therefore, just as through one man death entered into the world, and that through sin, so death spread to all men, *in whom* [Adam] all sinned."

The more accurate translation of the verse reads:

> "Therefore, just as through one man death entered into the world, and that through sin, so death spread to all man, *for that* [or *in that*] all sinned."

What is the difference between the two translations? In the version available to Augustine, the passage states that *all humanity* had sinned *in Adam* (or in *Adam's* sin). [7] In other words, when Adam disobeyed God, he "stained" the seed that would produce all succeeding generations, and thus Adam's *personal* sin becomes our personal sin.

The correct translation does not allow for such an interpretation. The more accurate text teaches that Adam's sin carried *death* to all creation, and that although our sin is evidence to this death, *it is not* Adam's specific transgression that we have inherited.

The inference drawn from the Latin translation is that all mankind, in its very nature, has become "sin infected" through Adam's first transgression (Original Sin). Due to *the wrong* choice of the father humanity, *every* one of his later "children" will be born *innately* sinful and *utterly* depraved. This means that every person, before any independent and willful act of his own is a genetic inheritor of *Adam's personal* sin and guilt. According to this view, from the very moment of conception, every human being shares Adam's guilt.

Eastern Christianity admits to the reality of Original Sin, but not to this "inherited stain" version of the doctrine. The East, being quite familiar with the original Greek of the disputed passage, always understood Romans 5: 12ff as teaching that Original Sin passed on *mortality* and *death* —not total depravity. We can summarize it as: Death is the *consequence* of sin, and each individual's *personal sin* is the consequence of that death. Man's *natural state, however, is not sin itself.*

Original Sin, therefore, is the transgression of pride and selfishness that fractured man's communion with God, others and creation. Yes, the Fall blurred the image of God within man, but it did not obliterate it. The Fall could never be the contraction of Adam's *personal* sin or guilt. How could it be? How can one inherit the personal responsibility or the guilt of *another*? Guilt can only be the result of an act which the person himself has freely committed. No one can sin *for* another. Man needs a Savior to escape death and to be forgiven of *his own* transgressions, but not to be forgiven of *Adam's* first transgression.

WHAT CHRIST DID TO SAVE US

Christ did not save us just by going to the cross and dying for us. His *whole* life was redemptive. Without the incarnation, He could not have had a ministry. Without His ministry we would be unprepared for the meaning and significance of His death. Without His resurrection, His death would hold no meaning. Without His ascension, the Spirit would not have been sent, and we could not have been adopted as sons of God (Rom. 8:15).

In saying this, I do not mean to discount the fact that there were some specific moments within Christ's life on earth that were especially important in His redemptive ministry. His incarnation, death, and resurrection, for example, embody the purpose and character of Christ's ministry like no others. These deserve special attention, for the whole scope of salvation comes into focus in them. For this reason, I will commit the next section of this chapter to the ancient Church's unique perspective on these saving events.

THE INCARNATION:

OUR SALVATION IS IN OUR UNION WITH HIM

> "Since then the children share in flesh and blood, he Himself likewise also partook of the same, that through death He might render powerless him who had the power of death, that is, the devil." Heb 2:14,15

> "who, although he existed in the form of God ... emptied Himself, taking the form of a bond-servant, and being made in the likeness of men. And being found in appearance as a man, He humbled Himself by becoming obedient to the point of death..." (Phil. 2:7, 8)

Both of the above passages speak clearly of the need for Christ to have taken on our humanity. In the incarnation we marvel at the depth and intensity of God's love to save. We marvel at the amazing humility that love inspired. How incredible! Christ, the One through Whom all things were created, became a divine-human embryo in the womb of Mary. For what purpose? Christ shared our flesh and blood that we may have a way to share in His divine life. [8]

Our salvation could never have occurred if Christ had not been *fully* God and *fully* Man. [9] Why? Our fallen humanity made it impossible for us to restore ourselves. We had to be restored by *God*. We also had to be restored by a *perfect* Man. Only one who could identify with us in *every way as a human* could bring us back into union with the Father. God had to become Man and yet remain God so that we, through His humanity and divinity, would be able to come into communion with His divinity as humans.

A God far off and detached cannot communicate His personal life. Only the incarnation —the union of humanity with divinity— can cure what is defective in our humanity. Jesus Christ—the Word, the Eternal Son—is the exact Image of the Father (Heb. 1:3); therefore, *He* is able to restore a reflection of that image within man. The God-Man embraces us, and the breach caused by man's rebellion is healed. St. Athanasius summarizes this brilliantly in his *On the Incarnation:*

> The Word of God came in His own Person, because it was He alone, the Image of the Father, Who could recreate man made after the Image. In order to effect this re-creation, however, He had first to do away with death and corruption. Therefore He assumed a human body, in order that in it death might once for all be destroyed, and that men might be renewed according to the Image [of God].[10]

THE SIGNIFICANCE OF CHRIST'S DEATH

A MYSTERY OF LOVE

Eastern Christianity refuses to give a definitive explanation of Christ's death because it is a saving mystery no analogy or interpretation can ever capture. The cross is not only the place where sins are transferred, God's justice reckoned, or spiritual debts paid. *Its significance is much deeper, and its meaning is much greater.* Gregory of Nazianzus awakens us to the depth of the mystery of Christ's death when he rhetorically asks to whom was the death offered (to satan?, to God?), and for what specific purpose was it intended (to pay a ransom?, to satisfy an angry God?):

> To whom, and why, is this blood poured out for us and shed, the great and most precious blood of God, the High Priest and Victim?...We were in the power of the Evil One, sold to sin, and had brought this harm on ourselves by sensuality ... If the price of ransom is given to none other than him in whose power we are held, then I ask, to whom and for what reason is such a price paid?... If it is to the Evil One, then how insulting is this! The thief receives the price of ransom; he not only receives it from God, but even receives God Himself. For his tyranny he receives so large a price that it was only right to have mercy upon us ... If to the Father, then first, in what way? Were we in captivity under Him?... And secondly, for what reason? For what reason was the blood of the Only Begotten pleasing to the Father, Who did not accept even Isaac, when offered by his father, but exchanged the offering, giving instead of the reasonable victim a lamb?..."[11]

Christ did indeed take upon Himself the sin of the world, but He did not do this *because* the Father had a thirst for human suffering. God never desires *anyone* to suffer. He *grieves* over human suffering! Neither is death a *condition* for God's *love and acceptance!* God is not like the god of the pagans who hungered for "human sacrifice." He sent an angel to hold Abraham's hand from sacrificing Issac, and He expressly commanded His people never to sacrifice their young. How could God want the death of

His Eternal Son, when God's love for Abraham and Isaac led Him to reject the sacrifice of a mortal child?!

The question isn't whether Christ's death was a ransom to the devil or a sacrifice to the Father. Christ did not die on the Cross to "pay off" the evil one, or to quiet the Father's rage. The sacrifice was for *our* sake (not satan's or the Father's) and as an offering for *our* sins. We must not go any further than this. We cannot know how Christ's death grants us communion with God.[12] We do not *need* to know. But one thing is certain: God's love, not legal negotiations, has saved us.[13]

Indeed, the law does not tell God how, when or why He should love. His love is greater than the Law. Love will always go *beyond what the law requires.* Christ did not go to the cross because the law *made* Him do it. Love led Him to *the Cross.* He did not die to balance the sin ledgers in heaven. He died because His love would not allow *Him to give us any less than His life.* "Greater love has no one than this, that one lay down his life for his friends." (Rom. 5:8).

The Eastern Fathers did not see sin simply as a transgression of the Law, but as a personal alienation and as a barrier to communion. One is separated from God because he lives in *contradiction to His life,* not simply because he has committed a legal "wrong." It is not merely a broken rule that violated our relationship with God, but an attitude which concludes in the way of death. A legal imperfection did not send God running away from *us*, but an attitude of going *our own way* (Isa. 53:6) led us to race away from *Him.*

Yes, sin is a broken law, but even more basically, it is the breaking of the current of love and life in which God had once allowed us to share. Sin, therefore, is our resistance to communion, and the fruit of this isolation leads not only to imperfection ("unrighteousness") but to every profanation of love (selfishness). Likewise, God does not "give" us punishment for our offenses, so much as He allows our own rebellion and sin to dispense its own penalty. He will not *make* us commune with Him. If we want to stew in our own juice, as much as it grieves Him, He'll let us —even if it be for all eternity.[14]

God is not and never was our enemy. Man may make himself an enemy of God (Jas. 4:4), but He will never be our adversary. Thus, our salvation is not dependent on *our* finding a way to reconcile ourselves with an angry God. Reconciliation is something that *God* does for us, not something *we* do for Him. [15] Paul does not tell us that we must reconcile ourselves to God, but rather "that *God* was in Christ *reconciling* the world to Himself" (2 Cor. 5:19). Not one aspect of God's plan of redemption is for *His* sake (i.e., to get from us what we owe Him). Salvation was not designed by the mind of God as a way His anger could be appeased, or as an opportunity for Him execute His vengeance. His *chief motive* in redemption was to restore our *communion* with Him. It was yet another expression of God's creative love and concern for us; He did it all for us, not any of it for Himself.[16]

God's forgiving love, therefore, is not testified to by the cross alone. "The whole work of God in Christ is a work of forgiveness."[17] Christ's ability to dispense God's forgiveness was real and actual *throughout* His earthly ministry.[18] Wherever sin brought death, Christ always brought with Him the power to communicate life.

HIS DEATH SAVES US

Even though the cross is only one of many images of redemption, it is an indispensable one. *Within the context of Christ's entire life*, the cross alone stands as the culmination of His ministry (Jn. 12:27). In the mystery of Jesus' death, God "cancelled out the certificate of debt ... against us...[and] has taken it out of the way, having nailed it to the cross" (Col. 2:14). In the rite of crucifixion, the crimes of the sentenced were inscribed on a tablet ("the certificate of debt") and hung over the head of the one executed. Above Jesus' head also hangs a tablet. But *His* crimes are not written there, *ours* are. And it is this list of offenses that God tore up and disposed of in His Son's death.[19]

Even though this is an unfathomable mystery, we can still receive a glimpse of how it is that the miracle of Christ's incarnate death could bring us into wholeness. Christ was perfect, in both divinity and humanity. Therefore, no inherent necessity caused Him to die (He did not need to pay "the wages of sin" [Romans 6:23] for Himself). His communion with God (Life) was never interrupted. (If it had been, He would have ceased to be divine). However, in death there *is* a separation, and in the death of the Lord, His body and soul were certainly separated. But even in His death, His divinity and humanity *remained in communion within* His Person. This communion of divinity with human death *imparted life to death* itself![20] He swallowed the live coal of death, and through the Divine Life that remained within Him, He extinguished its black flame. "Thus it happened that two opposite marvels took place at once: the death of all was consummated in the Lord's body; yet, because the Word [the Eternal Son] was in it, death and corruption were in the same act utterly abolished'."[21] In His divine-human identification with death, we are saved.[22]

The sacrifice symbolized in the cross, then, is of *God offering Himself to us by assuming all that we are, even the curse of death.* There is an expiatory dimension to this, but not in the terms of Anselmian justice. Christ assumed the *consequence* of sin: that is *death.* And He assumed the sting of that death to the very end, even to the farthest regions of the cosmos.

Given this perspective, Christ's *death* must be viewed as a victory in and of itself. In it, Christ is not the passive victim; He is the Conqueror. He knew that the humiliation of the cross would be no mere endurance of obedience. It was the *very* path of Glory, the attainment of *ultimate* victory. The purpose and result of the Crucifixion are seen in this: Christ accepted death not to be "beaten up" by God, but to destroy death in the resurrection.

THE RESURRECTION

THE DEFEAT OF DEATH AND SATAN

It is the resurrection that makes it clear that Christ's death has a saving significance. For this reason, it is not surprising to learn that the early Church chose to emphasize this particular moment of redemptive history above all others. [23] In it, humanity's liberation from the chains of death and the plundering of Satan's dominion became obvious.[24] This turning of tables on the devil was foreshadowed in Genesis 3:15, the passage that prophesies that a woman's seed (Mary's) would one day inflict a mortal blow on the "serpent's head" (satan). Christ fulfilled that prophesy in His resurrection. Satan was and is overthrown from his "throne of death", the risen Jesus having "rendered *powerless* him who *had* the power of death" (Heb 2:14). Christ now declares before him and all demons: "*All* authority has been given to *Me* in heaven *and* on earth" (Matthew 28:19).

In the resurrection, we now have the confidence that *no one* has to die. The One who shared our humanity has "tasted death for everyone" (Heb 2:9), and has risen victorious from the grave. He now tightly holds the "keys of death and Hades" (Rev. 1:18), and they will never be taken away from Him. And now we, too, in union with Christ, can walk in the likeness of His resurrection Life (Rom. 6:5).

The reality of the resurrection also makes it clear that God has put satan's mastery over us to an end. "The Son of God appeared for this purpose, that He might *destroy the works of the devil* " (1 John 3:8). The "ruler of this world" has been judged and cast out (John 16:11, 12:31). Now, in Christ, our deliverance from satan can and will be experienced on every level: spiritually, physically, psychologically, interpersonally. [25]

The significance of Christ's resurrection triumph is brilliantly painted by a Fourth Century Eastern Orthodox Easter sermon, an excerpt from it follows:

> Let no one mourn that he has fallen again and again; for forgiveness has risen from the grave. Let no one fear death; for the Death of our Savior has set us free. He has destroyed it by enduring it. He spoiled Hades when he descended it. He vexed it even as it tasted of his flesh. Isaiah foretold this when he cried, Thou, O Hades, has been vexed by encountering Him below. It is vexed; for it is even done away with. It is vexed; for it is annihilated. It is vexed; for it is now made captive. It took a body, and, lo! it discovered God. It took earth, and, behold! it encountered heaven. It took what it saw, and was overcome by what it did not see. O death, where is thy sting? O Hades, where is thy victory? Christ is risen, and you are annihilated. Christ is risen, and the evil ones are cast down. Christ is risen, and the Angels rejoice. Christ is risen, and life is liberated. Christ is risen, and the tomb is emptied of the dead; for Christ, having risen from the dead, is become the first-fruits of those that have fallen asleep. To him be glory and power forever and ever.[26]

The Byzantine spiritual writer Nicholas Cabasalas (*c.* 1322), masterfully summarizes Christ's saving ministry in these stanzas:

> Christ overcame *sin* through the *Cross.* Christ overcame the *fallen nature* by *assuming our nature,* Christ overcame *death* through *His death* ... and in His *descent into Hades and His resurrection, Christ overcame Satan and his power.*

THE NATURE OF SALVATION

GENERAL MEANING

The Hebrew word for salvation can be translated as "to be wide," "roomy," "to be free, well off", or "prosperous." In this sense, the Israelites were *saved* from the hand of the Egyptians (Ps 106:7-10; Ex. 14:30), *saved* from the domination of death (Ps. 6:4, 5; 107:13, 14)), *saved* from their enemies (Ps. 106:10) and *saved* from sickness (Isa. 38:21). The Greek word *soteria* (σωτηρία) has many of these same meanings [27] including preservation, bodily health, safety (Acts 2: 40; 27:31; Heb. 11:7) and deliverance from sickness (Matt 9:21). In short, salvation connotes *wholeness.*

This wholeness, however, is not focused on one's personal well being, or on the restoration of one's relationship with God alone. God's desire is that wholeness (salvation) clothe His entire creation as well, both man and creation being renewed by Him Who made it in the beginning. As Adam's sin passed death on to all humanity, and reverberated throughout all of creation ("Cursed is the ground because of you", Gen. 3:17), the redemptive life man receives will likewise fill out and restore God's created order.

> For the anxious longing of the creation waits eagerly for the revealing of the sons of God... in hope that the creation itself also will be set free from its slavery to corruption into the freedom of the glory of the children of God. (Romans 8: 19, 20)

This reveals something important about the nature of God's salvation. Salvation is not zeroed in on the individual alone; [28] it is both *manifold* and *communal.* In the Restoration, *all things* will be subjected to Christ, that "God may be all in all" (I Cor. 15:28).

SALVATION IS COMMUNAL, NOT INDIVIDUALISTIC

I have spoken of the communal dimension of salvation extensively throughout this book. Let me here mention just a few additional things about this dimension that I think merit our attention. Sin led man away to pursue his "own thing" in isolation from God and others. The first stage of conversion therefore, is when one realizes that such an existence is impossible. When man realizes that he is *not self*-sufficient or autonomous, and that he cannot survive outside of interpersonal communion with God and man, he looks again to the Source of true life. There he sees God and His love for us, and the union He has within Himself and with those made like Him.

Christ came to heal man's self-centeredness, and His cure is found within His divine love and communion. In this sense, love "saves" us. Within the environment of this love—the Church—that this salvation is realized.[29] Without this healing love, salvation is impossible. Here both the "lover" and the "one loved" experience and manifest the healing power of God. Love, as salvation, is *by nature communal.* Orthodox theologian Dumitru Staniloae seizes upon this vision of salvation in the following excerpt from his book *Theology and the Church*:

> Christ did not bring us salvation so that we might continue to live in isolation, but that we might strive towards a greater and ever more profound unity which has as its culmination the eternal Kingdom of God. We see this reflected in the fact that we cannot gain salvation if we remain in isolation, caring only for ourselves. There is no doubt that each man must personally accept salvation and make it his own, but he cannot do so nor can he persevere and progress in the way of salvation unless he is helped by others and helps them himself in return, that is, unless the manner of our salvation is communal. To be saved means to be pulled out of our isolation and to be united with Christ and the rest of men. [30]

"The new life given in Christ is unity and oneness: 'That they may be one *as we are*' (John 17:11)."[31] "It is remarkable that in the New Testament the name 'saint' is almost exclusively used in the plural, saintliness being social in its intrinsic meaning."[32] This is the sense one gleans from John, the beloved Apostle:

> "what we have seen and heard we proclaim to you also, that you may have *fellowship with us*; and indeed our fellowship is *with the Father, and with His Son Jesus Christ* " (1 John 1:3).

Salvation is not just the forgiveness of sins or one's escape from Hell, as important as these may be. We are not just saved *from* something, we are saved *in Someone,* Jesus Christ. Redemption is not just to get rid of evil's residue, it is to impart to us life, goodness, and joy. This life is possible only through our union with Christ, Who is Himself the resurrection and the life (John 11:25).

> "For the atonement made necessary by our sins is not an end but a means, the means to the only real goal... union with God. What does it matter being saved from death, from Hell, if it is not to lose oneself in God?"[33]

Christ in us, us in Christ: this is the mystery and glory of salvation (Eph. 1:18-23). John Chrysostom summarizes our place in Christ in one of his sermons based on Romans:

> We have been freed from punishment, we have put off all iniquity, and we have been born from above (Jn. 3:3), and we have risen again. With the old man buried, we have been redeemed, we have been sanctified, we have been given adoption into sonship, we have been justified, and we have been made brothers of the Only-begotten. We have been constituted joint heirs and one body with Him and have been perfected in His flesh, and have been united to Him as a body to its head. All of this Paul calls an 'abundance of grace', showing that what we have received is not just a medicine to counteract the wound, but even health, beauty, honor, glory and dignities ... For Christ paid out much more than the debt we owed, as much more as the boundless sea exceeds a little drop. [34]

THE CONSEQUENCES OF SALVATION

MAN BECOMES WHAT HE WAS MADE TO BE

The Eastern-minded Christian does not see salvation as something alien to his human nature, but as a process whereby man becomes what *he was made to be,* a mirror of God's "image and likeness." The creation account makes it clear that God *made man to be in union* with Him. Man's restoration to God in Christ is *natural;* separation from God is *abnormal.* [35] If one does not participate in God's life, there is something *in* - human about him, something "missing" in his very nature as a human being.

RESTORATION OF OUR NATURE AND WILL

Therefore, to be in Christ is not a *negation* of the human will, but an *empowering* of it. The Christian, in communion with God, regains the ability to voluntarily and freely harmonize his will with God's intentions. This was the state of Adam and Eve before the Fall, each readily *desiring* to grow in a greater and deeper union with God. In Christ, the symphony of the human and divine will, evident in Adam's and God's relationship before the Fall, is again "realigned." Jesus' human will freely and intelligently *follows* His divine will. What does this mean for us? Those *in* Christ can now have the power to attune their human wills to the Divine will, just as Christ did. Such a harmony and co-operation is *natural* for every family in heaven and on earth who has derived its name from the Father (Eph. 3:14,15). [36]

MAN'S PARTICIPATION IN THE LIFE OF GOD

The significance of all of this is astounding: man can *participate in the very life of God!* Because of the communion of humanity and divinity in the Person of Jesus, man can share in *God's* immortality, *His* properties and power. By this I do not mean to imply that human beings can become God, or that anything finite can *possess* God. My only point is that God shares Himself—personally, intimately and directly— with His creation. "It is God *Himself* who acts and participates in man's own salvation." [37]

Christ became man that man might, *by His gift of communion,* share in Him and thus be *like* Him. Christ's divinity assumed our humanity and thus healed and restored it. Because of this, in a manner similar to the way He was (and still is) a partaker of the human nature, Christians are now "partakers of the divine nature" (2 Peter 1:4). The only difference between the way we participate in His divine nature and the way He participates in our human nature, is that Christ possesses both natures *as His own.* (We, on the other hand, do not possess Christ's divinity as our own.)

This concept can be better illustrated by explaining what the Eastern Christian Fathers referred to as the "essence" and "energies" of God. The *essence* of God is that in which no human will ever be able share, His infinite, "inner" Person. [38] God's *energies*, in contrast, are those aspects of His being which we *can* perceive and experience, those ways in which He is *known* by us (His love, wisdom, healing, revelation, creative power, etc.). This understanding of our relationship to God can be summarized by the saying, "One can share in a person's *life* (his *energies*), but one cannot participate in his *person* (his *essence*)."

This distinction between essence and energies is not to imply that there are two parts to God; God is Three Persons Who is *as* divine in His essence as He is in His energies. The only difference between essence and energies is that His essence is unapproachable by man, and His energies are "participatable." [39] Why make such a seemingly "hairsplitting" distinction? This whole manner of speaking seeks to protect the mystery of God's communion within creation, without falsely equating creation itself *as* God.[40] It affirms that an immediate knowledge of God *is* possible, and, at the very same time underlines the truth that the finite will never encapsulate the Infinite God. Thus, God's presence is both *entirely* inaccessible and *entirely* accessible.

OUR "THEOSIS"

A Christian's union with God in Christ makes it possible for him to continually be transformed to become more and more like God. The Eastern Fathers called this process *theosis* or "divinization." [41] Once again, to be absolutely clear, this does not mean that man "becomes" the Divine essence. It does mean what the Scriptures teach in numerous places: one's union in Christ allows him to participate in Christ's divine energies. "Theosis means no more than an intimate communion of human persons with the Living

God... [and to] ... be with God means to dwell in Him and to share His perfection." This is possible only because of the incarnation. To quote St. Athanasius, "Through the 'flesh-bearing God' we have become 'Spirit-bearing men' and 'sons of God in the likeness of the Son of God'."[42] In this communion of God's energies, the Christian is continually healed, restored and made whole.[43]

HOLINESS

It should be obvious from the above that to be *in* (union with) Christ can only mean to be *like Him*.[44] Therefore, sanctification (theosis) and salvation are inseparably related.[45] Like salvation, theosis is a *gift,* not a reward for one's personal achievement. Holiness—the fruit of theosis—is realized in the life of the believer because the Holy *One* lives in communion with him; it is manifest only because of this *relationship.* In our union in Christ, we actually share in His life and love. His character of love no longer is His alone, for as we live in Him, it gradually becomes *ours* as well.

A good analogy of how holiness is acquired through our theosis in Christ is illustrated in the writings of St. Athanasius and other early Fathers. It describes the two natures of Christ, and how they constantly participate in each other. Christ's human nature is like an iron sword, and His divine nature is like a fire. If one were to place the sword in a blazing fire, the fire would soon permeate the iron sword without changing the essential nature of iron or fire in the process. Both His humanity and divinity permeated each property, while both at the same time still remained distinct from each other (i.e., the fire does not become iron, and the iron does not become fire.)

Borrowing from this metaphor, a Christian's union in Christ and his subsequent theosis is like the iron in the fire of divinity. In the flame's engulfment, he partakes of the divine nature and is thus continually transformed into His likeness, "being transformed into the same image from glory to glory" as St. Paul says (2 Cor. 3:18). To the extent that the Christian makes himself open to participate in Christ's healing warmth and illuminating light, to that same intensity is God's holiness manifest. Conversely, those who remove themselves from the Divine Flame through selfishness and pride, become cold and no longer exhibit its characteristics. Therefore, the one who does not abide in Christ cannot reveal His holiness. "Abide in Me, for apart from Me, you can do nothing." (John 15:5)

RIGHTEOUSNESS

The Christian's righteousness is not just put on him like one puts on a coat; he cannot be "labeled" righteous and yet have his inner constitution remain unchanged. In other words, one is not "saved" no matter what kind of moral life he chooses to live.[46] Yes, Christ has justified man before God's law, but it is because of Christ's union with man that man is righteous, not because of some abstract decree to that effect.[47] Through Christ's union of divinity and humanity, our "human nature has indeed become holy and righteous in its very root."[48] But this righteousness is not valid because someone "says" it is so. We are righteous because we live in communion with Christ. "The whole problem is not a juridical and utilitarian one — what is sufficient and what is not — but rather a question of the original human destiny, which is to be *with* God and *in* God."[49]

Perhaps this can be better illustrated by looking at how the words "righteousness" and "justification" are commonly understood in the New Testament. Both these words come from the same New Testament Greek word, *dikayosinee* (δικαιοσύνη). Given this insight, let's look at Rom. 3: 21, 22:

> "But now apart from the Law, *the righteousness [justification] of God* has been manifested, being witnessed by the Law and the Prophets; even *the righteousness [justification] of God* through faith in Jesus Christ for all those who believe..."

The phrase "the righteousness (justification) *of* God" in the Scriptures does not have a legal, systematic definition; instead, it points to a field of reality. The phrase can accurately be interpreted either as "the righteousness which *belongs* to God", or as "the righteousness which He *bestows and which is from Himself.*" Actually, *both* interpretations are correct and complementary. Our union with Christ *creates and transforms us into conformity with His righteousness.* This is a *transmitted* righteousness, one *He* gives from Himself. This is a righteousness which is *recreated in us*, one which becomes *our own through our communion with Him* .[50] Neither righteousness is earned. Neither righteousness is possible without faith.

This, however, is at odds with the teaching that says, "God acts as if ("pretends) we are righteous, when He really knows that we are not."[51] This is a nominalistic interpretation of the passage, and it assumes that God denies reality.[52] God does not "overlook" sin, He forgives it. God does not ignore death, He transfigures it into genuine life. Our righteousness is in our *union* with Christ, something which our theosis with Him actualizes.

In this context, the controversy of "faith and works" is seen in a completely different light. The Christian does "good deeds" to be a source of blessing to others, not because he wants to get to heaven. To impart God's life to others is synonymous with having a saving union with Christ; it is not a "tack on." In the Christian's fellowship with the "Author and Perfecter" of his faith, one's heart is enlarged to love, and in this he testifies that God lives within Him. As love was God's motive in giving His Son, so love is integral to the saving experience itself.

Similarly, there is no such thing as "passive" love. An attitude of ready obedience always accompanies a life of communion.

> "He who believes in the Son has eternal life; but he who does not obey the Son shall not see life..." (Jn 3:36)

> "By this we know that we are in Him: the one who says he abides in Him ought himself to walk in the same manner as he walked." (1 John 2:5)

> "No one who abides in Him sins [here meaning, "makes a practice of sin"]; no one who sins has seen Him or knows Him." (1 John 3:5)

To say this is not to say that our salvation is *conditional* on our performance of works, but that they *always accompany* it.[53] It is not a question of whether it is faith *alone*, or faith *and* works that saves. To speak in this way is to make faith an entity in and of itself, something apart from faith *in Christ.* It is not faith *in our faith* in Christ which saves, it is our union with Christ which saves, and this saving union is accomplished through our faith *in Him.*

Actually, it is faith *and love* that saves, for a life not characterized by love cannot be a life *in Christ* ("Christian"). God's salvation is not selfish or self-centered, nor can it be secretly locked up in one's "private" soul. Can one be saved and not live a life of love, i.e., giving, caring, sharing? There is no such thing as a union in Christ which refuses to bear the fruit of love.

HOW WE APPROPRIATE SALVATION

IN SYMPHONY WITH OUR WILL

As can be gathered from all the above, salvation is not forced upon us. God does not coerce His creation into a saving intimacy with Himself.[54] Love never imposes itself on anyone. If it does, it ceases to be love, for love reveres the freedom of each individual. For this reason, God will *always* yield to man's will.[55]

> God becomes powerless before human freedom; He cannot violate it since it flows from His own omnipotence. Certainly man was created by the will of God alone; but he cannot be deified [divinized] by it alone. A single will for creation, but two for deification. A single will to raise up the image [the general resurrection of the just and the unjust], but two to make the image into a likeness [the glorification of those in Christ]. The love of God for man is so great that it cannot constrain; for there is no love without respect. Divine will always will submit itself to gropings, to detours, even to revolts of human will to bring it to a free consent.[56]

God works *together* with man— in symphony *with* man's will—to realize salvation in his life. Eastern theologians refer to this process as *synergy* ("to work together"). The following passages from Scripture give us a few examples of that cooperation:

> " For we are *laborers together with* God..." (I Corinthians 3:9)
>
> "And we sent Timothy, our brother and God's *fellow worker* ..." (2 Thessalonians 3:2)
>
> "work out your own salvation ... for it is God who is at work in you, both *to will and to work* for His good pleasure." (Phillippians 2:12)

The synergy pictured in the Phillippians passage is not to be construed as making a case for "saving ourselves." It merely expresses the truth that God gives us the strength and desire to live in communion with Him (to be saved). Because God asks us to cooperate with Him does not mean that we must perform a certain work requirement or uphold our own end before He can save us. It is not as if God does half of the saving work and we do the other half. God does *all* the work. Christ *alone* saves us. But, if we are in communion with Christ (are saved), it only makes sense that *we must respond to Him* —with our *whole* self, with faith and in *application* of that faith. Therefore, God saves us 100%, but to experience His redemption, we must be willing to respond to Him 100%. In this very action—a continuing choice for God—God is able to infuse our will with His presence. We grow in a firmer resolve to be like Him, and His image is thus restored within us.

Humankind inherited corruption from Adam, and all of us since that time have voluntarily decided to take the way of pride for ourselves. In Christ, however, the Spirit gives the Christian *true* freedom, i.e., the desire to live in communion and godliness. This is salvation. Salvation is not God acting *on* man, or only on his behalf, as if human beings were unresponsive stones. People have wills which act, receive, initiate, and respond. Salvation embraces and provides healing for all the dimensions of man, including his will. If sin and death are slavery (Rom. 6:16; Heb. 4:14, 15), then, of course, salvation must be a *release and restoration of human freedom.*

THE PROCESS OF CONVERSION

Before the Eastern Christian understanding of conversion can be grasped, the reader must again be reminded that salvation is not a judicial formula or a legal contract. It is a saving *relationship* with a *saving Person.* How does the Scripture tell us if one has eternal life? "He who *has the Son* has the life (1 John 5:12)." Salvation is realized through an unfolding relationship of trust in Christ, not just by a commitment to one moment of His ministry (i.e., the cross).

In today's Evangelical-Fundamentalist context, almost every question asked in reference to salvation is centered around how one "gets to heaven." Salvation, however, pertains not only to where one will spend eternity, but how the Christian *lives in Christ now.* Wholeness is not intended just for heavenly citizens; it is something which "earth bound" believers should taste as well. Because salvation is *union in Christ* (i.e., theosis, holiness, love, and communion), it is not an experience reserved solely for those behind the heavenly gates, neither is it a possession (I have "it", he doesn't have "it"). Salvation is a *relationship* with a *Person,* a relationship which begins this side of eternity. Jesus Christ is the core of the salvation experience. As Vladimir Lossky notes,

> After the fall, human history is a long shipwreck awaiting rescue: but the port of salvation is not the goal; it is the possibility for the shipwrecked to resume his journey whose sole goal is union with God. [57]

Certainly it is important whether one will be in heaven or not. Christ did come to deliver us from the eternal bondage of satan, but salvation is not just an escape; it is an entrance into the life of God. To come to Jesus *only* to "get to heaven" is to use and exploit Him (an impossibility, I might add).

When many Christians quit their pursuit of God after they are "saved," they act like the cold person who marries only to be taken care of by his or her mate. He does not care about the quality of the love, trust or communion in the relationship, only that the relationship is "legal" and gets him what he wants. Salvation, however, does not begin and end at the moment a Christian says, "I do", to Christ. It is a *continuing* process of healing and wholeness *which comes through an ongoing, deepening relationship with Him.* It should not just be a matter of whether one is "saved" (going to heaven), but whether, through his ongoing communion with God, he is *being* saved day to day (growing in wholeness: mentally, spiritually, psychologically, in relationships, etc.). Saving faith in Christ, therefore, involves a *continual* disposition of trust. In this relationship of personal reliance, one is both saved and being saved, a process that begins now and culminates in eternity.

Repentance ("to return") should likewise be a constant disposition within the Christian life. To repent means to give oneself to a radical, continuous dynamic change in mind and action. Faith, always accompanying this change, constantly nurtures the Christian's communion with God and his brethren. In this light, conversion must be both instantaneous *and* gradual; demanding a constant attitude of saying, “yes,” to communion and, “no,” to selfishness, transcending a single "moment of decision" and requiring daily affirmation. [58]

Certainly, if one is a Christian, he does not turn to Christ merely *once* in his life, he *constantly* readjusts his heart and mind toward Christ. [59] In this life of repentance, our awareness of both God's love, and the love of the brethren, is continually restored. Each moment of life can be another opportunity to be plunged more deeply into the fire of divinity. This way of life makes it evident to both us and others that salvation is not just forgiveness, reconciliation, or justification, but union with God and one another. This is something even Adam could not know in Paradise because he been united with the Incarnate Christ. It is no wonder that the mystery of salvation is something "into which even angels long to look" (1 Pet. 1:12)!

NOTES FOR CHAPTER FIFTEEN

1 "In the Eastern Church there is no official pronouncement on the doctrine of salvation. The tradition of the Church concerning our reunion with God in Christ, our redemption or salvation or justification by God in Christ, has not been challenged in the East. It is for this reason that one does not find any fixed doctrine even among the ancient Fathers, but only a common tradition." Savas Agourides, "Salvation According to the Orthodox Tradition," *Ecumenical Review* (July 1969), Vol. XXI, Number 3, p. 190

2 "...[Luther] emphasized that Adam's state as one who was created in the divine image was no longer even intelligible to fallen man, who had no experience of it; much less was it correct to say that the image was still present, for 'it was lost through sin in Paradise'. ... Luther's understanding of the image of God is this: that Adam had it in his being and that he was good, but that he also lived a life that was wholly godly; that is, he was without the fear of death or any other danger, and was content with God's favor.' All of that was lost and would be fully restored only after the Judgement Day. In its place had come death and the fear of death, blasphemy, hatred toward God, and lust: 'These and similar evils are the image of the devil, who stamped them on us'." Jaroslav Pelikan *The Christian Tradition: Reformation of Church and Dogma (1300-1700)* (Chicago and London, The University of Chicago Press, 1983) p. 142 citing Luther's *Lectures on Genesis*, Genesis 1:26 *D. Martin Luthers Werke.,* Vol. 42:45-46

The belief of man's utter depravity is also, of course, echoed in Calvin's theology of salvation which can be summarized as follows: a) man is totally depraved, b) thus man can do nothing to be saved; it is God alone who unconditionally elects those destined for salvation c) making Christ's atonement limited to only these elect and d) because of this specified election and atonement (predestination), the true saints can be assured that they will persevere in the faith until the end.

3 "The term 'satisfaction' was first introduced into Christian thinking by the North African lawyer and Christian, Tertullian (220). It appears to have come from its use in Roman private law, where it referred to the amends one made to another for failing to discharge an obligation, or from Roman public law, where it could be interpreted as a form of punishment. In the West the term satisfaction became a term for the reparation made necessary by sins after baptism. Hillary of Potiers (367) was the first who equated 'satisfaction' with 'sacrifice' and interpreted the cross as Christ's act of reparation to God on behalf of sinners." Jaroslav Pelikan, *The Christian Tradition: The Emergence of the Catholic Tradition (100-600)* (University of Chicago Press, Chicago, 1971) p. 147

4 "The ancient Fathers would reject any theory of salvation according to which the main purpose of Christ's mission among men was to reconcile humanity with God by reconciling God's love for man with God's justice hurt by man's disobedience. Such a theory has never been supported by Orthodox (Eastern) theology." Savas Agourides, "Salvation According to the Orthodox Tradition," *Ecumenical Review*, (July 1969) Vol. XXI, Number 3, pp. 190, 191

5 "The Greek *amartia* means 'to miss, miss the mark, miss the road, to fail of doing, fail of one's purpose, to miss one's point, fail, go wrong, to fail of having, to be deprived of, to lose, err, sin." Maximos Aghiorgoussis, "Sin in Orthodox Dogmatics", *St. Vladimir's Theological Quarterly*, (Crestwood, N.Y., St. Vladimir's Press, 1977) Vol. 21, Number 4, p. 179

6 "According to St. Athanasius, the human fall consists precisely in the fact that man limits himself to himself, that man becomes, as it were, in love with himself. And through this concentration on himself man separated himself from God and broke the spiritual and free contact with God. It was a kind of delirium, a self-erotic obsession, a spiritual narcissism. One can say it was a de-spiritualization of human existence. All the rest came as a result - the death and decomposition of human structure. In any case, the fall was realized first in the realm of the spirit, just as it already was in the angelic world. The meaning of Original Sin is the same everywhere - self-eroticism, pride, and vanity. All the rest is only a projection of this spiritual catastrophe into the different areas of human structure. ... It was the infidelity of love, the insane separation from the Only One who is worthy of affection and love." Georges Florovsky, *Creation and Redemption*, (Belmont, MA., Nordland Publishing Company, 1976) p. 85,86

7 Although this idea did not completely originate with Augustine, it was through his influence that both this doctrine and this exegesis came to be accepted as church dogma — to the exclusion of any alternative.

8 "What are the characteristic features of Christianity? The innermost center and the whole substance of the Christian Good Tidings is the boundless *condescension of God,* the inrush of God into the world, the concrete, historical, supreme and unique revelation of God's infinite love, the Son of God having descended to become one of us and ascended, thus enabling us to ascend with Him." Nicholas Arseniev, "Characteristic Features of the Christian Message," *St. Vladimir's Quarterly* , (Crestwood, New York, St. Vladimir's Seminary Press, 1962) p. 55

9 "Luther ridiculed the scholastics for investigating the relationship between the two natures of Christ and branded such investigation as 'sophistic.' 'What difference does that make to me?' he continued. 'That he is man and God by nature, that he has for his own self; but that he has exercised his office and poured out his love, becoming my Savior and redeemer-that happens for my consolation and benefit'." Jaroslav Pelikan, *The Christian Tradition: Reformation of Church and Dogma (1300-1700),* (Chicago and London, The University of Chicago Press, 1983), p. 156 citing Luther's *Church Postil, D. Martin Luthers Werke,* Vol. 10-1-1:147)

10 St. Athanasius, *On the Incarnation* (Crestwood, New York, St. Vladimir's Seminary Press, 1983) p. 41

11 Georges Florovsky, *Creation and Redemption* (Belmont, MA., Nordland Publishing Company, 1976) p. 103 citing St. Gregory of Nazianzus, *orat.* XLV, *in S. Pascha,* 22, *M.G.* XXXVI, 653

12 "The wealth of our salvation in Christ is so rich that it cannot be expressed completely in any one single formula, nor even in all of them together. It is a mystery which can never be completely understood or defined. St. Gregory Nazianzen, for example, after he has treated briefly of the work of salvation accomplished by Christ, declares: "Let us respect what remains by our silence", for "nothing can equal the miracle of my salvation." The exclusive use of any term, especially if it becomes the key to interpret all other terms, will inevitably enclose us within a very limited understanding of this ineffable mystery." Dumitru Staniloae, *Theology and the Church* (Crestwood, N.Y., St. Vladimir's Seminary Press, 1980) p. 183

13 This is not to discount that the Eternal Word *had* to become incarnate and suffer death in order for us to be saved. Athanasius makes this point brilliantly in his answer to the question,"Why could not God have simply willed our salvation instead of sending the Son?"

> They will say that , if God wanted to instruct and save mankind, He might have done so, not by His Word's assumption of a body, but, even as he at first created them, by the mere signification of His will. The reasonable reply to that is that the circumstances in the two cases are quite different. In the beginning, nothing as yet existed at all; all that was needed, therefore, in order to bring all things into being, was that His will to do so should be signified. But one man was in existence, and things that were, not thing that were not, demanded to be healed, it followed as a matter of course that the Healer and Saviour should align Himself wit those things that existed already, in order to heal the existing evil...It was not things non-existent that needed salvation, for which a bare creative word might have sufficed, but man—man already in existence and already in process of corruption and ruin. It was natural and right, therefore, for the Word to use a human instrument and by that means unfold Himself to all... the need, therefore, was that life should cleave to it in corruption's place, so that, just as death was brought into being in the body, life also might be engendered in it. If death had been exterior to the body, life might fittingly have been the same. But if death was within the body, woven into its very substance and dominating it as though completely one with it, the need was for Life to be woven into it instead, so that the body by thus enduing itself with life might cast corruption off.

St. Athanasius, *On the Incarnation* , New Edition (Crestwood, New York, St. Vladimir's Seminary Press, 1983) pp. 80,81

14 "For God did not send the Son into the world to judge the world; but that the world should be *saved through Him.* He who believes in Him is not judged; he who does not believe *has been judged already*, because he has not believed in the name of the only begotten Son of God (John 3:17, 18)."

"Indeed, 'eternal damnation' is not inflicted by 'the angry God.' ... 'Damnation' is a self-inflicted penalty, the consequence and the implication of the rebellious opposition to God and to His will." Georges Florovsky, *Creation and Redemption* (Belmont, MA., Nordland Publishing Company, 1976) p. 257. The retribution of the Lord, and the eternal destruction that the unbeliever will experience (and in part, is experiencing now) results from his being "excluded from the presence of the Lord (2 Thess. 2:8-10)." The Lord's vengeance is manifest in this: the consequence of man's turning away from God's love. Unbelievers will reap the penalty which their self-imposed isolation has led them, and they will be tormented forever, contemplating their pride in Hell, " where their worm does not die, and the fire is not quenched" (Mk. 9:48).

15 Col. 1:20, 22; Rom. 5:10, 11; 2 Cor. 5:18.

16 "God in his great love for us is not concerned with himself in even the slightest degree, but only with us. Christ does not become incarnate and die simply for the sake of an external reconciliation with us and in order to make us righteous before him. ... The purpose of the incarnation was our deliverance from eternal death, our complete and eternal union with Him." Dumitru Staniloae, *Theology and the Church* (Crestwood, N.Y., St. Vladimir's Seminary Press, 1980) p. 197,198.

17 Savas Agourides, "Salvation According to the Orthodox Tradition", *Ecumenical Review* (July 1969) Vol. XXI., Number 3, p. 198

18 Lk. 7:44-48; Matt. 9:2-6; Jn. 8:3-11

19 Joachim Jeremias, *The Central Message of the New Testament,* (Philadelphia, Fortress Press, 1981) p. 37

20 "In other words, though separated in death, the soul and the body remained still united through the Divinity of the Word, from which neither was ever estranged. ... This does not alter the ontological character of death, but changed its meaning. This was an 'incorrupt death', and therefore corruption and death were overcome in it, and in it begins the resurrection. The very death of the Incarnate reveals the resurrection of human nature." Georges Florovsky, *Creation and Redemption* (Belmont, MA., Nordland Publishing Company, 1976) p. 136

21 St. Athanasius, *On The Incarnation*, New Edition (Crestwood, New York, St. Vladimir's Seminary Press,1982) p. 49

22 "Why had the true life to be revealed through the death of One, Who was Himself 'the Resurrection and the Life'? The only answer is that Salvation had to be a victory over death and man's mortality. The ultimate enemy of man was precisely death. Redemption was not just the forgiveness of sins, nor was it man's reconciliation with God. It was the deliverance from sin and death. ... Thus, according to St. Athanasius, the Word became flesh in order to abolish 'corruption' in human nature." Georges Florovsky, *Creation and Redemption* (Belmont, MA., Nordland Publishing Company, 1976) p. 225,226

23 "When a modern Western Christian turns to the Christian writers of the second and third centuries for their understanding of salvation in Christ, it is . . . their emphasis on the saving significance of the resurrection of Christ that he will find most unusual. So great was that emphasis in the soteriology of many church fathers that the definition of salvation through Christ's victory over man's enemies has been called "the classic" theory of the atonement. To be sure, other ways of speaking about the atonement were too widespread even among the Greek fathers to permit us to ascribe exclusive or even primary force to any one theory, but Christ as victor was more important in orthodox expositions of salvation and reconciliation than Western dogmatics has recognized." *The Christian Tradition: The Emergence of the Catholic Tradition (100-600)* (Chicago, IL, The University of Chicago Press, 1971) Vol. 1, p. 149

24 "...the Fathers spoke of a *personal* power of death and corruption, that of the Devil. This is from whom and from what Christ came to liberate man." John Meyendorff, *The Catholicity and the Church,* "The Significance of the Reformation in the History of Christendom, St. Vladimir's Seminary Press, (Crestwood, New York), 1983, p. 72

25 Verses 5 and 6 of Isaiah 53 capture the various dimensions of salvation in Christ's death made available to us.

He provided *forgiveness* and the *restoration of our relationship* with God...

> "But He was pierced through *for our transgressions*, He was crushed for our iniquities."

He made our *personal, psychological and physical wholeness* once again possible...

> "The chastening for *our well-being* fell upon Him, And by His scourging we are healed"

Christ's victory over satan in our lives is also emphasized in the Matt. 8:16, 17, a passage looking back to Isaiah 53 for its context. In these verses it becomes plain that Christ came to deliver us from the spiritual, physical and psychological afflictions of satan:

> "And When evening had come, they brought to Him many who were demon-possessed, and He cast out the spirits with a word, and healed all who were ill; in order that what was spoke through Isaiah the prophet might be fulfilled, saying, "He Himself took our infirmities, and carried away our diseases."

26 The following is based on the translation appearing in *The Greek Orthodox Holy Week and Easter Services Book,* compiled by Rev. George L. Papadeas (New York, New York, 1973) p. 482

27 Lk 1:69, 71; Lk. 6:9; Acts 7:25; 1 Cor. 16:2; Heb. 5:7; Jas. 4:12; 5;20; 1 Cor. 5:5

28 Claude U. Broach and F. Burton Nelson, both Evangelicals themselves, aptly criticize the contemporary problem of the "individualized" view of salvation endemic within our Western culture:

> The emphasis upon the individual causes all too many of us, as Baptists, to think of the Gospel of Christ in the narrow terms of individual salvation and grace. We think of the Gospel as something for us - for me, for *my* salvation, *my* wholeness, *my* oneness with God, *my* ticket to heaven! We are not trained and conditioned to think of the Incarnation in terms of God's plan and purpose for the whole Creation; we are not inclined to think of the whole Church as an instrument of Divine grace, designed to carry out the mission of redemption for a lost world. Emphasis upon individual responsibility has been allowed to create a mood of pre-occupation with individualistic piety and moralism.

Claude U. Broach, "Introducing Southern Baptists", *The Greek Orthodox Theological Review* (Brookline, MA., Holy Cross Press, Winter 1977) Volume XXII, Number 4, p. 374

> The hallmark of evangelicalism has been its emphasis upon the experience of personal salvation - individual commitment to Jesus Christ as personal Savior. This emphasis is central to any vital experience of Christian faith. But whenever this focus becomes exclusive - i.e. whenever salvation is understood "solely as an individual, spiritual, and otherworldly matter to the neglect of the corporate, physical, and 'this worldly' - there is something seriously lacking. In other words, the "Call to Holistic Salvation" points to the debilitating polarization of what should be a holistic Christian life embracing the full range of human experience - individual, and corporate, spiritual and material, temporal and eternal.

F. Burton Nelson, "A Call to Church Unity" , *The Orthodox Evangelicals* , Robert Webber, Donald Bloesch, eds., (New York, Thomas Nelson, 1977) p. 95

29 Love always draws together. Acts. 2: 42-45, "And those who believed were **together**, had all things **in common** and they began selling their property and possessions, and were sharing them with all,

as anyone might have need." The total opposite is the foolish, rich man who lost his soul through his self-sufficiency (Luke 12:15-34).

30 Dumitru Staniloae, *Theology and the Church* (Crestwood, N.Y., St. Vladimir's Seminary Press, 1980) p. 204

31 Alexander Schmemann, "Toward a Theology of Councils", *Church, World, Mission* (Crestwood, New York, St. Vladimir's Press, 1979) p. 164

32 Georges Florovsky, *Bible, Church, Tradition: An Eastern Orthodox View* (Belmont, MA., Nordland Publishing Company, 1972) p. 62

33 Vladimir Lossky, *Orthodox Theology: An Introduction*, (Crestwood, New York, St. Vladimir's Press, 1978) p. 111

34 St. John Chysostom, *The Epistle to the Romans,* Hom. X., 17 based on the translation appearing in J. B. Morris, Philip Schaff, ed., *The Nicene and Post-Nicene Fathers* (Grand Rapids, Michigan, Wm.. B. Eerdman's Publishing Company, 1979 reprint) p. 403

35 "When the New Testament speaks of the Holy Spirit offered to the believer, this Spirit is not to be regarded as an incidental entity, added over and above man's own nature. Not even the most obnoxious sin can expel from man the Spirit in all his totality. A trace of the Spirit must always remain to remind man of his origins and to make him capable of repentance... Adam's fall has not completely detached the Spirit from man. Logic itself requires us to believe that the Spirit remains in man as the source of his life and intelligence. ... Were the Spirit to abandon the sinner completely, God could then expect nothing of him, and punishment would have no real meaning." Emilianos Timiadis, "The Holy Spirit and the Mystical In Orthodox Theology", *Lutheran World* (1976) Vol. 23, Number 3, p. 175

36 "One has to distinguish most carefully between the healing of nature and the healing of the will. Nature is healed and restored with a certain compulsion, by the mighty power of God's omnipotent and invincible grace. The wholeness is in a way forced upon human nature. For in Christ all human nature (the "seed of Adam") is fully and completely cured from unwholeness and mortality. This restoration will be actualized and revealed to its full extent in the General Resurrection, the resurrection of all, both of the righteous and of the wicked. No one, so far as nature is concerned, can escape Christ's kingly rule, can alienate himself from the invincible power of the resurrection. But the will of man cannot be cured in the same invincible manner; for the whole meaning of the healing of the will is in its free conversion. The will of man must turn itself to God; there must be a free and spontaneous response of love and adoration. Only by this spontaneous and free effort does man enter into that new and eternal life which is revealed in Christ Jesus. A spiritual regeneration can be wrought only in perfect freedom, in an obedience of love, by a self-consecration and self-dedication to God." Georges Florovsky, *Creation and Redemption*, (Belmont, MA., Nordland Publishing Company, 1976) p. 147,148

37 John Meyendorff, *The Catholicity and the Church,* "The Significance of the Reformation in the History of Christendom, St. Vladimir's Seminary Press, (Crestwood, New York), 1983, p. 73

38 "Divine transcendence is not due, as in Augustine, to the limitations of our fallen state, or to our bodily existence, but because God is *above* creature." John Meyendorff, *The Catholicity and the Church,* "The Significance of the Reformation in the History of Christendom, St. Vladimir's Seminary Press (Crestwood, New York), 1983, p. 71

39 The nature of God is both the participable and the non-participable elements of God. Both His essence and his energies are uncreated and fully God. His energies are not His "acts", they are what we can experience of *Him.* In His energies we are brought into union with Him, and He is manifest to our spirit, mind, body and consciousness. God is beyond understanding, and not definable apart from man, but neither is He separate from Him. This way of illustrating the mystery of God as essence and energies makes it clear that God is not exiled in heaven.

40 "For His being in everything does not mean that he shares the nature of everything, only that He gives all things their being and sustains them in it. Just as the sun is not defiled by the contact of its rays with earthly objects, but rather enlightens and purifies them, so he Who made the sun is not defiled by

being made known in a body..." St. Athanasius, *On the Incarnation* (Crestwood, New York, St. Vladimir's Seminary Press, 1983) p. 46

41 It very interesting that many Anabaptists had a strikingly similar approach to the Ancient Eastern Church in this respect:

> Whereas in the Magisterial Reformation grace was looked upon from man's side as God's act of forensic justification in which the sinner is declared righteous without actually being made so, in the Radical Reformation grace was rather regarded as the act whereby God through the agency of the Holy Spirit brought about an actual ontological change within the nature of man himself. Through the Holy Spirit the image in man which was lost through the fall is restored, and the believer is made a participant in the divine nature itself. Thus, the result of grace in man is a reversal of the incarnation in which the eternal Word becomes man in order that man may become God.

Alvin J. Beachy, *The Concept of Grace in the Radical Reformation* (Harrisonburg, U.S.A., 1976) pp. 70-71

42 Georges Florovsky, *Creation and Redemption*, (Belmont, MA., Nordland Publishing Company, 1976) pp. 240, 75 citing St. Athanasius, *De incarn. et c. arian.*, 8, c. 996

43 "In the process of theosis the human person is 'divinized,' that is assumed into the higher and internal life of God, and by no means de-humanized or bereft of its human qualities and properties. On the contrary, concomitant to divinization is the process of true humanization, because man comes closer to God the Omega, God the Fulfiller, the ground of being and perfection and therefore comes closer to the real self." Edited By: David Neiman and Margaret Schatkin, *The Heritage of the Early Church,* (Pont. Institutum Studiorum Orientalium, Roma, 1973) p. 352

44 As in the Person of Christ, however, our humanity does not become Divine because of our union with Him. Christ's humanity participates in Divinity by way of its "energies", never in its essence. If divinity and humanity were to merge, Christ would neither be God, nor man, but a "being" foreign to either natures. Christ's two natures cannot be mixed or confused, He remains *one* Divine Person *in* two natures (human and divine). He is truly man, His manhood being the same as ours (yet without sin), and He is truly God in that His Divinity is consubstantial with the Father. As the Chalcedonian confession (451) makes clear, He is to be...

> "acknowledged in two natures, without confusion, without change, without division, without separation; the distinction of natures being in no way abolished because of the union, but rather the characteristic property of each nature being preserved, and concurring into one Person and one subsistence (hypostasis), not as if Christ were parted or divided into two persons, but one and the same Son and only-begotten God, Word, Lord, Jesus Christ..."

J. Stevenson, *Creeds, Councils and Controversies* (London, S.P.C.K., 1966) p. 336-337

45 Many Reformed theologians often equate the Eastern understanding of "divinization" with what they would mean by "sanctification," and overall this is a good analogy. There is one significant distinction to be made in this parallel, however. In the East sanctification (theosis) and salvation are not distinguished. Thus, one who is "being saved" is *also* one who is being *sanctified* in life and attitude. It is for this reason that Orthodox use the word "salvation" interchangeably with "theosis" (sanctification), and this has been a cause of confusion for some Christians in the West. Salvation in the East, however, does not hold *just* a forensic meaning (forgiven of "sin", a "debt" is paid, a pardon from "condemnation" given), but *also* carries the more expansive sense of *communion* and *participation in God's life*.

46 In the scholastic view, the spiritual man and the "human" man are divorced, saving grace being understood as something which can only change one's "spiritual" standing but incapable of bringing about an actual transformation in the nature of a person himself. "....'God reckons imperfect righteousness as perfect righteousness and sin as not sin, even though it really is sin'. And Luther himself, in the course of an academic disputation, did use the concept of the alien righteousness; outside ourselves,' to prove that justification must be through faith alone, without works, since these could not take hold of such a

righteousness." Jaroslav Pelikan *The Christian Tradition: Reformation of Church and Dogma (1300-1700)* (Chicago and London, The University of Chicago Press, 1983) p. 142 citing Luther's *Disputation on Justification*, 27-29, *D. Martin Luthers Werke.*, Vol. 39—I:83 and Luther's *Commentary on Galatians* (1535) 3:6, *D. Martin Luthers Werke.*, Vol. 40-I: 367-368

47 "In Luther and Zwingli this doctrine of imputed righteousness is logically combined with and supported by the doctrines of total depravity, the bondage of will, and sovereign , unconditional election. In such a pattern, justification and actual sanctification are separated and especially in Luther, the former becomes dominate; the latter tends to become secondary." Kenneth Ronald Davis, *Anabaptism and Asceticism* , (Scottdale, Pa., Herald Press, 974), p. 130

48 Dumitru Staniloae, *Theology and the Church* (Crestwood, N.Y., St. Vladimir's Seminary Press, 1980) p. 63 This is in contrast to the Reformation doctrine of a righteousness separate and distinct from who we are as persons. Dietrich Bonhoeffer summarizes this doctrine well when he says, "The Reformers expressed it this way: Our righteousness is an 'alien righteousness," a righteousness that comes from outsied of us (*extra nos*)." *Life Together*, (Fortress Press), p. 22

49 John Meyendorff, *The Catholicity and the Church,* "The Significance of the Reformation in the History of Christendom, St. Vladimir's Seminary Press, (Crestwood, New York), 1983, p. 73

50 "In Christ, indeed, man is given justification before God's law. But he is also restored into the fellowship of God and the participation in divine life: the original relationship is not only re-established but now man can become as 'God.'" John Meyendorff, *The Catholicity and the Church,* "The Significance of the Reformation in the History of Christendom, St. Vladimir's Seminary Press, (Crestwood, New York), 1983, p. 72 I shall speak more about this under the discussion of *theosis* which follows.

51 " A man's faith makes him just, brings him God's holiness and forgiveness of sins.. ...Out of this...came Luther's doctrine of justified man, as at one and the same time both just and a sinner (*simul justsus et peccator*)...[communicated by] three essential elements : 1) the principle of gratuity (*sola gratia* -grace alone), the principle of faith (*sola fides* -faith alone) and the principle of God's Word (*sola Scriptura* -scripture alone). ... Calvin is one with Luther in believing that when a man is justified, he remains *simul justus et peccator*, a sinner and yet just because in Christ God imputes justice to him." William A. Scott, *Historical Protestantism: An Historical Introduction to Protestant Theology* (Englewood Cliffs, N.J., 1971) pp. 8, 46

52 Some have even made a case from Luther's nominalism that his teaching on "justified by faith and still a sinner" is more a matter of Occam's influence on him than the Scripture's. Here is Bouyer's analysis:

> "Inside ...[this nominalist] framework, the sovereignty of God is no more than a total independence of all that could be considered as laws of reality, whether the moral law, or the logical principles indispensable to thought. To say that God is all–powerful would amount to saying that he could make good evil and *vice versa*, making a being other than it is; otherwise it means nothing at all. For if being is no more than a word without content, infinite being cannot be other than the indefinite, pure and simple. In such conditions, it seems quite natural that God may 'declare just' the sinner, leaving him as much the sinner as before, that he may predestine some to damnation, just as he predestines others to salvation. If he did not do so, nothing would distinguish him from us, his transcendent sovereignty would disappear. Doubtless he could remain greater than, but within the same order. He would no longer be sovereign. In the same way, the Word of God can only be the Word of *God* if it remains transcendent, external to us or any other authority..."it becomes a dictamen from above....the Word is totally inexpressible in human ideas and language. Man can only receive it blindly..."

Louis Bouyer, *The Spirit and Forms of Protestantism* (Westminster, Maryland, The Newman Press, 1956) pp. 154,155

53 Peter Davids, in his excellent commentary (*New International Greek Testament Commentary on James*), harmonizes the seeming contradiction between faith and works in the following exposition of James 2:22: "You see faith was working with his works, and as a result of the works, faith was perfected."

> James states that Abraham's faith is perfected through his works (doubtless meaning it is brought to maturity, and thus indicating the unfinished state of faith without works) through his works (ἐκ τῶν ἔργων). Here, then, is a balanced statement. James wishes to reject *neither* faith *nor* works. Both are individually important. Yet for the person to receive God's declaration that he is righteous (James 2:21 presents the goal) they must mix together. Faith assists works, works perfects faith.

Peter Davids, *New International Greek Testament Commentary on James*, (Grand Rapids, MI., Eerdmans Publishing Co., 1983) p. 128

54 "The fall of man consisted in man's preference to compete with God, to be His equal instead of participating in His gifts...he became enslaved to the power of death because he did not possess immortality as a property of his own." John Meyendorff, *The Catholicity and the Church,* "The Significance of the Reformation in the History of Christendom, St. Vladimir's Seminary Press, (Crestwood, New York), 1983, p. 72 The consequence is the distortion of our once perfect and divinely given human nature. Although man is fallen, he is not totally depraved. Because traces of the divine image remain, man is still spiritually and morally free. He has the ability to choose or reject communion with God, grace (God's presence in relationship and communion) is able to be resisted.

55 "It does not depend upon our will whether we shall rise after death or not, just as it is not by our will that we are born. Christ's death and resurrection brings immortality and incorruption to all in the same manner, because all have the same nature as the Man Christ Jesus. But nobody can be compelled to desire. Thus Resurrection is a gift common to all, but blessedness will be given only to some. One has to die to oneself in order to live in Christ. Each one must personally and freely associate himself with Christ, the Lord, the Saviour, and the Redeemer, in the confession of faith, in the choice of love, in the mystical oath of allegiance. Each one has to renounce himself, to "lose his soul" for Christ's sake, to take up his cross, and to follow after Him. The Christian struggle is the "following" after Christ, following the path of His Passion and Cross, even unto death, but first of all, following in love. This is no mere ascetical or moral rule, not merely a discipline. This is the ontological law of spiritual existence, even the law of life itself." Georges Florovsky, *Creation and Redemption* (Belmont, MA., Nordland Publishing Company, 1976) pp. 148, 149

56 Vladimir Lossky, *Orthodox Theology: An Introduction* (Crestwood, New York, St. Vladimir's Press, 1978) p. 73

57 Vladimir Lossky, *Orthodox Theology: An Introduction*, (Crestwood, New York, St. Vladimir's Press, 1978) p. 84

58 "We should rid ourselves of the all too usual tendency to oppose either sudden or gradual conversion, and should try to understand that one is impossible without the other. The biblical use of the term 'ἐπιστρέφειν' [to return] if understood aright, denies a radical separation between the two; 'ἐπιστρέφειν' should be understood as signifying a continuous act of being on the way back after one has taken the decision to return. To introduce a separation between the two and give preference to the once for all 'sudden' decision of conversion is to take a one-sided radical position. For a Christian who studies conversion it is not only the sudden decision which is interesting, but also what follows this decision. For him conversion is a continuous growing in maturity in all realms of life as a responsible member of the Christian community and through it of the world-wide, human society." Nikos A. Nissiotis, "Conversion and the Church", *The Ecumenical Review* , p. 261

59 "The responsibility of a Christian is to continue to become more and more what he already is, to become a Christian throughout his every day life. A Christian is in a constant status of becoming. His task is to always become more Christ-like . . . " Bishop Maximos Maximos Aghiorgoussis,, "On Being A Christian", *The Illuminator* (August-Sept. 1981) p. 8

CHAPTER SIXTEEN

BAPTISM (PART I):

THE DIFFICULTIES WITH AGE RESTRICTIVE BAPTISM

Most modern Evangelical-Fundamentalists assert that adult "believers" baptism is the *only* acceptable mode of Christian baptism. To these Christians, baptizing an infant is unbiblical, illogical and, perhaps, even irreverent. This was the position of the Anabaptists,[1] those of the Radical Reformation with whom many of today's Baptists identify.[2] Indeed, the Anabaptists' exclusive acceptance of adult-believer baptism is interpreted by many as a direct response to New Testament teaching. But was their rationale for an age-restrictive baptism based solely on the New Testament, or were there other factors?

Anabaptist theology and practice were greatly influenced by what the Radical Reformers saw of Post Reformation Christianity in Europe: a stronger, hard line Medieval Roman Catholicism, moral laxity by those both within and without the Reformation, and a resurgence in the ideals of monasticism. Concurrent with these trends, the course and emphasis of the Radical Reformation were also significantly influenced by Erasmian humanism, an outlook which influenced their views on the Church, the sacraments, and almost every other doctrine unique to that movement.

In the first part of this chapter I will explore the significance these historical factors had on the Anabaptist doctrine of baptism. What did they believe the doctrine symbolized? Why did they feel adult baptism was necessary to restore New Testament Christianity? And how did their theology shape their thinking on both of these issues? In the remainder of the chapter, I will evaluate the doctrine as it is practiced today among modern Evangelical-Fundamentalists, by taking a closer look at some of the premises behind the doctrine.

THE SETTING

The Roman Catholicism of the Sixteenth Century saw baptism as possessing the power to save one from eternal retribution. According to the teaching, only through baptism could one enter into a "salvation contract" with God. The stain of Original Sin was too great for God to overlook. If baptism were not administered to erase its curse, even a child of Christian parents who died without the rite would suffer punishment.

The Reformation corrected some elements of this theological reasoning, but it remained ineffective in bringing about a significant moral reform.[3] Actually, the Reformers never advanced a theological reformation to bring about a moral awakening. To them, theology and piety were two different things.[4]

At that time, however, there were many Christians who embraced an ascetic and moral vision for reform. When they saw that the Reformation had failed to address their concerns, they left the movement in frustration.[5] It was this concern which led many of them to look to Anabaptism as a platform to advance the holiness they eagerly desired.[6]

Because holiness was the greatest of concerns for the Anabaptist, they saw the Magisterial Reformers—men like Luther, Calvin and Zwingli who aligned their movements with secular governments—as corrupters of the pure spirit of the Gospel.[7] As light has nothing in common with darkness, they reasoned, neither can the Truth be "married" to the State. This union of Church and Nation, coupled with the Reformers' failure to balance justification by faith with a doctrine of lived-out holiness, compelled a segment of Christians sympathetic to the need for church reform, to leave the major Reformation streams and begin the Anabaptist movement in its stead.

THE REASONS BEHIND THE ANABAPTIST STAND ON BAPTISM

INFANT BAPTISM AS AN IDENTIFICATION WITH A FALLEN CHURCH

The Anabaptists believed that the fundamental reason for the corrupt state of European Christianity lay in the indiscriminate admission of all to its ranks. What were the qualifications for baptism by the church bodies of the time? In essence, if one were a citizen of a "Christian" nation, one was a Christian. In this setting, baptism was understood as signifying one's allegiance not only to the *State's* church, but to the *state itself.*

To the Anabaptists, this was not Gospel baptism but *State* baptism.[8] "God does not recognize *secular* baptism, but *Christian* baptism," they boldly asserted.[9] It was inconceivable for them to imagine that the True Church could ever allow such a practice. The fact that Luther and Zwingli later advocated beheading, burning, or drowning Anabaptists as heretics *and* political traitors, encouraged them to believe this all the more.

It is important to note that before this persecution, several Anabaptist groups had no theological or moral difficulty with baptizing infants.[10] Up to this time, their primary concern had been only that the children of *believing* parents be admitted to baptism. This later oppression by the Reformed church, however, encouraged almost all Anabaptists to reject infant baptism of *any* kind. More and more, the baptism of children came to be equated with the rite of a fallen and discredited "church", one willing to murder all those who did not affirm its legitimacy.

Although baptism would eventually symbolize what Anabaptists stood for, baptism in and of itself was not originally their major issue.[11] *The initial thrust behind Anabaptism flowed, not from a New Testament conviction that adult-believer's baptism alone was acceptable, but from its repudiation of a church which compromised its message for the sake of political advantage.* Infant baptism became the emblem of the unholy union of church and state. For Anabaptists, such a marriage was an impossibility. Hence, baptism became the catalyst for the discussion, but the crucial issue was what "church" is the True Church. As Anabaptist Church historian Franklin Littell notes:

> Baptism became important only because it was the most obvious dividing line between two patterns of church organization. ... The real issue between the Anabaptist and the other reformers was on the question of the type of Church which should take the place of the old Church.[12]

THE TRUE CHURCH IS A VISIBLE CHURCH; THUS, INFANT BAPTISM HAS NO PLACE

Luther, Zwingli, and Calvin defended infant baptism on the grounds that since the elect were destined to be saved anyway, and since God alone knew who those elect were, there was nothing inappropriate in administering baptism to all who presented themselves for the sacrament. God gives the benefits of baptism only to members of the true, "invisible" Church, and thus the practice did not compromise the Church's membership in any way. Whenever baptism was given to those predestined to judgment, there was no benefit because the sacrament had no power to change his spiritual state one way or the other.

The Anabaptists countered this line of reasoning by asserting that the Church is a *visible* entity, *not* an invisible one. There is only one Church, the Church of the *saints.* There is no "church" of unbelievers. To them, such a "church" was only a lapsed, human institution, not the Body of Christ. *This contradictory view regarding the nature of the Church -not baptism itself- provided the major reason for the split between the Reformers and the Anabaptists.*[13]

Because only those committed to living a Christ-like life were members of the Church, only these should be baptized. Similarly, a logical means of protecting the purity of the Church was to prohibit the baptism of those who might one day reject the way of discipleship (i.e., infants and children). To the Anabaptist, infant baptism promoted a corrupt, unregenerate and lukewarm church, whereas adult baptism challenged both the State church's moral compromise and their divided loyalty to the kingdom of God.[14]

Both Reformer and Radical Reformer agreed on one thing regarding baptism; the baptism of infants was *the* link between church and state. To the Anabaptist, adult baptism was a call *out* of this world; infant baptism was an adulterous union *with* it. The doctrine of adult-believer's baptism stood against the State-instituted church and its claim that it alone had the power to invest power in the sacraments.[15] The Anabaptists offered an alternate view of the Church and the meaning of the Christian life, both of which were summed up in their doctrine of baptism. For this reason, Conrad Grebel (1498-1526), a key leader of the Swiss Anabaptists, saw baptism as the central issue of the Radical Reformation:

> The medieval order can be laid low in no more effective way than by abolishing infant baptism.[16]

A SIMPLISTIC METHOD OF INTERPRETING THE SCRIPTURES

The Anabaptists were not interested in the "theology" of either Rome or the Reformers; they simply wanted to live a godly Christian life.[17] This attitude tended to translate into a predominantly moralistic approach in their reading of the Scriptures.[18] The Scriptures were seen primarily as a book of ethics and morality, not of doctrine.

"Most of the partisans [of Anabaptism] were simple-minded people who took the Bible literally and wished to embody its teachings in everyday realities without making the necessary ... effort at translation and understanding."[19] The study of ancient languages, Church history, or the writings of Biblical scholars in order to understand the Scriptures was a waste of time to them. All one needed was the Spirit and the collective voice of their local fellowship to interpret the Bible.

This anti-academic bias toward the Scriptures was held both by Zwingli, and by the Anabaptists. Consequently, both had much in common in the way they understood and interpreted the Bible. This agreement should not startle us; the original leaders of Swiss Anabaptism had themselves been Zwingli's disciples at one time. Both believed the Bible was the sole authority in the Church, and that anything not specified in the Scriptures should be eliminated in Church practice. All who read the Scriptures, if humble and pious, would agree upon its interpretation. [20]

According to this approach to the Bible, an age restrictive doctrine of baptism can be extracted from the Scriptures without difficulty. [21] As Conrad Grebel stated in one of his "Programmatic Letters", "...that which is not taught by clear instruction and example we shall regard as forbidden to us--just as if it stood written, Do not do this..."[22] From *this* line of reasoning, the baptism of children must be prohibited. Where in the scriptures does it *specifically* record an infant baptism? Where does the Bible say something like, "And the newborn child of Crispus was hence baptized by Peter." Nowhere. Thus, according to this method of interpretation, the Bible says that children and infants should not be baptized.

HUMANISTIC INFLUENCE

The Anabaptists' literal and moralistic system of Biblical interpretation was derived straight from Erasmus' humanism. Erasmus' influence on the movement was only natural since he had a great deal of direct and indirect contact with Zwingli and many of the founding leaders of Anabaptism. His teaching profoundly molded both Anabaptism's moral interpretation of the Scriptures, and its theology in general. [23] How significant was his influence? *Almost every element of Erasmus' personal theology was similar to Anabaptist positions.* [24] Here are a few examples:

> Erasmus believed that the Bible "interpreted itself," that the primary emphasis of the Scriptures was ethical, not doctrinal, and that a devotional -not an intellectual- approach to the Scriptures was clearly superior. For these reasons, he dismissed the input of Biblical scholars. [25]
>
> Erasmus disdained theology (he once described a contemporary as "a scab of a fellow, theology incarnate"),[26] emphasized personal piety, [27] advocated a lay asceticism, [28] elevated morality over doctrine,[29] and defined the church more in ascetic terms than in political or institutional ones.

> Erasmus separated the spiritual from material, "external" things,[30] taught the primacy of an inner faith over ritual, and denied a "real presence" in the Eucharist.
>
> Erasmus proposed pacifism, refused to accept only a "legal" understanding of justification (Christ's righteousness is not just "inputted" by faith, it must be demonstrated), rejected predestination, and suggested the re-baptism of adults.

Zwingli, also an avid pupil of Erasmus, faithfully re-enforced Erasmian teaching in a study group he led in Zürich. [31] Within this group, the seeds of Anabaptism were deeply sown, and all of its members were to become the leading proponents of Anabaptism: Conrad Grebel, Felix Manz, and Balthalzar Hübmaier. [32] Whether it was expressed by Zwingli, or the Radical Reformers, the mainstream of Anabaptist ideology flowed from Erasmus. What Erasmus taught privately, (but avoided teaching openly out of deference to the Roman Church's authority), Zwingli taught publicly both within his study group and from the pulpit. What Zwingli taught but did not implement out of deference to State authority, the Anabaptists practiced openly, refusing to honor the "government of men." [33]

MONASTICISM'S INFLUENCE ON ANABAPTISM

Erasmus' most important contribution to Anabaptist thought lay in his teaching on the nature of the Church. In this respect more than any other, he is the forerunner of Anabaptism.[34] The Church, in Erasmus' view, should be a Brotherhood separate from the world, one committed to holiness and ascetic discipline. In this regard, the true Church is much like a monastic Order; it is a distinguishable brotherhood under the "rule" of the Gospel. This discipline would be reflected by a true inner devotion, and a repudiation of externals such as wealth, luxury, and fancy clothing. Intemperance, gambling, and dancing would also be prohibited to promote a lifestyle that would more responsibly "imitate" Christ's own.

How does this ascetic outlook tie into a vision of adult-only baptism? Erasmus maintained that, in baptism, the Christian should understand himself to be making a "vow" to Christ, to the brotherhood (Christians within a specific community), and to a life of holiness. In this light, baptism would be similar to a monk's commitment to an Order as a "novitiate." This is the motivation behind Erasmus suggestion that those who had been baptized as infants re-enact their baptism as adults, a view obviously very sympathetic to Anabaptist sentiments. [35]

From Erasmus' ascetic premise Anabaptists reasoned that infants were unable to meet the criteria of baptism. How can a child be baptized when he is unable to make a "vow" to holiness and to his brethren? The only way to correct this moral neglect in the Church, the Anabaptist deduced, would be to disallow infant baptism.

Erasmus' emphases were clearly ascetic, but how deeply did monasticism affect Anabaptism in general? *Very, very* deeply. Another Anabaptist historian, Kenneth Ronald Davis, makes this exact point in the following:

> Asceticism clearly dominates the theology, soteriology, sacramental teachings, ecclesiology, eschatology, and even the unique principles of biblical interpretation of Evangelical Anabaptism.[36]

The Anabaptists' central vision was aimed at the creation of the new man in Christ. This was not just a theology of holiness through regeneration, but the *demonstrable ascetic* theology of holiness. Holiness was not only emphasized, it governed every other aspect of Anabaptism's theology. [37] Baptism was a commitment to that ideal of holiness, and those who forsook that ideal would be swiftly disciplined. [38]

Monastic influence did not gain prominence among the Anabaptists through Erasmus alone. *Many* of the Anabaptist leaders were themselves former monks. [39] "More than coincidence is involved in the fact that literally thousands of evangelical preachers and teachers were recruited from the ranks of the monks, friars, and hermits...."[40] For example, Michael Sattler, an ex-prior of St. Peter's near Freiburg in Breisgau, was the most significant leader of the Anabaptist Swiss Brethren; his refining and unifying of doctrine and practice still remains with Anabaptism today.[41]

This heavy monastic flavor all the more emphasized their perspective on baptism. The Church, not just the monastery, should be composed only of those who had voluntarily decided for a life of spiritual discipline. In other words, the ascetic ideal became a non-optional requirement for membership. If one were not committed to live a holy life, how could he be one of Christ's disciples?

> What is implied is that the Anabaptists not only proclaimed the Reformation doctrine of the priesthood of all believers, but also the "monkhood,' in its laicized sense, of all true believers. This is the older Franciscan ideal from the ascetic tradition taken to its logical and ultimate conclusion. Not only is the ascetic life now possible and encouraged for all Christians, but it is *required,* absolutely necessary, as the only road to salvation.[42]

By 1525, the Anabaptists expected all true believers to demonstrate their submissiveness to the will of God by voluntary participation in a believer's baptism. Those who abstained from this action could not be "of the Fold." Following the ascetic pattern, the "church as institution" was rejected for "the church as Brotherhood." True Christians would now give themselves to each other in love, and thus, as in a religious Order, willingly share their goods with one another in a common trust and common lifestyle. Again, because an infant or small child could not give himself to such an ideal, he should not be given baptism—*the* symbol of an ascetic way of life.

A SUMMARY AND SOME OBSERVATIONS ...

The Anabaptist view of baptism is not the same at every point as the Evangelical-Fundamentalist perspective, but it still stands as its chief cornerstone. Because of this, and because many of the arguments behind "adult-believer only" baptism today are fueled by Anabaptist thinking, it is important to recount the influences which affected Anabaptism's perspective on the doctrine. After such an analysis, the reader will be in a better position to evaluate his own thinking in light of the arguments presented in the remainder of this chapter.

Anabaptist history makes one thing undebatably clear: *the core of Anabaptist thinking on baptism was cast in ascetic and Erasmian molds.* This attitude affected their approach toward baptism in four major ways:

1) *The exclusionary baptism of adults was motivated by a desire to make sure the Church remained holy and pure.* The vision of the Christian life as an ascetic discipline led Anabaptists to see baptism as a vow to a specific life-style, and, therefore, adult-believer-only baptism was enforced to achieve this end.

2) *Adult-believer only baptism occurred in strong measure as a reaction to the undiscerning acceptance of any "Christian citizen" (believer or unbeliever) into the Church's membership.* The practice of both Roman and Reformed Churches of admitting any and all to their ranks provoked the Anabaptists to see age-exclusionary baptism as a safeguard. Membership in the Church was not the birthright of all born into a "Christian" nation; it was the free, voluntary choice of each individual.

3) *Anabaptism understood infant baptism to be the symbol of a fallen church's merger with the world.* The Radical Reformers were primarily concerned that the Church be free and in no way subject to the State. Anabaptists judged the alliance of the Church and State evil, and, therefore, renounced their former ties with this "church's" baptism. In its place, they promoted a "*true* " baptism by a "*true* " church made up of "*true* " believers.

4) *The baptism of adult-believers only was derived by Anabaptists through ascetic, humanistic, and anti-intellectual methods of Biblical interpretation.* While the Reformers and Roman theologians tended to neglect piety in their pursuit of "truth," the Anabaptists neglected creeds, Church Fathers, and scholarship in favor of good deeds. Intellectual disciplines aiding one's understanding of the Scriptures were discouraged.

All the above makes it clear that *the primary motivation and energy behind the practice and defense of baptizing believing adults only, lay in a moral and ethical impulse, not a doctrinal one.* Adult-only baptism was an act of piety. The practice did not come about as a result of a new exegetical find, an insight once forgotten but now rediscovered through the availability of the Scriptures to all. It did not emerge through the discovery of a lost ancient Biblical manuscript. Nor was this teaching the fruit of a more thorough study of the Bible's original languages. In short, *the practice of baptizing adults only was not stimulated by the Bible's teaching on the subject.*

PROBLEMS WITH AN ADULT "BELIEVERS" ONLY APPROACH TO BAPTISM

Anabaptists, as well as the many Christians today who hold an age restrictive view of baptism, are certainly to be commended in their desire to defend the Gospel's integrity. Yet, as one takes a closer look at adult-only baptism, one cannot help but see certain contradictions. On a number of points, age exclusionary baptism actually *counters*

Christian doctrines professed by the very groups who practice this mode of baptism. On other points, the philosophy behind the doctrine appears to be more humanistic than Biblical. Let's look at some of these problems now.

FAULTY PREMISES BEHIND AGE RESTRICTIVE BAPTISM

RATIONALISTIC FAITH IS NOT BIBLICAL FAITH

Oftentimes, the argument for an age exclusionary baptism is based on the belief that only adults can have faith. This understanding of faith, however, is not Biblical; it is humanistic. It stems from the philosophy that defines man only in rationalistic terms: Man is man *only because* he has the ability to reason. [43] Similarly, man's capacity for faith exists in direct proportion to his ability to *use his mind or will.* Therefore, if man does not reason or use his will for a conscious purpose, he neither exists as rational-man, nor can he possess faith. This is the rationalistic definition of "faith" and "man" which was (and still is) often *read into* the Scriptures wherever words like "faith" or "believe" appear, e. g. "Believe" (with your mind and will) and be baptized (Mk. 16:16). *This is not the Biblical conception of belief.*

The word for "faith" and "belief" comes from the same Greek word (pistis [πίστις]). And in most cases can be equally and accurately translated as "trust" or "confidence." Seen in this light, faith is obviously not a rationalistic concept. Rather, it expresses a *relationship of trust.* As faith in another human is a bond of trust and love (not primarily a product of analytical reasoning), so is one's faith in God. Therefore, one's ability to use his mind and faculties is not *the* requirement of faith. The orientation of one's heart and trust is the requirement. It is only this latter sense of faith —as trust— that the Scriptures illustrate. [44]

The Biblical meaning of faith is not restricted to those with an adult intellect, or only to those who can express their faith verbally, but to those who trust. In Psalm 22:9, the quality of faith is ascribed to a nursing infant, "Thou art He who didst bring me forth from the womb; Thou didst make me *trust* when upon my mother's breasts." And in Matthew, Jesus referred to a little child whom He held in His arms as "one of these little ones *who believe in me* " (Matthew 18:6). [45]

ONE CAN HAVE COMMUNION WITH GOD WITHOUT A RATIONALISTIC FAITH

Why should communion with God be given only to those who have the ability to reason as an adult? Cannot a child truly experience the Lord through his Christian parents? Must he first have the ability to cognate and analyze before he can know the love of God? Is God prevented from having communion with the human spirit of a child until his brain is fully developed? Do not both the Scriptures and our experience testify that even a very young child's spirit is vulnerable to the spiritual environment around him, either to the presence of Christ or to the presence of evil? Has age *ever* prevented one from having a relationship with God? Did not John the Baptist leap for joy at the presence of the Lord, when he was still in his mother's womb?

The one who accepts only a rationalistic definition of faith is left with more difficult questions to answer. Doesn't this perspective force one to conclude that one's trust in and experience of God is directly proportional to one's intellectual abilities? If so, what about the Christian who has grown senile in old age? Does his relationship with God weaken with the infirmity? Or conversely, can we say that a Christian with a higher I.Q has the potential to know and experience God more deeply than the one with only average intelligence?

Please do not misunderstand me at this point. Our ability to reason is not unimportant (we should use everything in our power to better know and love God), but does God classify us according to our rational abilities? Of course not. The irrefutable fact is that intellectual reasoning —rationalistic faith— does not save. Only *union with Christ* saves. And this union is a reliance upon Him. It is not dependent on a rationally validated will or a cluster of adult brain cells.

HOW FREE WILL IS NOT VIOLATED IN THE BAPTISM OF INFANTS AND CHILDREN

But doesn't baptizing a child, even of Christian parents, violate the child's free will? The assumption behind this question is also based on an unbiblical, rationalistic understanding of man. This perspective of the human will teaches that a person can only demonstrate his freedom if, when a "temptation" confronts him, he makes a rational "decision" either for or against the enticement. But what does this really mean about the nature of man's will? Is man only free as long as he has the opportunity to sin?

In heaven there will be no option to choose evil. Does this mean we will no longer be free? Quite the contrary! In heaven we will experience a *greater* measure of freedom than ever before. No, freedom is not given to us *in* the occasion of sin, it is given to us *in communion with God.* The closer one is to Christ, and the more intimate his union with Him, the freer one is from the sin which binds him and his will.

The true Christian "chooses" to live the way of love even in the absence of temptations. His union with God is freely based on his *relationship* of love and faith, not because he can *decide* to sin! He does not wait for us to have a relationship with Him until the time we can choose against Him. God desires this communion with us from the very instant of our conception.

ADULT ONLY BAPTISM DENIES THE PERSONHOOD OF CHILDREN

A child is not a "blob" at birth, a non-spiritual entity that only evolves into a person once he begins to reason. Even in the womb, the Scripture makes it clear that a child is a person: *body, soul* and *spirit.* The child is a human being not because he can prove it by his powers of reason, but because he has been made *in the image and likeness of God.*

For these reasons, the Early Church did not discriminate between her child members and her adult members. *Both* were considered equal members of the Body of Christ. The ancient service of baptism testifies to this: it was the same exactly for adults and children in every way.[46] By this practice, the Primitive Church declared that *all* her members had equal access to God.

EXCLUSIONARY BAPTISM DENIES THE EXISTENCE OF CHRISTIAN CHILDREN

Age restrictive baptism ostracizes the child from his own Christian family by excluding him from Church membership. If baptism is indeed symbolic of one's entrance into the fellowship of believers (a point clearly taught by Romans 6), what then is symbolized by *withholding* baptism from children of Christian parentage? It cannot mean anything other than, "This child is not one of us."

Exclusionary baptism on the basis of age puts a division where God intended union. As such, it is a violation of God's command "that there should be no division in the body, but that the members should have the same care for one another..." (1 Cor. 12:25, 27). As God's love calls the family to be in union with each family member, so is this the predominant bond in the Church.

Frankly, the faulty premises behind "believer's" only baptism lead one into many problems. To follow a doctrine of baptism that is determined by age and a rationalistic understanding of faith will invariably lead one to contradict the Bible, ancient Christian doctrine, and common sense. I will now show how this is the case.

ADULT ONLY BAPTISM CONTRADICTS CHRISTIAN NURTURE

It is God's will that a child of a Christian family not only be recognized as a person, but that he be *raised as a Christian.* A child should not have to grow older, fall away, and *then* repent before he can be recognized as one of the Fellowship. Although their doctrinal dispositions frustrate its expression, a number of sincere Christians clearly sense this truth.

Most modern Baptists, for example, do indeed relate to their children as if they were Christians; this is plainly evidenced by the way they nurture them in the faith. Ironically, their theology of baptism and conversion should logically prevent them from taking such an approach. Southern Baptist Findley B. Edge in his article "Christian Nurture and Conversion" makes this point well:

> Traditionally Southern Baptists have rejected the theology which underlies this view of Christian nurture and have insisted upon the necessity of the conversion experience. However, in recent years, with our emphasis on enrolling the babies, with our "centers of interest" approach to teaching in the elementary departments, we perhaps are utilizing the "Christian nurture" approach as effectively as any other religious group. So much is this true that our friends in other religious groups are saying that our theology of conversion and our program of religious education for children are inconsistent. For example, they are saying, "You Southern Baptists are doing an unusually effective piece of work in the area of religious education for the small child. From infancy and through earliest childhood you teach the child that Jesus is his best Friend. You teach him that God is his loving

> Father; you teach him to pray to God, and teach him to sing, 'Jesus loves me.' This teaching goes on throughout his early years. But then somewhere around the age of ten (or perhaps a year or two before or after), you take the child and thrust him out of the Kingdom and say to him, 'You are lost; you need to be saved!' The child is confused, puzzled, perplexed. He says, 'What do you mean, I'm lost? What do you mean I need to be saved?' You say to him, 'You must love Jesus, You must trust Jesus.' But the child says, 'I *do* love Jesus. I *do* trust Jesus. I always have.' What will you say to the child then? [47]

The contradiction resides in imposing a practice intended for adults *outside of the Church* (i.e., "repent and believe") upon a child who *already* identifies with Christ. To do so is to twist the child's experience to conform to an ill-fitting theological assumption.

It is interesting to note that as Baptists have gained an internal sense of the reality of a child's faith, and as time has removed them more and more from the controversies the Radical Reformers faced, the age requirement for baptism has steadily lowered. For example, among Anabaptists, the age requirement was first twenty years old. Later on it was lowered to somewhere between thirteen and fifteen years. Now, in many Evangelical-Fundamentalist congregations, one can be baptized anywhere from the ages of nine to twelve—in some places it is even younger.[48]

The faith of a child is, in essence, the same faith as that of an adult. Yes, it matures, develops, and intensifies, but, at its core, it is still faith.[49] Faith must grow or it ceases to be alive, but to reject a child's faith on the premise that it is not yet "adult like" enough, is to impose an unbiblical standard of measurement on it.

Actually, *at each age* one is faced with opportunities for greater maturity in his faith, and each opportunity is as important to his spiritual health as the one before it. Similarly, there is not a time when faith is too "green" for God to accept. If one gauges faith to be only an adult phenomenon, then an exclusionary perspective of baptism makes sense. [50] But this is not the case. God does not relate to us in this way. A child's faith is *real*, and within the context of his believing family, he is a partaker of God's covenant.

The debate regarding nurture and conversion (i.e., which of the two brings one to Christ?) is of little importance. In the Nineteenth Century, evangelisitc revivals expounded an Augustinian view of Original Sin which maintained that man was *so* depraved, it was *impossible* for him to be nurtured into the Faith. His will was too feeble to reach out to God on his own. He needed a power from outside of himself to say "yes" to Christ. Only a radical, instantaneous conversion experience brought on by the Holy Spirit could ever grant the sinner this ability.[51] The testimony of the children from Christian homes who now live for Christ, though unable to pinpoint the time of their conversion, are living witnesses to the fallacy of such a teaching.

In reality, it is not an either-or situation. The Christian life is a life of *both* constant repentance, *and* constant growth through nurture. One should reaffirm his union with Christ continually, at *every* stage of life *—no matter how young or how old he is.* Likewise, the process of one's growth and trust in God should never peak or plateau. Faith in Christ is a *continuing process.* "In the New Testament, the faithful Christian is one who *has* believed *(pesteusas),* who now *believes (pistuon),* and *who goes on believing (pepisteukos)...*"[52]

Free Church minister Donald Bridge, and Anglican David Phypers, jointly wrote *The Water That Divides,* a book which objectively describes and discusses many of the important issues surrounding the baptism debate. In the following excerpt, they point out the inherent contradiction of those who hold an adult-only view of baptism, yet who, at the same time, ignore the theological implications behind the practice of Christian nurture:

> If baptism is to be administered at the time of conversion and if baptists refuse to baptize children younger than fourteen (or thirteen, or twelve, or whatever) then they are implying that all such children cannot be converted and must, therefore, for the sake of consistency, be treated as outsiders. Initially, of course, the question is raised, at what age can a child consciously believe? Little children of three and four are often far more conscious of the reality and nearness of Christ than their parents; should they be baptized? Could it be that a serious attempt by baptists to baptize on conversion according to the New Testament pattern, would lead them inexorably, and perhaps very rapidly, towards a position of child baptism, little different from infant baptism? The conclusion seems inescapable. Why then do baptists shrink from such a conclusion? Because their children might later repudiate their baptism on growing up? But then, many who are baptized as adults repudiate their baptism in later years.[53]

ONE CANNOT BE A NON-CHRISTIAN AND YET "SAVED"

Many Evangelical-Fundamentalists believe that a child who has not reached an age where he can reason between right and wrong ("the age of accountability") is automatically saved. Curiously, the same passages that are often quoted to support the legitimacy of infant baptism, are quoted in this context to support the claim that children of immature reasoning abilities are already involuntary members of the Kingdom. [54] In the Middle Ages, this perspective was clearly a reaction to the Medieval Roman Catholic view insisting that unless a child were baptized, it would perish in Hell or end up in *Limbo*. The consequence of this reaction, however, was a theological contradiction for the Anabaptists: a child (especially of Christian parents) is saved, but is still not a member of the Church.[55]

The Reformers addressed this dilemma by insisting that a child is baptized, not because he will suffer eternally if he dies without it, but because the child's identification with his family has already included him in the New Covenant (Col. 2:11, 12).[56] For the Anabaptists to accept this answer, however, they would also have to accept the validity of a corrupted State-church and its negligence regarding moral discipline. This was too great a price to pay for merely having a child receive a baptism which "had no effect on his salvation" one way or the other. [57]

To say that a child is "saved" (if only "for a while") *because* he is a child makes no sense Biblically. There is no "saving limbo" that God has exclusively set aside for children. Can a person experience salvation other than through Christ? No. "There is no other name under heaven by which we must be saved (Acts 4:12)." Can one be saved without a faith in Christ? [58] No. "For you all are all sons of God *through faith* in Christ Jesus" (Galatians 3:26). The way an adult is saved is the same way a child is saved. *Nowhere in Scripture are there "exception clauses" for children.*

What was "it" that was "saving" the child before the age of accountability that somehow expires when one reaches the age of accountability? What was "it" that made him complete before but spiritually deficient later? What is "it" that loses its power to save once the young person reaches adolescence? Grace? What does this mean? Can a person be saved by "grace" but not by "Christ?" Of course not. Grace is not a thing; it is a *relational union* with God through Christ. "It" is only *Christ* who saves, and His salvation is not conditioned upon one's age or intellect.

If one were to ask the average Evangelical-Fundamentalist if it were possible to be "saved" and yet still not be a Christian, the answer, of course, would be "no." But to affirm that a child is saved and still not a Christian, is to affirm that very contradiction. How can one be "saved" and yet not be a member of the Body of Christ (the Church)? The child is either a member of Christ's Covenant, or he is not.

The line of reasoning is simple: If one is to say a child is saved, it must be through Christ. If it is through Christ that the child is saved, the child is a Christian. If the child is a Christian, the child must be a member of the Body of Christ. And if the child is a member of the Body of Christ, the child's baptism simply proclaims what already is the case in the eyes of God and the Church. If all this be true, how can a Christian child be denied baptism?

AGE EXCLUSIONARY BAPTISM DENIES THE REALITY OF THE CHURCH AS THE BODY OF CHRIST

I have emphasized how age-restrictive baptism was greatly fueled by the compromises of the State church, the lack of moral improvement within the Reformation, and by Anabaptist asceticism. As a means to preserve the Gospel way of life, the Anabaptists gave themselves heart and soul to the task of building a "pure Church." The problem with this strategy, however, is that the Church is not an institution or a corporation which can be created by planning and strategy, i.e., *man cannot build God's Church.* The Church is a divine-human *organism with Christ as her head,* a Living Being which only the Spirit of God can build and sustain. For this reason, human efforts can never *modify* the Church's purity one way or the other. *The Church is by nature pure —she is in union with Christ.*

Therefore, there is no such thing as an "impure" Church and a "pure" Church. There is *the* Church, and it is always pure. Yes, members *within* the Church must always strive to realize this purity. But even if each Christian were to live a perfect life, this is not what makes the Church holy. The believer's union with *Christ* give the Church (the saints) her holiness.

To the Anabaptist, the Church was an *ascetic* assembly, and each member's *personal* holiness made the Church pure. This misconception of the Church led them to commit at least four serious errors: 1) the redefinition of baptism *as if it were an "entrance rite" into a monastic Order;* 2) seeing holiness as something which one *brings to* the Church as opposed to something which *resides within* the Church (the Body *of Christ*) 3) forsaking the Biblical image of the Church as a genuine spiritual union of Christ with His people in favor of a more institutional portrayal; and 4) the abandonment of baptism as the actualization of this union.

The focus of baptism should not be on its *timing*, but on *the relationship of trust it signifies.* When the chief attention given to baptism centers around an individual's age, rationalistic faith, and one's volitional commitment to the ascetic practices of a particular assembly, the idea of the Church as primarily a spiritual union with Christ and His body is diminished. The Church is a relational entity, not an Order based on adult codes of behavior. For this reason, the *entire* Christian family —inclusive of its children—has a place in God's family, the Church.

INCONSISTENCIES AND CONTRADICTIONS OF AN "AGE OF ACCOUNTABILITY" DOCTRINE

• THE AGE OF ACCOUNTABILITY DOCTRINE IS UNSCRIPTURAL

Surprisingly, justification for the "age of accountability" doctrine was actually born from within Medieval Roman Catholicism. Let me explain. For the first 1,000 years of the Church's history, children were free to receive of the Eucharist in both the East and West. During the height of scholastic reasoning, however, theologians began to prohibit children from receiving the Eucharist on the basis that they could not understand what they were doing. They found support for their argument in 1 Corinthians 11:29, "For he who eats and drinks, eats and drinks judgment to himself, *if he does not judge the body rightly.*" The verse, interpreted from a Western rationalistic bias, was understood to mean that anyone who could not reason ("judge") the bread of the Lord's Supper as being the actual transubstantiated body of the Lord would be condemned if he received it. The only logical conclusion from such a line of reasoning would be to ban children from taking the eucharistic bread. [59] When a child was old enough to "discern" this transformation, he could then be permitted to receive Communion.[60]

This Eucharistic age restriction definitely set a precedent for the "age of accountability" theory. If the Roman Church were justified in limiting reception of the Lord's Supper until one could understand what he was receiving, how could the Anabaptists be criticized for using the same logic as a rationale for excluding children from baptism? Both perspectives reduced faith, and the spiritual relationship which the sacraments symbolized (union with God and His people), to rationalistic systems of logic.

• THE AGE OF ACCOUNTABILITY DOCTRINE WRONGLY TIES FAITH TO AN AGE LIMIT

Even if the age of reason doctrine is unscriptural, doesn't restricting the age of one's baptism still have some practical utility? For example, can't it at least on some level ensure that the one who is contemplating a commitment to Christ will do so with a greater seriousness than one who is less mature in years? The assumption here, of course, is that with the increase of years, one's past experiences will have made him more consummate in his understanding of both life's temptations, and Christ's call to discipleship. But this conclusion is without basis. Let me explain why.

If this line of reasoning is valid, why not carry the principle further and *raise* the age limit on baptism? If one is more experienced and wise at age twenty than at age ten, why not carry this principle further and delay baptism and Church membership until age thirty? At thirty, one will have had more time to study and digest the Scriptures than he did at age twenty. His experience in married life will also have given him a clearer sense on how living for Christ could impact his role as a husband and father (or her role as wife and mother). Or better yet, how about age forty? After having experienced the temptations and trials more specific to this season of life (wealth, status and recognition, "mid-life" crisis, etc.), would not his decision for Christ and his faith be more "tested" than it would have been at age thirty?

Of course, trying to determine when one's faith is the *most* real, genuine and mature is foolish. The increase in one's age is never a guarantee of sincerity or depth of commitment. It is impossible to define exactly when a person becomes "accountable."

All who ascribe to an age of accountability doctrine admit that they cannot know the *exact* moment when one's faith is mature, for only God knows our hearts. But if we cannot specify when a child moves from being a responsible child to being a morally responsible person, doesn't our inability take away the practical purpose of the doctrine? If we mortals do not know when one is accountable and thus "spiritually responsible," how can the Church (also made up of fallible human beings) be certain when to baptize? In other words, how can the Church *be sure* that when it accepts a person for baptism, it is accepting one whose "time" has come, and not someone who is still unaccountable? The argument for an age of accountability easily leads one to such futile speculations.

There are other pointless questions this doctrine must force us to ask: Just what *is* the minimum age allowable for baptism? Exactly when does the child become capable of the *beginning* of faith? How far back can we go? Exactly what should we use to draw the line? How can we differentiate between rational "faith", and a child's imitation of the faith of their parents? What yardstick should we use to discern genuine, mature faith—when the child begins to pray for himself, or psychological testing?

A better question is, "What in the Scriptures compels us to draw *any* line for faith based on age?" Again, faith is not primarily a function of a rational mind; it is an expression of trust, love and vulnerability. It is not an abstract analytical concept. It is a *relationship*. And as a mother can have a relationship with her child right from birth (actually, even before birth), so can God. Doctrines of accountability and rationalistic views of faith contradict Scripture; faith understood as a relationship of trust does not.

• AN AGE OF ACCOUNTABILITY DOCTRINE GRANTS NO INSURANCE OF A "PURE" CHURCH

As disconcerting as it may seem to some, the New Testament gives no foolproof way of screening "the wheat from the chaff." We will all have to wait until the Day of Judgment before we can know who is "in" and who is "out." There are no empirical tests we can employ to *ensure* that all who profess to be members of the Church are indeed members. Even the New Testament Church was not "pure." The Christians in Galatia, Corinth, Ephesus, Smyrna, Pergamum, Thyatira, Sardis, Philadelphia and Laodicea all were aware that there existed a number within their ranks that were impostors (2 Corinthians 11:20; Galatians 1:6-7; 3:1; 4:10,11; Revelation 2:1,4-5, 9,14-16, 20-22; 3:1-4).

This isn't to say that the Church has no safeguards whatsoever, for she surely does. However, her protection is not secured through any technical or clinical means, but by *spiritual ones*. Such things include the clear proclamation of God's Word, each member's personal responsibility to love the Lord and each other, and each Christian's openness to the fruit, gifts, and ministry of the Holy Spirit. Church discipline, including excommunication for serious matters of unrepentant heresy, immorality, or factiousness, has clear biblical and historical precedent. When we falter in our practice of such spiritual means to deal with blatant sinfulness in the Church, there are no administrative guarantees to fall back on.

• AGE OF ACCOUNTABILITY IS NOT A PROTECTION AGAINST SPIRITUAL COMPROMISE

How does one answer the charge that allowing the baptism of children and infants encourages spiritual stagnation? Let me answer that question with another one: "Are there any Christian assemblies which exclusively practice adult baptism that are spiritually stagnant?" Of course there are. Indiscriminate baptism, whether it be of adults or children, coupled with the compromise of Christian discipleship, certainly inflicts spiritual damage. But just as adult-only baptism does not ensure spiritual life, neither does a baptism open to all ages ensure spiritual death. Many other factors always enter in.

Unquestionably, a congregation's "reflex-action" to baptize *any* child or infant outside the context of a spiritual and personal relationship is potentially harmful and unbiblical. Discerning the spiritual health of the family presenting the child should not be left to chance The pastor and his congregation have a responsibility to discern, to the best of their abilities, that the baptism of the child truly reflects the life of Christ already present within the family.

When a child of an unbelieving family is baptized, the sacrament is blatantly derided, and its meaning mocked. This, however, should not blind us to the fact that adult baptism *can just as easily be abused.* If an adult is baptized in Christ's name and then later lives a life in contradiction to discipleship, has he not blasphemed the significance of baptism just as much as the unbelieving family's baptism of their child? Unfortunately, baptism, whether it be age-restrictive or open to all ages, has been sorely abused by many within our generation.

The solution to this profanation has nothing to do with setting an age requirement for baptism. *The answer lies in the Church living up to its call as the body of Christ.* The Church is a true communion with God and one another, and *it must demonstrate this reality.* It is an environment where God dwells, and where each member is united to Him and to one another; *it must continually actualize this.* Within the Church is a divine life of love, communion, and trust; *it must manifest this.* The way to disclose this beauty is not found in any external rule, but in each member's constant co-operation with the Holy Spirit. This is a summons which *all* her members (children and adults) at *every* phase of their lives must answer.

NOTES FOR CHAPTER SIXTEEN

1 "The word "Anabaptist" is a Latin derivative of the Greek original, *anabaptismos* (re–baptism). The German form, *Wiedertäufer*, means "one who re–baptizes." Lutherans and Zwinglians applied it in the beginning to those who separated themselves from the main body of the state churches. As for the radicals themselves; "They repudiated the name, insisting that infant baptism did not constitute true baptism and that they were not in reality re–baptizers. Their argument was of no avail. The name was so conveniently elastic that it came to be applied to all those who stood out against authoritative state religion. The radicals wanted to be known only as "Brüder' (Brethren) or by some other nonsectarian name, ..." Franklin H. Littell, *The Origins of Sectarian Protestantism* [New York, The Macmillan Company, 1964] p. xv; Austin P. Evans, *An Episode in the Struggle for Religious Freedom:the Sectaries of Nuremberg, 1524-1528* [New York: Columbia University Press, 1924) pp. 14-15]

"The term ... was invented for the purpose of condemning those who believed in adult baptism, even though they believed in only one baptism and preferred to be called simply 'Baptists.' The Anabaptists were severely persecuted by the civil authorities as well as by the Catholic and Protestant churches." Harold J. Grimm, *The Reformation Era 1500-1650* (New York, The Macmillan Company, 1965) p. 268

2 "Baptist church historians are in accord with others, engaged in Anabaptist research, who see in the movement the beginning of the modern Free Church movement." Torsten Bergsten, *Balthasar Hubmaier-Anabaptist Theologian and Martyr*, W.R. Estep, Jr., editor (Valley Forge, Judson Press, 1978) p. 41

"However difficult it may be to establish a succession of men or congregations from the Anabaptists to the English Baptists, still it remains a fact that this teaching was in the air and regardless of how it was transmitted, the modern Baptists are in the direct line of the Anabaptist tradition." Charles A. Arrington, "The Anabaptists: Their Relation to the Early Church and to Modern Baptists ", Thesis submitted to Faculty of Union Theological Seminary (New York, Department of Church History, 1948) p. 42

3 "...as Luther himself admitted, it [the Reformation] failed to bring about the substantial increase in general piety ... Many who had initially supported Luther noted this failure with concern....this concern becomes a major factor in the emergence of Anabaptism as an alternative, reform movement." Kenneth Ronald Davis, *Anabaptism and Asceticism* (Scottdale, Pa, Herald Press, 1974) p. 64

4 Luther declared that even if Rome had observed the traditional religion with the discipline of the hermits, Jerome, Augustine, Gregory, Bernard, Francis, and Dominic, its false doctrine would still have made the Reformation necessary. And those within the Calvinist sphere were quoted to have said, "The Calvinists want men to be judged not on the basis of their morals but according to their beliefs..." Steven Ozment, *The Intellectual Origins of the Reformation*, pp. 146, 148 from the Commentary on Galatians (1545), *W A 40, p. 687=Lw* 26, p. 459 and the citation of *Contra libellum Calvini,* E 8 b respectively.

5 "The Christian ascetic tradition was still profoundly influential in the religious thinking and the aspirations of many in Europe at the beginning of the sixteenth century. As a reforming impulse it moved mainly in two directions during the fifteenth century: toward monastic reform by a return to a more faithful and rigorous keeping of the 'Rule' of the Order, and toward an internalization and spiritualization of the monastic ideals and their extension to lay society. The latter trend received its principle impetus much earlier from Francis of Assi (1182-1226), but was maintained in varying degrees by the Tertiaries and in the Brethren of the Common Life, one of laicized asceticism's most influential expressions in the fifteenth century." Kenneth Ronald Davis, *Anabaptism and Asceticism* (Scottdale, Pa, Herald Press, 1974) p. 293

6 "...was there really a sufficiently vigorous *ascetic* revival, especially of lay piety, in the 15th century to anticipate that some, even in the new Protestantism, would demand an alternative on this ground to Luther's particular vision of Christian reform and experience? The answer of all 576 scholars (reported as a consensus — a rare thing among historians) at the 1972, University of Michigan, conference on late medieval religion was 'yes'." Kenneth R. Davis, "The Origins of Anabaptism: Ascetic and Charismatic Elements Exemplifying Continuity and Discontinuity," in *The Origins And Characteristics of Anabaptism,* ed. Marc Lienhard (The Hague, Marinus Nijhoff, 1977) p. 34

7 The Lutheran, Swiss and later Anglican Reformation were magisterial as they advocated an orderly reform under the sanction, support and protection of town councils, princes and kings. In contrast to this policy, the Radical Reformation basically supported the separation of its conventicle churches from the national or territorial state government's support or association.

8 The Anabaptists believed that it was this merger between Government and Church which destroyed the Christian witness in the Fourth Century under Constantine, and that its continued insistence upon it by the Reformers of their time similarly distorted the faith. The Anabaptists did not just desire the reformation of the Church, they wanted its restoration. John Christian Wenger, *Even Unto Death* , (Richmond, Virginia, John Knox Press, 1961), p. 79

9 The Reformers hesitated to abandon infant baptism, in part, from the belief that such a move would jeopardize their plan to establish Christian nations in accordance with Reformation doctrines. To this the Anabaptists answered, "'But who cares about rebuilding Christendom?..Uncommitted people *are* pagans, whether they live in Germany or China'...This was the REAL baptismal controversy. " Donald Bridge, David Phypers, *The Water That Divides* (Downers Grove, IL., Inter-Varsity Press, 1977) p. 100-102

10 Philipp of Hesse (1509-1567) advanced a compromise agreeable to both the Lutheran Church and numbers of Anabaptists which illustrates this point. Whereby numbers of Anabaptists returned to the Lutheran Church. The Church of Hesse adopted certain measures which to this day give it a special structure: an active practice of church discipline and the service of confirmation (this later practice later picked up by other Protestant territorial churches in Germany and Switzerland).

> The original suggestion seems to have come from Schwenckfeld, during the Strassburg debates of 1533: 'If you won't agree to eliminate Infant Baptism, at least there should be set up a ceremony whereby the baptized children, when they have reached the right age, will be dedicated to Christianity.' ... The Hessen Agenda of 1574 made it a permanent institution in the church. In the meantime confirmation was adopted by the Genevan Church Order of 1537 and in the Württemberg Church Order of 1545 (signed by Luther, Bugenhagen, Cruciger, Maier, and Melanchton). Schwenckfeld's suggestion, popularized by Butzer's *Ad Monasterienses* (1534), thus became one of the most permanent contributions of the Protestant radicals to the life of the established churches.

Franklin H. Littell, *The Origins of Sectarian Protestantism* (New York,The Macmillan Company, 1964) pp. 35-36, citing "Konfirmation." in *ML* [Hege, Chritian, and Neff, Christian, ed., *Mennonitisches Lexikon*] (1937) II, 533-36

11 "To the Anabaptists, however, the fundamental issue was not baptism. More basic was their growing conviction about the role the civil government should play in the reformation of the church. Late in 1523, intense debate on this issue broke out in Zürich. At that time it became clear that the Zürich city council was unwilling to bring about the religious changes that the theologians believed were called for by Scripture. What then? Should one wait, and attempt to persuade the authorities by preaching? This was the view of the Zürich Reformer, Zwingli. Or should the community of Christians, led by the Holy Spirit, initiate Scripture-backed reforms regardless of the views of the council? So argued Zwingli's radical disciples..." John H. Yoder and Alan Kreider, *Eerdmans' Handbook to the History of Christianity*, "The Anabaptist," (Grand Rapids, Michigan, Wm. B. Eerdmans Publishing Company, 1977) p. 399

12 Franklin H. Littell, *The Origins of Sectarian Protestantism* (New York,The Macmillan Company, 1964) pp. xv, xvii

13 "They said of Luther that he 'tore down the old house, but built no new one in its place,'..." Franklin H. Littell, *The Origins of Sectarian Protestantism* (New York,The Macmillan Company, 1964) pp. xvii, 2 citing *The Anabaptist* (London: James Clarke & Company, 1935) pp. 14-15 and Josef Beck ed., *Die Geschichts-Bücher der Wiedertäufer in Oesterreich-Ungarn* (Vienna: Carl Gerold's Sohn, 1883) p. 12 fn. 2

14 Luther and Zwingli believed this too and were fearful that if the church-state union were broken society would be in total chaos. The Anabaptist position on baptism " drove a wedge into the traditional

notion of a commonwealth that was at once both religious and political, and the composition of which was monolithic." Hans J. Hillerbrand, *Men and Ideas In The Sixteenth Century* (Chicago, Rand McNally, College Publishing Company, 1969) p. 88

15 "The Reformation was influenced by the growing interest in the natural as opposed to the supernatural, and the assertion of individual independence which marked the later Middle Ages. This favoured views of baptism which removed mystery, and which made it the sign, not of a man's dependence on, but of his adhesion to the Church." James Hastings, ed., *Hastings Encyclopedia of Religion and Ethics* (New York, Charles Scribner's Sons, n.d.) p. 406

16 'Infant Baptism is a supporting pillar of the papal order. As long as it is not removed, there can be no Christian congregation,' agreed Hans Sockler, and by 'the papal order' he meant Christendom, whether Catholic or Protestant. " Donald Bridge, David Phypers, *The Water That Divides,* (Downers Grove, IL., Inter-Varsity Press, 1977) p. 106,107

17 It should be noted that, given the scholastic setting of both Roman Catholic and Reformed theologies, the Anabaptist was forced to see doctrine as only an intellectual science. No longer is theology understood as a reflection of one's union with God, nor as a means for growing in greater communion with Him and the brethren.

18 "It is apparent that the Anabaptists were less interested in theology than in the practical application of Biblical teachings to the affairs of this world. Despite the fact that Grebel had been a humanist and was skilled in the use of Latin, Greek, and Hebrew, his teachings were not based on any of the intellectual currents of his day but solely on the early Reformation doctrines of Zwingli and his own independent study of scripture." Harold J. Grimm, *The Reformation Era 1500-1650* (New York, The Macmillian Company, 1965) pp. 267-268

19 Jean Rillet, *Zwingli: Third Man of the Reformation* (The Westminster Press, 1959) p. 139

20 Disagreement was fleshly and "disunity could only mean some alien influence was present." Kenneth Ronald Davis, *Anabaptism and Asceticism* (Scottdale, Pa., Herald Press, 1974) p. 90

21 It seems likely that Zwingli himself taught against infant baptism before the Radical Reformation:

> According to Hübmaier [a leading Anabaptist who had been strongly influenced by Zwingli], he and Zwingli discussed in detail a number of articles which he, Hübmaier, had drawn up on a slate. Among these was the question of infant baptism. On this point Zwingli had admitted that children should not be baptized until they had been instructed in the faith. In 1525, Zwingli himself admitted in print that "a few years ago" he was in favor of adult baptism. As a result of Zwingli's spiritualistic emphasis with relation to the sacraments, baptism (whether of infants or of believers) was to him of secondary importance. He regarded faith as the necessary element. Water was merely a sign required by "austic man" that he had been purified inwardly by faith.

Torsten Bergsten, *Balthasar Hubmaier-Anabaptist Theologian and Martyr,* W.R. Estep, Jr., editor (Valley Forge, Judson Press, 1978) pp. 80-81

22 Conrad Grebel, *Conrad Grebel's Programmatic Letters of 1524,* translated by J. C. Wenger (Scottsdale, Pa., Herald Press, 1970), p. 21

23 "It is common knowledge that the leaders of South German Anabaptism, Conrad Grebel, Simon Stumpf , Hübmaier Sattler, Wilhelm Reublin, Hans Denk (1495-1527) and probably Mantz, all drank deeply of a reform vision drawn directly from Erasmian circles." Kenneth R. Davis, "The Origins of Anabaptism: Ascetic and Charismatic Elements Exemplifying Continuity and Discontinuity," in *The Origins And Characteristics of Anabaptism,* ed. Marc Lienhard (The Hague, Marinus Nijhoff, 1977) p. 35

24 His "private" theology differed from his "public" theology. "He combined two theologies in much of his writings: a personal one and a moderate one, and did so from conviction not guile or cowardice. But since he was seeking converts and thus to change eventually the official teaching (which he publicly upheld in the meantime) to his personal and Biblical one, his closest, younger followers mostly took up Erasmus'

own personal theology and dropped the other completely." Kenneth R. Davis, "The Origins of Anabaptism: Ascetic and Charismatic Elements Exemplifying Continuity and Discontinuity," in *The Origins And Characteristics of Anabaptism,* ed. Marc Lienhard (The Hague, Marinus Nijhoff, 1977) p. 36

25 "An interesting and significant point, which is strongly reflected in Anabaptist hermeneutics, especially during its Zürich beginnings (for example, in Grebel's "Letter to Münster"), is Erasmus' insistence that Christ's teaching shall not be mingled with human teaching. The learned give uncertain counsel, for the light of faith does not shine in them." Kenneth Ronald Davis, *Anabaptism and Asceticism* (Scottdale, Pa, Herald Press, 1974) p. 291 citing H. von Heinhold Fast's article, "The Dependence of the First Anabaptists on Luther, Erasmus, Zwingli," *Mennonite Quarterly Review,* XXXV (April 1956) p. 109

26 Henry Chadwick, *The Reformation.* , p. 33

27 In his *Paraclesis* he states : "In my eyes he is a true theologian who, not by syllogisms craftily turned, but in affection and in his very countenance and eyes and in his very life teaches that riches are to be scorned..that injuries must not be revenged...that death is to be longed for..If anyone displays these qualities in his moral conduct, he , in short, is a great doctor." Brian A Gerrish, ed., *Reformers in Profile* , (Philadelphia, Fortress Press, 1967) p. 76

28 "... in Erasmus' "philosophy of Christ" the innovative, ascetic idealism of the *Devotio Moderna* is not only reflected but extended. The simple, moderately ascetic, devout piety of the *Devotio Moderna* , coupled with humanistic biblical "primitivism" applied to asceticism and perhaps with some Neo-platonism, influenced Erasmus to support iconoclasm, sacramentarianism (a denial of the real presence). and even to reject music in worship... The trend towards a revived , primitive, biblical asceticism is associated largely with the *Devotio Moderna,* which upheld a moderation, laicization, personalization, and internalization of ascetic ideals and practices." Kenneth Ronald Davis, *Anabaptism and Asceticism* (Scottdale, Pa, Herald Press, 1974) p. 64

29 "The reformers did not permit ethics to sit in judgement on the truth of their doctrine. It became the hallmark of the Anabaptist, Spiritualist, and rational critics of the Reformation, almost all whom were deeply influenced by the work of Erasmus, to make good deeds the true test of true creeds and to criticize the followers of Luther and Calvin for failing to improve the moral quality of life. Steven Ozment, *The Intellectual Origins of the Reformation,* p.148

30 "The strong moralistic strain and the nonspeculative cast of his thought combined with a Platonic spiritualism to color Erasmus' entire reading of Paul." Brian A Gerrish, ed., *Reformers in Profile* , (Philadelphia, Fortress Press, 1967) p. 76

31 Zwingli, from 1514 onwards, reflected Erasmus' moralist "philosophy of Christ." "That his attitude to scripture was basically Erasmus' own is hardly to be questioned." Bernard M.G. Reardon, *Religious Thought In The Reformation* (New York, Longham Inc., 1981) p. 32

32 "Until recently the origins of the Anabaptist Movement lay in darkness. But the subtle researches of Fritz Blanke have shown that the first Anabaptist communities constituted a revival movement called into being by the preaching of Zwingli." Gottfried E. Locher, *Zwingli's Thought: New Perspectives* (The Netherlands, E. J. Brill, Leiden, 1981) p. 70

33 "At the outset it is important to recall again Zwingli's own judgement about the Swiss Brethren (including Conrad Grebel as chief), in which he states that the teaching of the Brethren did not differ from Zwingli's own views on any major point of Christian doctrine. ... The differences between Zwingli and Grebel lay primarily in the sphere of the doctrine of the church ... and its relation to the state and the social order, and in the sphere of Christian ethics. ... In the matter of ordinances, only in baptism was there a cleavage, and even there it was not on the general character and function of ordinances, but rather on the specific meaning of baptism and the requirements for baptism." Harold Bender, *Conrad Grebel,* (Herald Press, Scottsdale, Pa., 1971), pp. 203-204

34 "The Anabaptists should be characterized essentially as, apart from their own creativity, a radicalization and Protestantization ... of the lay-oriented ascetic reform vision of which Erasmus is the

principal mediator." Kenneth R. Davis, "The Origins of Anabaptism: Ascetic and Charismatic Elements Exemplifying Continuity and Discontinuity," in *The Origins And Characteristics of Anabaptism,* ed. Marc Lienhard (The Hague, Marinus Nijhoff, 1977) p. 41

35 "Bainton refers to Erasmus as radical for his advocacy of a second baptism. Since, unlike the Anabaptists, Erasmus never totally repudiated the external rite of infant baptism, his stress on personal involvement and spiritual participation if any external rite is to be effective forces him to advocate a re-baptism or second baptism in such cases. His second baptism then becomes very close in meaning to Anabaptist baptism. At the age of puberty, he suggests, the rite of baptism should be solemnly, personally, and publicly reenacted, after thorough instruction relative to the meaning of the baptismal vow. He writes:'...how much more glorious a spectacle to hear the voices of so many youths dedicating themselves to Christ, so many initiates pronouncing their vows, renouncing the world, abjuring Satan; to see new Christians bearing the mark of the Lord of their foreheads, to behold the great crowd of candidates coming up from the sacred laver, to hear the voices of the multitude acclaiming the beginners in Christ!...If this were done, we should not have so many at the age of fifty who do not know what was vowed in baptism..." Kenneth Ronald Davis, *Anabaptism and Asceticism* (Scottdale, Pa., Herald Press, 1974) p. 288 citing Ronald Bainton's article, " The Paraphrases of Erasmus," *Archiv für Reformationsgeschichte*, LVIII (1967) p.73 (*Opera Omnia,* VII, 3 verso, preface to Matthew).

36 Kenneth Ronald Davis, *Anabaptism and Asceticism* (Scottdale, Pa, Herald Press, 1974) p. 217

37 The means to attain this holiness are also clearly ascetic: the imitation of Christ ideal (a popular ascetic discipline), the laicization of the three vows of obedience, chastity, and poverty, the necessity of a communal environment for the development of the social virtues for holiness, and the societal exemptions previously given to monks (i.e., exemption from vows, service in government positions and military service).

38 "The idea of a covenantal relation to God and one's fellows became the foundation for the Anabaptist community, and through it came the use of the Ban (spiritual government). The Anabaptists said repeatedly that true baptism was that submission to the divine authority described in I Peter 3:18-22, the responsibility of a good conscience toward God. They saw that this brotherly admonition and exhortation, the practice of intentional fellowship." Franklin H. Littell, *The Origins of Sectarian Protestantism* (New York, The Macmillan Company, 1964) p. 85; "As an agency of progress in sanctification, the brotherhood functioned ... as an agency of spiritual discipline, restraint, chastisement, and correction. ... The willingness to submit to such group discipline is part of the promise or vow of submission which must be voluntarily rendered at baptism." Kenneth Ronald Davis, *Anabaptism and Asceticism* (Scottdale, Pa, Herald Press, 1974) p. 183

39 A few examples of leaders who were monks: *Hans Altenbach* (was baptized in 1525) was an active Anabaptist leader and had been a monk for nineteen years. A portion of those years he had held the office of subprior. *Johannes Krüsi* (also called Hans Kern) joined the Anabaptist movement in 1525 and also was a former monk. He was one of the most active and influential leaders and proselytized with great success. He worked closely with with two other ex-monks, *Sebastian Ruggensberger* (former prior of the monastery of Sion in Klingau) and *Wolfgang Ulimann.* See Kenneth Ronald Davis, *Anabaptism and Asceticism* (Scottdale, Pa., Herald Press, 1974) pp. 109-113

40 Lewis W. Spitz, *The Renaissance and Reformation Movements* (Chicago,Il., Rand McNally and Company, 1971) p. 317

41 On February 24, 1527, he presided at an Anabaptist meeting at Schleitheim, ...and the Anabaptists present adopted a confession of faith which he had written, entitled *Brotherly Union of a Number of Children of God Concerning Seven Articles.* ""The whole document is nothing less than a manifesto for moral separation on lay, ascetic terms." Kenneth Ronald Davis, *Anabaptism and Asceticism* (Scottdale, Pa, Herald Press, 1974) p. 116

42 Kenneth Ronald Davis, *Anabaptism and Asceticism* (Scottdale, Pa., Herald Press, 1974) p. 195

43 Edmund Schlink, *The Doctrine of Baptism* , (St. Louis, Concordia Publishing House, 1972) p. 136

44 Matt. 8:10, 26; 14:31; Lk 17:19; Acts 3:16; Acts 20:21; 24:24; Rom. 4:20; 9:32; 14:23; 1 Cor. 2:5; 12:9; 13:13; 2 Cor. 4:13 , 5:7; Gal. 2:16; 5:5, 6; Eph. 3:17; Col. 2:12; 1 Thess. 1:8; 3:5-7, 10; 1 Tim. 1:14; 3:13; 2 Tim. 1:13, 15; Heb. 11:3-4, 7-9, 17-, 24, , 1 Pet. 1:21

45 Larry Christenson, "What About Baptism?", (Minneapolis, MN., Bethany Fellowship, Inc. 1973) p. 13

R.C.H. Lenski in his commentary, *The Interpretation of St. Matthew's Gospel* (Minneapolis, MN., Augsburg Publishing House, 1964), complements that thought in his exegesis of Matthew 19: 13, 14:

> Then there were brought to him little children in order that he might put his hands upon them and might pray; and the disciples rebuked them. But Jesus said, Suffer the little children and stop restraining them from coming to me; for of such is the kingdom of the heavens. And having put his hands on them, he went from there.' The scene loses a good deal of its beauty when it is supposed that superstition prompted these parents to bring their children, and that they supposed that the touch of Jesus' hands had magical power. We may be sure that, if this had been the case, Jesus would himself have rebuked these people and would not have touched a single child. To place the hand upon someone in connection with prayer is a symbolical act, it is an invoking of the divine blessing upon the person touched. Matthew writes *paidia* , 'little children,' for which Luke 18:15 has τα βρέφη, 'their babes' or 'sucklings.' Because they were so tiny, it was, of course, impossible for them to understand what Jesus was doing for them. When Jesus saw what the disciples were doing, he was indignant. The disciples are to stop restraining the children from coming to Jesus. The implication is that children, and this includes babes, are ready to come to Jesus and need only that men let them do so. The conclusion is justified that, like the other synoptists, Matthew records this incident as the answer to the question whether infants are to receive baptism. The use which Tertullian (born about 160) makes of this account as a substantiation of infant baptism is evidence that long prior to his time the church so understood the words and the actions of Jesus.

46 There *never* existed a "special" or differentiating baptismal service for infants in the Early Church. This is still the Eastern practice today.

47 Findley B. Edge, " Christian Nurture and Conversion", *Review and Expositor*, Vol. LIII, (April, 1956), No. 2, pp. 188,189

48 In " Children and the Church: A Baptist Historical Perspective," G. Thomas Halbrook recounts the historical and current trends within Southern Baptist congregations to progressively lower the age limits to membership and a greater openness towards children. I present a lengthy excerpt from his interesting and informative article below:

> Baptists have taken one of four basic approaches. With regard to their relationship to the church they have viewed children primarily as (1) nonmembers, (2) prospects, (3) potential disciples, or (4) maturing participants. This is the order in which the approaches arose historically. Although there is inevitable some overlap in any such attempt to categorize, the basic emphases of each approach remain clear.
>
> Baptists had their beginnings within English Puritanism in the early seventeenth century. Their major point of difference with the Puritans was their demand for a completely regenerate church membership, which led them to reject the baptism of infants. They restricted baptism and church membership to regenerate, professing believers only. John Smyth, their founder, proclaimed, "The church of Christ is a company of the faithful; baptized after confession of sin and faith." Consequently, baptism "does not belong to infants." Infants could not be members of the church. The General Baptists followed Smyth, and about three decades after the General Baptists the Particular Baptists began. Both Particulars and Generals agreed that in no sense could children be considered as members of the church. Baptists in America followed their English forebears. During the 17th and 18th centuries the great majority of those received into church membership

were probably twenty years of age or older. As time passed children were still viewed by Baptists as nonmembers, although a few had professed their faith and become members of the church. If it was possible for these few, why could not others do so? Was it necessary to consider most children as nonmembers? The stage was set for the development of a second approach to the relationship of children to the church. This was the approach of children as prospects.

Charles G. Finney, a leading revivalist, suggested that one could not know when children became moral agents and accountable to God, but serious consideration would "doubtless lead to the conviction, that children become moral agents much earlier than is generally supposed." Thus children were appropriate prospects for conversion and church membership.

The children-as-potential-disciples approach emphasized conversion as a total commitment of one's life to Jesus Christ as Lord. Since conversion was primarily a commitment to discipleship, children were capable of making a profession of faith only when they were capable of making such a commitment. "Thus the quest for the age of accountability," according to L. Craig Ratliff, "is a quest for disciple-ability. Such "disciple-ability" required the ability to understand abstract ideas, the development of selfhood and independence from parents, and social maturity. On the average a child would come to disciple-ability between the ages of thirteen and fifteen.

The most recent approach to develop among Southern Baptists was that of children as maturing participants. Children were to be considered related to the church in a way similar to that of catechumens in the early church. This approach sought to take seriously biblical insight, the practice of the early church, the findings of developmental psychology, and ecumenical discussions regarding a theology of the child. It remained a minority position, but William E. Hull recently espoused it in "The Child in the Church," a paper presented at the meeting of the Baptist World Alliance in 1980. Hull contended that Baptists need a theology of the child that recognized the Old Testament insight of nurture within the community and the New Testament insight of the necessity of conversion. A theology of the child recognizing the insights of both, however, would also parallel the findings of developmental psychology. Such a theology would recognize the profound effect of the setting into which a child was born. It would affirm the childhood task of understanding, accepting, and affirming this complex inheritance. It would declare this affirmation to be "the foundation on which to build a true sense of autonomy." Following these biblical and developmental insights, Hull proposed a "pattern for relating the child to the church." In infancy the church would stress the religious heritage, including among other aspects "an act of dedication on the part of the parents which affirms that their offspring is holy by virtue of its solidarity within a Christian home." In childhood children would be given the opportunity to affirm this heritage and their commitment to the faith. Baptism and church membership would come in the middle of childhood, approximately ages nine through twelve.

Historically, Southern Baptists have taken the four approaches delineated above, but in the twentieth century they have held only the last three - Children as prospects, children as potential disciples, and children as maturing participants. All of these views are currently held. All three assert the innocence of children until the age of accountability. All affirm the necessity of conversion. They differ, however, on the age of accountability, the nature of conversion, and the relationship of children to the church throughout the process.

The amount of support for each of these approaches varies considerably among Southern Baptists. The great majority still hold to the children-as-prospects approach. Although this approach has been modified in the last two decades, it remains more in accord with the traditional views of evangelism and conversion. The children-as-potential-disciples approach is supported by a substantial minority. It is most in harmony with the church renewal emphasis of the past two decades. A smaller minority advocate children as maturing participants. This newest approach, however, is most in harmony with the recent research being done in the area of faith development. That such diversity exists is not surprising. Southern Baptists have only recently engaged in genuine theological discussion on the issue. It is encouraging that Southern Baptists are now giving serious consideration to the issue of children and the church.

G. Thomas Halbrooks," Children and the Church: A Baptist Historical Perspective", *Review and Expositor* , (Spring 1983) pp. 179-187

49 "The idea that there are different degrees in faith can be found in the Synoptics: they talk about 'little faith' (Mt. 6:30 and parallels) and 'great' faith (Mt. 15:28); and they also realize that full faith comes from Jesus' intervention (Lk. 17:5)." J. Duplacy, *Baptism In the New Testament* , (Baltimore - Dublin, Helicon, 1956, trans. 1964), p. 139

50 "It is the *particular* definition of faith that results in a certain kind of baptism. Where faith is dependent on the competence of the individual soul, where it is the fruit of an effort of man's will, where it is in part an intellectual achievement, maturity of years is regarded understandably as a requisite." Martin E. Marty, *Baptism* (Philadelphia, Fortress Press, 1962) pp. 44-45. Italics mine.

51 See Thomas H. Groome, *Christian Religious Education* , (San Francisco, Harper & Row Publishers, 1980) p. 116

52 J. Duplacy, *Baptism In the New Testament* , (Baltimore - Dublin, Helicon, 1956/ trans. 1964), p. 153

53 Donald Bridge, David Phypers, *The Water That Divides,* (Downers Grove, Il., Inter-Varsity Press, 1977) p. 173

54 "Menno Simons, in his book entitled *Christian Baptism* , 1539, wrote: But little children and particularly those of Christian parentage have a peculiar promise which was given them of God without any ceremony, but out of pure and generous grace through Jesus Christ our Lord who says, "Suffer little children and forbid them not, to come unto me; for of such is the kingdom of heaven." Matt. 19:14; Mark 10:14; Luke 18:16. ... therefore such parents have in their hearts a sure and firm faith in the grace of God concerning their beloved children, namely that they are children of the kingdom, of grace, and of the promise of eternal life through Jesus Christ our Lord and not by any ceremony." John Christian Wenger, *Even Unto Death* , (Richmond, Virginia, John Knox Press, 1961), p. 75

55 Not all Anabaptists, however, immediately accepted the fact that children would be automatically saved. Hübmaier is a case in point: "As for the fate of children who died before being able to give that 'inward yes,' Hubmaier confessed: 'I can neither pronounce [them] saved, nor can I damn them. I leave all of that to the judgement of God'." Jaroslav Pelikan *The Christian Tradition: Reformation of Church and Dogma (1300-1700)* (Chicago and London, The University of Chicago Press, 1983) p. 318 citing Balthasar Hubmaier's *A Discussion of Zwingli 'On Baptism'* , 4, in *Quellen und Forschungen zur Reformationsgeschichte. Gütersloh* (1911) 29:201

56 "'...the children of believers are baptized not in order that they who were previously strangers to the church may then for the first time become children of God, but rather that, because by the blessing of the promise they already belonged to the body of Christ, they are received into the church with this solemn sign'." William A. Scott, *Historical Protestantism: An Historical Introduction to Protestant Theology* (Englewood Cliffs, N.J., 1971) p. 47, citing John Calvin's Institutes of the Christian Religion, IV, 15, 10, IV, 15, 10, LCC, XXI, p. 1311, edited by John T. McNeill and translated by Ford Lewis Battles. The Westminster Press. 1960, W.L. Jenkins.

57 "In 1523 Grebel had accepted Zwingli's teaching that children were saved by Christ and His redemptive work on Golgotha, and needed no ceremony to "seal" salvation to them." Conrad Grebel, *Conrad Grebel's Programmatic Letters of 1524,* translated by J. C. Wenger (Scottsdale, Pa., Herald Press, 1970), p. 9

"The whole of Anabaptist soteriology presupposed the forensic atonement of all mankind through the work of Christ on Calvary, something different from the forensic justification of the individual believer, as in

Lutheranism: hence the refusal of the Anabaptists to impose a purificatory baptism on new-born infants, already cleared of Adamic sin by the will of God and the deed of Christ." George Huntston Williams, *The Radical Reformation*, (Philadelphia, The Westminster Press, 1975) p. 839

58 To this question, as remarkable as it may seem, Grebel answered, "Yes." The child is a special exception. , faith is not necessary for a child to be saved:

> Christ is the New Adam who has restored their [the children's] ruined life, for they would have been subject to death and damnation only if Christ had not died. Also they have not yet grown up to the infirmity of our broken nature--unless indeed we could be shown that Christ did not suffer for the children! But if the objection is raised that faith is demanded of all who are to be saved, we exclude children from this requirement, holding that they are saved without faith.

Conrad Grebel, *Conrad Grebel's Programmatic Letters of 1524*, translated by J. C. Wenger (Scottsdale, Pa., Herald Press, 1970), p. 31

59 Continuing on in this scholastic mode of thought, the Roman Church for a time did permit the child to receive of the Chalice, however. Why? Because Christ, when speaking of the Cup said "Drink from it, *all* of you" (Matt. 26:27). Thus, children (as one of "the all" in this passage) were permitted to receive.

60 Baptism, confirmation, and reception of the eucharist were not separated from each other in the Early Church, nor were they each understood to "carry" a distinct grace. Each sacrament testifies to one's union with Christ and His Body (the Church).

CHAPTER SEVENTEEN

BAPTISM (PART II):

THE MEANING OF BAPTISM IN THE ANCIENT CHURCH

Which is correct: infant baptism or adult "believer's" baptism? The question would have struck the Early Church as strange. Of course, both means are appropriate. Whether an adult or the child of Christian parents, the one baptized is called to give himself to Christ, the Church, and to Christian discipleship for his entire life. [1]

The issue for the Christian of the first centuries was not *when* someone was baptized, but what baptism *signified* for every Christian. As this chapter will show, to set one form of baptism against the other is a betrayal of baptism's very meaning: union with Christ and the brethren. If this is true, it makes no sense to ask, "Why is it *necessary* to baptize children?" A better question would be, "Why" (given the symbolic meaning of baptism) "do some conclude that it is necessary *to exclude* children of Christian parentage from baptism?" In this chapter, I will explain why there is no Biblical, theological, or historical reason to make such an exclusion, and why the inherent meaning of baptism actually commends itself to believers of all ages.

THE MEANING OF BAPTISM

UNION WITH CHRIST

Baptism in the Early Church was not a merely a sign of one's confession of Christ. Baptism was (and is) the *symbol of Christ Himself.* [2]

> The one baptized is *united with* and *engrafted into* Christ (Roman 6:5; 1 Cor. 12:13; Rom. 11).
>
> "All who were baptized into Christ have *put on Christ.*" (Gal. 3:27).

Our baptism is a complete *identification* with Christ, not an "add on" to our faith. Our baptism is *in one Lord and one faith* (Eph. 4:5); it is integral to our *calling upon the name of the Lord* (Acts 22:16). For this reason, our baptism is *in Christ's name.* [3] This explains why no Christian within the New Testament ever abstained from baptism.

The symbol-reality of Christian baptism depicts and makes present all that it means to be "in Christ", [4] and this union saves us. To be baptized is to realize the truth of our union with Christ. In baptism, *Christ's* death becomes *our* death, "having been buried with Him in baptism." (Col. 2:12) [5] In baptism, *Christ's* resurrection life becomes *our* resurrection life, "For if we have become united with Him in the likeness of His death, certainly we shall also be in the likeness of His resurrection." (Rom. 6:5) [6]

NEW LIFE AS EXPRESSED THROUGH THE SYMBOL OF WATER

Although it is just as true today, the agrarian culture of the New Testament period was much more aware than most modern Western nations that all life is dependent upon water. They saw what effect a draught could have on their crops, livestock, and even their own lives: death and destruction. It makes sense, therefore, that the people saw water as the source of life. Likewise, those within the Church saw the water of baptism as a type of life that only God could give.[7]

> "...but whoever drinks of the water that I shall give him shall never thirst; but the water that I shall give him shall become in him a *well of water spring up to eternal life.*" (Jn. 4:14)

> "He who believes in Me, as the Scripture said, 'From his innermost being shall *flow rivers of living water*'. " (Jn 7:38)

> "...that He (Christ) might sanctify her, *having cleansed her by the washing of water* with the word" (Eph. 5:26)

> "...for the Lamb in the center of the throne shall be their shepherd, and shall guide them to *springs of the water of life* ..." (Rev. 7:17)

"By the word of God the heavens existed long ago and the earth was formed *out of water and by water.* " (2 Pet. 3:5) The Church understood God's Spirit in the waters of Creation to be life-giving, "and the Spirit of God was moving over the surface of the waters" (Gen. 1:1), and so, too, they recognized His enlivening Presence within their baptismal waters. As God's Spirit gave life to creation through water, now He uses water to actualize new life in the Christian's restoration and re-creation (2 Cor. 5:7).[8]

The water of Christian baptism discloses and re-presents many aspects of this divine reality:

our regeneration...

> "He saved us, not on the basis of deeds which we have done in righteousness, but according to His mercy, by the washing of regeneration and renewing of the Spirit." (Titus 3:5)

forgiveness...

> And Peter said to them, 'Repent, and let each of you be baptized in the name of Jesus Christ for the forgiveness of sins; and you shall receive the gift of the Holy Spirit." (Acts 2:38)

new life...

> Jesus answered, 'Truly, truly I say to you, unless one is born of water and the Spirit, he cannot enter into the kingdom of God. (John 3:5)

sanctification...

> that He [Christ] might sanctify her [the Church], having cleansed her by the washing of the water with the word. (Eph. 5:26)

and our deliverance from death.

> ... who once were disobedient, when the patience of God kept waiting in the days of Noah, during the construction of the ark, in which a few ... were brought safely through the water. And corresponding to that water now saves you—not the removal of dirt from the flesh, but an appeal to God from a good conscience—through the resurrection of Jesus Christ. (I Peter 3:20, 21)

To Paul, the water of baptism was more than just a prop required for a religious ritual. It communicated the very redemption which Israel's crossing of the Red Sea foreshadowed.

> For I do not want you to be unaware, brethren, that our fathers were all under the cloud, and all passed through the sea; and all were baptized into Moses in the cloud and in the sea; and all ate the same spiritual food: and all drank the same spiritual drink, for they were drinking from a spiritual rock which followed them; and the rock was Christ. (1 Cor. 10:1-4)

The context of this chapter makes it plain that the "spiritual food" and "spiritual drink" referred to is the Eucharist (1 Cor. 10:16ff). Similarly, Israel's being "baptized into Moses" in their crossing through the Red Sea is a type for Christian baptism. Moses, here, is clearly understood by Paul to be a type of Christ.[9] In both instances, it is not food, drink, or water that is the ultimate focus; it is *Christ*. In all these things, Christ was revealed, and He is what each sacrament reveals. They ate and drank Christ, and passed in and through Christ to get to the home God prepared for them. *He* was Israel's life, food, and salvation, even though they did not recognize it at the time ("and the rock was Christ").

This Corithinans passage teaches that, as those who crossed through the Red Sea entered into the Promised land, those who now pass through the waters of baptism enter into God's Kingdom.[10] This understanding does not give water any inherent power outside of Christ; water cannot save.[11] Neither is the water of baptism substantially changed into something else than what it was before. It is water before a person's baptism, it is water afterward.

What is the significance of water in baptism, then? It, as a type of all creation, anticipates the day when the entire material universe will be clothed with Christ.[12] And in this, it presents us again with the spiritual and material reality inherent in all sacramental symbolism - in this case, water and the Spirit. As the matter of water naturally cleanses and gives life to the body, so the Spirit, by transcending and enveloping the baptismal waters, communicates spiritual cleansing and life to all those who therein wash themselves by faith. Do we place faith in the water? Of course not. To be baptized is to be baptized *into Christ, an identification and union which is only possible by a relationship of faith in Him.*

THE INFLUENCE OF THE WESTERN UNDERSTANDING OF "ORIGINAL" SIN ON INFANT BAPTISM

Infant baptism is justified by many Christian groups in the West as a way of dealing with the curse of Original Sin (the sin and guilt of Adam's transgression passed on to the human race). They believe that if the stain of Original Sin remains on an unbaptized child's soul, he will be immediately doomed to hell (or, at best, limbo) if he should die.

The growing predominance of this view began to de-emphasize baptism as a revelation of one's union with Christ within Community. Instead of this communal conception, baptism came to be understood in more individualistic terms. Baptism was something "done to" a person, a means to get rid of Adam's curse. It was less and less understood as an induction into a life of communion with God and the brethren.

THE RELATIONSHIP OF BAPTISM TO THE CHURCH

Whereas Augustine saw the baptism of infants as a means to cancel out the *negative* effects of Original Sin, Eastern Christianity sees baptism as primarily *positive.* In the ancient Eastern Church, baptism was administered to children to actualize their *union with Christ and the Church,* not to absolve them of Adam's guilt. The child is baptized because they believed that the fruits of this union— power over sin, death and the devil—could be realized from his earliest days.

This is not all. The baptism of a child of Christian parents symbolizes that his place is *not* of the world, but *in Christ.* [13] In the same way a child becomes part of the Christian *family's environment* without his cognitive assent, so in his baptism is he set within the *Church's environment.* He is not isolated or "on his own": he (in his family) is a part of a loving people. God's Kingdom is reflected on earth by such a communion.

Of course, all of this assumes that the infant is being baptized into a genuine Christian *community,* rather than just a denominational association, or a twice–a–week gathering of believers having no interpersonal commitment and communion. Whether adult or child, one cannot have a New Testament baptism unless it occurs in a New Testament Church, i.e., a Church of love, life and devotion.

New Testament baptism is indeed a baptism into *the Church* ("For by one Spirit we were all *baptized into one body.*" 1 Corinthians 12:13). As may be remembered from chapter 10, the first Christians had a clear sense that their commitment to Christ was a commitment to His Community. The align oneself with the covenant name of Jesus was to align oneself with Christ's *Body.* The first Christians were baptized into the "name of Jesus," and thus, entered into fellowship with Christ *and* His brethren (Acts 2:38, 42).

Baptism is not a private matter between the person and God alone because salvation is not a solitary thing; it involves the entire Church.[14] Hence, baptism, Church membership, and one's Christian profession cannot be detached from each other; they are all interrelated. One cannot be baptized without being a member of the Church. One cannot be a member of the Church without being baptized.

> ... Baptism, far from being a private, personal, individual affair ("between me and God alone"), is rather at once and continually an existence "in fellowship" (1 John 1:3-7). It is societal, communal - in the truest sense "churchly". This existence begins in community, is maintained in community, functions in community, and is fulfilled in community.[15]

For this reason, baptism in the Early Church was performed *only* in the context of corporate worship. By so doing, the members of the congregation symbolized their solidarity with the newly baptized, expressed their commitment to support him in the Christian life, and were thus reminded of the communal significance of their own baptism. The Fellowship's familial love made it clear to them that, in baptism, the Church was embracing a new brother or sister into the Family of God. This is why not only the candidate, but the *whole Church* prepared itself for the baptismal ceremony with prayer and fasting.

All of this has a direct bearing on how one views infant baptism:

> Infant baptism is not performed in a vacuum, but upon the explicit profession of faith by parents, sponsors and the very community itself, gathered to celebrate the mystery, each time reaffirming its faith, pledging itself to provide an environment of continued Christian witness for its new members, regardless of their age and circumstance. ...Baptism is not an entrance into some universal and abstract idea, but into the life of a concrete local community, where the business of dying and rising daily in Christ is experienced. The baptismal liturgy rightly belongs to the whole Church; it is not a private act.[16]

THE PLACE OF THE EUCHARIST AND CONFIRMATION IN BAPTISM

Some Evangelical-Fundamentalists criticize denominations which permit infant baptism by saying, "If you say a child is able to be baptized, what criteria do you use to reject him from the Lord's Table?" This is a valid question, and the answer many Christian bodies give in response to it is indeed contradictory. How can one say that a child is a member of the Body of Christ (by baptism), and yet refuse him admission to—and within—the Eucharist (the Body of Christ)?

As stated in the last chapter, the practice of the Ancient Church was to allow the baptized to participate in the Eucharist *regardless of age.* Both baptism and the Eucharist are communal mysteries as both reveal one's membership to Christ as a union with His Community. It is obvious. If the child is a member of the Body of Christ, his communion with Christ and the Church is already a matter of fact. When one is baptized into the Body, he should be allowed to participate in the Eucharist, the chief symbol of the Christian community into which he has *just been baptized.* This is still the practice of the Eastern Church today.

What about confirmation? Wasn't this practice "invented" in recognition of the fact that each person who was baptized needed to make a personal response of faith later in life? No. As stated previously, confirmation, the Eucharist, and baptism were all celebrated *together and as a unity* in the Early Church. Confirmation was not a sacrament set aside to accommodate a "rational" expression of faith. It, too, symbolizes the Spirit's presence among and within the members of the Church.[17] *Each* sacrament— in association with the other two — unveils the Christian's anointing with the Spirit, his union with the Body, and his communion with the Trinity. Baptism, confirmation, and the Eucharist must stand *together*, for to separate them is to forget that salvation is union with Christ (and thus, with His body as well).[18]

THE NECESSITY OF FAITH

Baptism does not *make* one a Christian; it *exemplifies, actualizes, and manifests* the union with Christ which already exists in the life of the believer. The Church can only baptize those who *already belong to her.* Only those of the Faith can be baptized in the Faith. There is no "baptism" for a non-Christian.

Whether adult, child, or infant, faith and a life lived in symphony with that faith are essential if baptism is to hold any meaning. But how can this be understood in the case of a child? When Jesus stressed that one must first "believe and be baptized" (Mark 16:16), he was not addressing infants. He was addressing unbelieving adults who needed to forsake trust in themselves and trust Christ instead. The Christian infant does not need to first repent before he believes. What is he to repent of? It is inappropriate to apply a Biblical passage intended for unbelieving adults to the infants of believers.

This is not to say that the Early Church did not see faith as an absolute prerequisite for baptism, for it surely did. Therefore, it did not baptize just *any* child. Pre-adult baptism was limited *only* to those who were under the care of Christian adults.[19] In such cases, the Church affirmed that the child's faith *had begun,* and that She, along with the family, would provide an environment where that faith would be nurtured. The parents, and the entire fellowship would commit themselves to the child and his growth in the faith.

As a child matures, the conditions for his participation in the fellowship change in accordance with his increased capability. At *every* age and *every* stage of life, the faith of the child is expected to mature: in his commitment to Christ, in his understanding of Christian teaching, and in his continual need for repentance.[20] Whether an adult or child, it is logical to expect that the way his baptismal faith is expressed will differ in accordance with his state in life.

> What an infant has to do is different from what his adult guardians have to do. What a senile old person has to understand and confess is not the same as that of a young person ... Conditions for sacramental participation in the Church differ between the intelligent and the retarded, the neophytes and the mature, the young and the old, the strong and the weak. [21]

A SACRAMENT EACH PERSON'S FAITH MUST COMPLETE

Although it is not its primary meaning, baptism is a demonstration of one's "pledge" to Christ. [22] It is up to the one baptized to be faithful to that pledge throughout life.[23] If that resolve is ever forsaken, the redemptive significance of his baptism is likewise abandoned.

Christian baptism, therefore, only *begins* with the administration of the rite. The Eastern Christian sees baptism as something that is to be *lived.* Only as one *identifies* with Christ day to day is the sacrament realized. Each Christian has the responsibility to live a life that says, "It is no longer I who live, but Christ lives in me." Only in this is the Spirit's ministry, given in one's baptism, able to be completed.

In order for this or any other sacrament to be "worthily" received, its reception must always be wedded with an inner resolve to *live* in Christ. This means that one should not approach the mysteries if he is not, by this action, ready to express his identification with Christ. Each one must personally and freely associate himself with Christ in the confession of faith, and in the choice of love. This is not an ascetic or moral rule of discipline, it is a real bond and communion with Christ. If it is real, one's participation in the sacraments will effect a genuine transformation and healing. If it is not, no amount of tactile contact with any sacrament will be of any benefit.

BIBLICAL ILLUSTRATIONS OF BAPTISM WITHOUT RESPECT TO AGE

The Scriptures nowhere specifically speak of *infant* baptism. Nor do they specifically speak of *age-restrictive adult* baptism. The Scriptures speak about *Christian* baptism. Period. This should be our point of focus. When we look at the subject in this way, we can see that an age-exclusive baptism contradicts the *nature* of Christian baptism. A baptism open to all ages embraces it. I will further illustrate this point by looking at three important factors: 1) the Bible's view of family solidarity; 2) the nature of covenant; and 3) the significance of the Bible's silence on the subject of adult-only baptism.

FAMILY SOLIDARITY

"In early Israelite thought the clan or the family was the fundamental unit, not the individual."[24] This fact sheds light directly on the Bible's understanding of the child's relationship within his family, the link that exists between his faith and his family's faith, and the meaning of baptismal faith. A child was not perceived as an independent being, somehow spiritually and socially removed from his parentage. He was an organic part of his family, and the faith of the child was always understood as inseparable from his family's faith. [25]

> The idea that a parent should enter a religion or covenant-relation with God as an individual merely, i.e., by himself as distinct from his immediate

> family, would never occur to the ancients, least of all to a Jew. There were no 'individuals' in our sharp modern sense of the term. Hence to any one familiar with the modes of antique thought, no proof in any given case is needed that children from their birth were regarded as sharing their parents' religious status.[26]

There is nothing in the New Testament to indicate that this child-family relationship changed. As the parents related to God on behalf of their family within the Old Covenant, so they continue to do so within the New. The parents' faith sanctifies the child. This explains why Paul could call the child of a believing parent "holy," a term derived from the same Greek word translated as "saint" (1 Cor. 7:14).[27] Because his family has extended Christ's covenant to him as a member of *their household,* the child is a "saint," a "holy one."

Household. This word's appearance and meaning in the Scriptures is itself a testimony against age-restrictive baptism, and a strong witness of family solidarity. The Greek word *eekos* (οἶκος), translated "house" or "household," has always been traditionally understood as a designation for the family— *inclusive* of *every* member of the family (i.e., infants and children). If this is the case, the following passages make it more than probable that the offspring of believing families were baptized along with their parents.

> Now I [Paul] did baptize the *household* of Stephanas... (1 Cor. 1:16).
>
> [An angel spoke to Cornelius saying] 'Send to Joppa, and have Simon, who is also called Peter, brought here; and he shall speak words to you by which you will be saved, and all your *household.*' (Later, when Peter arrived at Cornelius' household) '... he ordered them to be baptized." (Acts 11:13b, 14; Acts 10:48a)
>
> "And when she [Lydia of Thyatira] and her *household* had been baptized ... (Acts 16:15a)
>
> "Believe in the Lord Jesus, and you shall be saved, you and your *household* ... and immediately he was baptized, he and all his *household.*" (Acts 16:31, 33b)

But how do we know that "household" *always* has an inclusive meaning? At least four reasons help us assert that this is its intended meaning:

> 1) There is *no* evidence of "household" being used in either secular Greek, Biblical Greek, or in the writings of Hellenistic Judaism which would *in any way limit its meaning to adults alone.*[28]
>
> 2) The Old Testament Hebrew equivalent of this word ("bayit") always refers to the *entire* family (even inclusive of up to four generations).[29]
>
> 3) The Greek translation of the original Hebrew manuscripts (completed in 250 B.C.) uses *oikos* to translate this Hebrew word as meaning a *complete family* (men, women, children, infants).[30]

4) The phrase "he and his house" in the Old Testament particularly refers to the *total* family, not just to its adult members. Any number of definitive examples could be cited where this usage clearly mentions children and infants in this context. [31]

Even if one were to assume that the Bible does not mean to include children under "the age of accountability" in *each* usage of "household", this does not change the strength of the argument for age-inclusive baptism. Actually, it does not really matter whether there were specific infants included in the instances where this word appears or not. *What is significant is that the word household is used in the context of baptism at all!*

> In the recorded instances of such household baptisms, the primary question is not to decide finally whether or not they included infant children for sure. The thing which is emphasized is the organic idea of family units, the whole family participating in the faith of the parents. The record clearly indicates faith on the part of one parent, and baptism of the whole house. These are the facts without anything else read into it.[32]

BAPTISM AS AN ENTRANCE INTO THE COVENANT

Both the Old and New Covenants are covenants of God with a *people*, not just with individuals. Where in the Scriptures does it say that the Old Testament was exclusively a corporate covenant to God, whereas the New Testament is only a covenant for individuals? Nowhere. A covenant is still a covenant, whether it is of the Old Dispensation or of the New. Both —*as covenants* — were intended to establish *a people* for God.

In reality, there is only *one* covenant: God's covenant in Christ. He is the common foundation for both Old and New Covenants. The Old Testament looked forward to Christ in the New; the New receives and realizes Him after discerning His presence foreshadowed in the Old. The New Covenant is a *fulfillment* of the Old, not an alien *individualization* of it. In many respects both Covenants are similar. As salvation was by faith in the Old (Gen. 15:6), so is it still in the New (Rom. 3:22, 23). The Old Covenant stressed individual responsibility to God as a people (Ez. 18), and, although each must personally seal his covenant in Christ, the New Covenant establishes this person's faith *within a people* (1 Peter 2:19). This Covenant in Christ allows the Church to be seen as "the Israel of God" (Gal. 6:16).

Therefore, the covenantal and communal nature of salvation is as real now as it ever was.

> The covenant was central in Peter's very first sermon after Pentecost (Acts 3: 12-26). It was the starting point for Stephan's address (Acts 7: 2-8). Paul affirms the permanence of the covenant (Galatians 3: 17), and teaches that Christian believers are the children of Abraham (Galatians 3: 7,26,29; 4: 21,23,28). ... Paul speaks of the apostles as "ministers of the covenant" (2 Cor. 3:6). Despite the vast differences in administering the covenant under the new dispensation, it is clearly the same covenant of grace in force. [33]

Therefore, if a child born within the former Covenant were viewed as a participant in its blessings, why should it be different with the child of the New? If Moses did not ask the parents to leave their children on the shores of the Red Sea because they could not articulate a rational faith in the Old Covenant, how can Christian parents justify the exclusion of their children from Christian baptism because their children cannot "explain" the Gospel? The nature of Covenant makes one fact clear. As the infants of the Old Covenant received "Moses' baptism", so should the children of the New Covenant receive Christ's baptism, the fulfillment of that which Moses testified was to come. [34]

Circumcision was the Old Testament symbol of initiation that sealed one into God's Covenant. This was not merely an ordinance or ceremonial law, its significance lay much deeper. In the rite of circumcision, the saving presence of God foreshadowed what Christian baptism would later signify: the acceptance of God's Covenant through our union with Christ's death:

> "in Him you were circumcised with a circumcision made without hands ... the circumcision of Christ; having been buried with Him in baptism.." (Col. 2:11, 12).[35]

Now through Christ, not just Israel, but all peoples can enter into the saving Covenant. This entrance is what circumcision then *anticipated*, this entrance is what Christian baptism now *fulfills*.

> The sign and seal of the covenant ratification was circumcision. And this sign and seal was to be received, not only by Abraham the believer, but also by his infant children as rightful heirs of the covenant promises. Circumcision was thus not an enactment of the Law of Moses. It was given 400 years before Moses, to Abraham. In the Old Testament period there were two sacramental ordinances of particularly great importance, circumcision and the Passover. Correspondingly, in the New Testament period there [is] ... baptism and the Lord's Supper. [36]

If baptism into Christ is "New Testament circumcision," how can there be any objection to a Christian family baptizing their pre-adolescent child, and thus "sealing" him? [37]

THE BIBLE'S SILENCE ABOUT AGE RESTRICTIVE BAPTISM

The Bible speaks against using age as a criterion for baptism not only by what it *does* say, but by what it *does not* say. Certainly, if it were forbidden to baptize a child under "the age of accountability," one would expect to read an injunction to that effect: "Do not bring your children to baptism until they confess Christ for themselves." Or, at least one would expect to read of "exception clauses" forbidding baptism to the infants of Christian families: "Go therefore and make disciples of all the nations, baptizing them —*except* for the infants of those families..." [38]

"But they did not need such a command," some may say." They already knew better than to present their young children for baptism." Actually, it would have been more natural for the Jewish Christian to present the child for baptism than it would have been to withhold him. If the Early Christians recognized Christian baptism as the fulfillment of circumcision, and if they always understood their children as being included in their faith via the rite, what theological reason would they have to begin viewing it in a completely different way? If there were at least *some* reason why they should change their view, or if their were *some* way that they should express their faith differently, it would only be normal that something would have been said to correct this approach. But there was nothing said. There was nothing that needed to be said.

The Scriptures say *nothing* to lead us to conclude that age-restrictive baptism is theologically appropriate. *Nothing* in the Scriptures testifies that it was the practice of the time. And there is *nothing anywhere* in the Scriptures which expressly forbids the baptism of infants of Christian families. Without doubt, if baptism were intended for adults alone, we would at least expect to see a case where a child of Christian parents was later baptized as an "accountable" adult.[39] There are no such cases. We would expect the Scriptures to give us a different view of covenant and the solidarity of the family. It does not.

HISTORICAL TESTIMONY TO AGE-INCLUSIVE CHRISTIAN BAPTISM

If there were no age restrictions on baptism, we would expect to see this borne out in the history of the early Church. This is indeed what the historical account shows.

- There is no recorded incident in the earliest Christian history giving evidence that baptism was refused anyone on the basis of age (inclusive of "the age of reason").

- There is nothing to substantiate that the right of a Christian parent to have his children baptized had ever been challenged or renounced.

- At *no place* and at *no time* was there *anyone* in the Early Church who viewed the practice of open-aged baptism as something *new.* If the practice was indeed an innovation, certainly there would have been some record as to when and why it began, but there is no such testimony.[40]

- *There is no evidence of any Christian protest against the validity of infant-child baptism for 1500 years.*[41] If it had been viewed as something incongruent with Apostolic teaching, one would think that it would have been challenged by someone within the Early Church as soon as it appeared.

- There is not *one* example in Early Church history showing a Christian family postponing their child's baptism to a later time.[42]

Besides these historical facts, many noted teachers within the Church of the Second and Third centuries give ample reason to question the legitimacy of age discriminatory baptism. Let us look at just five examples from the first three centuries of the Church.

Polycarp of Smyrna (155, d.)

The very early date of his martyrdom, along with other historical data, shows that Polycarp was eighty six at the time of his execution. At his martyrdom, Polycarp affirmed, "*Eighty six years I have served him,* and he never did me any wrong. How can I blaspheme my King who saved me?" In order for him to make such a statement, he would have had to understand himself as being a Christian *from birth.* Certainly, he could not have made such a declaration if he believed that faith began only at a certain age. What it meant to be a believer then is what it means to be a believer now: identification with Christ and inclusion into the Christian Community. *This* is the meaning of baptism. Thus, whether Polycarp was baptized with his "household" upon the conversion of his parents, or within the context of a Christian family, in either case the point is clear: he had been baptized at a *very young* age and in this act he saw the beginnings of his Christian life.[43]

Justin Martyr (100-165 A.D.)

In his understanding of baptism as Christian circumcision, Justin speaks of the impropriety of restricting baptism to those meeting a certain age requirement:

> ... in Christ the Son of God, who was proclaimed as about to come to all the world, to be the everlasting law and the everlasting covenant, even as the fore mentioned prophecies show. And we, who have approached God through Him, have received not a carnal, but spiritual circumcision, which Enoch and those like him observed. And we have received it through baptism...[44]

Justin also, like Polycarp, is a testimony to the existence of "pre-adult" Christianity when he states, "And many, both men and women, who have been Christ's disciples from childhood, remain pure at the age of sixty or seventy years..."[45]

Irenaeus (120-202 A.D.)

Irenaeus, a disciple of Polycarp, rightly believed that Christ identified with all aspects of our humanity. He was one of us, and as a human being He could pass through all that we as mortals now experience at various ages. Irenaeus, wrote:

> He [Christ] came to save all through Himself - all I say, who through Him are reborn in God - infants, and children, and youth, and old men. Therefore He passed through every age, becoming an infant for infants, sanctifying those who are of that age, and at the same time becoming for them an example of piety, of righteousness, and of submission; a young man for youths, becoming an example for youths, and sanctifying them for the Lord.[46]

This insight holds a great deal of significance for our understanding of Christian baptism. Christ does not have a commonalty with only the adults among us, nor is His salvation confined solely to those physically and mentally developed. He saves *all* those in *union* with Him. The incarnation stands strongly against any idea of an age selective salvation (the union of the divine with humanity). As it was possible for Him to identify with all of us, so too is it possible for all of us—regardless of age—to be one with Him. This is the nature of redemption, this is what it means to be baptized *in* Christ.

Hippolytus' (170-236 A.D.)

Hippolytus wrote many things regarding the worship practices of the Early Church. In speaking about the proper procedures to follow regarding baptism, he instructs the following:

> "Baptize first the children; and if they can speak for themselves, let them do so. Otherwise, let their parents or other relatives speak for them." [47]

Obviously, children who do not yet have the ability to speak are well below what many would ascertain to be the "age of reason."

Cyprian of Carthage (200-258 A.D.)

In the Third Century, Bishop Cyprian had presided over a synod of sixty-six bishops (256 A.D.) which ended up making a strong statement against an age-restrictive view of baptism. At the conference it was discussed whether or not the Church should change the customary practice of baptizing children on the *third* day after birth or postpone baptism until they were *eight days* old, as was the case with Old Testament circumcision. They unanimously concurred that the practice they had followed for years was adequate.

This was the only discussion of an "age-restrictive" baptism in the Early Church! And what they believed about limiting baptism to anyone on the basis of age— even if only by five days— was obvious. Baptism was not to be forbidden at any age.

CONCLUSION

The very meaning of baptism naturally contradicts an age restrictive view. If one can identity with and be in union with Christ at any age, baptism—the very symbol of that union—cannot be prohibited to anyone on the basis of his mental or physical development. Baptism is a symbol of one's engrafting into the Church, an environment of love where caring relationships are to support the baptized Christian in his efforts to live a sincere Christian life (1 Cor. 12:13). If baptism is not administered in this context, it is not baptism. If it is, the fruit of the sacrament will be obvious.

The real reasons for "age of accountability" baptism are due to past abuses, not theological or Biblical reasons. Given the lack of spiritual life we see within a great number of Christian bodies, this is an understandable reaction. However, it is not a *justifiable* reaction.

Yes, baptism has been abused, and this abuse must be corrected. But it is corrected by believers manifesting the Christ's Church as it is, and is to become—an *environment* of faith and trust. It is remedied by families becoming serious in their resolve to make their homes a place where Christian love and faith can grow, not by relying upon the rite to do something on its own, apart from this context. The sacrament should not be modified in individualistic terms, rather, the sacrament should redirect Christians into becoming communal people once again. This corrective begins in the resolve of each Christian to end his prideful isolation and to *daily live out* his baptism *within* a body of believers.

And lastly, for the meaning of baptism to be regained, one type of baptism should not be argued over another. They *both* have their place in the Church. If "infant" baptism is exclusively practiced, it becomes obvious that a particular congregation's evangelistic consciousness is sorely ill. If only adult baptism is permitted, theological and Biblical distortions regarding the nature of faith, one's communion with God, the Church, the family, personhood, and redemption are fostered. Unquestionably, when both types of baptism are properly practiced, and when what they symbolize is lived out in the lives of the faithful, there will be no need for debate. Then, baptism will not be a "topic" for "doctrinal discussion." Baptism will be an encounter with God, a union with Christ and His Church — a manifestation of the Kingdom of God.

NOTES FOR CHAPTER SEVENTEEN

1 "When the expressions 'infant baptism' and 'believers' baptism' are used, it is necessary to keep in mind that the real distinction is between those who baptize people at any age and those who baptize only those able to make a confession of faith for themselves. Both forms of baptism require a similar and responsible attitude towards Christian nurture." "Baptism, Eucharist, and Ministry," Faith and Order Paper No. 111 (World Council of Churches, Geneva, Switzerland, 1982) p. 11-12

2 "St. Paul did not have to justify or defend the practice of baptism. It never seems to have occurred to him, so far as this rite was concerned, to separate the act from its implication: the two were one. The rite and its meaning were, for the thought of the Apostle, an indissoluble unity." W. F. Flemington, *The New Testament Doctrine of Baptism* , (London, S.P.C.K., 1964) p. 82

3 Acts 2:38; 10:48; Acts 8:16; 19:5; 1 Cor.1:12-16

4 Rom. 6:3; 16:3, 7; 2 Cor. 5:17; 12:2; Gal. 1:22

5 Note Mark 10:38, 39 is also a reference to the death which each Christian is to undergo in his baptism:

> "But Jesus said to them, 'You do not know what you are asking for. Are you able to drink the cup that I drink, or to be baptized with the baptism with which I am baptized?' And they said to Him, 'We are able.' And Jesus said to them, 'The cup that I drink you shall drink; and you shall be baptized with the baptism with which I am baptized'".

6 "It can be said that baptism is a sacramental resurrection in Christ, a rising up with Him and in Him to a new and eternal life... Co-resurrected with Him precisely through burial: for if we be dead with Him, we shall also live with Him' 2 Tim. 2:11." Georges Florovsky, *Creation and Redemption*, (Belmont, MA., Nordland Publishing Company, 1976) pp. 149,150

7 A few other related passages...

> "And after being baptized, Jesus went up immediately from the water; and behold, the heavens were opened, and He saw the Spirit of God descending as a dove, and coming upon Him." (Matt. 3:16)
>
> Jesus answered, 'Truly, truly, I say to you, unless one is born of water and the Spirit, he cannot enter into the kingdom of God." (Jn. 3:5)
>
> "And who is the one who overcomes the world, but he who believes that Jesus is the Son of God? This is the one who came by water and blood, Jesus Christ; not with the water only, but with the water and with the blood." (1 John 5:5, 6)
>
> "And the Spirit and the bride say, 'Come.' And let the one who hears say, 'Come.' And let the one who is thirsty come; let the one who wishes take the water of life without cost." (Rev. 22:17)

8 "The miracle stories of the Synoptics with their healings and exorcisms were fit just for those prepared for Baptism. Enlightenment of the whole nature, healing from sickness, exorcism from demonic powers—all these, organically connected with the rite of initiation, reveal another dimension of Baptism, namely that of the *natural* or *cosmic*. This dimension is easily forgotten in the discussions about Baptism. And yet, not only did it very early form part of basic liturgical acts entailed in the rite of Baptism, but it was a fundamental element in the baptismal typology of the Primitive and Early Church." As P. Lundberg (*La typlogie baptismale dans l' Eglise ancienne* , Leipzig and Uppsala, 1942, pp. 10ff.) made clear some years ago, the water symbolism attached to Baptism from the beginning was taken over from the creation and the deluge, to come through the filtering of the Passion of Christ into Baptism and thus bring the whole of creation into the baptismal reality." John Zizoulas, "Some Reflections on Baptism, Confirmation

and Eucharist", A paper prepared for the Study Commission on Worship of the Commission on Faith and Order of the World Council of Churches, p. 648

9 See Walter Lewis Wilson, *Wilson's Dictionary of Bible Types* (Grand Rapids, MI., Wm. B. Eerdmans, 1957), p. 313

10 "St. Paul looks back to baptism as that which marked for each Christian the inauguration of the New Age, the transition from the old life to the new. Everything began for the convert when he came up out of the water and robed himself afresh in his garments. ... By that act he came to share in all the privileges of the new life; he was an heir, he was free, he was a son. (Rom. 6: 1-4)" W.F. Flemington, *The New Testament Doctrine of Baptism* , (London, S.P.C.K., 1964) p. 59

11 Gregory of Nyssa (335-395), a respected theologian of the Eastern Church, comments that water is a symbol of great significance, but that its property *as water* is not what in and of itself makes it important:

> It is not the water that bestows this gift (for in that case it were a thing more exalted than all creation), but the command of God, and the visitation of the Spirit that comes... But water serves to express the cleansing. For since we are wont by washing in water to render our body clean when it is soiled by dirt or mud, we therefore apply it also in the sacramental action, and display the spiritual brightness by which is subject to our senses. ....'Unless one is born of water and the Spirit, he cannot enter into the kingdom of God' (John 3:5). Why are both named, and why is not the Spirit alone accounted sufficient for the completion of Baptism? Man, as we know full well, is compound, not simple: and therefore the cognate and similar medicines are assigned for healing to him who is two fold and conglomerate: — for his visible body, water, the sensible element,— for his soul, which we cannot see, the Spirit invisible, invoked by faith, present unspeakably. ....He blesses the body that is baptized, and the water that baptizes.

Gregory of Nyssa, "Christian Baptism in the Old Testament Types and Prophecies: From A Sermon of St. Gregory of Nyssa, "For the Day Of The Lights", *Coptic Church Review*, (Winter 1983) Vol. 4, No. 4, pp. 10, 11

12 The water of baptism is a type of all creation which will one day be redeemed and completed in Christ.

> ...water is the source of life for the entire cosmos.... Instead of dominating man, nature becomes his servant, since he is the image of God. The original paradisiac relationship between God, man, and the cosmos is proclaimed again: the descent of the Spirit anticipates the ultimate fulfillment when God will be 'all in all.' This anticipation, however, is not a magical operation occurring in the material universe. The universe does not change in its empirical existence. The change is seen only by the eyes of faith—i.e., because *man* has received in his heart the Spirit which cries: 'Abba, Father' (Gal. 4:6), he is able to experience, in the mystery of faith, the paradisiac reality of nature serving him and to recognize that this experience is not a subjective fancy, but one which reveals the ultimate truth about nature and creation as a whole. By the power of the Spirit, the true and natural relationship is restored between God, man, and creation.

John Meyendorff, *Byzantine Theology,* (New York, Fordham Press, 1979) p. 170

13 Larry Christenson, a noted Lutheran pastor and teacher, illustrates this very aspect of baptism from his own impressions of the Eastern service of baptism:

> The most ancient liturgies of baptism lay special stress on this point: the child is 'snatched from Satan's clutches,' into the protective bosom of the church. At an ecumenical conference on baptism in Germany, a theologian of the Eastern Orthodox Church described this particular aspect of baptism, as it occurs in the baptismal liturgy of his church. The child is delivered into the arms of the priest, at which point the parents turn and "spit on the devil." At another point, there is a threefold exorcism, whereby the child is delivered from the power and authority of Satan. The central emphasis of the

baptismal service is upon the victory of Christ over the powers of darkness, the deliverance and rescue of the child into the company of God's people. After the lecture, a Baptist minister said, "Now *there* is a case for infant baptism!"

Larry Christenson, "What About Baptism?" (Minneapolis, Minnesota, Bethany Fellowship, Inc., 1973) p. 14,15

14 "Christ's action for the salvation of man is not an individual action; He extends His grace in a corporate fashion...He aims not only at uniting man with Himself, but also men among themselves." Metropolitan Emilianos Timiadis, "The Eucharist: The Basis of All Sacraments and Union With God," *The Patristic and Byzantine Review* (Kingston, New York) Vol. 3, No. 3, 1984, p. 183

15 Richard Jungkuntz, *The Gospel of Baptism* , (St. Louis, Concordia Publishing House, 1968) pp. 92-93

16 Comments regarding "The Lima Statement on Baptism", *St. Vladimir's Seminary Quarterly* (1983) Vol. 27, Number 4, p. 259

17 "Confirmation, whether administered by the laying-on of hands or by Chrismation, was from the beginning understood as the bestowing of the Holy Spirit upon the baptized. This understanding was for a long time common between East and West. But it is important to notice that in the history of this understanding, the emphasis was gradually directed in the West towards the idea of *perfection* of Baptism by Confirmation. ... This as expressed even more by the adoption of the term *confirmatio* , which seems to have been used for the first time (in verbal form) by Leo the Great and officially by the Council of Riez in 430 (Canon 3). By the final adoption of this term in the West the implication was becoming clearer that Confirmation is necessary because something is lacking in Baptism, either in the rite itself or in the person who received it (e.g. age). This easily opened the way towards an understanding of Confirmation as basically an opportunity of *response* of the adult faithful, especially if he had been baptized as a child." John Zizoulas, "Some Reflections on Baptism, Confirmation and Eucharist", A paper prepared for the Study Commission on Worship of the Commission on Faith and Order of the World Council of Churches, p. 649

18 On this see 1 John 1:3, 4; John 17:21; Eph 1:7-10; 1 Cor. 12:25; Eph. 4:15, 16, Col. 2:9

19 "If there are no adults to care for the children's spiritual life and churchly upbringing, then it is normally understood by the Orthodox that such children ought not be baptized. Baptism is not magic. It is not an act in which something happens to a person in isolation from the ongoing life of the Church into which the person is born in the baptismal mystery." Thomas Hopko, *All the Fulness of God* (Crestwood, N.Y., St. Vladimir's Seminary Press, 1982) p. 130

20 "The response to God is first made by one's parents ... who acknowledge Christ and pledge to Him as it were: "This young person is yours!' Afterwards, the goal of Christian life is to become aware of Christ and the Holy Spirit actively and consciously. As the baptized Christian grows from child to adult, and participates in the sacramental life of the Church, his personal response to God becomes crucial. Each Christian must personally re-affirm the baptismal pledge and himself say by free choice to Christ: 'Yes, I am yours!' " Anthony M. Coniaris, *These Are the Sacraments* , (Minneapolis, Minnesota, Light and Life Publishing Company, 1981) p. 28

21 Thomas Hopko, *All the Fulness of God* (Crestwood, N.Y., St. Vladimir's Seminary Press, 1982) p. 133

22 Evidence from ancient papyri gives reason to believe that the word "appeal" in 1 Peter 3:21 (that baptism is "an appeal to God for a good conscience") can be translated as "agreement" or "pledge." "In the early Church, baptism was viewed as a seal of contract. Therefore, the phrase 'a pledge to God for a clear conscience' suggests renunciation of 'human passions' and of the gentile way of life (4:3), and a promise to live a life of obedience to Christ (1:2) and of doing 'right' (3:17)." Joseph J. Allen, ed., *Orthodox Synthesis: The Unity of Theological Thought*, Veselin Kesich , "I Peter and the Doctrines of Primitive Christianity" (Crestwood, N.Y., St. Vladimir's Seminary Press, 1981), p. 139

23 Georges Florovsky, *Creation and Redemption*, (Belmont, MA., Nordland Publishing Company, 1976) p. 231

24 J. D. Douglas, Ed., "Symbol", A. A. Jones, *The Illustrated Bible Dictionary* , (Leicester, England, Inter-Varsity Press/Tyndale House Publishers, 1980) Vol. 3, p. 1498

25 "The parent dealt with God on behalf of his children, and the parent also dealt with the children on God's behalf, instructing them and seeking to lead them to a personal knowledge and acceptance of this covenant as their God and Redeemer." Dwight Hervey Small, *The Biblical Basis for Infant Baptism*, (Grand Rapids, MI., Baker Book House, 1968) p. 55

26 James Hastings, *Encyclopedia of Religion and Ethics* , "Baptism in the Early Church', Kirosopp Lake (N.Y., Charles Scribner's Sons, n.d.), p. 379

27 As in Judaism the child's objective status was conditioned by circumcision, it is natural to suppose that in the Church it was so conditioned by baptism (Col. 2). We look further into circumcision's relationship to baptism later in the chapter.

28 See Joachim Jeremias, *Origins of Infant Baptism* (Great Britain, SCM Press, 1963), p. 16

29 The application of the word in the Old Covenant was far from being in any way restrictive. On the contrary, it 's meaning was *very expansive* .

> The Old Testament pictures the household ("bayit" in the Hebrew) as including several generations in a family. In the book Anthology of the Old Testament, Hans Walter Wolff observes that "A household usually contained four generations, including men, married women, unmarried daughters, slaves of both sexes, persons without citizenship, and 'sojourners,' or resident foreign workers." Old Testament Scripture confirms again and again the significance and uniqueness of the household and the family. God's original promise to Abraham included the provision that through him " . . . all families of the earth shall be blessed'."

Win Arn, Charles Arn, *The Master's Plan For Making Disciples* , (Pasadena, CA., Church Growth Press, 1982) pp. 37-38

30 Joachim Jeremias, *Origins of Infant Baptism* (Great Britain, SCM Press, 1963) p. 21

31 Genesis 46:5,7,27; I Samuel 22:15-19; II Kings 9:8; Deuteronomy 12:7, 14:26, 15:20; Genesis 36:6; cf. Exodus 1:1; II Samuel 2:3, 15:16; Genesis 7:1, 12:17,34:30, 17:23,18:19; I Samuel 27:3, 25:6; II Samuel 6:11; Jeremiah 38:17 ; Judges 18:25, 15:15; Esther 4:14; Joshua 24:15; I Chronicles 10:6

32 Dwight Hervey Small, *The Biblical Basis for Infant Baptism*, (Grand Rapids, MI., Baker Book House, 1968) p. 103

33 Dwight Hervey Small, *The Biblical Basis for Infant Baptism*, (Grand Rapids, MI., Baker Book House, 1968) p. 38,39

34 A significant parallel also exists between early Christian baptism and *Jewish proselyte baptism* , a rite where Gentiles are received into Judaism. The similarities between the two are striking; the terminology which is used, the symbolism employed, the meanings assigned to each and even aspects of the rite itself are much the same in both "baptisms." What is especially significant is that children and infants were baptized *with* the convert's family. Why would the very early Church (which was in great measure made up of Christian Jews and Gentiles familiar with the practice, Acts 6:5), choose to change this attitude toward their children when there was no inherent reason to change but many theological reasons to commend its continuance? See Joachim Jeremias, *The Origins of Infant Baptism* , (Great Britain, S.C.M. Press Ltd., 1963) p. 28

35 "... it must be emphasized that the understanding of Christian Baptism as a fulfillment, and thus a repeal, of Jewish circumcision is not just a theological foundling, appearing only at a late date after the Apologist Justin; nor is it just a supplement designed to support Christian Baptism. This conception is

already present explicitly in Col. 2: 11, and implicitly especially in Rom. 2: 25, 4:1, Gal. 3:6, and Eph. 2: 11. A fundamental kinship between circumcision and Christian Baptism is thus apparent." Oscar Cullmann, *Baptism in the New Testament*, (Philadelphia, PA., The Westminster Press, 1950) p. 56,57

36 Dwight Hervey Small, *The Biblical Basis for Infant Baptism*, (Grand Rapids, MI., Baker Book House, 1968) p. 17,18

37 "In these three passages (2 Cor. 1: 21-22, Eph.1:13-14, Eph.4:30) the verb 'to seal' is used. It seems almost certain that the word is to be understood as a reference to baptism. St. Paul uses the word "seal" (*sfragis*) of circumcision in Rom. 4:11, speaking of Abraham, "he received the sign of circumcision, a seal of the righteousness of the faith which he had while he was in uncircumcision.' From the way in which the word seal is used by Christian writers in the second century A.D. it is clear that by that time it had become a recognized synonym for baptism. The implication is that at some date previously the term seal, originally used of circumcision, had been transferred to the Christian counterpart of the Jewish rite." W.F. Flemington, *The New Testament Doctrine of Baptism* , (London, S.P.C.K., 1964) pp. 66-67

38 "The fragment in St. Matthew's Gospel which discusses 'all nations' would be the place where exclusive clauses would be expected. Go and baptize whom? Adults? Those who have reached the age of reason?" Martin E. Marty, *Baptism* (Philadelphia, PA., Fortress Press, 1962) p. 23

39 " Such records would have been possible by the time the Book of Acts was written. Absence of any such references is further evidence that there apparently were no baptisms of adults who had thus grown up in covenant families. Presumably they were baptized as infants. All the New Testament records of Christian baptism are in connection with its application to converts. These were all adults. ... there is no suggestion of exclusion from baptism of those below a certain age." Dwight Hervey Small, *The Biblical Basis for Infant Baptism*, (Grand Rapids, MI., Baker Book House, 1968) p. 100

40 It is noteworthy, however, that history does tell us when and why the practice of "infant dedication" began, a practice clearly having no precedent in either the Bible or early Church history. The practice began with the Anabaptist, Balthalzar Hübmaier (around 1525) in Walshut, Switzerland. He offered a dedication service in place of the baptism for the children of families within his congregation. "Hübmaier reports that he had publicly declared that according to Christ's teaching children should on no account be baptized. Instead of baptizing children, he blessed them, reading the gospel in the vernacular while the whole congregation knelt in prayer for the child." Torgsten Bergsten, *Balthasar Hübmaier: Anabaptist Theologian and Martyr* (Valley Forge, PA., Judson Press, 1978) p. 185

41 This was even the case among the heretics. Neither the Ebionites, Novatians, Arians, Donatists, Montanists, nor any other early heresy refuted infant baptism (many were even noted as practicing it themselves).

Tertullian (160-230), is often pointed out as an exception to this as he was the only early Christian teacher who questioned the wisdom of infant baptism. The bulk of his objection, however, was not the result of a conviction that Scriptures either forbade it or that rational faith must first be demonstrated. His opposition stemmed from the heretical belief that many of the sins committed after baptism were unforgivable. For this same reason, he opposed the baptism of any *unmarried* person, thinking them to be more prone to sin. He believed that one who was baptized and later led away by his passions into sin would receive a much greater condemnation than the single person who had refrained from baptism altogether. For this cause, he advocated that one not be baptized until he was married.

42 Although several examples exist from the Third century of the children of Christians being baptized as infants, in all of the literature and collections of inscriptions from that century there is not a single example of Christian parents delaying the baptism of their children. Joachim Jeremias, *The Origins of Infant Baptism* , (Great Britain, S.C.M. Press Ltd., 1963) p. 53

Those like Chrysostom, Gregory of Nazianzus, Jerome and Basil the Great were all raised in Christian families but had postponed baptism. Why? They postponed their baptisms in an effort to minimize the times they sinned after baptism, believing that such a practice would grant them eternal benefit. *This erroneous belief* led them to be baptized as adults, *not* because they held an infant-child baptism to be invalid on the grounds that the child had not yet reached an "age of accountability." Gregory and Chrysostom were baptized at 30 years, and Jerome and Basil at 20 and 27 respectively. Certainly, were rational "belief" the criterion of baptism, they would have been old enough to participate in the sacrament before these ages.

43 Joachim Jeremias, *The Origins of Infant Baptism* , (Great Britain, SCM Press, 1963) p. 58 There are other testimonies similar to Polycarp's testimony . Jeremias also mentions Polycrates of Ephesus who, in testifying in 190 A.D. to have lived "65 years in the Lord," also reckons himself to have been a Christian from the time of his birth (125-126 A.D.). Justin Martyr

44 Justin Martyr, *Dialogue With Trypho,* XLIII, Alexander Roberts, James Donaldson, eds., *The Ante-Nicene Fathers* , (Grand Rapids, Michigan, Wm.. B. Eerdman's Publishing Company, 1971 reprint), p. 216

45 Justin Martyr, *Apology I.,* c. XV., Alexander Roberts, James Donaldson, eds., *The Ante-Nicene Fathers* , (Grand Rapids, Michigan, Wm.. B. Eerdman's Publishing Company, 1971 reprint), p. 167

46 *Irenaeus Against Heresies* , II:22:4, *The Ante-Nicene Fathers* , (Grand Rapids, Michigan, Wm.. B. Eerdman's Publishing Company, 1971 reprint) p. 187

47 Hippoytus of Rome, *The Apostolic Tradition* , 394i, [21], William A. Jurgens, *The Faith of The Early Fathers,* Vol. I., (Collegeville, MN., The Liturgical Press, 1970), p. 169

> ... he [Hippolytus] considers that infant baptism is a tradition from the apostles as does Origen, who remarks, "For this reason the church received a tradition from the Apostles to give baptism to infants too." ... Jeremias has correctly argued that this attitude on the part of Origen and Hippolytus would be difficult to explain had not these scholars themselves received baptism in the period of their infancy.

Jack P. Lewis, "Baptismal Practices of the Second and Third Century Church" , *The Restoration Quarterly* , (1983), Vol. 26, pp. 14-15 (Hippolytus, *Apostolic Tradition.*, 21.3-4)

RECOMMENDED READING LIST

St. Athanasius, *On the Incarnation* (Crestwood, New York, St. Vladimir's Seminary Press, 1983)

St. John of Damascus, *An Exact Exposition of the Orthodox Faith* , *The Nicene and Post-Nicene Fathers*, Vol. IX, S.D.F. Salmond trans., (Grand Rapids, MI., Eerdmans Publishing Company, 1979)

Carnegie Samuel Calian, *Icon and Pulpit* (Philadelphia, PA., The Westminster Press, 1968)

Georges Florovsky, *Bible, Church, Tradition: An Eastern Orthodox View* (Belmont, MA., Nordland Publishing Company, 1972)

_____________, *Creation and Redemption* (Belmont, MA., Nordland Publishing Company, 1976)

Vladimir Lossky, *In The Image and Likeness of God* (Crestwood, New York, St. Vladimir's Press, 1974)

___________, *Mystical Theology in the Eastern Church* (Crestwood, New York, St. Vladimir's Press, 1976)

___________, *Orthodox Theology: An Introduction* (Crestwood, New York, St. Vladimir's Press, 1978)

John Meyendorff, *Byzantine Theology* (New York, Fordham Press, 1979)

___________, *The Catholicity and the Church* (Crestwood, New York, St. Vladimir's Seminary Press, 1983)

___________, *Living Tradition* , (Crestwood, New York, St. Vladimir's Seminary Press, 1978)

___________, Joseph McLelland, eds., *The New Man: An Orthodox and Reformed Dialogue*, (New Jersey, Standard Press, 1973)

Jaroslav Pelikan, *The Christian Tradition: The Spirit of Eastern Christendom (600-1700)* (Chicago and London, The University of Chicago Press, 1974)

A. J. Philippou, ed., *The Orthodox Ethos* (Oxford, England, Holywell Press, 1964)

T. F. Torrance, *Theology in Reconciliation: Essays Toward Evangelical and Catholic Unity In East and West*, (Grand Rapids, MI., William B. Eerdmans Publishing Company, 1975)

Robert Webber, *Common Roots* (Grand Rapids, MI., Zondervan Publishing House, 1978)

__________, Donald Bloesch, eds., *The Orthodox Evangelicals* (Nashville/New York, Thomas Nelson Publishers, 1978)

Christos Yannaras, *The Freedom of Morality*, (Crestwood, N.Y., St. Vladimir's Seminary Press, 1984)

John D. Zizioulas, *Being As Communion* (Crestwood, N.Y., St. Vladimir's Seminary Press, 1985)